OLYMPIC
Battleground

OLYMPIC
The Power Politics of Timber Preservation
Battleground

SECOND EDITION
CARSTEN LIEN

THE
MOUNTAINEERS

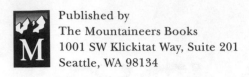

Published by
The Mountaineers Books
1001 SW Klickitat Way, Suite 201
Seattle, WA 98134

© 2000 by Carsten Lien

First edition, 1991, by Sierra Club Books. Second edition, 2000.

Published simultaneously in Great Britain by Cordee, 3a DeMontfort Street, Leicester, England, LE1 7HD

Manufactured in Canada

Project Editor: Dottie Martin
Cover designer: Peggy Egerdahl
Cover photograph: *Olympic National Park, Wash., old growth forest*
    © Pat O'Hara

Library of Congress Cataloging-in-Publication Data

Lien, Carsten.
    Olympic battleground : the power politics of timber preservation /
    Carsten Lien.—2nd ed.
        p. cm.
    Includes bibliographical references and index.
    ISBN 0-89886-736-3 (pbk.)
    1. Olympic National Park (Wash.)—History. 2. Olympic National Forest
(Wash.)—History. 3. United States. National Park Service—History. 4.
United States. Forest Service—History. 5. Emergency Conservation
Committee—History. I. Title.

F897.O5 L54 2000
979.7'98—dc21

                                                            00-041867

CONTENTS

FOREWORD

First published in 1991, *Olympic Battleground* was immediately recognized as one of the most important books ever written about the national parks. It was recognized by everyone who values history as a window on the truth and who, like Carsten Lien, understands that history has the power to haunt the future.

In the case of Olympic National Park, the threat comes from opponents still maintaining that the park has protected far too much. No national park in the American West is more blessed with an abundance of natural diversity. Any novice would think the park was planned that way, that is, expressly to be diverse. Not so, this book reminds us, getting to the heart of its contribution. Olympic National Park might just as easily have been a pittance—not the crown jewel we know today. This jewel required activists committed to raising the political stakes. Welcoming controversy, they fought for a park that mattered biologically, determined that it recognize the great rain forests of the Pacific Northwest. A national park worthy of this region should include every life zone between the Olympic Mountains and the sea, the activists believed.

Seeking consensus, the National Park Service preferred its tradition of including more "sample" landscapes, which enhanced its reputation as the guardian of scenic wonders. By only glorifying mountains, preservationists themselves had come late to the realization that nature is more than merely high-country inspiration. Now moving to include unique vegetation and animal habitat within the national parks, they directly challenged logging, mining, grazing, and settlement of the public lands. Lowlands and foothills—not commonly thought of as purely inspirational—had always been reserved for exploitation. It was inconceivable—even to the National Park Service—that wilderness should protect trees and wildlife, not just mountain and canyon scenery.

Thus evolved the battle, and the battleground, that became Olympic National Park. Now that the battlefield had grown in value, so also had the battle turned controversial.

Normally, the establishment of Olympic National Park in 1938 would have signaled a victory for preservationists. But again, there was nothing traditional about this park's values, especially regarding the many acres of old-growth forests. Serving the park as a seasonal naturalist, Carsten Lien learned the meaning of that distinction. He expected the National Park Service to think idealistically, eagerly welcoming the broadening of its mandate. Instead, in 1954 he witnessed a parade of logging trucks carrying off thousands of ancient trees. Incredible as it seemed, the park superintendent had not only instigated the logging, but the director of the Park Service himself promoted it. Carsten Lien then committed himself to what became a lifetime project, writing a history of the sources of controversy that still portended the park's destruction.

Upon its first publishing in 1991, this book's honesty became a source of controversy, dismaying the National Park Service that its leadership could be corrupted, too. Or was the corruption out of character?, Carsten Lien further dared to ask. Has the agency uniformly defended the national parks against all special interests or itself willingly bent to whim and politics when the bureaucracy sees a benefit?

Apologists for the National Park Service would still prefer to argue that the problem is with the messenger. History again says otherwise, reminding those making excuses that they also undermine the public trust. American culture maintains that national parks should be held inviolate, an interpretation that is hardly unique to Carsten Lien. If no one escapes his scrutiny, it is because no one should—or can.

History is not about giving comfort but rather expunging myth. The myth under scrutiny here is that the National Park Service always pursues the public interest. Another myth I would challenge is that the agency welcomes and believes in scholarship. To the contrary, what might be called its conscience has consistently evolved outside— nurtured by scientists, historians, and social activists willing to accept that government is never perfect. Like any bureaucracy, public or private, the National Park Service looks only for approval. "Did we do that? You must have it wrong," the service rebuffs.

Carsten Lien handles the problem as any scholar should, basing all interpretation on the standards the National Park Service alleges it upholds. Where the agency has failed those standards, history offers that the public interest has not been served. The point of criticism remains whether the Park Service's standard was followed or ignored.

Thus this second edition of *Olympic Battleground* reminds us of ongoing claims against Olympic National Park—again, claims that a strong and committed National Park Service should never have entertained. A notable example is the Quileute tribe, which still asks for hundreds of acres within the park's boundary. History grants that all of North America was previously inhabited by native peoples. The question is how that entitles their descendants to repossess significant portions of our national parks. Is that justice to the past, or merely another setup against the future? History would remind everyone that conquest and dispossession are universal sins of humankind. Meanwhile, population has conquered the world far more significantly than any army. We cannot turn back the clock. The gravest injustice the future could possibly imagine is to make the national parks another victim of our duplicity, allowing the dismantling of a public trust to appease those posturing a superior place in history.

In support of a common inheritance, no claim can be above another, which is why this book remains exceptional, not merely informative or just worthwhile. In preservation, either that is the standard—and the standard speaks for itself—or else there cannot be national parks. Anything less demeans the standard, and with it, all value of the inheritance. By failing the parks, we fail ourselves, destroying the best of who and what we are. The tragedy is that any of our parks ever served as battlegrounds, demanding a need for the irrefutable lessons we are given here.

Alfred Runte

ACKNOWLEDGMENTS

I gratefully acknowledge the generous personal contributions that a number of people have given to this work. In a crucial period when Rosalie Edge was alive, Liz Cushman Titus arranged for a research grant from the Student Conservation Association which enabled me to spend part of the summer of 1959 with Rosalie Edge at the Emergency Conservation Committee in New York. She in turn gave unstintingly of her time and insights which provided essential hooks to hang the data on as they later passed before my eyes as I labored through the archives. Without her input, the conceptual framework of this study would have been inaccurate. Rosalie Edge's son, Peter, graciously provided me with a copy of his mother's autobiographical account, *An Implacable Widow*, about her years in conservation. Her account clarified and provided detail which otherwise would have been lacking.

Irving Brant spoke to me constantly from beyond the grave as I synthesized the data at hand. As James Madison's principal biographer, Brant had such a keen sense of what historians need from manuscript material that he annotated his own papers before his death. These annotations provided detail, clarification, insight and sometimes marvelous wit. I never stopped feeling that it was I for whom he went to all that effort in the twilight of his life. I thank him for his generous contribution. Brant's daughters, Ruth B. Davis and Robin Lodewick, willingly provided a draft manuscript of their father's book, *Adventures in Conservation*, about his years in fighting for environmental causes from which detail and clarification to the Olympic battle emerged. Geographical proximity to Robin Lodewick enabled me to interview her as well.

Dave Brower, then executive director of the Sierra Club, arranged for Allan Sommarstrom to help during a summer in the National Archives, help that enabled me to find some useful and obscure data that I might otherwise have missed. Several Park Service officials, including Olympic Park Superintendents, participated through the years by sharing information of importance. Their input has been gratefully received. The persons I formally interviewed are listed separately.

An enormous assist to the process of writing was given by Professor Robert G. Lee and Dean David Thorud of the University of Washington's College of Forest Resources. They opened up the resources of the university with an appointment as Visiting Scholar with the full knowledge that the college had been an actor on the Olympic stage, all in the tradition of what a great university is all about. Two directors of the University's Institute of Environmental Studies, Professors Gordon Orians and Conway Leovy, extended my appointment and provided office space and support in the unfounded but persistent belief at the time that something of environmental interest might in the end emerge from my efforts. Their contribution saved incalculable time in the writing process by putting me immediately adjacent to the leading research library in the region.

Wally Smith enabled me to produce this work now instead of later. Al Williams, with enormous energy and contributions of vast amounts of personal time, applied his considerable skills with the computer to organize things technically so that the manuscript could be printed on a laser printer, thereby dramatically improving its appearance.

Above everyone else, my wife, Cristi, toiled endlessly at the word processor to get the manuscript into print.

The following persons generously agreed to read the draft manuscript of this work. Some were participants in the events, some were themselves authorities in other ways in aspects of the work. Many of these persons offered invaluable suggestions, guidance, and sometimes provocative challenge to what I had written. This contribution enabled me to rethink what I had said and in some cases to see that I needed to document the text more thoroughly than I had originally thought necessary. I am grateful to them all for agreeing to read the manuscript and for the gifts of generous contributions of time and effort that many of the readers made.

Dave Brower, Richard A. Cooley, Ruth B. Davis, Donna De Shazo, Gordon Dodds, Polly Dyer, Peter Edge, Gunnar and Frances Fagerlund, Harry and Sharon Francis, Guy Fringer, Michael Frome, Glenn Gallison, Patrick Goldsworthy, Robert G. Lee, Conway Leovy, Dave Lester, Robin Lodewick, Harry Lydiard, Harvey Manning, Grant McConnell, Grant Sharpe, Paul Shepard, Ben Twight, Vim Wright and Phil Zalesky.

PREFACE

WHEN, IN THE 1950's, I discovered the National Park Service was logging Olympic National Park, I knew there had to be a story behind it. As the Park Service issued adamant statements about its preservation role, all the while logging was going on, the conflict between rhetoric and action amazed me. I began then to research the organization behavior to account for this conflict.

Little did I realize then where this small effort would lead. Early on, I discovered that parts of the story led back to the battle to create the Olympic Park in the 1930's. With the assistance of a grant from the Student Conservation Association, I arranged to spend part of the summer of 1959 with Rosalie Edge and the files of the Emergency Conservation Committee in New York. One day, during one of many rambling conversations with her on park issues and the ECC, she said to me in her precise New York accent, reminiscent of Mrs. Roosevelt, "Well, you know the Park Service fought the creation of Olympic National Park from the start." I was so taken aback by what she said that I responded with youthful dismay. "You're kidding me," I said. Chagrined at my reaction, Edge told me with even more preciseness, "I most assuredly am not *kidding* you. The record will show it absolutely when you get to it." Indeed the archives did show as clearly as she said they would that the Park Service had fought furiously to keep Olympic National Park as it now exists from ever coming into being. The question then became why.

So it went. For every new disclosure there were further questions that were left unanswered that had to be explored. Layer after layer had to be peeled away until there were no more to peel. In the process of peeling away layers to account for various occurrences in Olympic National Park, I became aware that I was rewriting the history of the Park Service and of Stephen Mather and Horace Albright, its first two directors, as well. And in addition, I discovered that three other Park Service directors had gone to personal disaster over Olympic National Park. None of this had ever been disclosed before. Even Gifford Pinchot and John Muir turned out to be players in the drama of the Park Service and Olympic National Park in totally unanticipated ways. In fact Pinchot so much so that if anyone could be said to be the father of the National Park Service itself, it would be he. His demands that the parks be logged, and his continuing attempts to gain control of them to fulfill that demand, contributed the impetus which ended in the final passing of the Park Service Act of 1916. As all of this unfolded, while attempting to find the answers that drove the Park Service's organization behavior in Olympic, I became aware that I was in fact rewriting the whole of American conservation history. And a topsy turvy rewrite it is. The story turns out to be one of citizen activism fighting bureaucracy and the timber industry, tenuously winning only to be defeated and forced to fight all over again. Over and over.

Everyone who comes to the story of what happened in Olympic National Park will come with a preconceived bias. Either one believes that what was set aside to be preserved was too much, depriving the local area of a chance to maximize its industrial economic development potential, or that it was not too much, that the fraction of the forest type that was preserved was appropriate to the urban society we have become. Because the story told here is the story of the clash of two ideologically based value systems, vying at all times in our society, I had to choose to write from a position. Readers need to know that I personally believe that we have not set aside too much. In spite of this bias, I have attempted to be scrupulously honest in the documentation of what occurred. For the people who played roles in the unfolding drama of forest preservation, I have attempted to reflect as accurately as the archives will allow what each of them did and the circumstances under which they did it. I have not made any attempt, however, to write a balanced account of any of their careers. As accurately as I could, I have attempted to reflect only on what they did in relation to Olympic or in a situation which in turn relates to Olympic.

Here then is the hundred-year-long story of efforts to preserve trees on the Olympic Peninsula and the national conflict that was generated as powerful forces moved to prevent that from occurring. In uncovering this story, I have relied principally on primary source material — material that provides a startlingly different version of events than that which is promulgated by governmental agencies and the folklore surrounding various officials of those agencies. This primary source material includes the letters, official documents, and other materials produced by the actors on the Olympic stage as the drama was un-folding.

In order for readers to have the sharpest focus on the value conflict involved, I have opened each chapter with the actual words of those engaged in that conflict.

1 UP FOR GRABS

. . . the sacred duty of so using the country in which we live that we may not leave it ravished by greed and ruined by ignorance, but may pass it on to future generations undiminished in richness and beauty.[1]   JOHN MUIR

I do not believe that there is either a moral or any other claim upon me to postpone the use of what nature has given me, so that the next generation or generations yet unborn may have an opportunity to get what I myself ought to get.[2]
SENATOR HENRY M. KELLER, COLORADO

A POWERFUL and ever-present urge in the American population from the earliest of times has been to preserve part of the natural landscape. Even when government policy ran in the opposite direction, there was a strong undercurrent of concern for preservation. As early as 1865, Frederick Law Olmstead expressed this societal concern openly in his plan for the protection of Yosemite. "The first point to be kept in mind," he said, "is the preservation and maintenance as exactly as is possible of the natural scenery."[3]

In the mid-nineteenth century, the U.S. government allowed railroad companies and timber syndicates to acquire title to millions of acres of the most valuable forests in the American West. This inspired a preservation movement that is still growing today.

The battle began in 1870, when Franklin B. Hough, superintendent of the Census Bureau, read a paper before the American Association for the Advancement of Science called *"The Duty of the Government in the Preservation of the Forests."* He had collected statistical data for the first time on forest land in the 1870 census and wanted to alert the public to the rapid shrinkage of the nation's forests.

In 1876 John Muir proposed the appointment of a national commission to inquire into the "wastage of forests" (Muir's phrase) to take a survey of existing forest lands in public ownership and to recommend measures for their conservation. The following year, Secretary of the Interior Carl Schurz advocated the withdrawal of all timberlands still belonging to the federal government from entry under the homestead and pre-emption laws. But the immediate result, the Timber and Stone Act of 1878, made the privatization of the public forests easier. It made available to individuals land that was considered "unfit for cultivation" and "valuable chiefly for timber." An individual could acquire 160 acres for as little as $2.50 per acre—a price that was unrelated to the value of timber. And for the first time an individual could buy government timber directly. Almost immediately crews of ships touching every northwestern port were hired to enter 160 acres in the General Land Office and immediately deed the land to a timber company in return for fifty dollars.[4] The company history of Pope & Talbot, a large timber operator on the Olympic Peninsula and Puget Sound, laughingly explains the reason so much of their timberland was located near tidewater was that the owners were afraid the sailors might get lost if they went too far into the woods.[5] In this way, 15 million acres of the nation's timber vanished from the public domain. Not a single quarter section of California's redwood forests remained in public ownership by the end of the century.

During the nearly twenty years that had gone by since the data in the 1870 census had confronted the nation with its forest policy, increasing numbers of bills had been introduced in Congress calling for some form of forest protection. None had gotten anywhere. In 1888 a bill appeared in Congress which would have given the president the power to proclaim forest reservations to be administered by the government. It did not pass, but it laid the groundwork for an approach that would later be used to create what is today the national forest system and much of the national park system.

When Iowa lawyer John W. Noble was appointed Secretary of the Interior in 1889, forest conservation had a real advocate. He was also part of an exclusive group of wealthy men of education, position, and influence brought together by Theodore Roosevelt the year before as the Boone and Crockett Club. Many of this group had been involved in earlier efforts to protect Yellowstone and would continue that and other national park activity as members of the club. This group would, through the years, become a major force for preservation on many fronts and would keep close watch on one of the richest stands of conifers in the world — Washington's Olympic Peninsula.

In 1891 a seemingly inconsequential bill entitled "An Act to Repeal Timber Culture Laws and for other purposes" was amended to include a section introduced as a separate bill earlier without success by Senator Cushman K. Davis of Minnesota. A few words in the amendment changed the course of conservation history: " . . . the President of the United States may from time to time, set apart and reserve in any state or territory having public lands bearing forests, any part of the public lands, wholly or in part covered with timber or undergrowth, whether of commercial value or not, as public reservations and the President shall by public proclamation, declare the establishment of such reservations and the limits thereof."[6] Here finally was what John Muir and his colleague Robert Underwood Johnson, editor of *Century* magazine, and much of the nation's intellectual press had been working for decades to achieve — the withdrawal from entry of the public's forestlands.

Muir had worked to pass the Yosemite National Park bill in October of 1890, and Johnson had provided Muir with a nationwide forum through the pages of *Century*. By chance, Johnson met Secretary of Interior Noble at the Yale commencement in June of 1891 where both were to receive honorary degrees. Johnson grabbed at an opportunity. "I had acquainted him with Muir's convictions on an urgent need for a radical policy to save the national forests," said Johnson later, "and we had correspondence about the Sequoia, General Grant, and Yosemite national parks, where he instituted an effective system of patrol."[7] Muir now had a direct pipeline, through Johnson, to the government official whose department would be preparing whatever proclamations would be issued to breathe life into the bill allowing for forest reservations.

Johnson kept in communication with Noble during the period when the reservations which followed the passage of the bill were being proclaimed. "When I spoke to the Secretary in advocacy of Muir's idea of reserving the whole of the upper regions of the Sierra," Johnson said, "he was most sympathetic, but although he consulted me about some details, I had no idea to what length he would go in his recommendations to President Harrison." When a friend suggested to Johnson in casual conversation that he hoped the Grand Canyon would not be forgotten, Johnson wrote at once to the Secretary. "I told him . . . that there was not a great deal of timber in the Canyon and while the scenery itself could not be injured, it seemed important that provisions should be made against spoilation of the best points of view and against the possible incursion of ugliness in the environs."[8] Two days later, Secretary Noble wrote back expressing doubt about his authority to prepare proclamations because there was so little timber involved. He would, he said, take the risk anyhow. A Grand Canyon reservation became fact, thereby, along with the Sierra and Yellowstone reservations. President Harrison proclaimed the forest reservations as presented to him by Secretary of the Interior Noble, who in turn got them from Johnson and he in turn from Muir.

Here was launched the citizen activism which became an inseparable part of U.S. forest policy-making and administration. And the preservationists had triumphed for the moment. No timber could be cut, no forage could be grazed, no minerals could be mined, nor any road built in the reserves. But the purposes of the reserves were undefined, and life went right on as before for those who lived next to the reserves. Sheep grazed, trees were cut, and rivers dammed. Only the privatization process had been stopped.

Muir believed in the preservationist nature of the timber reserve proclamations. Of Yellowstone, he wrote that the park "was to all intents and purposes enlarged by Yellowstone National Park Timber Reserve . . . its geographical position, reviving climate, and wonderful scenery combine to make it a grand health, pleasure and study resort, a gathering place for travellers from all the world."[9]

Muir was not alone in his belief that the 1891 act was to be used for preservation. Judge James Wickersham, who led expeditions into the Olympic Mountain Range in 1889 and 1890, concluded that "A more beautiful national park cannot be found" after exploring the upper Skokomish River basin and descending the Dosewallips. When his article promoting the cause of an Olympic National Park, sent to editor Robert Underwood Johnson in April of 1891, failed to appear in *Century* as he thought it would, he moved aggressively towards Washington, D.C. Aware of the new law providing for reservations by proclamation, Wickersham sent maps and his article "descriptive of a proposed Olympic National Park" to Major John W. Powell, superintendent of the U.S. Geological Survey. "I am informed," he said, "that you are preparing to recommend several reservations, under the act of March 3, and I send you this with the hope that you may be induced to make the proposed park."[10] He was not alone in promoting a park. Lieutenant Joseph O'Neil, who led an 1890 Olympic expedition, concluded that the Olympics "would serve admirably as a National Park."[11] Wickersham and O'Neil were grasping at the same straw that Muir and Johnson had grasped at when they proposed reservation status for the Grand Canyon.

In 1889, with the potential for closing the public domain fast developing, an explosion of excitement and change was underway in western Washington. The Olympic Mountains for the first time were being explored, the last area in the continental United States to hold that

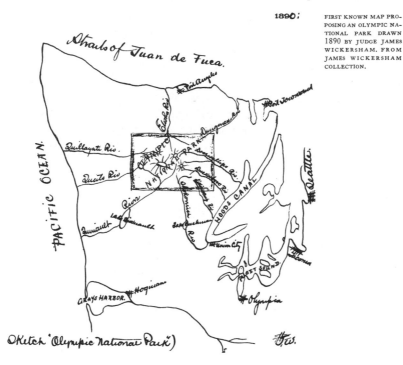

1890:   FIRST KNOWN MAP PRO-
POSING AN OLYMPIC NA-
TIONAL PARK DRAWN
1890 BY JUDGE JAMES
WICKERSHAM. FROM
JAMES WICKERSHAM
COLLECTION.

The O'Neil and Wickersham Expeditions of 1890 both produced national park recommendations for the Olympics. Wickersham prepared this map for the Geological Survey.
The Living Wilderness, Summer-Fall 1961; Wickersham Collection, National Archives.

distinction. A transcontinental railroad had arrived six years earlier,
linking Puget Sound to the east. Statehood would arrive in November.

On the Olympic Peninsula, Port Townsend, until recently Washington's leading city, lay doomed by the railroads that would never be able
to link to it across Puget Sound. A future Secretary of the Interior,
Richard Ballinger, decided to join the exodus from Port Townsend and
packed up his law practice to seek whatever fame and fortune Seattle
had to offer. Seattle had grown from a town of 3,500 to a city of more
than 40,000 in the preceding decade.

Meanwhile, in 1890, the first settlers headed for the rain forests of
the western Olympics. Some landed in schooners at Sand Point and
hauled their goods through three miles of dense rain forest jungle to
the shore of Lake Ozette, where they settled. Others landed at the mouth
of the Ozette River with a fleet of nine canoes hired from the Indians
at Neah Bay. This party ferried the lake and settled at nearby Big River.

For thirty-six years, or until the country road was completed to Swan Bay on Lake Ozette in 1926, the settlers had no way to reach civilization except by trail.

The state's timber and the land on which it grew was rapidly shifting away from public ownership and into the hands of timber speculators and corporations. Every shipload of sailors increased the flow as each of them was marched to the local General Land Office to file for another 160 acres. When the battle began to preserve something for the future, the corporations and speculative syndicates involved on the Olympic Peninsula, and indeed in all of the West, were driven by one all-powerful commitment to short-term self interest. The corporate call to arms in the 1890's was, "If I do not take all that I can get, somebody else will get something."[12] Keeping the public timberlands in public ownership was the issue. How would the country administer them? And for whose benefit? Future generations or the present?

The presence of reservations spurred onward all the diverse groups who wanted more. Robert Underwood Johnson worked out a plan with Charles S. Sargent, professor of arboriculture at Harvard, to use the National Academy of Sciences to form a Forest Committee. The committee would not only recommend new reserves but also would deal with policy and legislative recommendations. Johnson was requested by Sargent to take on the task of inducing President Cleveland's Secretary of the Interior, Hoke Smith, to request of the National Academy of Sciences that such a committee be formed. Johnson finally got to see Smith at eleven o'clock at night and during the next two hours convinced him to request the appointment of the committee. When Smith's letter of February 15, 1896, arrived at the president's desk, the committee was formed. Gifford Pinchot was coming into prominence as a forester at that time and although not a member of the National Academy of Sciences, became secretary of the Forest Committee.[13]

Johnson personally took on the effort to secure an appropriation for the committee work as well. Searching for the $25,000 that Sargent believed would be necessary, Johnson went to Washington and called on Joseph G. Cannon, then chairman of the House Appropriations Committee. The conversation began in his office and continued in the street as Johnson walked with Cannon back to the Normandie Hotel. Johnson's persuasive powers prevailed. The committee got its appropriation after Cannon accepted Johnson's argument that it was really an economy measure—"there would never be another opportunity to obtain without compensation the professional advice on this subject from so many distinguished experts."[14]

The committee was a distinguished group: Dr. Walcott Gibbs, president of the National Academy of Sciences, appointed himself along with Sargent, General Henry L. Abbott of the Army Corps of Engineers, Dr. Alexander Agassiz of Harvard, Dr. William H. Brewer of Yale, Arnold Hague of the U.S. Geological Survey, and Gifford Pinchot. Muir joined the committee informally in Montana in July to assist the survey. The beginning biases of the committee were all strongly oriented towards the non-use, preservationist viewpoint to be backed by the use of the army. But "Pinchot knew that public opposition to the forest reservations had to be taken into consideration. . . . He argued for the opening of the forest reserves to regulated use under the supervision of a staff of trained government foresters. This, he felt would assure protection for the forests while deriving maximum benefits from them and win friends instead of enemies for the principles of forest preservation."[15] Pinchot wanted to use the committee to "get ready for practical forestry."[16]

Muir and Pinchot met in the summer of 1896 when both were involved in the field work of the Forest Committee. They took an instant liking to one another: "a most fascinating talker, I took to him at once," said Pinchot. At the time, Muir seemed much closer to Pinchot than he would later. Just the year before, Muir had written, "The forests must be and will be, not only preserved but used . . . the forests, like perennial fountains may be made to yield a sure harvest of timber, while at the same time all their far-reaching beneficent uses may be maintained unimpaired."[17] This was exactly the "we can have our cake and eat it too" position the timber industry would embrace in later decades. This was also the position at the moment that was going to prevail on the Forest Committee to Muir's anguish. A year later, whatever peace and cordiality had existed between Muir and Pinchot in the beginning was shattered when Muir stopped in Seattle on his way home from Alaska. Muir was startled and then angered by an interview with Pinchot that appeared in Seattle's morning paper. Pinchot was quoted as saying that sheep grazing in the reserves did little if any harm. Because some of the most powerful politicians in Washington State were sheep ranchers and cattlemen or closely allied with livestock corporations, Muir saw this as a sellout by Pinchot. Realizing that Pinchot was also in Seattle, Muir went straight to Pinchot's hotel. In the presence of newspaper reporters in the lobby of his hotel, Muir confronted Pinchot, "Are you correctly quoted here?" Pinchot admitted he was. "Then, if that is the case I don't want anything more to do with you,"[18] Muir said.[19]

Whatever preservationist sentiment existed when the committee's work began, it did not find its way into the committee report. The Pinchot viewpoint triumphed, and was reflected in the Forest Committee's recommendations:

1. That details of troops protect the reserves until a permanent forest bureau in the Department of the Interior has been authorized and thoroughly organized.
2. That the Secretary of the Interior be authorized to issue the necessary rules and regulations for the sale of timber firewood, and fencing . . . for allowing the public to enter and cross the reserves . . . for rights of way for roads, for rights of way for ditches, flumes and pipes and for reservoir sites, to locate mining claims.
3. That a bureau of public forests shall be established in the Department of the Interior.
4. That a board of forest lands shall be appointed by the President to determine what portions of the public domain should be reserved permanently as forest lands.
5. That lands more valuable for the production of timber than for agriculture or mining shall be withdrawn from sale, settlement, and held for the growth of timber.
6. That Mt. Rainier and the Grand Canyon be set aside as national parks.[20]

Not only did the Forest Committee present a full plan for the immediate economic utilization of the reserve's resources and a plan of administration to serve those purposes, but they also presented draft legislation to implement each of their recommendations.

The Forest Committee also recommended the creation of thirteen additional forest reserves, including an Olympic Forest Reserve, adding 21,279,840 acres to the 17,564,800 acres already set aside. By the time the Forest Committee was doing this work on the adding of forest reserves, it was clear to everyone that a new era had already dawned and that the additions would simply be a part of it. Forestland for the taking was almost a thing of the past. In spite of the progress being made, however, Muir continued his attacks on the corporations and wealthy speculators who fought on to continue their private amassing of public wealth. Muir charged:

> The outcries we hear against forest reservations come mostly from thieves who are wealthy and steal timber by wholesale. They have so long been allowed to steal and destroy in peace that any impediment to forest robbery is denounced as a cruel and irreligious interference with vested rights . . . [21]

Frederick Weyerhaeuser, then sixty-five years old, and the lake states' timber industry, as the *National Geographic* described it, had "nearly completed their virgin cut, under methods so suicidal that sandy wastes of worthless brush have been substituted for what might have been well

stocked young pine forest . . . "[22] By the time Weyerhaeuser was com-
pleting this cut, the Northern Pacific Railroad had received in land
grants approximately 40 million acres, an area equal in extent to the
states of Maine, Vermont, New Hampshire, Massachusetts, and Connecticut combined. In Washington State, the railroad had been given
alternate sections in a swath eighty miles wide plus an indemnity strip,
the land which the railroad could claim if land inside the eighty-mile
swatch had already been claimed. With the Northern Pacific Railroad
land grant went a vast volume of timber.

The Weyerhaeuser timber syndicate and the Northern Pacific Railroad shared the same key set of common stockholders, and the companies, both headquartered in St. Paul, worked closely together.[23]

After Frederick Weyerhaeuser's arrival in St. Paul in 1891, he enjoyed
a close friendship with James J. Hill of the Northern Pacific Railroad.
Two years later, Weyerhaeuser moved next door to Hill on Summit
Avenue. Their common business interests prospered.[24] In 1894, Hill sold
Weyerhaeuser 990,000 acres of timberland from the old St. Paul and
Pacific grant for two dollars an acre.[25] Later, F. E. Weyerhaeuser, Frederick's son, appeared on the Northern Pacific Railroad board of directors. The closeness of these companies allowed Weyerhaeuser to jump
from the denuded hills of Wisconsin and Minnesota to the heavy timber of the Pacific Northwest, for Hill was moving to privatize publicly
owned timber out of the northwest's forest reserves.

In 1896, Hill moved to make a national park out of Mount Rainier,
which the Forest Committee itself had recommended, and which would
at the same time provide the vehicle by which he could proceed with
his plan. In January of 1896 Congressman William H. Dolittle of Seattle introduced the bill to create Washington National Park. Section 3
of the bill allowed the railroad to exchange its checkerboard sections
in the park, most of which were rock, ice, and alpine meadows, for "an
equal quantity" of public lands, "whether surveyed or unsurveyed." By
specifying an equal quantity, he could exchange rock and ice for heavy
lowland timber without reference to value. By specifying "unsurveyed,"
his timber of choice was available ahead of everyone else; all other claim-
ants would have to wait until surveys were completed. Because the railroad ran only eighteen miles into Oregon, from Goble to Portland,
access to Oregon's heavy west-side timber had always been unavailable
to the Northern Pacific Railroad. Hill's park bill specified that selections could be made "within any state *into or* through which the railroad . . . runs."

Four months later, the Northern Pacific Railroad's park bill emerged
from the Public Lands Committee with eight additional words, *"also
the lands in the Pacific Forest Reserve."* The railroad could exchange, if

the bill passed, not only lands in the proposed park but also lands throughout its holdings in the whole of the Pacific Forest Reserve, equal area of rock and ice for heavy timber. It could even make those choices in the heavily timbered lowlands of western Oregon. The bill also specified that "the mineral-land laws of the United States are hereby extended" to the park. This opened the park to miners and gave them free timber to cut in the park. The railroad, also on amendment, had the right to build a railroad and a tramway into or through the park.

The Northern Pacific park bill sailed through Congress and went to President Cleveland's desk, but Cleveland refused to have anything to do with the bill and it died in a pocket veto as Congress adjourned. Then, on Washington's birthday, February 22, 1897, just ten days before he left office, Cleveland proclaimed all of the reservations recommended by the Forest Committee. The legal descriptions of these reservations, written by Gifford Pinchot, he left unaltered. This protected 21,279,840 acres of public forest from the privatization process, a process that had accelerated in anticipation of the president's action. The corporations and the western legislators in both Houses who were beholden to them, were outraged. That the Forest Committee had recommended opening up the reserves to commercial exploitation made no difference. The issue was the privatization of the public domain itself—the land and the resources on it. Having government involved in determining who could use what and under what circumstances was a radical and foreign concept, completely out of character with the American frontier past. Those profiting from the unfettered exploitation on public lands were not about to have the rules change now.

Washington State's Congressional delegation and those of the other western states attacked Cleveland: " . . . this ignorant act of a corrupt Executive shall be overturned,"[26] said South Dakota's Congressman Richard Pettigrew. William C. Jones of Washington bemoaned that George Washington's birthday "should have been desecrated by the most despotic act that has ever marred our history."[27] Cleveland had upset the special privilege that the mineral laws had conveyed on the public domain. And the companies that had profited from this advantage were not about to give up without a fight.

Six days after Cleveland issued the proclamations creating the reserves, Senator Clark of Wyoming moved to nullify them all, restoring them to the public domain. His amendment passed the Senate the same day. But Congress rejected the Clark amendment because of the threat of a presidential veto. "Amend the Sundry Civil Bill, will they?" Cleveland said, "Well, if they do, I will veto the whole damned Sundry Civil Bill."[28] Senator Pettigrew said, "A President who would make that threat, a President who would allow it to be made, disgraces civilization and the American Republic."[29] Cleveland let it be known of this direct confrontation with Congress that this event was one of the most important in his administration and was one of those of which he was most proud. Congress did accept the Lacey amendment to open the reserves to economic exploitation, but Cleveland left office not having signed the bill, his pocket veto saving the day for both the Muir camp and the Pinchot group.

"Cleveland's veto," said Pinchot, "was by far the biggest thing any President had yet done for Forestry. It put Forestry on the front page all over America, and made it, for the first time, a generally recognized national question."[30]

Cleveland's proclamations had interrupted the flow of resources to those who once had the power to capture them. The lumber, mining, and stock syndicates had not had enough time to get what they had staked out when the proclamations were issued. Senator Richard Pettigrew of South Dakota, a forest reserve hater and defender of the interests of the Homestake Mining Company, the largest gold mining firm in the country, assumed the leadership role in Congress to undo everything Cleveland had put into place.

Exactly two months from the moment he assumed the presidency, McKinley presented to Congress his own amendment to the Sundry Civil Bill. Prepared by Secretary of the Interior Bliss and the Congressional delegations from each of the states containing reserves proclaimed by Cleveland, Senator Pettigrew introduced the administration's amendment. McKinley's amendment "restored to the public domain the [reserves] as though said orders and proclamations had not been issued." Giving the corporations a year to make their claims, McKinley then provided that any lands "not otherwise disposed of before March 1, 1898, shall again go into the reservations." Gifford Pinchot succeeded in getting into the amendment the sale of "the dead, matured or large growth of trees" everywhere in the reserves, a move that preempted John Muir and the other preservationists.[31] Mining companies, settlers, and prospectors continued to get free timber. The Northern Pacific Railroad, having failed to obtain the right to exchange rock and ice for timber when the Mount Rainier Park Bill died two months earlier, now had that power restored by McKinley in the amendment. All the waters on all the reservations "may be used for domestic, mining, milling or irrigations purposes" was another provision that removed forever Muir's vision of wilderness in the reserves.[32]

Even though Pettigrew had introduced the administration's proposals for economic utilization, he fought on for total permanent abolishment of the reserves. Even he, however, caught a glimmer of the political reality to which McKinley was responding—the one-year suspension was about as far as McKinley dared to go on behalf of the corporations. Pettigrew lamented that "all the Eastern newspapers are opposed to any change whatever. The *Forest and Stream,* the *New York Tribune* are opposed vigorously to vacating these orders. . . . They insist that this whole area in my state . . . shall be locked up; that there be no revocation of the order; and the pressure is tremendous. The pressure has been so great that since the 22nd of February, although we have urged constantly the revocation of the order, we cannot get it revoked."[33]

The corporations now had what they wanted and the explosive opposition died away as they could continue to capture for the moment the resources they wanted. After that, all the resources in the reserves would be available to them even though ownership of the land was not. In spite of this, McKinley came so close to revoking the reserves that it was only the personal intervention of Professor Sargent himself that prevented him from doing so. McKinley did warn the Forest Committee members to either accept the Pettigrew amendment or risk losing the forest reserves.

While Congress and McKinley were holding the door open for the "greedy forest grabbers" (as the Muir camp called them), the "grabbers" became so emboldened by their success that a group of them tried to get Congressional authority to cut the General Grant Sequoia Grove in California.

The moving of the forest reserve issue to the forefront of the national agenda had given Muir his chance to fight for preservation. All along he knew that the forest reserves were never going to exist solely as great preserves, and this was clear from his stated view that "it is impossible in the nature of the things to stop at preservation . . . the forests, like perennial fountains, may be made to yield a sure harvest of timber . . . "[34] But it had never occurred to him that Pinchot's concept of economic utilization of all the resources of all the reserves now written into the law of the land through the passing of the Pettigrew amendment to the Sundry Civil Appropriations Act of June 1897 (30 stat 34–36) would so thoroughly prevail. The *Century,* the widely read national periodical, had been working continuously for Muir's brand of preservation for some time. Joined by many of the rest of the nation's intellectual press, the *Century* was now not alone. Muir was invited to address the readers of *Harper's Weekly* with an article defending the reservations, appearing in June of 1897. "Probably more than ninety percent of the people in the States in which the new reservations lie are in favor of them," he wrote, and he began to attack Gifford Pinchot. "Much is said on questions of this kind about the greatest good for the greatest number, but the greatest number is too often found to be number one."[35] Two months later in his August 1897 article in the *Atlantic Monthly,* Muir wrote

> Any fool can destroy trees. They cannot run away; and if they could they still would be destroyed — chased and hunted down as long as fun or dollar could be got out of their bark hides, branching horns, or magnificent bole backbones. Few that fell trees plant them; nor would planting avail much towards getting back anything like the noble primeval forests. During a man's lifetime only saplings can be grown in the place of the old trees—tens of centuries old—that have been destroyed.[36]

Muir's January 1898 *Atlantic Monthly* article began to entice readers to the marvels awaiting them in the forests and mountains of the reservations. "The tendency nowadays to wander in Wilderness is delightful to see," Muir wrote. "Thousands of tired, nerve shaken, over civilized people are beginning to find out that going to the mountains is going home; that wildness is a necessity; and that mountain parks and reservations are useful not only as fountains of timber and irrigating rivers, but as fountains of life."[37]

Muir's articles had had an impact on American public opinion beyond anything imagined possible when he began. The editor of *Atlantic Monthly* reported "enormously" increased circulation as a result of them. When March 1, 1898, arrived and the suspension of the Cleveland reserves expired, the Senate again passed an amendment to abolish them altogether. Public enthusiasm for forest reserves had become so strong that the House, more nearly reflecting this sentiment, voted down the Senate's amendment by a vote of 100 to 39. Forest reserves were here to stay.

But Gifford Pinchot had triumphed. The reserves were now open to economic exploitation. "The Pettigrew Amendment to the Sundry Civil Act of June 4, 1897," he said proudly, "was and still is the most important Federal forest legislation ever enacted."[38] Later Pinchot dubbed it *The Forest Management Act of 1897.*

There were problems in the amendment for the Northern Pacific Railroad, however. The railroad's plan to exchange rock and ice for timber, not just in the Pacific Forest Reserve but now in all the forest reserves, was moved directly from the vetoed Mount Rainier Park Bill and into the Pettigrew amendment. It was now the law of the land. But the language of the amendment was ambiguous. First, the in-lieu section of the amendment had presumed selection from surveyed timber lands because it had not specified otherwise. The railroad wanted to select from the especially valuable unsurveyed lands. Second, in regard to exchanged lands, the law had used the phrase "not exceeding in area" leaving the Northern Pacific Railroad with the future possibility of deal-ing with an unequal value legal challenge. Third, with forest reservations then being created in the political climate of 1898, the Northern Pacific Railroad wanted to make explicit that public domain forestland was to be available for exchange. This was critical because James J. Hill had previously accelerated the flow of public timberlands into private ownership, using the forest reserves themselves as the device. Hill wanted the ambiguities of the amendment removed, and the simplest, easiest way by which that could be done was to resurrect the Mount Rainier National Park bill.

Senator John L. Wilson of Washington introduced the same park bill that Cleveland had vetoed earlier. When Senator Wilson asked unanimous consent of the Senate to pass the bill, he attempted to down-play its importance by saying, "It is a little bill that has passed the Senate twice."[39] The House Committee on Public Lands was handled by Wash-ington's Congressman James Hamilton Lewis. He assured Congress in the committee's report that "the railroad lands within the proposed park are in large part very heavily timbered, and hence their exchange for other lands will in no way injure the United States, but be a direct pub-lic benefit."[40] This fraudulent report was calculated to obscure the rail-road's intent to exchange rock and ice for timberland, acre for acre, without concern for value.

McKinley signed the bill; it provided for a railroad and tramway into or through the park, for the mineral laws to apply, and for the North-ern Pacific Railroad to exchange "equal quantity," "surveyed and un-surveyed," from within any state *into or* through which the railroad runs." The last provision opened up the rich forest lands of western Oregon.

Within three days of the passage of the Mount Rainier National Park bill, the railroad released 450,000 acres for exchange, testifying to the high level of company activity that had to have immediately preceded its passage. The heavily timbered lands it received in exchange were in large part sold to the Weyerhaeuser Timber Company. Within a de-cade, Weyerhaeuser and his associates had acquired 1,945,000 acres con-taining 228.5 billion board feet of Pacific Northwest timber; 80 percent of that came from the Northern Pacific Railroad,[41] thanks in part to the creation of Mount Rainier National Park and the in-lieu clause in the Pettigrew amendment.

Everything had gone as the railroad had planned except for the mountain itself. Mount Rainier National Park contained 17,318 acres of glaciers which the railroad fully expected to exchange for timber-land. Public opinion intervened however, causing the government to change its course. In the face of popular sentiment, the government moved to retain Mount Rainier's glaciers in public ownership, arguing that within the concept of the Northern Pacific Railroad land grant they were not "land." The railroad contended that there was land under the glaciers somewhere, and proposed to relinquish title to the glaciers and select in-lieu lands elsewhere. The Northern Pacific Railroad actually contended that it had contemplated going into the ice business and had plans to cut off and market "ice from the glaciers" and establish a pleasure resort on the summit of Mount Rainier. It claimed the summit, contending that it stood within an odd section. Asserting also that if an exchange of glaciers for other lands was not acceptable, then the glaciers must still remain in the ownership of the railroad. The Department of the Interior concluded finally that the glaciers more nearly resemble rivers and streams than land, holding that they were not covered by a grant of land and could not be used as a basis for making in-lieu selections. (See 40 Land Decisions 441, 1912)[42] The public opposition to the Northern Pacific Railroad's attempt to keep Mount Rainier itself was so great that the railroad decided not to appeal the General Land Office decision against its claim of ownership.

In spite of the loss of 17,000 acres of the timberlands it expected to get for the rock and ice of Mount Rainier, the Northern Pacific Railroad fared remarkably well. Its successful promotion of the park bill netted it lands and timber worth billions today. By 1915, the enormity of the public loss was common knowledge. Congressman Thomson of Illinois described for the record the results of the Northern Pacific Railroad's in-lieu legislation efforts. "Mountain peaks, barren hillsides, lava beds, swamp lands and other valueless holdings . . . were released and the most valuable timber, coal and oil lands within the public lands were taken in exchange . . . when Mr. Hitchcock became Secretary of the Interior, he held the Lieu Land Law allowed exchange with any 'owner.' The bars were let down for wholesale fraud and a national scandal resulted."[43]

2 GONE FAST

To leave the boundaries unchanged would work immeasurable injury to the settlers by arresting the development of the communities through checking the growth of schools, markets, roads, and society.[1]   SEATTLE CHAMBER OF COMMERCE

. . . the only interests which are suffering in the slightest degree are those of the lumbermen and millmen, who are desirous, naturally, in having large areas of the best timberland in this reserve set apart from it.[2]   CHARLES D. WALCOTT,
U.S. GEOLOGICAL SURVEY

THE OLYMPIC FOREST RESERVE, one of thirteen that President Cleveland proclaimed, was the most valuable by far. Containing 2,188,800 acres, three fourths of the Olympic Forest Reserve timber volume lay in the lowland valleys and foothills. It was flowing rapidly to the timber companies and speculators by way of the Timber and Stone Act.

The Forest Committee, in its report on Olympic, identified in advance of Cleveland's proclamation the massive problems that lay ahead:

1. This proposed reserve no doubt contains for its area the largest and most valuable body of timber belonging to the nation; and here is probably the only part of the United States where the forest unmarked by fire or the ax still exists over a great area in its primeval splendor.
2. There is no agricultural or grazing land whatever in this proposed reserve, and no traces of precious metals have yet been found in it.
3. The character of its forests, which can be made to yield permanently vast quantities of timber, its wildness, the picturesqueness of its sur-

face, and its remoteness make the proposed Olympic reserve one of the most valuable of all the forest reserves which have been made or proposed.[3]

When John Muir heard that an Olympic Forest Reserve had been created, he prophetically saw what was coming. "The Olympic will surely be attacked again and again for its timber."[4]

During the Congressional debate that followed Cleveland's proclamations, it was widely alleged that the committee members had viewed the local areas only from railroad trains when they made their recommendations. To quiet these accusations and to provide a review of the committee's recommendations, special Interior Department agents were hired to investigate these reserves on the ground after the Pettigrew amendment passed in June of 1897. With the reservations suspended so that the privatization of their resources could continue for a year, Pinchot secured an appointment as one of these agents. He headed west into the new Olympic Forest Reserve in the summer of 1897.

Arriving August 19, Pinchot proceeded westward from Port Angeles to Lake Crescent where he picked up Al Blackwood, "a first class woodsman," he said, as a guide. "So thick was the undergrowth," Pinchot wrote, "so formidable the down timber, and so dense the forest that it took us from ten in the morning until seven in the evening to make less than five miles." He described it as a "super magnificent forest." "And no wonder," he said, "many of the trees were 275 feet in height, and not a few of them were 10 or 12 feet through breast high or even more." "The overpowering sense of bigness which emanated from that gigantic forest I can never forget." They journeyed up the Soleduck Valley to Sol Duc Hot Springs and on to the High Divide of the Hoh "from which," he said, "the view of Mt. Olympus was beyond description." Pinchot and Blackwood then proceeded together down the Bogachiel River where "for three days we saw no trace of humans but only wolf tracks and the deep worn trails of the Olympic elk." The trip for them ended on a truly somber note when they finally reached Sappho on their way back. "Just the week before," Pinchot wrote, "a mountain lion had carried off a child. It was the only case I ever knew of, outside the nature fakers, and on the very spot it was extremely real."[5]

When Pinchot's report on the Olympic Forest Reserve was submitted the following March, he made it clear that even if the other reserves would survive, Olympic would not. No other forest contained such enormous dollar value. Every tree below 1,000 feet elevation was available for logging with the equipment then available. Every tree that met this criterion was the target of the timber industry. The creation of the

The climax growth in the nation's temperate rain forest occurred on the wet west side of Washington State's Olympic Peninsula in elevations lower than 1000 feet. *Copyright 1988, Seattle Times.*

Olympic Forest Reserve had made unavailable for privatization those very trees, and Pinchot's report seemed to promote, somewhat ambiguously, economic utilization:[6]

1. "The Olympic forest is finer and more productive than that of any other of the United States and may fairly be called magnificent."
2. "Individual acres bearing more than 100,000 feet of lumber are common, while in the neighborhood of Port Crescent one quarter section which had been lumbered is known to have yielded upward of 40,000 feet per acre of cedar alone."
3. Climax growth in all species regarding size, quality and volume occur here.
4. There are no agricultural values in the reserve. "The land itself, after clearing, is worth but a fraction of the cost of clearing it. The destruction of timber for this poor result is appalling . . . "
5. "Enormous quantities of timber have passed into private hands around the edges of the peninsula, and these supplies will be sufficient to meet all commercial demands for several years to come."

Pinchot believed that public ownership of all the forestlands still in public ownership was the first essential ingredient to the development of a national forest policy. Reforestation as a routine function of cutting and the governmental control of cutting on private lands were the mainstays of his program. Both put him into open conflict with the timber industry. Within the confines of these beliefs, Pinchot believed that anything short of economic utilization of resources in the reserves was wasteful and pandering to simpleminded sentimentalism.

1898 would begin the showdown between Pinchot, who wanted additions to the Olympic Forest Reserve, if any boundary changes were to be made at all, and a timber industry committed to the corporate acquisition of every acre of Olympic forest that could be logged profitably. The gentle, rolling flatlands between the ocean and the mountains which contained the rain forest were at stake.

In 1898, after filing his Olympic report, Pinchot accepted appointment as head of the Division of Forestry in the Department of Agriculture, and from this position he began his seven-year-long campaign to get control of the forest reserves and their transfer to the Department of Agriculture.

The Olympic Forest Reserve, encompassing 2,188,800 acres, now became the battleground of three government agencies. The General Land Office, corrupt, subject to local pressures, with untrained and politically appointed personnel, had charge of the administration of the reserves. The U.S. Geological Survey in the Interior Department, a group of professionals with good training, had charge of surveys in the reserves. Working quietly and without publicity, they made no attempt to affect public opinion. In the Department of Agriculture was the Division of Forestry, headed by Pinchot, which regarded as one of its tasks directing and educating public opinion as well as recommending the creation of new reserves and dealing with technical matters on the growing of trees.[7]

Senatorial patronage had provided most of General Land Office personnel with their jobs, and the agency worked faithfully to get heavily timbered townships out of the Olympic Forest Reserve under the aegis of the Pettigrew amendment. That amendment read, in part:

> Any public lands embraced within the limits of any forest reservation which, after due examination by personal inspection of a competent person appointed for that purpose by the Secretary of Interior, shall be found better adapted for mining or for agricultural purposes than for forest usage may be restored to the public domain.

The Pettigrew amendment required upon this finding the recommendation of the Secretary of the Interior and the approval of the president; the territory specified would then be excluded.

The first problem for the timber industry was that Gifford Pinchot, himself, had performed the examination on the ground and had found no minerals and no agricultural land. The General Land Office, which administered the reserves, making recommendations to a sympathetic Secretary of the Interior and president, would struggle with Pinchot. The second problem was Congress, and to marshall its forces there, the timber industry moved to replace Washington Senator John L. Wilson with a timber industry insider. The state legislatures voted U.S. senators into office at the turn of the century, and the industry controlled the state legislative vote. It would be fourteen more years before the constitution would be amended to change that.

The corporate designatee was Addison G. Foster, partner of Chauncy Griggs who earlier had been partner to James J. Hill himself. Both Griggs and Foster had been neighbors on St. Paul's Summit Avenue, with Frederick Weyerhaeuser and James J. Hill. Foster was part of the St. Paul railroad and timber crowd that moved west in 1888 with the construction of the Northern Pacific Railroad through the Cascades. In 1898 he was engaged in coal mine operations, railroad construction, and was a principal in the St. Paul and Tacoma Lumber Company, which he served as vice president. He was the very model of the turn-of-the-century entrepreneur.

Over pinochle one evening, Foster and his partner in the timber business, Griggs, agreed that it would be good for the country if he were a senator and good as well for the St. Paul and Tacoma Lumber Com-

A wall of wood up to 300 feet high confronted those who entered the Olympic Peninsula's west side forests. None was saved. Only the inferior fringe forest in the Olympic National Park can suggest what it was like. *Photo circa 1890. Bert Kellogg Collection.*

pany.[8] But the headlines and articles in the *Tacoma News* responded to his candidacy with disbelief. "REPUBLICANS ARE MYSTIFIED" said the headline, " . . . the politicians who have induced him to 'come out' have made him believe that the voice of the people is demanding him with thunderous accords. . . . Just why Mr. Foster should be trotted out when so much available timber was lying around loose seems very mysterious indeed."[9]

As soon as Foster took office, the demand for an Olympic Forest Reserve reduction began. The reduction was purportedly for the benefit of the settlers. Foster lobbied in the Senate to release the "vast agricultural lands that had been tied up by the outrageous act of creating an Olympic Forest Reserve." He knew where the heavy timber was located and he let both Binger Hermann, General Land Office commissioner, and the Secretary of the Interior, E. A. Hitchcock, know what he wanted removed—"all valley lands and foothills now inside the Reserve."[10]

Although Foster led and orchestrated the effort, he had with him the public officials of Jefferson and Clallam Counties, Congressmen Cushman and Jones, and the officials of the General Land Office, whom they controlled through patronage in staffing its field offices. They would try to overcome the resistance of the U.S. Geological Survey under Charles Walcott and Gifford Pinchot in the Division of Forestry. And that would be difficult. Pinchot had first-hand knowledge of conditions and could refute the charges that would be made to justify the reduction. The U.S. Geological Survey had detailed reports from its field men available.

Port Angeles dentist J. W. Cloes, supervisor of the reserve, was appointed to the General Land Office in 1897. A political hack willing to perform whatever functions industry asked of him, Cloes was the personification of the corruption of the General Land Office. He immediately recommended cutting down the size of the Olympic Forest Reserve. Clallam County Auditor, Thomas T. Aldwell, organized the local campaign to convince the doubtful in Washington, D.C., that the recommendations of Cloes, aligned as they were with various chambers of commerce and Senator Foster, were correct. Aldwell also warned of heart-rending disaster that would overtake everyone if economic relief were not granted immediately.

Aldwell and Cloes generated petitions addressed to Senator Foster and Congressmen Cushman and Jones for use in urging that the great error (creating the reserve) be corrected immediately to avert imminent disaster. The same petitions went to the Secretary of the Interior and commissioner of the General Land Office in the hope that the corrective action could occur as soon as possible. The grounds upon which these petitions were based were that:

1. The reserve included large areas of agricultural lands.
2. The settlers on them would suffer "immeasurable injury by arresting the development of their communities."
3. "The development of the agricultural resources of the counties affected should not be checked."
4. The tax base of Clallam and Jefferson Counties would be negatively affected if the land remained in public ownership instead of passing into the hands of "settlers."[11]

Director Walcott of the U.S. Geological Survey responded personally to the General Land Office when word of Cloes' recommendations reached him. "None of this land is suitable for agricultural purposes," he said, pointing out that in fact it "is so heavily forested as to preclude its being cleared for agricultural purposes." He also pointed out that on eighteen of the southern townships Cloes was recommending for elimination stood 8.6 billion board feet of prime timber. "It is apparent," Walcott said, "as in other cases from this region, that the purpose is not to make available for settlement, agricultural lands, but to obtain for the benefit of lumber companies and the men employed by

them, the timber upon these lands, which is precisely what the government wishes to prevent in setting them off as reserves."[12]

Walcott, knowing that Pinchot had been to the Olympic Forest
Reserve, asked him to submit a statement for the record to counter the
pressure that was building. Pinchot, noting that it was an honor to do
so, reviewed what he had found in his 1897 trip that covered much of
"the route passed over by Mr. Cloes." "Abandonment of claims was at
that time in full swing," he said, "and had been for some time before,
for the reason that the immense labor of clearing the enormously heavy
forest from the land was all out of proportion to the returns the cleared
land was capable of producing."[13]

Lawrence Rakestraw, in his history, describes well the unfolding of
the strategy devised to reduce the boundaries. "Dozens of other petitions
came into the land office in 1899, praying for relief from the hardships
wrought on the poor but honest settler by the reserve. The arguments
advanced here were plausible and at times heartrending. Homesteaders
who had spent the best years of their lives developing fertile farms in
the region found their investment was for naught, Clallam and Jefferson Counties had lost most of the taxable land in their counties, schools
would close and road bonds, owned by widows and aged people in the
east, would be defaulted; farmers already in the area would sell out for
lack of markets and in order not to be caught in enlargement of the
reserves. The Seattle Chamber of Commerce sent in a remonstrance,
as did Senator A. G. Foster."[14] When Cloes became discredited, D. B.
Sheller, superintendent of Washington's forest reserves, began making
his own recommendations. A former member of the legislature and
also a political appointee, Sheller struggled in a job for which he had
no training and no support. He was unable to get convictions for forest trespass because of local hostility, and he worked without support
from the General Land Office and even from his own subordinates.[15]

In the same area that Cloes found 100 settlers, Sheller found only
eleven. But when it came to making recommendations, he also concluded by asking for revision of the reserve boundaries. With Sheller
supporting the boundary revisions, the local clamor for boundary adjustments reached a crescendo. Clallam County Auditor Aldwell wired
the congressional delegation, "Hundreds of settlers waiting to file
homesteads in reserve" and demanded immediate relief from what
would otherwise "badly retard growth of county." This was a complete
fabrication.

Senator Foster referred the telegram directly to Secretary Hitchcock,
demanding action. Chambers of commerce on the Olympic Peninsula
began communicating directly with the secretary, presumably because

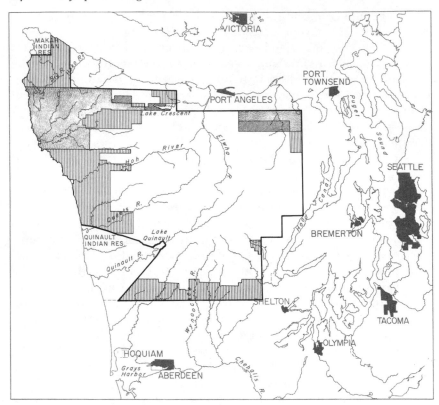

OLYMPIC FOREST RESERVE ELIMINATIONS OF 1900 AND 1901

In 1900 and 1901, President William McKinley accommodated the timber companies and wealthy speculators with proclamations eliminating three fourths of all the timber by volume from the Olympic Forest Reserve. These companies wanted the fraudulent privatization process then underway to continue. *OFR Reductions.*

they were not getting anywhere with the General Land Office and the U.S. Geological Survey, headed by Henry Gannett.

Lawrence Rakestraw's account recorded that "Sheller's report was backed by that of the field men of the Geological Survey, Theodore Rixon and Arthur Dodwell, who had just completed their examination of the area. They reported that the lumber industry had no immediate future there; there was no market for hemlock, and the fir and spruce were of poor quality. They also believed that the reserves were holding up development of Clallam County. . . . Gannett [of the Geological Survey] denounced both reports. Sheller, he said, was not a qualified observer as to the value of the timber there, which field notes of the

Geological Survey indicated was much higher in value than his estimate; and he also had a wrong idea as to what constituted agricultural land, believing that any level ground was agricultural. . . . As to Dodwell and Rixon, they had been swayed by the protests of the settlers."[16]

With Senator Foster now working furiously for the revision, and the U.S. Geological Survey working as furiously to head it off, Secretary of the Interior Hitchcock apparently ordered that the General Land Office and U.S. Geological Survey agree on a boundary revision. The two agencies met on March 15 to agree on areas for exclusion from the reserve. On April 7, 1900, by proclamation, President McKinley reduced the reserve by 264,960 acres. A year later, on July 15, 1901, another 456,960 acres were returned to the public domain.

It had taken the corporations and timber speculators only two years and four months to remove from the Olympic Forest Reserve three fourths of its timber by volume, everything that was considered merchantable at the time. 126 square miles of this heaviest of all timber in the United States went to the Milwaukee Railroad alone. Driving the privatization process was the U.S. Geological Survey's description of the Olympic Forest Reserve, which it said "is by far the finest body of

Clearcuts of 20,000 acres or more became common after speculators and timber companies succeeded in privatizing three fourths of the Olympic Forest Reserve's timber during the McKinley administration. *Photo circa 1900. Bert Kellogg Collection.*

Future Generation: *Did All This Happen Within Your Time, Grandpa?*
Present Generation: *Yes, My Boy.*
Future Generation: *What Did You Let 'Em Do It For?*

From The St. Paul Pioneer-Press.
1909.

By 1910, the loss of 520,000 acres of the heaviest timber the world had ever seen in the Olympic Forest Reserve through Timber and Stone Act fraud was but one of many timber scandals under Congressional investigation. It was too late by then to undo the loss of finest of the nation's forest heritage. Pinchot, *Breaking New Ground.*

timber yet remaining in the possession of the United States." Small remnants of the enormous rain forest trees in pockets in the low valleys,
inaccessible to the forestry technology of the turn of the century, remained in the reserve.

Congressional investigators later disclosed that ten years after the
reduction, the following "settlers" were included in the list of corporations which had acquired the lands of the reserve:[17]

	acres
Milwaukee Land Company (railroad)	80,630
Weyerhaeuser Timber Company	15,560
Simpson Logging Company	12,360
Polson Logging Company	10,040
Puget Mill and Timber Company	5,760
Merrill and Ring Company	4,160

Ten years after the boundary reduction about 600 acres of the elimination had been cultivated; title to 523,720 acres had passed into the
hands of the large owners. Three companies held 178,000 acres.[18] All
of this heavily timbered land was released as agricultural and fraudulently acquired under the Timber and Stone Act which required an
oath that it was "unfit for cultivation" and "valuable chiefly for timber."
In 1901 the commissioner of the General Land Office dismissed the
Olympic Forest Reserve reduction in his annual report, for 1901: " . . . the
timber in the extreme northwest corner of Clallam County was not
worth preserving, as it would be destroyed by storms and it was good
for farming."[19] In 1904, Senator Foster returned to the vice presidency
of the St. Paul and Tacoma Lumber Company full time as soon as his
Senate term expired, his Olympic mission accomplished.

By 1910, Congressional investigations and the eastern press turned
public attention towards the massive give-aways of public resources in
the previous decade. While these exposés were unfolding, Thomas
Burke of the Seattle Chamber of Commerce spoke for those who had
been the recipients of the bounty:

> The people of today have a right to share in the blessings of nature . . .
> there is a determined purpose not to let a band of well meaning sen-
> timentalists rob the present on the plea that it is necessary to hoard the
> nation's riches for unborn generations.[20]

3 A PRICE TO BE PAID

There are trees in heaven that are safe from politicians and fire but there are none here.[1]   JOHN MUIR

There has been a fundamental misconception that conservation means nothing but the husbanding of resources for future generations. There could be no more serious mistake.[2]
                                                            GIFFORD PINCHOT

THE OLYMPIC FOREST RESERVE eliminations contributed mightily to Gifford Pinchot's hatred of the Interior Department with its corrupt relationships with corporations operating on the public domain and the incompetence of its patronage employees. He attacked the Olympic eliminations as having been put through in his absence and without his knowledge on the utterly imaginary ground that it was more valuable for agriculture than for forestry. "Nearly every acre of it," Pinchot said, "passed promptly and fraudulently into the hands of lumbermen."[3] And he attacked everyone who had anything to do with Interior Department employment. "The Interior Department's field force on the Forest Reserves was enough to make angels weep," he said, suggesting that the real men of the West "could have nothing but contempt for a service manned by the human rubbish which the Interior Department had cheerfully accepted out of Eastern and Western political scrap heaps and dumped into the Forest Reserves."[4]

He was going to have an opportunity later to imprint the Forest Service with this and other personal viewpoints. But first he had to get the forest reserves, which remained in the Department of the Interior, transferred to the Department of Agriculture. From the moment he took over the Division of Forestry in 1898, he began the politicking to achieve that singular goal. With the same end in mind, he was able, with great political skill, to outmaneuver Muir. While Muir's campaign to keep sheep out of the reserves was having some effect, Pinchot was undoing it at every turn. When grazing was prohibited in the Arizona reserves by the Secretary of the Interior in 1900, Pinchot inspected the area and decided that grazing would not damage water supplies and persuaded the secretary to admit cattle and sheep. From 1901 on, the powerful National Livestock Association passed resolutions recommending transfer of the reserves to the Department of Agriculture and expressing confidence in Pinchot's views.[5]

Support was needed from lumbermen, too. In October of 1903, lumbermen held a conference with Pinchot and protested the further extension of forest reserves in Washington. Pinchot told the lumbermen that if they would cooperate with the government, these reserves would not be used as a means to keep stumpage values low. In other words, the government, by withdrawing timberlands from entry and keeping them off the market, would aid in appreciating the value of the newly acquired and now privately owned timber.[6] President Everett Griggs of the St. Paul and Tacoma Lumber Company, acting for the Pacific Coast Lumber Manufacturers' Association, said a short time later that the association was "working in harmony with Mr. Pinchot." Frederick Weyerhaeuser and his associates were "in sympathy with the work and plans of the bureau of forestry and stood ready to do whatever is in their power to cooperate in them."[7]

By bartering with the key corporations and associations on how the resources then in the Interior Department would be managed if he got control of them, Pinchot gained year by year their support for the transfer. Underlying all of his political maneuvering by then was the widely known fact that Pinchot stood for economic utilization of the resources in the reserves. He had no patience with Muir's concept of resources being held in trust for future generations. "The first principle of conservation," Pinchot said, "is development, the use of the natural resources now existing on this continent for the benefit of the people who live here now."[8] This was attractive to those corporations which stood at the ready to begin that development.

In 1905, when Pinchot had gained enough support from the corporations and trade associations of the West, there were enough votes in Congress to transfer the forest reserves to the Department of Agriculture. The nation's heritage of primeval land was being transferred to a man committed to preserving nothing. Only the small group of national parks then in existence remained inviolate. Muir, from that point on, relentlessly pursued the concept of preservation through national parks. However, every new park would have to be created out of an existing forest reserve and the reserves were now Pinchot's domain.

With the creation of the Forest Service barely underway in 1906, Pinchot made the first of several moves that would make him father of the National Park Service, still a decade away. Flushed with success from getting the reserves transferred to the Department of Agriculture, basking in the power conferred on him by President Roosevelt, and relishing nationwide publicity, he proceeded to confront Muir head on — in Yosemite National Park.

Acting on his own from his position as the president's only advisor on conservation matters ("I have put my conscience," President Roosevelt had said, "in the keeping of Gifford Pinchot"), Pinchot began urging on the city of San Francisco that it secure a water supply in Yosemite National Park following its 1906 earthquake. "I hope sincerely that in the regeneration of San Francisco its people may be able to make provision for a water supply from the Yosemite National Park," he volunteered to San Francisco. "I will stand ready to render any assistance which lies in my power."[9] By the end of the year, he urged the city to continue on the assumption that the attitude of the new Secretary of the Interior, James Garfield, would be favorable. A close friend of Pinchot's, Garfield could be counted on not only to endorse the flooding of Hetch Hetchy Valley in Yosemite, but also to support Pinchot in his efforts to get the national parks themselves transferred to the Forest Service. Garfield had put into his annual report for 1909, "Another year's experience in the administration of the parks confirms my belief that all of them, except the Hot Springs Reservation, should be transferred to the Forest Service, under the Department of Agriculture, where they could be better handled in connection with the national forests."[10]

Pinchot was dismissed from office by President Taft for insubordination in 1910. This ended the pressure to transfer the national parks. In the five years that he had control of the Forest Service, his aggressive attempt to controvert the expression of any preservationist element in land use, epitomized by the dam at Hetch Hetchy in Yosemite National Park, resulted in a massive public reaction. But in that same period, Pinchot's organizational skills succeeded in imprinting the new Forest Service with a deeply embedded cultural imperative that demanded the economic utilization of all the resources under its control.

In all the years that Pinchot had been working to gain control of both the forests and the national parks, he had ignored the signals of societal change all around him. Not only was there a Sierra Club (1892) but similar grass roots organizations had sprung into existence from Seattle to Boston. A rising tide of these organizations, the Appalachian

Mountain Club (1876), the Campfire Club of America (1897), the Mountaineers (1906) in Seattle and many more, were all committed to wilderness and its preservation, and to political action to achieve that preservation when required.[11]

Pinchot's efforts to invade Yosemite activated a nationwide network of these preservationist organizations and brought into their ranks some distinguished allies — Henry Fairfield Osborn, president of the American Museum of National History; ex-Secretary of War Henry L. Stimson; and Horace McFarland, president of the American Civic Association, were only a few. The national press, including *Harper's Weekly, Atlantic, Century* and many others, continually extolled the virtues of national parks: " . . . there can hardly be too many, and it is gratifying to believe that the tendency toward establishing them is constantly growing," summed up this sentiment.[12] Glacier National Park emerged from the work of the Boone and Crockett Club in 1910 as did Mount McKinley National Park later. So strong had the preservationist sentiment grown in Seattle that the *Seattle Mail and Herald* openly editorialized as early as 1904, " . . . let us have a National Park in the Olympics by all means."[13] Muir's proselytizing and the rising urbanization of American society were having an effect. Pinchot ignored it all.

Pinchot had succeeded in getting Hetch Hetchy for San Francisco, but he also succeeded in creating the political constituency that would create a National Park Service. That constituency would take lands away from the Forest Service continually (the latest in 1986) and preserve them.

4 PRESERVATION COMES AND GOES

There are many great copper veins in that range and some are included within the boundaries of the Olympic National Monument. It doesn't seem right that over 600,000 acres of land should be set aside for the benefit of less than 500 elk. . . .[1]

F. H. STANARD,
SEATTLE CHAMBER OF COMMERCE

. . . the agitation in regard to the mineral wealth of the Olympic Mountains, which probably does not exist, might lead to something of a stampede and the taking up of considerable quantities of heavy timber under the mining laws.[2]

HENRY S. GRAVES,
CHIEF FORESTER

THE ELK OF THE OLYMPIC PENINSULA occupy an ecological niche so dominant that the very nature of the forest itself is defined by their presence. When they are present, the forest is open with vistas through the trees on the forest floor. When the elk are absent, an impenetrable jungle of understory vegetation covers every inch of ground, altering dramatically the whole growth pattern of the forest.

Hundreds of elk, perhaps well over a thousand, occupied the Ozette region at the time of the arrival of the first white men in 1890. At that time, the Ozette forest had the open understory characteristics of the Hoh Valley today. In an operation as ruthless as the slaughtering of the buffalo of the Great Plains, hide and teeth hunters moved into the area and killed most of the herd. Hides to be tanned for leather were

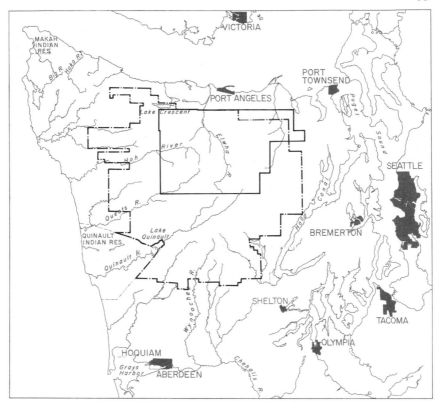

PROPOSED ELK NATIONAL PARK 1904

By 1903, the indiscriminate slaughter of the Olympic elk herd had reduced their number to about 500. The Elk National Park Bill of 1904 was doomed by its preservation of timber clause, put there on the premise that the saving of the elk required protecting their habitat.

shipped out by sailing schooner from a trading post at the mouth of the Ozette River. The two incisor teeth on each elk brought a good price as watch fobs. Walter Ferguson, who operated the trading post, reported with pride that he was able to kill seventy elk in a single day out of a band of 250 sighted at Swan Bay. The few surviving elk that were not killed later by Ozette homesteaders were doomed by the big blowdown of 1921 which marooned them and blocked their accustomed trails. With the elk gone, the Ozette forest reverted to the impassable tangle of understory which remains today.[3]

By 1903 there were "probably not more than 500 elk remaining" on the whole peninsula.[4] Nationwide concern that the largest band of free roaming elk would be gone forever produced fast action. In January of 1904, Congressman Cushman of Tacoma introduced the Elk National Park bill setting aside 393,600 acres "for the purpose of preserving the elk, game, fish, birds, animals, timber and curiosities therein." The bill, however, probably drafted by the Boone and Crockett Club, had a fatal flaw. It called for the preservation of timber on the assumption that the forest was an element essential to elk habitat. At that very moment, however, Gifford Pinchot was brokering with the timber companies for support in getting the forests transferred to the Department of Agriculture, which meant every tree would be available for logging. Within two months, Congressman Humphrey of Seattle made a move to counter the Elk National Park bill. He introduced a bill that would designate 750,000 acres as a game preserve "for the protection of game, animals, birds, and fishes in the Olympic Forest Reserve" with no mention of timber, leaving it open to logging in the future. On amendment, this was reduced to 450,000 acres.

When Humphrey made his move, the Elk National Park bill was well on its way, the House Public Lands Committee report appearing just a little over two months after it was introduced in 1904. The provisions of the bill were endorsed by both the commissioner of the General Land Office and the Secretary of the Interior. Speaking for the Public Lands Committee, Senator George Shiras said that "the creation of a national park in this locality will be a wise move and the conditions now existing are ideal for its present creation."[5]

The Port Angeles newspaper headline of March 11 said what everyone recognized: "INTRODUCTION OF AN OPPOSITION BILL BY HUMPHREY JEOPARDIZES THE PASSAGE OF THE CUSHMAN MEASURE ESTABLISHING ELK NATIONAL PARK." Everyone knew there had to be a reason for a competing bill, but it was hard to see. "Ulterior motives are alleged by some . . . " said the paper when an explanation was demanded by those supporting the park bill. Humphrey telegraphed, "Must be mistaken as to provisions of my bill, only intended to be in effect until Cushman bill is enacted." The Port Angeles newspaper raised the question which puzzled everyone: "Just how Mr. Humphreys (sic) expected to have his bill become a law and remain in effect temporarily pending the passage of another bill far in advance of it on the calendar and in the hands of the committee, is not explained."[6] As intended, the Humphrey "protect the animals but leave their habitat available for the timber industry" approach killed Elk National Park. Cushman never mentioned his bill nor any national park again. Stopping the Elk National Park bill kept the trees for the timber industry, but left the elk precariously on the edge of extinction. Killing the elk continued as before. The *Seattle Mail and Herald* in December of 1904 began a campaign to tell about what was happening to the elk. It asked for legislative relief from the state legislature as a stop-gap measure to protect them, and a national park in the Olympics for a permanent solution.

As part of a three-page editorial devoted to the elk and the need for a national park, the Seattle editor commented on letters from men who had returned from the Olympics. He said that "these letters tell a pitiful story of slaughtering elk whose carcasses are rotting in the Olympic Valleys." He went on to say, in part:

> These animals have apparently been shot down for the mere love of killing and in a great many instances not a pound of meat has been taken; nothing in fact except the horns and teeth; the carcasses have been left to rot.
>
> This, of itself, is a shame on humanity; it is a protest against useless slaughter; it is a louder protest against the existing conditions and an imperative cry for the protection of the largest game animal in the United States.
>
> The elk herds of the Olympics are swiftly and surely vanishing.
>
> It is absolutely necessary that action be taken . . . at the coming session of the legislature. Otherwise there will be no elk herds in the Olympics by the time the next following session of the legislature meets.

The Washington Seattle Game and Fish Protection Association was formed as a broad based, one-dollar-membership group "to force sane legislative enactments." It would be the organization to present a bill to the legislature.

> If this bill can be put through the Legislature it will be the first step in what will ultimately be the Olympic National Park. These things can't be done in a minute and we must preserve the game first and then get the Olympics set aside, or at least that portion of them that is necessary for a National Park, which shall protect the game there for all time to come and at the same time insure the people a playground and a recreation spot in what is one of the grandest little ranges of mountains on the globe.

Describing "the grandeur of that range, its ruggedness, its scenic beauty, its jewel like lakes, its glaciers, in short its own peculiar features, which are found nowhere else in the world," the three pages ended with a rallying cry for the city: "Let us preserve the game of the state and let us have a national park in the Olympics by all means."[7]

When the legislature met in January of 1905, the elk protective measure sailed through the legislative processes and it became unlawful to kill elk in Washington State until 1915. So popular had the Olympic elk become that the legislature promptly extended the killing ban again in 1915 for an additional ten years.[8] Five years after the killing ban had gone into effect, the Forest Service placed the total number of elk on the peninsula at 3,000 to 3,500, at least a doubling in number from what it had been.[9] They were no longer in danger of extinction.

Enthusiasm for an Olympic Park to protect the elk permanently in their forested habitat remained high. Congressman Humphrey reintroduced his industry-inspired, game-preserve-with-logging measure in 1906 (HR 15335) in the hope that it would quiet the demand. It didn't. Preservationism was now growing fast.

Meanwhile, in the short period that Pinchot had headed the new Forest Service, he had replaced the corrupt field force of the Interior Department with a group of college graduates committed to what they believed to be the public good. They moved to stop the corrupt practices that had become a way of life in the Interior Department. When life on the reserves began to be impacted by the organizational leadership of Pinchot, the corporations tried in Congress to limit the whole concept of government forests. They were still so influential that when the agricultural appropriation bill in 1907 emerged, it carried an amendment stripping the president of the authority to create any additional forest reserves in the six northwestern states.

Pinchot and Roosevelt were ready. Pinchot had long studied all the states involved for future possible additions to the forest reserves. Directing Pinchot to prepare the proclamations for the long-planned additions in 1907, Roosevelt signed the appropriation bill two days after he had signed the last of a series of forest reservation proclamations. Another sixteen million acres were added to the national forests, increasing them threefold.[10] This move gave Pinchot his chance to make some of the additions to the Olympic Forest Reserve he had mentioned in his 1897 survey report. He got 127,680 acres added and brought the forest to the shores of Hood Canal and put back some of the Soleduck Valley which had been eliminated by President McKinley.

The *Seattle Post-Intelligencer,* in response to Roosevelt's 1907 forest additions, ignored the rising preservationist activity all around it. It editorialized that "the growth of such a great state as Washington can no longer be hampered, and its development hampered (sic), to please a few dilettante experimentalists. . . . Their idea that the greater part of this state must be kept in primeval wilderness . . . does not appeal to the people of Washington, who are inviting immigrants to build up the country." And the governor of Washington stated at last in an interview that "Gifford Pinchot, the United States Forester, has done more to retard the growth and development of the Northwest than any other man."[11]

In 1908, when the furor had died down, Congressman Humphrey, four years after his first action to kill Elk National Park, again introduced another of his "save-the-wildlife-but-keep-their-habitat-available-for-the-timber-industry" game preserve plans (HR 14037). Again, it failed.

Later, in February of 1909, the three-year-old Mountaineers organization in Seattle began its first thrust into preservationist politics. Wealthy and influential Seattle attorney George E. Wright, on behalf of a committee of the Moutaineers, undertook to get a national park established on the Olympic Peninsula. The wide interest in a national park now had inspired a leading citizen with ties to the fabric of Seattle society. Wright wrote to Humphrey with the authority of God: "I am about to lend my support to the movement to create some kind of a National Park out of the main body of the Olympic Mountains." Humphrey read the message that a park was coming and he also got Wright's message about timber: "We can easily create a park having an area of between six hundred and one thousand square miles, without approaching the boundaries of the present forest reserves and without approaching merchantable timber."[12] In other words, whatever timber would be included would not be defined in the economy of 1909 as merchantable, but it would be included and preserved.

The Antiquities Act of 1906 had given the president the power to set aside by proclamation areas of public domain to be known as national monuments, to preserve objects of historic and scientific interest. It was intended for the preservation of the cliff dwellings and other Indian relics of the Southwest. But after struggling for more than five years to get some semblance of federal preservation into the Olympics, the Antiquities Act seemed a natural for Humphrey. Such presidential power could also head off a park bill that might propose to lock up much more. A presidential proclamation would be much more manageable.

Humphrey gathered up Pinchot to go with him to the White House to see what the lame-duck Roosevelt could do about it. "In my anxiety to do something towards preserving the Roosevelt elk of the Olympics . . . ," Humphrey said, "I thought of the statute that gives the President the power to set aside certain acres of land to preserve such features as were of great scientific value. I decided to ask the President to do this with this region. I requested Mr. Pinchot, who was interested always in game protection, to go with me to see the President for this purpose.

"I shall not forget that visit. It was as I recall, the second day of March, two days before the end of the Roosevelt administration and the beginning of the Taft administration. I was waiting in the Cabinet room when the President came in. . . . Without waiting for any formal greeting, as soon as he entered he called to me across the room, 'Tell me what you want, Mr. Humphrey and I will give it to you. Do not take time to give me the details, simply tell me what you wish me to do.' I said, 'Mr. President, I want you to set aside as a national monument, 750,000 acres in the heart of the Olympics.' He replied, 'I will do it. Prepare your order and I will sign it.'"[13]

Pinchot returned to his office to draft the proclamation, which would have to define the 750,000 acres to which Roosevelt had agreed. Humphrey had spent the last five years of his career in a continuous effort to keep timber from being preserved as a fall-out from efforts to save the elk. Here he seemed to support a measure that would do just that. But Pinchot was not about to be involved in the preservation of trees. When Pinchot's boundaries for the monument emerged in the proclamation, the boundaries included approximately 600,000 acres instead of the 750,000 agreed to by Roosevelt and expected by Humphrey. Pinchot excluded the west-side valleys of the Hoh, Bogachiel, Queets and Clearwater rivers where the major elk populations resided and which also contained the heaviest timber stands. In purpose and intent, the Antiquities Act required complete preservation of everything. In the face of this constraint Pinchot quietly added a clause to the proclamation that would make the monument meaningless:

> The reservation made by this proclamation is not intended to prevent the use of the lands for forest purposes under the proclamations establishing the Olympic National Forest, but the two reservations shall both be effective on the land withdrawn, but the National Monument hereby established shall be the dominant reservation and any use of the land which interferes with its preservation or protection as a National Monument is hereby forbidden.[14]

Absolutely contradictory, calling for the cutting of the trees in the monument while forbidding anything that interfered with their preservation, the clause took Humphrey off the hook with the timber industry and gave to Pinchot's Forest Service the power eventually to log while maintaining an illusion of preservation to placate the national park forces. At the time, Pinchot must have felt strongly the great political power of the Boone and Crockett Club connection as well. President Roosevelt, the key Public Lands Committee leadership in Congress, and both Congressman Humphrey and he, himself, were members. The club had been working to get protection for the Olympic elk for years and was behind the Elk National Park effort of 1904. Congressman John Lacey, author of the Antiquities Act, under which the monument was proclaimed, was also a member. By sabotaging the monument in the provisions of the proclamation, he avoided the complications of negatively entangling himself in the massive legislative power represented by the Boone and Crockett Club of 1909. Because he intended to remain as chief of the Forest Service, it was a prudent move, even in the face of internal opposition to the concept of a monument in his own organization.

Nearly everyone now believed that the Olympics had its national park with the elk and its habitat fully protected at last. "It is a region of wild natural beauty," extolled *Colliers Magazine.* "Seattle is unique as being the only city in the country which has a national park within sight of its front yard."[15] Even the industry-dominated Washington State Legislature got on the bandwagon. The day after Roosevelt signed the monument proclamation, the Washington State Legislature sent House Joint Memorial Number 5 to Congress calling for an Olympic National Park around the shores of Lake Quinault "containing 1,322.55 acres more or less."[16] This message to Congress defined what the timber industry might be willing to support in the way of a park for the Olympics if pushed hard by public opinion.

Pinchot and Congressman Humphrey had carefully structured the proclamation creating the monument so that it was "not intended to prevent the use of the lands for forest purposes." In other words, it could be logged just as any other part of the national forest. Humphrey also believed that the presence of the monument would not prevent mining and prospecting within the limits.[17] The monument as orchestrated by Pinchot and Humphrey was a sham to placate the rising national park movement in Seattle and throughout the state. All its resources could be used, they believed, exactly as if the monument boundaries were not there. It seemed to be a successful culmination of the Humphrey game preserve bills which had been appearing since 1904.

But shock waves passed through the Seattle business community when former Seattle mayor Richard Ballinger, now Secretary of the Interior, unexpectedly took the position two months after its creation that because the monument was created under the Antiquities Act, there could be no "prospecting for or working of mineral deposits" in the monument. This rigid preservationist viewpoint about the meaning of the Antiquities Act, later upheld many times, nullified the effect of Pinchot's forestry clause which he believed would leave the monument open for logging.

Ballinger's successor, Walter L. Fisher, himself a close ally of Pinchot's, took the same position on the monument in 1911 that Ballinger had taken. Several billion board feet of timber now lay preserved at Seattle's doorstep; the real national park that the preservationists had been working for since the Elk National Park bill of 1904 was a reality. The absolute preservation imperative of the Antiquities Act had been affirmed by two Secretaries of the Interior.

By 1909, the timber companies had gained title to almost all of the

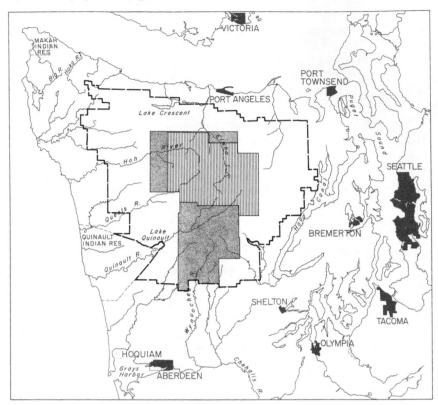

MOUNT OLYMPUS NATIONAL MONUMENT ELIMINATIONS OF 1915
A Seattle Chamber of Commerce committee, sponsored by the timber industry, demanded the elimination of all of the then merchantable timber in the Mount Olympus National Monument as established in 1909. In 1915, the Forest Service gave them everything they asked for and threw in another six square miles of the heaviest timber as well.

forests eliminated from the forest reserve. Just eight years earlier the last of these forest reserve eliminations had occurred. Still in place were all of the individuals who had so successfully achieved the spectacular result — the elimination and privatization of three fourths of the timber in the original Olympic Forest Reserve, everything that was merchantable. What had changed was that there now was widespread knowledge that "the agricultural lands" that "the settlers" had been deprived of were public forestlands that were now in hands of timber syndicates. In fact the interests of "the settlers" had become a kind of standard joke when referring to the timber companies. If the timber this time was going to come out of the monument, a new and more credible reason would be needed.

Before the new approach would emerge, Pinchot and Ballinger engaged in what became known as the Ballinger-Pinchot controversy. Pinchot was publicly dismissed by President Taft from his office as chief of the Forest Service for insubordination and Ballinger resigned from office after Pinchot had tarred him with the brush of corruption, a charge that was never sustained.[18]

At the moment of Pinchot's firing, the Seattle Chamber of Commerce, fronting for the timber and mining companies, began an attack on Pinchot, all of Roosevelt's resource policies, and on federal ownership of resources. In an attack on the Mount Olympus National Monument, one of the Seattle chamber's pamphlets called for continued privatization of the public forests. "The greatest advantage that would result from opening the forest reserves and the phoney (sic) national parks," it said, "would be to the state; it would increase the amount of taxable land . . . " indicating their attitude toward Pinchot, " . . . we hope it will be a long time before another millionaire's son, with a fad for forestry, gets control of the power to put us back in the reserve." In case anyone wondered what was intended, the chamber's pamphlet explained, "the reserves of a state should be under the control of that state," a view which reflected how successful Pinchot and the Forest Service had been in eliminating the corrupt patronage positions beholden to Senators and Congressmen who were in turn beholden to the corporations.[19]

The chamber charged that, "Any policy that would seal up or unnecessarily retard the use of nature's wealth not only would be of no benefit to the present or future generations but would be a positive injury to both."[20] Ironically, the Seattle Chamber of Commerce was saying exactly what Pinchot believed and had attempted to achieve for them in the proclamation creating the monument. The attacks on Pinchot personally and on the Forest Service now began in Congress, led by Humphrey on behalf of Washington State's industries.

Pinchot's Forest Service successor, Henry S. Graves, took over an organization under constant attack from the industrial users of public lands who now wanted those lands transferred to the states. He also found himself with a full-blown national park movement on his hands. The preservationist power had grown to the point where a separate service to administer and preserve the parks was about to emerge. Both movements could be laid at Pinchot's doorstep. His failure to acknowledge the validity of any thought of preservation had created the park movement. His incessant demands for control of cutting on private lands and for sustained-yield cutting in the national forests had led to the state ownership demands. Graves had inherited it all and would begin to fight for the Forest Service's life.

With a national park movement gaining strength daily at both the national and local levels, and the existence of the Mount Olympus National Monument under attack by the Seattle Chamber of Commerce, Congressman Humphrey decided to move. He introduced a bill early in 1912 that would convert the monument into a national park, getting rid of the "preserve everything" Antiquities Act underpinnings of the monument at the same time. His bill provided that the Secretary of the Interior "may also sell and permit the removal of such matured or dead or down timber as he may deem necessary or advisable for the protection or improvement of the park," almost word for word out of the Pettigrew amendment of 1897. No one really believed there were any minerals worth finding but he gave to those who wanted to try the provisions necessary for entering mining claims which also gave the timber to those who succeeded. For good measure he threw in provisions allowing for the leasing of summer home sites. Washington's Senator Wesley L. Jones introduced the same bill in the Senate a few months later.[21] Humphrey now was back to where he and Pinchot were when they presented Roosevelt with the monument proclamation: a park in name only.

Two factors immediately killed the bills. The preservationist forces had grown so strong that a bill to create a Bureau of National Parks with its own Park Service was about to surface. They weren't about to let a bill that would set the precedent of Hetch Hetchy, then being fiercely fought, take over the whole park system. Most importantly though, the timber industry and the chambers of commerce had discovered, as a replacement for "settlers and agricultural land," that the Olympics were absolutely laden with valuable minerals. The old drama began again. Government reports abounded with data that there were no mineral resources of any commercial value anywhere in the Olympics, just as similar reports earlier had stated that there was no agricultural land. If the necessity for immediate relief from the lock up of agricultural land in the forest reserve could succeed, why couldn't relief from the lock up of minerals in the monument succeed, even in the face of the same reports? The leaders of the "eliminate the monument movement" were right out front with the issue of minerals in the monument from the start. "The trouble with the Humphrey bill," said Asahel Curtis of the Seattle Chamber of Commerce, "is that it includes a lot of land that has no special attractions but is of value for its timber and for agriculture."[22]

The secretaries of the Departments of Agriculture and Interior and the chief of the Forest Service were besieged with petitions for relief from the burden that the presence of the monument was putting on the development of the country. A self-appointed committee of three undertook, on behalf of the Seattle Chamber of Commerce, the task of defining for the country what should be removed from the monument. Asahel Curtis represented the timber-dominated Seattle Chamber of Commerce. C. J. Kelly represented the Seattle Commercial Club, which was never at variance with the chamber. F. H. Stanard, whose office was in the Lumber Exchange, identified himself as "Representing Mining Interests of the Olympic Mountains." All went to work to free the monument's timber. They issued their report in January of 1912. It represented the maximum that any industrial forest-user could expect to achieve. It eliminated from the monument every tree that had commercial value. To reassure the national park movement, this committee of three recommended that what remained be made into a national park. To reassure those who might think that they wanted a real national park, they added that the proposed park should provide for "the entry of mining claims both lode and placer," cutting of timber, the use of water power, and "the right to build and operate any class of transportation . . . through or out of the proposed park."[23] Curtis, Kelly and Stanard accounted for their recommended eliminations on the basis of "commercial timber." When local pressure in Seattle wanted the "barren peaks," on the Olympic skyline but outside of the monument, added to the park recommendations, this committee of three explained away the impossibility of such an action by a simple declarative statement. "We find on careful investigation that such an extension of the limits would include a part of the valleys of four rivers, which valleys are heavily timbered."[24]

Two days later, the *Seattle Post-Intelligencer,* reporting the committee's recommendations, said "NEW NATIONAL PARK PROPOSED" and "WOULD RESTORE RIGHTS," presumably of the timber industry to the timber.[25] Not one word about the needs of the elk appeared anywhere in the report. "It seemed to be assumed that the protection of the elk was a matter of winter range," reported Forest Supervisor P. S. Lovejoy, "and that it would be impossible to include sufficient winter range in the Park without including improper and prohibitive amounts of timber and other resources."[26]

F. H. Stanard began travelling throughout western Washington, drumming up support from the chambers of commerce and commercial clubs for the boundary revisions as proposed by his committee. He managed to get their petitions and resolutions in support of an "Olympus National Park" to specify always "under the conditions and privileges set forth" in the committee's recommendations. Attorney George Wright of the Mountaineers, still working for a real park, became convinced that Stanard "represents some interest which he is keeping undercover" because the state geologist, Professor Henry Landes of the University of Washington, had already determined that the Olympics generally were "absolutely barren" of minerals.[27] No one doubted that the timber industry employed Stanard.

Asahel Curtis took on the task of reaching the preservationists who had national constituencies that might be used to thwart the monument reduction. To both William E. Colby and E. T. Parsons of the Sierra Club, he presented the issue as an attempt to create a national park because "the Monument has no legal standing and can be set aside." "I can assure you," he said, "that the park set aside as requested will be a very beautiful one and we are not giving up anything that would be of material benefit to it."[28] He failed to mention that logging, placer mining, and road building were contemplated for it.

Curtis ran into problems when he tried to get the Mountaineers to support the work of his committee in reducing the boundaries. Not only did they reject out of hand his committee's recommendations, but also "since that time," said Curtis, "have made a determined effort to have a National Park established with the same boundaries as the National Monument." "I believe that the action of the Club," wrote Curtis to Enos Mills, "has been influenced in a measure by a number of the members who have taken a strong dislike to me."[29] In part he was driven from the Mountaineers, in which he had been a charter member. He spent the rest of his life fighting every preservation proposal involving trees that came to his attention and was rewarded by having a Forest Service campground named after him near Snoqualmie Pass in Washington State.

In effect a real national park, Mount Olympus National Monument, with over 600,000 acres, existed. It protected everything within its boundaries from economic exploitation. The local preservationists, using their new voluntary organization, the Mountaineers, became the focal point of citizen action to continue its protected status, but as a national park. It was a pitiful effort and no match for the opposition. All the newspapers opposed them, and they had minimal contact with similar organizations.

The opposition to the preservationist efforts also centered on the creation of a national park, but only one whose territory lay in the center of the most mountainous region of the monument. All the resources in the recommended park, as well as what would be excluded from the existing monument, were expected to be available for economic exploitation. In agreement with this position were Seattle's and Washington's small-town business communities, their trade associations, chambers of commerce, commercial clubs, the Washington Congressional delegation, and the Forest Service.

Within four months of the issuance of the 1909 monument proclamation, the Forest Service regional office began a series of recommendations to abolish the monument. Over 7 billion board feet of timber in the Olympic National Forest were out of logging reach because of the monument. "Preventing use of the resources," "doesn't support the elk," "might appear that the Forest Service is fostering hunting grounds to the exclusion of the development of the natural resources," "splendid timber which should be open to development," were just some of the reasons given by the Forest Service for abolishing the monument.[30]

But the issue of Mount Olympus National Monument was a minor backwater affair for the Forest Service against the backdrop of what had been happening to it since Pinchot's departure. It was fighting for its very existence.

At the National Conservation Congress in 1910, James J. Hill, who had engineered the in-lieu legislation and then manipulated the creation of Mount Rainier National Park into a fortune in timber for the Northern Pacific Railroad and Weyerhaeuser Timber Company, wanted state control of the nation's forest lands. He was entirely opposed to the position of the conservationists and the Forest Service. Every large timber operator or owner was opposed to the Forest Service's policy of handling government timber whether as a government utility for present use or as a reserve for future generations.[31] This state-control movement had grown so strong by 1912 that Assistant Forest Service Chief William B. Greeley could say that "Debate on one of these measures clearly showed an astonishing amount of support for the idea that transfer to the states would be the ultimate disposition of the remaining public lands, the National Forests included."[32] With state ownership, there was a valid expectation that the privatization of the forest lands would continue. And there was a distinct possibility that the Forest Service would not be around.

In 1913, Congressman Humphrey, with a bill pending that would create a national park open to logging, began an open attack on the Forest Service, presumably to help the process of transfer of its forest lands to the states. On June 2, 1913, Humphrey stood up in the House and accused the Forest Service of having been responsible for the great timber monopolies in the West and for giving the railroads vast areas of the public domain. "It is today more largely responsible for the high cost of forest products than any one cause, and that in the name of conservation it annually keeps millions of dollars worth of timber off the market and permits it to rot in the forest."[33]

Increasing the cut on national forests was worth hundreds of millions of dollars to the industry and Humphrey set out to help them. Here is a fragment of what he had to say that day in June, 1913, when he launched his attack in Congress on behalf of the Seattle-headquartered timber industry:

It is the proud boast of the Forest Service that some time it will be self supporting. We heard this promise for many years, but it makes practically no progress in that direction. Under the present national forest systems how much shall it profit the people if it takes a billion dollars worth of property and a million dollars in cash each year to free the parasites that control it? Where do the people's interests come in? What would be thought of a guardian or an administrator that would take a billion dollars worth of standing timber and could not manage it in these times of high prices so that it would be self sustaining locking a million dollars each year? . . . Not only are these vast forests withdrawn from public use while the people are taxed a million dollars each year to pay the so-called foresters to care for them, although what these gentlemen do no man yet has ever been able to discover. . . . In the beginning the Western States were promised — and we believed that promise — that the States in which these national forests were located, in lieu of taxes, would receive a sum from the sale of the timber that would approximately equal that loss. That promise is still being repeated, as is the old, old promise that some day the Forest Service will be self-supporting. We no longer have faith in any such promise; in fact, we now know that it never will be kept.

Mr. Gifford Pinchot is probably the leading exponent in America of this national forest policy. . . . In a recent issue of Pearson's Magazine he discusses this identical proposition. In one portion of the article he did what a conservationist seldom does and what they should never do. It was a fatal mistake. He uses figures instead of adjectives. These figures given by him is the most scathing denunciation of the Forest Service ever uttered. If they did not come from the highest authority I would hesitate to use them. They demonstrate not only the utter worthlessness of the Forest Service but they further demonstrate that through the incompetency and negligence of this service millions of dollars worth of timber on the public domain in the State of Washington each year have been wasted. Let me read to you:

The facts are that in the eight years, 1905 to 1912, inclusive, during which the Forest Service has had charge of the national forests, 415,512,900 feet of timber has been sold from the national forests of the State of Washington. The average cut during that period was not seven but seventeen and a half million feet annually. For the last three years the cut has averaged a little over 30,000,000 feet, and during the last year it reached 37,000,000 feet. (Pearson's Magazine, May, 1913, p. 623.)

No enemy could have so convinced the Forest Service of criminal waste and stupidity as do these figures here given. What do these figures mean? They mean that in the most densely forested regions of the world, where 150,000 feet are frequently cut from a single acre, the Forest Service annually is cutting from each acre less than a foot and a half. They mean that in that bloated year of 1912, when the service was forced to sell some fire-killed timber, they actually cut from the forest reserves in the State of Washington at the rate of one plank for each acre, 3 feet 1 inch long, 12 inches wide, and 1 inch thick. They mean that on an empire containing 23,000 square miles — a region greater than Rhode Island, greater than Delaware, greater than Connecticut, greater than New Jersey, greater than Massachusetts, greater than all these States combined — the Forest Service in the name of conservation is annually cutting 350 acres of timber. They mean that a single mill in the State of Washington will cut the entire output from the national forest reserves in that State running less than three months each year. In the State of Washington the forests fully reproduce themselves in 16 to 20 years. How long at the present rate of cutting that has been practiced by the Forest Service for the last eight years, as pointed out by Mr. Pinchot, will it take to cut over once the national forests in the State of Washington? Only 35,000 years. That is all. Here in these figures proudly furnished by the chief prophet of the policy is demonstrated the supreme essence of "conservation" as it is practiced in all its sublime idiocy.[34]

Pinchot's turn-of-the-century understanding with the timber operators on the cutting of timber, which enabled him to get their support for transferring the forest reserves to him, now began to plague the Forest Service. By withholding government timber from sale, except in small quantities, the timber operators would not have to fear the value-depreciating competition of the Forest Service timber. But as the value of the privately owned timber, acquired by industry earlier, skyrocketed, the timber operators attempted to operate on cheap government timber. They could then wait to reap the harvest from the greatly increased value of their own timber later. The possibility of getting the Forest Service's timber transferred to the states meant being able to control the cut to maximize profits.

As these attacks continued, no one was certain, least of all Chief Forester Henry S. Graves, whether the attack might succeed and the forests vanish into the control of the timber industry at the state level. State control offered a happier prospect for the timber industry than did a continuation of the industry distrust imprinted on the Forest Service by Pinchot.

Albert Johnson entered Congress from Grays Harbor, Washington, in 1913. No one would ever represent the timber industry more vigorously than Johnson. He charged that "The Forest Service, we believe should be relieved from the administration of the national forests. The Forest Service should be a purely scientific bureau, such as the Bureau of Plant Industry and other bureaus in the Department of Agriculture."[35]

Johnson wanted the Forest Service transferred to the General Land Office in the Interior Department, Pinchot's enemy, and he introduced HR 6923 to accomplish it. Given the General Land Office's internal predisposition toward the disposal of public land, there would then be an agency in control of the forests favorable to a transfer to the states. The presence of Franklin K. Lane as Secretary of the Interior was encouraging also. Lane earlier had become city attorney of San Francisco and was the driving force with Pinchot behind the proposal to build the Hetch Hetchy dam; he had resolved in favor of flooding Hetch Hetchy Valley in 1913.

Johnson aggressively defended the by now notorious Olympic National Forest elimination. "It is true that lands eliminated from the Olympic National Forest," he said, "are now in the hands of private persons and corporations, some of these logging corporations. Being so, they are of some use to society. Had they remained in the national forests . . . they would have stagnated; their timber would have rotted. As it is, they are paying part of the tax burdens of the State, are contributing to the settlement and upbuilding of the Commonwealth, and are performing that duty which nature intended them to perform."[36]

Newly elected Congressman James W. Bryan, Washington's congressman at large, did everything possible to counter the timber industry's attempt to move the clock back as the sweet smell of rapidly appreciating timber values drove them onward. He charged that "the land grabbers know that they can strike a better bargain, as a rule, under State management than under Federal control." "The tax argument," he said, "is precisely urged on behalf of State and individual ownership. This means, of course, that if the State had control it would soon pass the timber land into private hands, and that the revenues of taxation would be greatly increased. It appears absurd to give away property in order to get the taxes. If the property were not worth more than the taxes, these timber operators would not want it."[37]

When Bryan charged that "under State control the most flagrant frauds were perpetrated" and that "collusion on the part of the State officers" was responsible for the Olympic forests passing "into the hands of large owners," Johnson blamed it all on the federal government. "There was some deceit practiced, it is true," he said, "but it was practiced by those forces in the control of the Federal Government."[38] The timber industry stood innocent.

While the debate raged on between what Congressmen themselves labeled the "anti-conservationists" and everyone else, Johnson finally got around to Mount Olympus National Monument. More than fifteen years had passed since the successful thrust to eliminate the forests from the Olympic Forest Reserve had begun. Johnson's argument, substituting minerals for agricultural lands, could just as well have applied to the earlier battle.

Speaking of the monument in the House in November of 1913, Johnson said:

> That monument comprises the great mountainous center of the vast Olympic Forest Reserve, which consists of nearly 1,600,000 acres, and under the monument act citizens are forbidden to wield a pick — almost forbidden to strike a match. In that monument, I am satisfied, exist semi precious minerals of many kinds. I believe that there is enough manganese there to supply the United States for 200 years. I believe that there are great quantities of fluorspar. . . . That great forest reservation has taken the heart not only out of the Olympic Peninsula, but also has taken the heart out of the prospector and the sturdy pioneer who settled in there, many of them over 20 years ago and who are still living far up in the trackless woods, waiting for the counties in which they live and for the State to whose charter they subscribe to build them roads over which they might haul in the necessities of life at less than 2 cents a pound and haul out the products which grew in such abundance in that, the richest soil in all the United States.[39]

Johnson spoke of the horrors of the Forest Service's presence on the Olympic Peninsula. "So much of its area [is] in the forest reserve — 100,000 acres in fact, that nothing is left but a little strip on the beach on the Pacific Ocean to the west and another strip on the shores of Puget Sound to the east; on a high hill overlooking the eastern shore of this great country sits in solemn grandeur the courthouse, slowly falling into decay because no taxes are available for its upkeep and no settlers are coming to that territory upon which the county had based its hopes of prosperity. . . . That county has been bankrupted by the Forest Reserve."[40]

Johnson never mentioned that all of Jefferson County's merchantable timber in the forest reserve as of fifteen years ago had presumably been put on its tax rolls in the forest reserve eliminations of 1900 and 1901. He kept defending the timber industry, even as the notoriety of the forest reserve "land grab" eliminations spread into nearly every environmental forum. The truth was that the Olympic Forest Reserve eliminations of the past were getting in the way of the industry agenda of the day — state control and then more privatization. When Johnson was confronted by the forestry committee report of the 1913 Conservation Congress that the Olympic forest "land fell into the hands of the big timber owners," he shot back that, "So it all did, much of it, but

I insist that the wages they pay in camps, mills and offices is to this day the principal support of the country in question. But for the withdrawal of 1901 another county would have been bankrupted."[41]

Congressman Bryan hoped the sheer magnitude of the statistics of the turn-of-the-century Olympic timber giveaway would deter another one. He charged that "523,720 acres passed into the hands of owners who are now holding it purely as a timber speculation. Three companies and two individuals own over 178,000 acres in holdings from 15,000 to over 80,000 acres."[42]

While Congress continued its debate between 1910 and 1914 over whether the Forest Service deserved to exist and whether the forests should go to the states or to the General Land Office, or somewhere else, Forest Service Chief Henry S. Graves fought as best he could on all fronts. Pinchot had unwittingly launched the national park movement which Graves had not been able to contain, and Graves himself as chief forester had added impetus for a park service. Graves had to face the seriousness of the on-going timber, mining and grazing industry attacks and these were having a profound internal impact on the organizational culture of the Forest Service itself.

Against this backdrop of crisis for the Forest Service, Graves saw the Mount Olympus National Monument reduction effort as another timber scheme, but which could prove to be serious in the context of the history of the earlier Olympic Forest Reserve reductions. Word was around that land eliminated from the monument would revert to the public domain and be open to the timber claims process. Attorney George Wright of the Mountaineers warned Graves that in view of the act of March 4, 1907, barring the creation of forest reserves in Washington without Congressional approval that "it may very well be that that part of the Presidential proclamation abolishing the Olympus Monument will be valid while that part of the proclamation 'restoring' the monument to the forest reserve may be wholly invalid. If such be the case, the result of such proclamation would be that by abolishing the monument the lands therein contained would be ordinary public lands open to entries of all sorts."[43]

In November of 1914, Graves wrote to the solicitor of the Department of Agriculture that if the monument is removed "it will undoubtedly cause a mining stampede, with the prospect of the location of a number of fraudulent mining claims to cover the heaviest and most valuable bodies of timber therein."[44] Graves had carefully analyzed the attacks on the monument and had identified three areas of concern to be resolved before he was willing to make any concessions on monument boundaries. He posed those concerns in the form of three questions to the departmental solicitor to be resolved legally:

1. "Whether if certain lands now included in the Monument are eliminated, they will remain unquestionably National Forest land."
2. "Whether, if the question arises, the Secretary of Agriculture can lawfully refuse to list, under the Act of June 11, 1906, agricultural lands within the area proposed to be eliminated from the National Monument if, in his judgment, they are needed to protect the breeding grounds of the elk and are chiefly valuable for that purpose."
3. "What legislation, if any, is necessary to properly safeguard these lands from fraudulent mining locations."[45]

No one in government service wanted any of the lands eliminated from the monument to end up in the hands of the timber operators as a repeat of the Olympic Forest Reserve eliminations. Graves had posed his questions to block the three avenues of access to the forests by which that repetition could occur. The continuing Forest Service debate in Congress, in which the earlier eliminations were prominently discussed, made the monument eliminations highly sensitive.

With answers in hand from the solicitor's office that the eliminated land would unquestionably revert to the Olympic National Forest, Graves knew that any move he made would have wide appeal. The small group of preservationists working for a real park with the boundaries of the monument could easily be ignored. They had no power and no local political support. The Forest Service local administration was vigorously opposed to the monument, so much so that Forest Supervisor Fromme had already decided to log it, had let one contract and was planning more in spite of the apparent Antiquities Act prohibition.[46] The Western Washington chambers of commerce, Governor Ernest Lister, commercial clubs and industries had all moved in concert for the second time to free the Olympic forests from the bonds of preservation.

Because of the battle then underway in 1915 over the creation of a National Park Service, Graves could not ignore the potential for park status for the Mount Olympus National Monument. He urged that it be considered for park status but that the remaining monument, after the reductions, be returned to the Forest Service and abolished if not ultimately made into a park.

With vigorous opposition to the monument coming from the local Forest Service administration, with violent opposition to the monument and the Forest Service itself coming from the timber industry and local commercial interests, with Congressional attacks underway on all fronts, Chief Forester Graves did what he thought he needed to do. After a field trip to study the monument for eliminations, he decided to give the timber industry what it wanted. He recommended for elimination, with one exception — everything the timber-industry controlled Seattle Chamber of Commerce had recommended for elimination. For good measure he removed another six square miles of the heaviest timber which they had not asked for. "Before long," Graves said, "there will be a demand for this timber."[47] Only trees without foreseeable commercial value would be left in the monument. The timber industry would again have available for logging everything of commercial value on the Olympic Peninsula. The attacks on the Forest Service began to subside after 1914.

Secretary of the Interior Franklin K. Lane and Stephen Mather, his assistant for parks, both fully concurred in Graves' forest elimination recommendations on Mount Olympus National Monument and President Wilson proclaimed them May 11, 1915.[48]

It had taken just three years from the time the Seattle Chamber of Commerce made its demands to eliminate all the commercially valuable timber in the monument until the timber industry got what it wanted. The needs of the elk had never even come up for discussion. As President Wilson signed the proclamation freeing the monument's timber from preservation, the National Park Service bill was on the verge of passing. It would become law the following year, 1916.

5 NATIONAL PARKS PRESERVED—ALMOST

The clearest way into the Universe is through a Forest Wilderness. Come to the woods, for here is rest. There is no repose like that of the green deep woods. These temple-destroyers, devotees of ravaging commercialism, seem to have a perfect contempt for Nature, and, instead of lifting their eyes to the God of the mountains, lift them to the Almighty Dollar.[1]

JOHN MUIR

It is the duty of the Forest Service to see to it that the timber, water power, mines and every other resource of the forests is used for the benefit of the people who live in the neighborhood. . . .[2]

GIFFORD PINCHOT

THE NECESSITY FOR RESOLVING the issues of management of the parks was created by Pinchot's maneuvering to log the parks' forests and otherwise utilize their resources economically. Right from the start, he separated himself from the preservationists and he antagonized them. In the proclaiming of the forest reserves in 1891 and 1897, the preservationists saw an opportunity to protect these reserves from commercial exploitation. Pinchot got them opened to grazing and logging. When the reserves were transferred to the Department of Agriculture in 1905 and the name "forest reserve" changed in 1907 to "national forest," he emphasized his development stand in order to gain support for his program. "The first great fact about conservation is that it stands for development," he said. "There has been a fundamental misconception that conservation means nothing but the husbanding of

53

resources for future generations."[3] Indeed, Pinchot atttempted early on to upset the New York state constitution of 1894 in which preservationist sentiment had gotten voters to prohibit all timber cutting in Adirondack State Park. For years he worked to allow logging the park but failed. However, this was not without cost to his reputation with the preservationists. Even as his reputation plummeted, in 1906 he launched the Hetch Hetchy battle to flood the floor of a mountain valley comparable to Yosemite Valley itself, for the benefit of providing power and water to San Francisco. The fact that there were less expensive sites which might have achieved the same end never deterred Pinchot in his quest toward economic utilization of Yosemite and all parks.

Pinchot began recommending in 1904 that the national parks be transferred to the Forest Service so that his economic development views could be imposed on them. He tried again in 1906 and 1907 but John F. Lacey, chairman of the House Public Lands Committee and the preservationists' leading congressional spokesman, successfully blocked his every move. In 1908 Pinchot actually got Secretary of the Interior Garfield, appointed originally because he supported Pinchot's views, to recommend that the Interior Department give the parks to Pinchot on the grounds that many of them "are connected with or surrounded by national forests." "These considerations lead me to recommend," Garfield said, "that the Congress be requested to enact such legislation as will make possible the transfer to the Forest Service of all the parks except the Hot Springs Reservation."[4]

With the specter of Hetch Hetchy hanging over the country, there was little doubt about what transfer of the parks to the Forest Service would mean. The national parks, Pinchot believed, should be utilized in the same way for timbering and grazing as the forests. Secretary Garfield reflected these views himself in recommending that timber be cut in the parks. When bills to create new parks did not provide for development, they were openly opposed by the Forest Service. When the Glacier National Park bill prohibited all commercial use except for the removal of dead, down or decaying timber by settlers, the Forest Service responded with a park bill which would have permitted the cutting of mature timber, water power development, and railroad construction within the park. When a bill to preserve the Calaveras Big Trees as a national park surfaced, Pinchot produced a counter bill to permit the cutting of any timber in the park except the Big Trees themselves.[5]

The preservationists began demanding the creation of a Bureau of National Parks largely in reaction to Pinchot. A national parks conference held at Yellowstone in 1911 attempted to bring together all the diverse pro-national-park groups to further promote the idea of an

agency dedicated to preserving the parks. Eugene S. Bruce, who identified himself as "Expert Lumberman, Forest Service," gave the atten-
dees a really clear vision of what the Forest Service specifically had in
mind for the parks as far as trees were concerned. "The mature, dead
standing and windthrown timber in the national parks," he said, "should
be sold and utilized wherever possible up to the point where such cutting and removal is liable to affect the scenic beauties of the park." To
make certain everyone understood the economic forces at work, he added, "In some of the national parks a large amount of the mature timber can be well utilized at the present time while in others very little
of it can be utilized on account of the timber being located in such
places that it is so inaccessible that it cannot be removed at a financial
profit. I believe that the sentiment of a majority of the thinking people
who have been instrumental in bringing about the reservation of national parks would be to the effect that wherever the mature, dead and
down timber could be cut and removed at a profit and where such
removal would benefit the commercial interests of the country without materially affecting the scenic beauties of the national parks involved that it should be done in every instance."[6] No one was persuaded
when in a later session Forester Henry S. Graves attempted to reassure
the conference. "In the parks," he said, "the question of scenic beauty
is first, and development and use of the natural resources is secondary."[7]

President Taft himself jumped on the preservationist bandwagon by
putting the White House solidly behind the separate bureau for national
parks idea. In a special message to Congress in February of 1911, just before Secretary of the Interior Ballinger's resignation, Taft recommended
the immediate passage of the Park Service bill. He called the parks, "wonderful manifestations of nature, so sterling and beautiful that everyone
recognizes the obligation of the government to preserve them. . . ."[8] Taft's
support of the national parks represented a rejection of Pinchot, whom
he had just fired for insubordination. Taft knew well that Pinchot's fon-
dest desire was to get Forest Service control of the parks.

To quiet the public furor over the Ballinger-Pinchot controversy, Taft
appointed a Pinchot man to replace Ballinger as Secretary of the Interior. Walter L. Fisher, at the time of his appointment, was vice president of the National Conservation Association, of which Pinchot was
president, and was viewed as a stand-in for Pinchot. In the April, 1912,
hearings on a bill to create a Bureau of National Parks, Fisher, speaking as Secretary of the Interior to the Senate Committee on Public
Lands, testified:

We have naturally quite a lot of timber in the parks, especially in sections away from the roads, that is maturing, where it happens to be of

a stand that is going to mature pretty much all at one time, where the
trees are large and are going to begin to decay much at the same time.
It is desirable to have that timber harvested and have it harvested in such
a way as will interfere as little as possible with the beauty of the park.[9](sic)

And the Park Service bills themselves contained the same Pinchot-
inspired terminology that had gotten into the act of 1897 and which
opened up the forest reserves to logging. It authorized the Secretary
of the Interior to "sell or dispose of dead or insect-infested timber and
such matured timber as in his judgment may be disposed of without
detriment" to the park.[10] As strong as the preservationists were, they
had not yet arrived at the place where they could keep authority to
log the parks out of a Park Service bill.

As the on-going Hetch Hetchy battle came to a head in 1913, the
preservationists, derisively dubbed "the nature lovers" just as environmentalists of later years were labeled "birdwatchers" by the timber industry, rapidly gained power. Nearly all the national press was opposed
to the Hetch Hetchy dam. When the final hearings began in 1913, the
saving of trees loomed as large as any of the issues of Hetch Hetchy.
The issue of logging in the parks had contaminated the Park Service
bills and was about to contaminate Pinchot's Hetch Hetchy efforts as
well. Pinchot became universally identified with the flooding of Hetch
Hetchy and the cutting of park trees. The public had never accepted
Pinchot's definition of conservation regarding trees, and emotions behind their cutting had led him to believe that the failure of the project
itself might be the result.

On June 25, 1913 Interior Secretary Franklin K. Lane spoke at the
final Hetch Hetchy hearings. Lane was in control of the national parks
but always opposed any concept of preservation regarding them. As
expected, he vigorously supported damming Hetch Hetchy Valley,
pointing out that he had supported it since he had worked on it as city
attorney of San Francisco. He was followed by Pinchot, who began with
his usual rhetoric about "conservation policy is that of use, to take every
part of the land and its resources and put it to that use in which it will
best serve the most people." Pinchot then launched his usual attack on
Muir and his "nature lover" cohorts. "I believe," he said, "if we had nothing else to consider than the delight of the few men and women who
would yearly go into the Hetch Hetchy Valley, then it should be left
in its natural condition. . . . I have never been able to see that there
was any reasonable argument against the use of this water supply by
the City of San Francisco. . . ."[11] The committee chairman, John Raker
of California, then invited Pinchot to present his views on the bill itself and the changes that should be made.

Pinchot dropped his bombshell:

MR. PINCHOT: On page 7, line 4, after the words, "Secretary of Agriculture," I would suggest inserting: *Provided. That no timber shall be cut in
the Yosemite National Park, except from lands to be overflowed, or such timber
as may be constituted an actual obstruction upon a right of way.*

In other words, I do not believe that a national park should be used
as a source of timber supply, and I understand the representatives
from San Francisco are entirely willing that that should be added.

MR. RAKER: There is already an act which permits them to dispose of it.
If there is down or dead timber you would not want them to go 5 or
6 miles? There is an act permitting that in the Yosemite National Park.

MR. PINCHOT: Then I am wrong about that.

MR. RAKER: There was a special bill passed two years ago permitting the
Secretary of the Interior to dispose of ripe, down, or dead timber in
the Yosemite National Park. You would not object to using that sort
of timber?

MR. PINCHOT: Not in a national park.

MR. RAKER: Dead and dying?

MR. PINCHOT: A place like a national park should be protected against
that. I think we can have a little timber fall down and die for the sake
of having the place look like no human foot had ever been in it. I
do not think that the national parks should be used as a source of
lumber supply.

MR. RAKER: Suppose the timber is ripe and ready to be disposed of, that
there is a tree which could be used, you would not want to leave that
there and go to the expense of going to some other place, if it does
not affect the scenic beauty of the park?

MR. PINCHOT: That does not apply to the national parks, but here is a different situation, here is one of the great wonders of the world, and I would
leave it just as it is so far as possible in the Yosemite National Park.

MR. RAKER: For instance, a tree falls down, one of the largest in the park,
that should not be left there to destroy the balance?

MR. PINCHOT: It will not destroy the balance.

MR. RAKER: I am just taking the statement of the others.

MR. PINCHOT: I will mention that among the greatest of the beauties are
some of the fallen trees. I would not touch one of them.

MR. RAKER: They would not want one of the great trees for building purposes?

MR. PINCHOT: No, sir. That does not apply to the national parks. The parks
are set aside for seeding purposes in the particular manner. I would
leave the trees alone. Outside of the parks I think the point of view
of use is the dominant matter which should control.

At that point in his testimony Pinchot got off onto another topic and dropped the discussion of trees. Later in Pinchot's testimony, John Raker of California, dumbfounded by what Pinchot had said and hardly sure that he had heard him correctly, brought the discussion back to trees.

> MR. RAKER: There was a bill passed three years ago, recommended by some department, in relation to the Yosemite National Park, that it would be a good thing for the park and would not affect the scenic beauty if the trees that were ripe and the dead and down timber should be disposed of. In constructing this work, if there are trees that are ripe — and, of course, that would have to be acted upon by the Secretary of the Interior or his agent — there would be no destruction of the scenic beauty by taking a few of such trees when it would not destroy the beauty of the park?
>
> MR. PINCHOT: I think it would largely reduce the beauty of the park. In the neighborhood of this right of way, the proposed reservoir, which would be in the neighborhood where most people would go, all the trees that are now standing should be left. It is not actually necessary to go all the way. I believe a provision of that kind would very largely detract from the beauty of the park, and furthermore, would tend to make the arguments of the nature lover very much more powerful.[12]

Strangely, Pinchot had given the exact testimony about trees in national parks that John Muir would have given. Because the cutting of trees "would tend to make the arguments of the nature lover very much more powerful," he felt the issue of trees might have enabled "the nature lovers" to kill the Hetch Hetchy bill. Pinchot had reversed himself on a major point in his traditional definition of conservation. Perhaps it was a desperate about-face to assure the construction of the Hetch Hetchy dam, which he had taken on as a deep personal commitment, or perhaps it was to get back at Muir to insure the passage of the bill. Ironically he was forced to join Muir in order to do it.

Nevertheless, when the Hetch Hetchy bill passed, it was a blow from which Muir never recovered. In a year he would be dead. He had spent his life working for the protection of Yosemite and now its other spectacular valley would be buried under 200 feet of water. Muir saw in the Hetch Hetchy fight the wedge of future efforts to destroy the national parks, to devour them piecemeal. Nothing would be safe, he thought, from commercialism.[13] Hetch Hetchy mobilized the entire preservationist movement around those fears.

When the Park Service bill was routinely reintroduced at the end of 1913, it included again the same authorization as before to log the mature, dead and insect-infested timber from the parks. The bill went nowhere.

With growing strength from what was being described as "the rape of Hetch Hetchy," and with the nation's proclaimed guru of conservation, Pinchot, having now declared his belief in the inappropriateness of logging in the parks, the preservationist forces finally were able to produce a park bill that was truly preservationist in focus. "The fundamental purpose" of the parks being defined in the bill as "to conserve the scenery and the natural and historic objects and the wildlife therein and to provide for the enjoyment of future generations." In contradiction to this constraint in the bill there remained the specific authorization to cut timber "to control the attacks of insects or diseases or otherwise conserve the scenery along with provision for the destruction of such animals and of such plant life as may be detrimental."[14] Both provisions would prove to be too much to handle for the organization that would emerge from the bill. The cutting of trees because they were "mature" would no longer occur, but the other timber-cutting provisions would create bitter controversy later.

Now Henry S. Graves had to face the fact that any new parks would be created out of territory administered by the Forest Service. He did what he could to get the Park Service transferred from the Interior Department to the Department of Agriculture. "It is essential," he said, "that there should be considered not only the park problem connected with the areas proposed as national parks, but also the problems of the national forests from which it is proposed to take such areas." Graves' concern was too little and too late, in the wrong time frame to have any impact.

The Forest Service wanted to retain Mount Olympus National Monument. The Secretary of Agriculture reported Graves' viewpoints on Grand Canyon and Mount Olympus to the Public Lands Committee. "Unquestionably, the Grand Canyon should be established as a national park" he said, but when it came to Mount Olympus he stalled. "The Mount Olympus National Monument, which is the only other monument under the administration of this department embracing any considerable area should be given careful consideration as a possible national park and if not included in such park by congressional action, should be restored to its original status as national forest land." Graves' views were rejected. The unanimous opinion of the Public Lands Committee was "that the time had already come to transfer the monuments to the Interior Department."[15] The power of the preservationist view had spread so widely that the report on the Park Service bill flatly stated that "The segregation of national park areas necessarily involved the question of nature as it exists. . . ."

6 THE PARK SERVICE VS. PRESERVATION

In order to adjust living conditions of species desirable for public observation and enjoyment, the enemies of these species must be carefully controlled.[1]　　HORACE M. ALBRIGHT
NATIONAL PARK SERVICE

It goes without saying that the administration should strictly prohibit the hunting and trapping of any wild animals within the park limits.[2]　　TRACY I. STORER & JOSEPH GRINNELL,
UNIVERSITY OF CALIFORNIA

THROUGHOUT HIS GOVERNMENT SERVICE, Pinchot had worked valiantly with all the influence he could muster to get the national parks transferred to the Forest Service. His failure to achieve that transfer reflected his failure to gain general public acceptance for his definition of conservation. "It stands for development," he said, and not "the husbanding of resources for future generations."[3] But Pinchot lived on in the Forest Service as the ideological fountainhead of its being long after his dismissal in 1910.

As the Park Service bill approached passage in 1916, Chief Forester Henry S. Graves again attempted to get the new Park Service assigned to the Department of Agriculture. "Most of the national parks that will be created hereafter," Graves testified, "will be located on acres now within the national forests."[4] That was the threat. It was obvious that the coming conflict could be much better contained within the Agriculture Department, where the Forest Service was already a powerful autonomous agency. In fact, the Forest Service by then generally controlled the actions of the Secretary of Agriculture as his actions might affect it.

So critical was the issue of future national parks to the Forest Service that it moved immediately with the full force of its political power and public relations machinery to define the nation's national park agenda before the new National Park Service was organized. It wanted a clear-cut policy, agreed to by all, as to when new national parks would be created. "The importance of a clear cut policy is evidenced by the efforts frequently made to secure the creation of national parks out of areas containing great bodies of timber, extensive grazing lands, and other resources, the withdrawal of which from use would be uneconomic and prejudicial to the local and general public interest,"[5] said the Forest Serivce in a paper prepared for the Secretary of Agriculture to promulgate in *American Forestry*.

Rather than let the preservationists and the new Park Service define the criteria for a new national park, the Forest Service took the initiative to head off any move in that direction that might be to its disadvantage:

1. "A national park should be created only where there are scenic features of such outstanding importance for beauty or as natural marvels that they merit national recognition and protection and, on this account, have a public value transcending that of any material resources on the same land.
2. The areas should be large enough to justify administration separate from the forests.
3. The boundaries [should be set] so as not to include timber, grazing, or other resources the economic use of which is essential to the up-building and industrial welfare of the country.
4. When parks are created from parts of the forests, the portions remaining as forests should not be left in a form difficult or impossible to administer.
5. Whether the National Park Service should be transferred to the Department of Agriculture is a matter for consideration."[6]

The new National Park Service was shaped to the Forest Service's program, but the public rejected these criteria repeatedly whenever it had any opportunity to influence pending park legislation.

Franklin K. Lane, President Wilson's Secretary of the Interior, held the concept of preservation for the national parks in contempt. Serving as city attorney for San Francisco, he participated early on in the attempts to dam Hetch Hetchy Valley and vigorously fought on behalf of the groups working to that end. As Secretary of the Interior and as the government official in charge of the national parks, he went to the

Hetch Hetchy hearing to throw the full weight of the secretary's office behind the project. He later ordered the national parks opened to grazing during World War I and approved the invasion of Yellowstone by irrigation interests and even went so far as to order the Park Service to report favorably on the Yellowstone irrigation project. Lane lined himself up on the side of oil men and assisted in drawing up the Ferris bill for the exploitation of public oil lands over the opposition of nearly everyone but the oil men. During his administration, Lane fought on the side of oil men against Pinchot, Secretary Daniels of the Navy, and Attorney General Gregory. He was committed to the disposal of the public domain and was no friend, therefore, of the Forest Service either. Pinchot was bitterly opposed to him, believing "he could not be trusted."[7] Early in his administration he had embraced selling the national parks trees to finance the purchasing of the private inholdings within them.

Ironically, Lane would be the man to whom the responsibility would fall to launch a new agency dedicated to preservation. He cared so little about the park system that in the fall of 1914, when he received a routine letter of complaint about the way the national parks were being run from Stephen T. Mather, whose name he recognized as a college classmate, he wrote back, "Dear Steve, If you don't like the way the national parks are being run, come on down to Washington and run them yourself."[8] The decision to hire Mather was made on Lane's personal whim; he had never had a discussion with Mather about the park system when the offer was made. All he knew was that Mather was an influential Chicago businessman and a millionaire.

When that discussion finally occurred, Lane introduced Mather to Horace Albright, a twenty-four-year-old fellow alumnus of the University of California, who was in Washington on a one-year internship. Mather convinced Albright to stay because of his familiarity with the Department of the Interior's procedures. The forty-seven-year-old, hand-shaking, backslapping Chicago millionaire and the twenty-four-year-old law student would launch the National Park Service.

What Lane found out about Mather's national park views fit perfectly with his own anti-preservation philosophy. "Golf links, tennis courts, swimming pools and other equipment for outdoor pasttime and exercise should be provided," for the parks, Mather said.[9] The preservationists were not reassured by Mather's business focus either. "Secretary Lane has asked me for a business administration," Mather said. "Our national parks are practically lying fallow and only await proper development to bring them into their own."[10]

Neither Mather nor Albright had been involved with the long, bitter struggle to protect the trees in the national parks from cutting. Nor had they paid any attention to the fact that Pinchot had been forced to capitulate on the cutting of trees in national parks in the Hetch Hetchy battle, then just concluded. Because of this lack of historical perspective, neither of them had even the most elementary background for stewardship of the nation's park lands.

Mather and Albright put themselves, even before the final passage of the Park Service bill, in the business of selling park trees to finance park acquisitions which lacked Congressional appropriations. They endorsed a bill drafted by Senator Walsh of Montana, S.5778, to allow the Secretary of the Interior to exchange mature, dead or decadent timber "in any part of Glacier National Park where it would not injure scenic values" for private lands, already a part of Lane's program. In other words, where the public generally would not see it, they would take the timber. There was a tract of privately owned land along the Glacier National Park road Mather wanted and by the passing of the bill, the Park Service itself entered the business of logging the very old-growth timber the park existed to preserve.[11] "It is most urgent that the Government be authorized to eliminate private holdings in Glacier National Park to prevent them from being denuded of the timber . . . " said Secretary Franklin K. Lane. But government land in the park could be denuded of its timber by the government itself.[12] To garner support from the timber preservationists, the Walsh bill offered the possibility of selling government timber from the national forests, not from the park — "the timber to be selected or exchanged may be taken from the Government lands within the metes and bounds of the National Forests within the State of Montana."

The Forest Service, seeing a precedent that would enormously strengthen the Park Service in establishing new parks in the future, responded in the Department of Agriculture's report on the bill that it questioned "the wisdom of trying to extinguish all titles in national parks for lands and timber within the national forests . . . readjustment of the boundaries would be a better method." To keep itself in control of timber exchanged from national forest land, the Forest Service wanted and got the bill amended so that Forest Service timber could be involved only with the approval of the Secretary of Agriculture.[13]

The endorsement by Mather and Albright of Senator Walsh's move to log the parks, endorsed by Lane since 1912, created a culture of ambiguity in the Park Service that lives on to this day. Mather and Albright had gone to Congress to get legislative permission to do what the organic act, which created the Park Service, had prevented — logging a national park. The park logging program that Pinchot had been forced to repudiate publicly in the Hetch Hetchy hearings just four years earlier was now a reality, ironically put in place by the new Park Service itself. President Wilson signed Senator Walsh's park logging bill into law on March 3, 1917.

Mather is the key to understanding the early Park Service. He was a fun-loving, gregarious, backslapping promoter who liked being the center of attention. Naturally flamboyant, he also clung throughout his life, some would say childishly, to the fun of adolescence. As a middle-aged man he vigorously participated in the activities of Sigma Chi fraternity, always wearing its pin, and even involved the fraternity in various ways in the Berkeley National Parks Conference.[14] To the dismay of his associates, there were never any boundaries in his life between his personal interests and his work interests. If the needs of the organization conflicted with his needs, he prevailed.

He spent money with great flair and drama, but with devastating impact on the development of the Park Service as an organization. He managed to make all of the Park Service's key staff dependent on him financially. When he disagreed with the government salary structure in place, he augmented Park Service salaries out of his own pocket. He personally provided, for instance, $5,000 a year to Robert Sterling Yard, his information officer. Albright received a monthly check to augment his salary as well. He gave Albright and Cammerer stock in his company so that the dividends would additionally supplement their salaries. The whole staff received a bonus at Christmas personally provided by him and he periodically footed a night out on the town in a nightclub. Mather's biographer, Robert Shankland, reports a typical incident: " . . . after Chief Ranger Forest Townsley of Yosemite had spent a month at the Grand Canyon reorganizing the ranger force, Mather sent him a personal check and asked him to take a trip to Oklahoma and see his parents. Nobody in the Park Service, Mather felt, was making half enough and he believed he had a clear duty to ease all the low income pains he could."[15]

When he wanted to buy the Tioga Pass Road in Yosemite and there was no government money available, he raised half the price from wealthy friends and paid the other half himself. Believing that the rangers in Yosemite ought to have a club house, he had one built with his own money and then stayed there himself instead of at hotels. "He liked to mix with his men."[16] And he personally bought revolvers for the Yosemite rangers when no funds were available for that purpose.

Mather's generosity was manipulative; his system of rewards, his impulsive and bullying managerial style corrupted the Park Service's normal organizational development.

Mather undermined subordinates continuously by going directly to the persons he wanted access to, preventing the organization from building its own internal management strength. Sometimes he sent Albright to do what should have been normal routine for the local park administrator, as when he sent Albright, who was superintendent of Yellowstone, to take over direction of a large fire burning in Glacier National Park. Any thinking manager would have left the task to the Glacier National Park superintendent because doing so would have strengthened the new organization.

Mather's managerial style was an administrative disaster. To this day the imprint of this heritage lingers strong in the Park Service where the attitudes, wishes, and whims of any key incumbent are the single most important predictor of what will occur. In the Forest Service by comparison, incumbency is nearly irrelevant to the management processes.

Ignoring rules, regulations, guidelines, and common understandings became Mather's prerogative in the Park Service. In the face of clear understandings of what a national park should be, Mather, on his own, in 1921, succeeded in getting an amendment to a Sundry Civil Appropriation Bill (1 Stat 41, 1407) that made the Hot Springs Reservation in Arkansas into a national park. The nation now had a national park comprised of some buildings in the middle of a fair-sized town. Deciding that the place needed more exhibits of plant life, he privately employed the foremost landscape architect in Chicago to come down and go to work.[17] All of this was flatly contradicted in the Park Service's own written policy.

The flaunting of rules, regulations, and the law early on in Mather's administration even attracted the attention of Congress directly. "The trouble with this service is that it does not imagine it is controlled in any way by either the limitation of law or the appropriation," charged Congressman John J. Fitzgerald in the Sundry Civil Bill Hearings of 1917.[18]

When Mather was struck down with one of his bouts with mental illness in 1917, the Park Service fell by default into the hands of twenty-seven-year-old Horace Albright. Without any prior management experience, he did the best he could to act in Mather's stead to continue the organizational processes then underway. Albright drew up a set of policy objectives for the Park Service which he believed accurately reflected Mather's ideas.[19] He took his cue from Pinchot, who had written twelve years earlier a similar set for the Forest Service to be sent to himself by the Secretary of Agriculture. Albright had his own guidelines sent to Mather as a directive from Secretary Lane. Albright did not understand that transmitting policy directives to any organization, especially new ones, has to involve clarity of purpose, lack of internal conflict, and the expectation that the organization's mission would be fulfilled in carrying them out. What he produced, instead, in one of the most important documents to affect the Park Service's future, was a group of conflicting policy guidelines that would influence the Park Service's inability to develop a consistent value system to support its purposes.

Here is what Albright wrote in his so-called Lane letter, one of the most basic of all the Park Service's management documents. Because of the protracted preservationist battle that had been underway over the parks for more than twenty years and which the preservationists had won, it was absolutely incumbent upon him to recognize that political reality, and he did.

> . . . the national parks must be maintained in absolutely unimpaired form for the use of future generations as well as those of our own time. Every activity of the Service is subordinate to the duties imposed on it to faithfully preserve the parks for posterity in essentially their natural state. The commercial use of the reservations . . . will not be permitted under any circumstances.[20]

John Muir could not have done better. But having paid obeisance to what public expectation demanded, Albright moved on to legitimize Mather's park program, which had nothing to do with preservation. The Lane letter

1. Permitted "the grazing of cattle in isolated regions not frequented by visitors, and where no injury to the natural features of the park may result from such use." This ignored the needs of the park's wildlife for the same forage and the destruction of wilderness values involved.
2. Legitimized the leasing of park lands "for the operation of hotels, camps, and transporation facilities." Mather's mass-use strategy required massive facilities of all kinds and required legitimization in the face of politically strong and rising interest in wilderness.
3. Approved the cutting of park trees when the "timber is needed in the construction of buildings or other improvements within the park."
   Approved "the thinning of forests or cutting of vistas" when the scenic features of the parks will be improved.
   Approved forest "destruction" when "necessary to eliminate insect infestation or diseases common to forests and shrubs." By the time Albright drafted the Lane letter, he no doubt had become aware of the public sensitivities involved in cutting park trees. The forestry journals were filled with it. He gave the Park Service a blank check to act in the face of those sensitivities.
4. "Every opportunity should be afforded the public, whenever possible, to enjoy the national parks in the manner that best satisfies the individual taste."

"Automobiles and motorcycles will be permitted in all of the national parks; in fact the parks will be kept accessible by any means practicable."

"All outdoor sports . . . will be heartily endorsed and aided whenever possible." Motoring was specifically defined as an outdoor sport, and the definition allowed for golf, tennis, and anything else normally done outside. Mather's mass-use strategy was diametrically opposed to what the preservationists who had created the Park Service expected. Albright gave to Mather the officially sanctioned guidelines he needed to develop full bore.

5. "You should diligently extend and use the splendid cooperation developed . . . among chambers of commerce, tourist bureaus, and automobile highway associations" to get more people to the parks. Albright succeeded in getting Mather's primary mass-use objective written into a policy directive from the secretary.

What Albright did in his Lane letter was to systematically prevent the organization from considering the management issues involved in preservation of the parks, even while promulgating preservation as the reason for the Park Service's existence. The Mather program had nothing to do with preservation; the policy guidelines are a monument to double talk.

To conclude the Lane letter, Albright adopted the Forest Service-devised national park program to head off the creation of new national parks.

6. "In studying new park projects, you should seek to find scenery of supreme and distinctive quality or some natural feature so extraordinary or unique as to be of national interest and importance. You should seek distinguished examples of typical forms of world architecture such as the Grand Canyon."

7. "The national park system as now constituted should not be lowered in standard, dignity and prestige by the inclusion of areas which express in less than the highest terms in the particular class or kind of exhibit which they represent." (Mather ignored this when he got national park status for Hot Springs.)

8. "It is not necessary that a national park should have a large area."

9. "You should engage in an investigation of . . . park projects jointly with officers of the Forest Service, in order that questions of national park and national forest policy as they affect the lands involved may be thoroughly understood."[21]

Albright had put the Park Service in the weakest possible position in dealing with the Forest Service on new parks, and it would be playing by Forest Service rules to minimize the creation of new parks.

When Mather returned he heartily endorsed the policy directive, and the Park Service absorbed into its very being all of the letter's hypocrisy and contradictions. The preservationists had won a hard and bitterly fought battle over many years to create a national park system focused on preservation. The triumvirate of Secretary Lane, Mather and Albright had succeeded in taking it away from them administratively in the very first years of the Park Service's existence. Mather was first and foremost a businessman and this orientation towards the park system affected most of the early management moves he made. His business goals were defined as soon as he arrived in Washington. They were to "develop to the highest possible degree of efficiency the resources of the national parks . . . for the pleasure of their owners, the people. . . . It is business to make these great public properties help themselves by adding to their yearly income provided by the government."[22] His strategy to achieve this profitability was mass use and he set for himself a goal to increase park usage immediately to ten times what it was when he arrived.[23] Mass use would also serve, he believed, to impress Congress with the need for dramatically increased appropriations. A born promoter, Mather not only knew how to achieve that goal, but also had the personal prestige that a flamboyant millionaire businessman could wield when dealing with other businessmen and politicians. He had access to everyone. Although Secretary Lane did not know what he was getting when he gave the parks to Mather, what Mather wanted to do fit perfectly with Lane's utilitarian value system. Mather's program could not have been further, however, from what the preservationists, who had worked for so many years to keep the parks away from Pinchot and the Forest Service, wanted. They were silenced for the moment by the charismatic excitement and national focus on the parks that Mather, ever the public relations expert, was able to generate.

Ironically, Pinchot and Mather held almost identical views on resource development, differing in little other than focus. Pinchot focused on maximizing economic return through industrial commodity production — timber, water power, and forage. Mather wanted to maximize the economic return from the retail marketing of tourism.

To achieve his mass-use goals, Mather arrived at a simple, straightforward, and workable strategy. He would focus on two development issues and make the management moves to deal with them:

1. How best to get visitors to the parks and to move them around once they are there.
2. How best to accommodate them during their stay.

The long preservationist battle over the cutting of trees in the parks, the preservationist triumph in getting into the Park Service bill the phrase "as will leave them unimpaired for the enjoyment of future generations," Mather ignored. He also failed to define the groups which had passed the preservationist-focused 1916 Park Service Act as part of the Park Service's natural constituency. Early in his administration the preservationists were derisively dubbed "the purists." Instead he turned to his home turf — other businessmen — for a Park Service constituency. He brought together chambers of commerce, park concessioners, tourist bureaus and the railroads to promote the parks and these became the Park Service constituency. He married the park system to the "See America First" promotion of the railroads in his first round of constituency building. So successful was Mather in this effort that the U.S. Railroad Administration actually set up a national parks and monuments division which launched a publicity campaign promoting the parks, publishing a series of national park booklets in the fall of 1918. He also brought the railroads together to make it possible for a traveler to reach Yellowstone by one railroad and leave by another at no extra charge. Mather's mass-use strategy proved successful beyond all expectations. He had demonstrated what all successful businessmen know — manage against achievable goals and success will result. People poured into the parks.

All the parks were opened to automobiles and a road building program was launched to make it easier for automobiles to get into parks. Mather believed that park tourism would increase if the emerging transcontinental highways were designed to go through the parks as well. When he decided that tourists were staying away from Glacier National Park because there was no highway through it in an east-west direction, he allocated funds for such a road and personally redesigned the road proposed by the engineers. He became so enamoured of the automobile that he determined that every park should have a road penetrating its most beautiful wilderness.[24] To placate the fears of "the purists" he reassured them that, "At the same time large sections of each park will be kept in a natural wilderness state without piercing feeder roads."[25]

The building of park roads produced internal stress in the Park Service organization. Road Engineer George Goodwin left the Park Service in disagreement with what he believed were the inappropriately high road standards and expensive methods of construction provided by the Bureau of Public Roads which Mather had embraced.

The automobile fast became the means for Mather to reach his mass-use goals. It was here he made his commitment, even to the point of sacrificing the most significant wilderness in each park, to maximize the quality of the experience for the motor traveler.

What Mather had lost sight of was historian James Truslow Adams's admonition that "because twenty people can enjoy a beauty spot, it does

Mather and Albright defined motoring as an outdoor sport having equal standing with mountain climbing, horseback riding and walking, which gave the automobile free run of the meadows of Paradise Valley below Mount Rainier. Bitter opposition from environmental organizations followed. The photo was taken in 1917. *Washington State Historical Society.*

not follow that two thousand can . . . if we go beyond a certain point instead of giving everybody everything, nobody has anything."[26] No better illustration of this admonition as it applied to Mather's policies is available anywhere than in Yosemite. One tourist compared the Yosemite Valley experience with similar conditions at Seventh and Broadway in Los Angeles. "The only difference between the locations," he said, "was there were trees and no traffic cop in Yosemite Valley, while in the city there were traffic cops and no trees. The population was about the same." He laid the trouble "in the Mather regime, and [it] goes deep throughout the entire service."[27]

By 1926 Mather had succeeded in turning Yosemite Valley into far more than traffic jams. It had become a tasteless honky tonk catering to concesssionaire profits, and the entertainment of urban-oriented mobs of people indifferent to the purposes of the park. Robert Sterling Yard describes the summer of 1926 which drew a crowd of 2,000 for the evening's entertainment at Camp Curry. "The specialities of a jazz band were followed by vocal solos, quartettes, and amusing stunts. One of the latter was so flagrantly vulgar that I wished myself out of

Director Mather measured successful local administration by how many visitors were attracted to each park. By 1929, even the newspapers questioned where this was leading. Directors Mather and Albright never did. *Oakland Tribune, November 2, 1929; National Archives.*

hearing but the crowd apparently adored it." Later the crowd drove two miles down the valley to witness the bear show: "The bears were fed from platforms on a clearing brilliantly lighted by electric lamps in trees. . . . They scrap delightfully. Believe me, with eight to a dozen bears gorging what the announcer calls 'swell swill' dumped on the platforms from a truck, it is some spectacle." The evening ended with dancing in the outdoor camps. "Once when I waked at midnight in my redwood cabin an eighth of a mile away, the air still palpitated with jazz. If only the Yosemite night could be transferred to an environ of New York City it would make its promoter a millionaire."[28]

In dealing with the second leg of his mass-use strategy, Mather decided that a monopoly would be awarded to one concessionaire. This concessionaire would then be in the position to offer the lowest possible prices and the best possible service to the travelling public, or so Mather believed. Two problems emerged. The competitive environment in existence in many parks had in fact produced already just what Mather said he was looking for—excellent service and reasonable prices. When the monopoly corporate concessionaires replaced the small local businessman, the drive to maximize the profits, or sometimes to stem losses, was irresistible. Rocky Mountain National Park and Mount Rainier National Park offer excellent examples of the many problems that Mather's monopoly policy caused the Park Service.

The monopoly concessionaire policy engaged Mather with the corporate giants he was most comfortable with, but the roughshod manner in which the monopoly policy was implemented and enforced resulted in enraged constituencies and media attacks nationwide.

In 1919 Mather secretly awarded a White Automobile Company subsidiary an exclusive transportation concession for hauling passengers and freight through Rocky Mountain National Park. No bids had been asked for and the public was not informed of the awarding of the concession until the operation of the summer's business opened, too late for any effective opposition. Enos Mills, "the John Muir of the Rockies," who had worked tirelessly for years for the creation of the park, was forced out of business by the award. Mills was the operator of a tourist hotel and had always provided transportation into the park for his guests, as had numerous independent taxi drivers operating out of Estes Park. As innumerable attempts were made by hotel operators and independent taxi drivers to exercise what they considered to be their rights, physical violence broke out as park rangers attempted to enforce the monopoly of Mather's concessionaire. The Park Service was now in the position of continuously arresting local citizens, often with attendant physical violence, for attempting to use the roads in the park they had always used but whose use was now denied as a result of the creation of the Park Service.[29] Mills asked that "there must be no poli-tics in the national parks" and that "the Park Service must take the pub-lic" into its confidence and "make no secret moves,"[30] a direct challenge to the way in which both Mather and Albright insisted on operating.

The roads in Rocky Mountain National Park were roads built by pi-oneers to open up areas where their private holdings were and by the county and state. A person going to his own private property in the park could no longer enter the park in any hired car not belonging to the White Motor Car subsidiary.[31]

Mills lost in court on his challenge that the monopoly had been ille-gally granted and was being illegally operated; but being a national figure in his own right, he caught the attention of the national media. By 1920 Mather was under attack for the arrogant and autocratic manner in which the park monopolies were being implemented and enforced. A St. Louis paper charged that "Monopolistic concessions in National Parks are given by a bureau, by an autocratic Director, who was not chosen and cannot be removed by the public he serves and rules. . . . Literally thousands of travelers through national parks have suffered from over-charge, insolence, carelessness of public servants there. Thou-sands of protests are made every summer and indeed in every season. The universal complaint is: 'the transportation company rules the park' . . . Bureaucratic administration, hand-in-glove with monopolis-tic concessionaires, is a combination that has not been broken."[32]

Mather was ignoring the constituency building which had made the Forest Service a powerful political force wherever it appeared. He in-stead was dooming the Park Service to a position of permanent weak-ness. It would always be at war with its natural constituencies while the Forest Service stood shoulder to shoulder with the resource exploiters it defined from the start as its own natural constituency.

Mather's management excesses in Mount Rainier National Park met the preservationists head on. Mount Rainier's presence affects nearly everyone in western Washington, always visible in clear weather and always of interest. What happened in Mount Rainier National Park affected the public's perceptions of the Park Service, which in turn would affect the battle to create an Olympic park more than twenty years later.

Mather's first concern for Mount Rainier was the construction of a full-fledged resort in Paradise Valley to replace the tent camp run by John Reese. Even though the Milwaukee Railroad had already built a good hotel at Longmire, it was not where the "scenery" was. In 1917, to bring business to the scenery, Mather convened a meeting of local busi-ness giants in Seattle's Rainier Club. He asked them to form the Rainier National Park Company to build an inn in Paradise Valley and he

"The Government must do its part," Mather said, "to make the national parks as cheap and as attractive as possible to the people, in order that the people, by coming in great numbers, may make business profitable for the concessionaires." Mather paved the meadows of Paradise Valley on Mt. Rainier with bungalows in 1917. *Washington State Historical Society.*

offered them concessionaire monopoly.[33] Among the group was C. D. Stimson, the president of the Stimson Mill Company, and Everett Griggs, president of the St. Paul and Tacoma Lumber Company. The timber industry appeared to be taking over everyone's favorite mountain at the very moment when the use of the automobile was causing rising antagonism towards the industry. The increasing use of the car had exposed to view the miles of rolling hills of stumps on every road out of every city in western Washington. Pressure to reform had grown as the use of the automobile exposed the environmental damage to view. The spokesman for the timber industry in resisting these pressures was Griggs. Speaking as president of the National Lumberman's Manufacturing Association, he met all challenges head on—the industry was not going to change its practices. "Reforestation will come when it is profitable," he said. Taking a hard economic line, Griggs announced that "the establishment of values will determine to what extent conservation will be practiced and reforestation followed."[34] Washington's recently deceased Senator Addison Foster, who had orchestrated the by-then notorious Olympic Forest Reserve eliminations, had been a vice president of Grigg's firm, the St. Paul and Tacoma Lumber Company, a fact widely known.

Mather had tied the development of Mount Rainier to the timber industry and he basked in the triumph of the Paradise Hotel as it was built. He knew that the monopoly would give the public the expanded facilities and services that would enable Mount Rainier to contribute to his mass-use goals. By 1922, however, his monopoly grant at Mount Rainier came under attack. Upon returning from Washington, D.C., its manager reported that the Park Service was "thoroughly demoralized and practically without friends in the House." The attacks on Mather's policies "has had such weight with the House [of Representatives] that there are few friends left for the Service. . . . Mather will probably resign. . . . "[35] He did not resign and instead pressed ahead to enforce the monopoly positions he had awarded. By the end of the year, the Mountaineers, a Seattle-based conservation organization, became so incensed at the monopoly policy as it was being applied in Mount Rainier that it mounted a nationwide attack on the Park Service.

Environmental groups fought the Park Service's plan to construct a road to Yakima Park (Sunrise), charging that it would end up urbanized as Paradise Valley had been earlier. They were correct. The photo was taken in 1932. *Washington State Historical Society.*

The Mountaineers were, as members individually and as an organization, major users of the park; their concerns were personal. Forming a special committee to document the activities of the Rainier National Park Company, the Mountaineers then distributed their report to every member of Congress and to every park-using group in the country. Charging that "government representatives in the parks are . . . regarded by the concessionaires as being employees of the concessionaires" and that the Park Service "acquiesces in this point of view," the attack continued to cite specific incendiary illustrations of Park Service application of rules to support its monopoly to the great detriment of the public. The Mountaineers had wanted to cross over a corner of the park, about five miles of road, in a bus from Seattle to get to a site where a pack train would then take them on an outing. The park superintendent determined he could not waive the transportation monopoly position of the concessionaire and allow it but offered to intercede on their behalf with the Rainier National Park Company. "Here is a case where the government found itself so hopelessly fettered by its own rule that it saw no other way to get relief than to go, hat in hand, to the Frankenstein of its creation and beg for leniency" charged the Mountaineers' pamphlet.

On Labor Day weekend of 1922, a group from Tacoma had planned to disembark on a three-day outing from a point about four miles inside the park boundary. They had rented a van and a small truck to haul their gear. The group was forced by the Park Service, enforcing the monopoly Mather had awarded, to unload their gear at the park boundary, load it onto a similar truck provided by the concessionaire and walk the four miles by road while their rented van followed them. Upon return they had to repeat the process in reverse. "This was a comedy worthy of being filmed, though the Park Service could hardly be expected to show the picture with their exhibition of films advertising the National Park attractions," said the Mountaineers' report. For fifteen pages, complete with texts of correspondence in an appendix, the report documented what the Mountaineers considered the outrageous administrative position of Mather's Park Service.[36]

What was especially galling to the Mountaineers was that Mather decided to protect the park concessionaires by not disclosing their profits. No matter how hard they tried "the Department has refused to divulge this information." "The concessionaires are given monopolies. The public has no chance to protect itself by patronizing somebody else. The government now refuses to allow the public to protect itself by having a voice in the discussion of the reasonableness of the charges which under government sanction are made by the concessionaires," charged the pamphlet.[37]

What emerged from Mather's concessionaire policies was contempt for the Park Service from the very preservationist groups that had led the fight to save the parks from commercial exploitation and which had created the Park Service itself. The creation of the Park Service was proving to be a devastating loss to them, affecting negatively even the normal use of the parks as they had been used before its existence. Objectors were dismissed as "purists." Mather did not want participation by the public in park policy.

And Mather created other enemies. He steered the new Park Service on a collision course with the scientific community over the killing of predators. The scientific community embraced the Park Service Act as it passed in 1916 requiring Mather to administer the parks to "conserve . . . the wildlife therein . . . as will leave them unimpaired for the enjoyment of further generations." Mather believed there were good animals and bad animals, the bad ones being those which ate others. He launched a greatly expanded carnivore extermination program throughout the park system. He got around the constraints of the law by defining wildlife in the law as "desirable species" and the carnivores as "enemies of wildlife."

Long before Mather appeared on the scene, however, national park lands had been ravished by predator-killing programs. As early as 1898, poison was used in Yellowstone when the shooting of individual animals was deemed not fast enough to meet the reduction goals for carnivores. Poisoned carcasses were found to be a successful method for killing coyotes and its use was expanded to Yosemite in the winter of 1910–1911. Strychnine became the poison of preference in Glacier National Park in 1914. That poisoning could be an effective mass killer was proved by continued use.[38]

Trapping was widely used from 1904 on in all the older parks and in the others when established. Trailing with dogs to kill cougars began with a pack of dogs purchased for that purpose in Yellowstone in 1893. Fifteen cougars were killed during the winter of 1903–1904 but by 1908 they were so scarce that only one was killed during the year.[39] All the while the elk population was exploding, a sign of the success of the program. Again in 1914, a paid hunter was brought in and he succeeded in killing nineteen cougars in that year. Shooting was probably the most widely used means of predator control.

Mather tackled the job of killing carnivores in the parks with the same energy that he pursued his mass use and road building strategies. The pressures to get on with the task of ridding the parks of the "enemies of wildlife" made it necessary to call in outside help because the new Park Service was not able to deliver the results that Mather wanted. Superintendent Ralston of Glacier National Park reported in

1916 that many coyotes were killed in the park by settlers. Also in Glacier National Park in the winter of 1916–1917, a number of cougars were killed "by hunters licensed by the service for this purpose." Mather reported in his 1918 report that a cooperative plan had been worked out with the chief of the U.S. Biological Survey for an intensive campaign for the destruction of predatory animals in Glacier National Park. At the same time hunters were detailed by the U.S. Biological Society to kill wolves and coyotes in Yellowstone, Rocky Mountain, Grand Canyon, Wind Cave, Mesa Verde, Mount Rainier and Zion national parks.[40] Ecological balances that had been in place for millennia were destroyed in the name of protecting the wildlife from its enemies.

Mather reported in 1919, "Our efforts to reduce the number of predatory animals in the national parks have met with unusual success during the past year, and in several of the bigger parks so many of those animals have been killed that there already has been a noticeable increase in the deer and other species that are usually their victims."[41] In 1920 he included in his report for Grand Canyon that "one government hunter bagged seven full grown lions in eight weeks work." He did not mention that Kaibab deer were destroying the forest. Although when pressed, he always denied he was after extermination, it crept into his reports and statements. "Predatory animals comprising cougar, lynx, bobcats, timber wolves, and coyotes are sometimes seen and an effort is being made to exterminate them," he reported for Crater Lake in his 1920 report.[42]

Illustrative of Mather's strange and convoluted thinking is the statement from Roger W. Toll, superintendent of Mount Rainier National Park, which Mather included in his 1920 report. Toll reported that "the reduction of the predatory animals in the park is very desirable in order that game and wildlife may be permitted to increase. This work can best be done by cooperation with the United States Biological Survey in placing the paid hunters in the park. These men should be adequately paid and devote their time exclusively to predatory animals, without the necessity of trapping fur bearing animals to supplement a nominal salary. The animals classed as predatory and whose presence in the park is detrimental to game and other animals are cougar, bobcat, lynx, coyote and wolf."[43]

Victor H. Cahalane, who was involved first-hand with Mather's extermination efforts, described the inner dynamics of how the program worked. "Control work was commonly regarded as rather arduous duty, frequently but not always worthy of special compensation. In some cases all of the resulting furs were sold, either in large fur markets or to operators of park curio stores, and the receipts deposited in the Federal Treasury. In other instances, however, all or part of the furs were turned over to the ranger or hunter taking them. This was especially true prior to about 1922, when game protection through predator control was assigned to the ranger force as a part of their regular duties when so directed. It was believed and hotly argued that, without special reimbursement by at least part of the fur take, the rangers would not pursue control work with sufficient vigor to meet the demands of the situation. In 1925 the Service ruled that employees designated as official hunters were to get one third of the hides secured, the exact percentage to depend on conditions of employment. Certain other employees who were allowed special authority to hunt predators in the parks were still officially permitted to keep all the furs they were able to take."[44] Mather knew, as a good businessman, that employee performance in meeting goals needed incentives.

In fact, the whole of the predator extermination program was another revenue source for the "business administration" Mather said Secretary Lane had asked for.[45] Mather had pledged in 1915 "to make these great public properties help themselves by adding to their yearly income provided by the government."[46] By 1922 the sale of hides of park carnivores, along with the sale of dead timber, had become one of the four major sources of Park Service revenue.[47] "The intensity of the campaigns carried on against park predators after . . . 1916," said Cahalane, "would seem to indicate that extermination was desired."[48]

In addition to the killing of predators, the Park Service began introducing exotics, that is, non-native trees, shrubs, and other plants, and began stocking park waters with non-native fish. By 1921, just five years into Mather's regime, the scientific societies began passing resolutions in opposition to what was happening in the parks. The Ecological Society of America attacked with a resolution affirming that "one of the primary duties of the National Park Service is to pass on to future generations, unimpaired the wilderness of the parks, including their native plants and animals" and "that the introduction of non-native plants and animals . . . be strictly forbidden." Albright responded that plantings of non-native fish would continue in those waters in which the plantings had already occurred. Dr. Charles C. Adams countered in a monograph on ecological conditions in the parks in the *Scientific Monthly* that "these exotic species, planted by error, should not be maintained in the parks at all, but should be reduced in every way possible, and no replanting of these species should be permitted."[49] The American Association for the Advancement of Science joined the attack on predator killing and exotic introduction with its own resolution in 1921, opposing it "and all other unessential interference with natural conditions and urges the National Park Service to prohibit all such introductions and interference."[50] Mather ignored all complaints.

By 1925 the wilderness movement organized the opposition to the Park Service's extermination program and its exotic introduction activities. The Boone and Crockett Club charged that "the importance of the national parks to science is bound up largely with the preservation of the balance of nature. The more this balance is kept free from man's interference, the better is the area for scientific study. That is, the less the natural conditions within the parks are interfered with the better. . . . The processes of nature are so delicately adjusted that when man interferes in one aspect he sets up a chain of consequences the end of which no one can foresee. Darwin's chain from cats to clover was cited as one of the best known examples. Cats eat mice, which eat the eggs and larvae of the bumble bees, preventing the development of the mature bees which collect the honey and at the same time pollinate the clover flowers. Thus the cat helps the clover crop by destroying the mice that destroy the bumblebees that fertilize the clover blossoms."[51] The American Association for the Advancement of Science and the Ecological Society of America now were joined by the American Society of Mammalogists, the Wilson Ornithological Club, New York Zoological Society and the Boone and Crockett Club. Finally, Mather was forced by the power of the opposition he had generated to concede in his 1926 report that "it is contrary to the policy of the service to exterminate any species native to a park area" but expressed the necessity for control so that the weaker animals would not suffer unduly.

By 1929 and 1930 the Park Service was deluged with resolutions and letters condemning predator control and Dr. Joseph Grinnell, director of the Museum of Vertebrate Zoology at the University of California, had intervened directly with the park superintendents to stop it.[52]

In 1929, after fourteen years as director, Mather was replaced by Albright, who could not withstand the pressure for reform. In 1931, Albright seemingly capitulated to the scientists. In a classic statement that never acknowledged that the Park Service had ever done anything but preserve nature as the Park Service Act of 1916 had intended, Albright referred to "widespread campaigns of destruction" as if these had occurred somewhere else rather than under his and Mather's orders:

> Certainly, one of the great contributions to the welfare of the nation that national parks may make is that of wildlife protection. It is one of the understood functions of the parks to give total protection to animal life. . . . Of late there has been much discussion by the American Society of Mammalogists and other scientific organizations relative to predatory animals and their control. The inroads of the fur trapper and widespread campaigns of destruction have caused the great reductions of some and the near disappearance of several American carnivores. The question

naturally arises as to whether there is any place where they may be expected to survive and be available for scientific study in the future.

The National Park Service believes that predatory animals have a real place in nature, and that all animal life should be kept inviolate within the parks.

Albright then proceeded to establish the "policies relative to predatory animals" which gave him enough leeway that he could continue the killing as he saw fit:

1. Predatory animals are to be considered an integral part of wildlife protected within national parks, and no widespread campaigns of destruction are to be countenanced. The only control practiced is that of shooting coyotes or other predators when they are actually found making serious inroads upon herds of game or other animals needing special protection.
2. No permits for trapping within the borders of a park are allowed. A resolution opposing the use of steel traps within a park was passed several years ago by the superintendents at their annual meeting and they are used now only in emergencies.
3. Poison is believed to be a non-selective form of control and is banned from the national parks except where used by Park Service officials in warfare against rodents in settled portions of a park, or in case of emergency.[53]

After seeming to have given the scientific community everything demanded, he actually had retained for the Park Service the freedom to continue the killing. And continue it did. The killing went on until 1936 when Albright's successor was forced to abandon it in the face of a national campaign by environmentalists.[54]

No government official has ever succeeded in wreaking havoc on any natural environment on the scale that Mather had with his carnivore-killing program in the national parks. It left the areas under his control permanently damaged and the program itself mocked the Park Service Act and individual park acts which required the preservation of wildlife.

In 1918, Mather and Albright started zoos for the entertainment of park visitors. Various park animals were held in cages in the most heavily populated park areas like Yosemite Valley, starting with a pair of cougar kittens captured near Wawona. Then Mather fenced in some of the Yosemite meadows to hold on display a herd of California Tule elk, which were not native to Yosemite but were brought in from the lowlands. All the criticism that was heaped on him, Mather ignored. Not only was the concept of a zoo in a national park an anachronism but also that anachronism was doubly confounded by the fact that animals not native to the park were involved, much to the continuing anguish of the scientific community.

Then there were the garbage-feeding amphitheaters. During the Mather/Albright administration, hundreds of tourists would gather at the posted feeding times to watch bears wallow in the garbage brought from the hotels and camp grounds. The garbage feeding in Yellowstone brought about unprecedented concentrations of bears in small areas and resulted in the spreading of disease and parasites among them. It introduced unnatural concentrates of rich foods that proved to be damaging to the bears. The feeding displays were scheduled for the tourist season rather than for the biological needs of the bears. As a result, the females went into hibernation in poor shape, and the cubs born in winter suffered. The garbage pits resulted in the desertion of the niche formerly occupied by the bears in the summertime and disturbed the bears' normal biotic relationship to the park. The garbage feeding attracted the bears to the food of campers and encouraged a lack of fear of man that ended in many bears being killed in order to protect visitors.[55]

Albright thought the garbage-feeding program was a wonderful addition to Yellowstone. "It is a wonderful sight to visit one of the bear feeding grounds in the evening, when from several hundred to a thousand people are observing the antics of the bears," he said. "The excitement of the audience caused by the appearance of a big old grizzly among a group of black bears is worth going a long way to see."[56]

The Mather/Albright years left the Park Service unfit to carry out the charge in the 1916 Park Service Act to administer "by such means as will leave [the resources] unimpaired for the enjoyment of future generations." The value system that emerged could with ease view such a charge with contempt. The ecosystems and biological balances in the parks were permanently damaged by Mather and Albright. The Park Service itself ended up with a value system irrelevant to preservation, if not indifferent or hostile to it.

And the law was ignored. Besides the 1916 Park Service Act, for example, many of the parks were bound by specifically restrictive wildlife laws as well. Typical of these laws was Section 4 of the act ceding exclusive jurisdiction in Mount Rainier National Park to the federal government. This law, which amounted to a contract between the federal government and the state over how the Park Service would administer the area of the park, specifically stated:

> That all hunting or the killing, wounding, or capturing at any time of
> any wild bird or animal, except dangerous animals when it is necessary

to prevent them from destroying human lives or inflicting personal injury, is prohibited within the limits of said park.[57]

Both Mather and Albright ignored this law and similar laws affecting nearly every park. By operating their tragic extermination program in the face of these protective efforts, the ecosystems of the parks were destroyed.

The creation of the Park Service had proved to be a disaster for the preservationists who had fought so hard for so long to preserve the national parks. Their dilemma was that there was no place else to go for preservation.

7 PRESERVATION AND RECREATION BE DAMNED

The lumber industry is spending millions of dollars in the effort to forestall or delay the public control of lumbering, which is the only measure capable of putting an end to forest devastation in America. It is trying to fool the American people into believing that the industry is regulating itself and has given up the practice of forest devastation.[1]   GIFFORD PINCHOT

You and I will have no disagreement over the importance of working with the lumbermen, educating them as we can, and being educated by them in turn. . . . The Forest Service has not the slightest idea of handing down a set of commandments from the mountain.[2]   WILLIAM GREELEY

WHEN PINCHOT GOT CONTROL of the nation's forests in 1905, he came to the role of chief with a vision and high organizational skills. He formulated that vision in a letter and had it sent from the Secretary of Agriculture to himself. Pinchot's letter had the power of secretarial policy and would be binding on the Forest Service into the future.

Pinchot's letter is a masterpiece of consistency and clarity. He wrote, "all the resources of forest reserves are for use, and this use must be brought about in a thoroughly prompt and businesslike manner." His vigorous attack on any concept of preservation, especially of trees, is a prominent feature of the Forest Service today. He defined what the

Forest Service's constituencies would be: "The continued prosperity of the agricultural, lumbering, mining and livestock interests is directly dependent upon a permanent and accessible supply of water, wood and forage . . . " And he defined what the management priorities would be for the local administrators in the decentralized Forest Service of his vision: "In the management of each reserve local questions will be decided upon local grounds; the dominant industry will be considered first. . . . " Pinchot even determined the organization structure that would deliver the "use" that he wanted: "these general principles . . . can be successfully applied only when the administration of each reserve is left very largely in the hands of the local officers. . . ."[3] Decentralization of administration thereby became the hallmark of the Forest Service.

Pinchot attracted an outstanding group of men who followed his leadership with high morale and absolute clarity about what they were trying to accomplish. Thornton T. Munger, who was present with Pinchot in the early Forest Service years, said of him long after he was gone that his "influence continued to be felt through the warp and woof of the Forest Service led by men trained by him and very loyal to him. Policies and procedures he so wisely founded continued to vitalize the Forest Service; the form and language to be used in correspondence, the policy of decentralized administration, the spirit of public service that pervades the personnel, the principle of conservation through use. . . ."[4] Pinchot had given purpose, direction and had developed the organization to deliver his utilitarian vision of use.

To make absolutely certain that the Forest Service delivered locally the immediate economic utilization he wanted, Pinchot wrote a "Use Book" for all employees. This manual eliminated any possibility of organizational deviancy towards the values of John Muir:

> All timber within the National Forests which can be cut safely and for which there is an actual need, is for sale.
>
> The prime object of the National Forest is use.[5]

This manual evolved into the Forest Service Manual of today.

In spite of his professional staff, high morale, and clarity of purpose, Pinchot had constructed a fatal flaw into the very fabric of the Forest Service organization. The decentralized administration he insisted upon, combined with his hierarchy of priorities in allocating resources locally requiring that "the dominant industry will be considered first," prevented the Forest Service from being able to differentiate the national interest from the narrowest of short-term local interests. This flaw would prevent the Forest Service from delivering on his well-known charge that "where conflicting interests must be reconciled the question will always be decided from the standpoint of the greatest good of the greatest number in the long run."[6] This left to the Forest Service itself the determination of what was the "greatest good." Cutting trees would always be its option of choice when "good" was considered. And this would result in the loss of millions of acres of the Forest Service's domain to the Park Service and to congressionally mandated wilderness withdrawals in the face of vigorous Forest Service opposition. The Forest Service was captured by those dominant industries Pinchot defined for it as the local administrators' first priority.[7]

The issue of forest depletion loomed over the Forest Service and began to tear it apart. By 1905, most of the nation's timberlands were in private ownership. The liquidation and devastation that followed were logical, given the desire to maximize profits. Nearly every forester believed something had to be done about cutting on privately owned timberlands to end the devastation and the famine to come. "Lumbermen . . . are not interested in what becomes of the land as *forest land* after cutting," charged H. H. Chapman of Yale's Forestry School. "Most of them will admit this and justify it. Many are interested in forestry, provided they themselves do not have to practice it."[8] Chapman had hit it on the head. No one was interested in forestry except the foresters. "Reforestation will come when it is profitable . . . it will not do to merely resolute and spread high sounding, well meaning platitudes on the records,"[9] said E. G. Griggs, president of the National Lumberman's Manufacturers Association in answer to the foresters.

The goal of the timber industry, to maximize profits in the face of a future timber famine, could only be dealt with the police power of the government. That was the firm belief of Gifford Pinchot and his successor, Henry S. Graves. Both had made control of cutting on private forestlands the Forest Service's focus for averting the coming timber shortage. In 1920 Graves told a meeting of lumbermen that regulation was necessary to stop destructive logging and asked their cooperation in working it out. Pinchot, with friends and supporters in Congress and old crusaders all around him, "demanded federal regulation of all private timber cutting in the United States. In earlier years he often referred to commercial forestry as a business 'that must pay its own way,' but he was impatient over the delay and inertia of the forest industries and their habitual defense that 'we cannot grow trees until they are worth the cost of growing them.' Pinchot was irritated by the alibi of hard times and tough competition in the lumber business. His crusading zeal demanded action now. He held that the public interest in all forest lands was paramount and must be protected whether the owner made money or went broke. Pinchot proposed to meet the competitive

William B. Greeley.
Forest History Society.

angle by the uniform imposition of cutting restrictions under federal
law. They would apply to all commercial forest operations and put all
competitors on the same footing. It would be like subjecting them to
a uniform federal tax but the money would go into future productive-
ness of their forests rather than the national treasury."[10]

Assistant Forester William Greeley disagreed fundamentally in every
way with the Pinchot approach. When Greeley's paper on the timber
industry[11] called for cooperation and support for the timber industry
as the route to get reforestation, Pinchot charged that Greeley accepted
the "commercial demands of the lumber industry as supreme over the
need of forest conservation and the rights of the public . . . and puts
the Forest Service in the position of throwing contempt upon its basic
reason for existence." And Pinchot reminded Graves, "You and I know
that the lumbermen have systematically played with the Forest Service
for years, and have directed their policy very ably toward getting all
they could . . . and giving nothing in return."[12] Pinchot's appraisal of
the timber industry proved to be prophetic. Greeley's ascendancy as
Forest Service chief in 1920 put him into position to implement his programs of cooperation with the timber industry. His ideas represented
an important departure from the second thoughts of Pinchot in his
last years as chief.

Greeley's program shifted the burden of forest ownership to the taxpayer at both the federal and state levels. It provided for state and federal moneys for fire protection and reforestation and tax relief legislation, all of which had the theoretical effect of enabling the industry to increase its profits in order that the industry might therefore do voluntarily what the public was demanding.

It took only three years of effort on Greeley's part to get through Congress, with the help of the timber industry, the legislation that would put a subsidy into the holding of private timberlands in the hope that a national goal of a continuing timber supply would result. At the hearings, Pinchot challenged all the premises upon which Greeley's program rested. He denied that fire prevention was the most essential feature in a reforestation program. Halting devastation, he said, was the key and that had to be accomplished by rigid national regulation. Pinchot saw duplicity in the lumberman's avowed eagerness to cooperate in a reforestation program in the light of their record of timber destruction. "Here are these lumbermen coming before you and asking to be controlled," he exclaimed before the committee members. "These are the men who have already destroyed in this country and reduced to desert conditions an area larger than the forests of Europe, excluding Russia. Now they ostensibly ask to be prevented from doing that very thing out of which they have made their money—that is, to be prevented from handling their lands as they choose." Why? Pinchot asserted that the reason Greeley's approach was so attractive was that the lumbermen would maintain their customary control over the state legislatures where they could prevent any action hostile to their interests and that this cooperative legislation would place control of the nation's lumber supply in the hands of the legislatures of Washington, Oregon and California.[13]

Pinchot had predicted accurately the outcome of Greeley's programs. After ten years of operation, even with public subsidy, fire damage was eleven times greater on private lands than on federal lands, less than one percent of private lands were managed to ensure continual growth of timber, and although private owners controlled 80 percent of the commercial forestlands, they now contributed only 7 percent of the total funds available for fire protection. In addition, the unstocked forestlands had gone from 81 million acres to 83 million acres.[14] The program was a failure and the public was saddled with a permanent subsidy to the timber industry. Because it greatly broadened the Forest Service's base of political support, however, it could claim success. Meanwhile, on the Olympic Peninsula, the timber situation was worse than ever as the maximization of profit during the roaring 1920's drove the forest liquidation strategies even harder. The Forest Service's own statistics for Grays Harbor County told it all. "In general, cut-over lands logged prior to 1920 have become better restocked than those logged since 1920. Because of the large scale of several of the logging operations in the county . . . clear cut areas of 20,000 acres or more in extent with practically no seed trees have resulted. This is particularly true in the Douglas fir zone of the central and eastern part of the county where 63 percent of the total area of 139,000 acres logged during the decade 1920–29 is nonrestocked, 24 percent is poorly stocked and only 13 percent are the coniferous reproduction stands satisfactorily restocked."[15] Clallam County's timber was receiving the same treatment. The Bloedel-Donovan Timber Company alone employed 1,500 men and by 1928–1929 were cutting 300 million feet per year in the rain forest at the west end of the county.[16] In the years 1925 to 1929, when the Greeley program was in effect, the forest depletion statistics for Washington State indicated that 1.9 billion board feet were grown and 7 billion board feet were cut annually, a cut of 3 ½ times growth.[17] Douglas fir loggers were leaving on the ground 20 percent of the timber that would be merchantable and used in most eastern operations. What was left on the ground, often running twelve or fifteen thousand board feet to the acre, provided the major fire hazard that Greeley now had public money to defend against.[18]

Greeley's policies, according to forester Robert Marshall, "involved the assumption that if the government patted the private owner on the back, and asked him politely to practice forestry, and helped him out with a substantial contribution of money for fire protection, research, and advice in regard to the management of his lands, the private owner would jubilantly and enthusiastically manage his woodlands to the perfect satisfaction of the forestry profession. . . . There was one serious fallacy which doomed it from the start. Lumbermen do not to any appreciable extent invest their extra profits in forestry. In fact, the more profitable it becomes for them to log, the more heavily they usually cut, and the fewer trees they leave on the ground after their operations are completed. As a result, in many cases where the markets were most profitable there was practically no provision made for a new stand. . . ."[19]

The industry had responded to Greeley's program just as Pinchot had predicted it would. The annual cut and the devastation accelerated. But with public money now flowing to the industry through the states, euphemistically called "cooperation" by Greeley, the industry asked for an expansion of the process to have the public pick up the costs of reforestation. The Milwaukee Land Company, which had been the largest corporate recipient of the west-side rain forest eliminations from the Olympic Forest Reserve thirty years earlier, with over 80,000 acres fraudulently acquired, now proposed that the present owners of cut-over Olympic forestland convey, under contract, to the state of

Washington "those lands suitable for reforestation." Under the contract the owners "would pay the state not to exceed five cents per acre per year during the life of the contract, the money to be used for . . . reforestation purposes. The present owners would have the right to repurchase these lands from the state, after a period of forty years, at the rate of one dollar per acre, plus fifteen percent of the gross value of the standing timber."[20] The plan would have enabled the Milwaukee railroad subsidiary to escape the land holding taxes and in fact would have externalized nearly all of the costs of forest land ownership while retaining the profit potential from the second-growth harvest. The state would have replanted this land, at five cents per acre per year, for the Milwaukee Land Company. The proposal went nowhere.

Inside the Forest Service, Greeley's efforts to bind the interests of the Forest Service and the public to those of the timber industry became known as "Greeleyism" and to its disparagers as "lumbermen leading the Forest Service by the hand."[21] Eight years in office had given Greeley ample opportunity to deal with the disparagers. His own men occupied most of the key positions. The Forest Service of Pinchot and Graves ended up as a Greeley Forest Service committed to industry cooperation and support by the time he left office in 1928.

Removing the highly regarded local men that Chief Foresters Pinchot and Graves had put in place did not happen as quietly as Greeley would have liked, however. District Forester C. M. Granger, in 1926, moved against those forest supervisors who had visibly emphasized forest recreational activities. Supervisor Rudo L. Fromme of Olympic Forest was summarily dismissed from office and asked to resign from the Forest Service, which he chose not to do. Supervisor Sylvester of the Chelan Forest faced removal and Supervisor Weigle of the Snoqualmie Forest faced disciplinary proceedings. "His principal offense," charged Asahel Curtis, "being that he is a member of the Tourist Committee of the Seattle Chamber of Commerce."[22] The dismissals and disciplinary actions were perceived by the local communities as being so patently unfair and even outrageous, that both Dean Winkenwerder of the University of Washington's College of Forestry and chambers of commerce throughout the state organized an active campaign to stop the dismissals. Greeley ignored them. When it all shook down, the forest supervisors with a visible interest in forest recreation had been replaced with a timber-production-oriented group loyal to Greeley and the 1905 guidelines laid down by Gifford Pinchot twenty years earlier. A decade later, in 1937, Greeley's actions in eradicating those who were seen as soft on recreation still hung heavy on the local scene. In speaking of Rudo Fromme, Superintendent Owen Tomlinson of Mount Rainier National Park said, "It seems that while in charge of the Olympic

Forest, he was not in sympathy with some of the plans for cutting, grazing, and other economic development and use. His outspoken disagreement with higher officials resulted in his transfer."[23] There is nothing
in the record to support Tomlinson's assertion but what is clear is that
Fromme had a soft spot in his heart for forest recreation as well as timber production. Greeley's dismissals sent a message to the Forest Service about what survivability in the system is all about, not to mention
promotability. The message was not only received but absorbed deeply
into its core.

On May 1, 1928, Greeley abruptly resigned to take up the work that
would occupy the rest of his life—heading the West Coast Lumberman's
Association. His major task in that role would be to keep government-
owned timber flowing from the public's forests to the mills owned by
his employers.

By 1929, just thirty years from the time of the scandal-ridden Olympic Forest Reserve eliminations, the privately held old-growth Douglas
fir was nearly exhausted on the Olympic Peninsula. There had been
virtual liquidation. Grays Harbor had, however, thirty-four sawmills and
thirty-seven other wood-using plants to feed. They were all hovering
on the brink of bankruptcy. Ten years later there would be ten mills,
20,000 parcels of tax-delinquent lands, and payrolls only 25 percent
of what they had been in 1929. In the meantime, having liquidated the
forest capital of the peninsula, the lumbermen moved in 1929 to capture the timber in Olympic National Forest that had not been included
in the eliminations thirty years before. Three fourths of all of the timber by volume in the Olympic Forest Reserve had been conveyed to
the lumbermen by the Timber and Stone Act fraud. The lumbermen
needed the remaining one fourth to keep their mills humming. And
humming they were. In 1926 alone, the Grays Harbor mills produced
1,557,223,000 board feet of lumber. 880 seagoing vessels that year hauled
it to the four corners of the world.[24]

Using the chambers of commerce of Grays Harbor County, the lumbermen prepared a brief with which to confront the Forest Service with
their demands that the overbuilt mill capacity of Grays Harbor be kept
going with public timber. "This brief prays for the allocation of the timber in the Olympic National Forest on the basis of maintenance of existing industry," it said in its opening paragraph. Their request included
all of the old-growth rain forests of the western and southern Olympics. Their surveys had shown, they said, that the only timber left was
federal and state timber and that "the lumber industry is at the mercy
of the government sale of this timber." Directing the Forest Service's
attention to the fact that the industry's investments were the result of
the "enormous stands of timber . . . peculiar to this territory" and that

they needed to be "protected by the allocation of timber . . . on the just premise that the people who have pioneered a country are entitled to first consideration in the distribution of such natural resources as may still be held by the government." The lumbermen believed the Forest Service "has sufficient power to carry out the allocation asked for . . . " but if not, they were "more than willing to sponsor legislation necessary to bring about the desired results."[25] It was a bold move and they had good reason for optimism. The flaw which Pinchot had programmed into the organizational development of the Forest Service—decentralized local control with the local forests' first priority defined for them as the dominant industry in the area—had by 1929 combined with Greeleyism—taxpayer support of the industry with subsidies for the costs of holding timberland. This new Forest Service with Greeley men occupying all the key roles was an unbeatable combination, with Greeley himself now representing the West Coast Lumberman's Association and able to deal directly with the very men he had put into place.

The chief of the Forest Service and Greeley's successor, Robert Stuart, announced the following year that the largest timber sale made during the preceding year was in Olympic National Forest, a sale of 852 million board feet. He made no pretense about why. "This timber was awarded . . . to a company which has cut nearly all the privately owned timber available to it and in default of obtaining public timber was faced with the alternative of ceasing operation and dismantling its plants, to the detriment of the community."[26] The interests of the Forest Service and the forest resources it held were now congruent with the timber industry. Hiring Greeley at the moment that much of the privately held old-growth forest had vanished was a brilliant move on the part of the lumbermen. Gifford Pinchot wrote to Robert Stuart, Greeley's successor as chief, that "under the leadership of Bill Greeley, the Service steadily put the interest of the lumbermen ahead of the interest of the country, and this poison is necessarily still hobbling the judgment of many men who under different leadership would have taken a totally different attitude."[27] But Forest Service employees continued to work for the benefit of the mill owner employers of their former chief. The rules laid down by Gifford Pinchot himself for the Forest Service in 1905 demanded it as well.

A proposal for an Olympic National Park, just over the horizon, threatened to disrupt the Forest Service and the mill owners. Almost immediately after becoming chief in 1920, Greeley moved aggressively against the new Park Service and its floundering leadership. Mather's Park Service was by then measuring the success of its administration by how many additional tourists had visited each park area compared with the year before, along with counting the number of predators

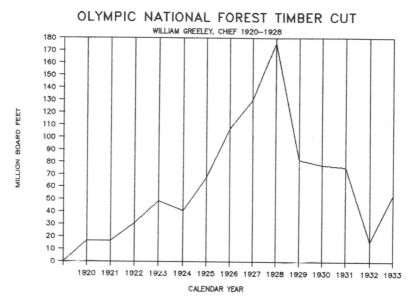

Chief Forester Greeley attempted to support the over-built and doomed Olympic Peninsula mills with publicly owned timber, clashing head-on with rising demands for wilderness and forest recreation. The mill owners hired him away from the Forest Service in 1928 to continue the effort. *U.S. Forest Service.*

destroyed to protect "the game." Greeley knew that the land and trees that might be added to the park system could come from only one source, the national forests.

Preserving trees in the national parks had been so completely accepted by the public, the Congress, and by Greeley himself, that by 1920 most believed that park logging was a dead issue. Trees removed from a park by a boundary adjustment were another matter, however. Trading national forest scenery, generally high altitude non-commercial areas, for the areas in the parks containing the most economically significant forests would be his strategy. The very forests that were the most valuable for preservation and for park purposes generally were also of highest commercial value for timber.

Realizing the potential political popularity of more national parks, Greeley moved to curb the burgeoning park movement by taking the initiative to define in every forum he could reach "the qualifications or specifications every national park should measure up to." "The first," he said, "is that the scenic attractions and national wonders and beauties of the area must be of such outstanding importance as to be distinctly national in their character. . . . The second general specification which it has seemed to me every national park should meet," he went on, "is that its value for public service in the form of recreation and natural beauty should be outstanding in importance as compared with the value of the commercial resources of the area."[28]

If these criteria were accepted, the Forest Service could resist future national park creations. It could argue both that the area under consideration was not of national significance and that the resources therein were of commercial importance to the region, thereby deflecting nearly any park thrust. But Mather took the bait. The Forest Service's park criteria became the Park Service's too. Albright, as Mather's successor, would find a decade later when he tried to extend the national park system what accepting these criteria meant.

Even the head of the National Parks Association was taken in. Robert Sterling Yard believed that "Greeley was the best advocate of national park standards I ever knew in official life."[29]

Greeley was so effective that a bill creating a greatly expanded Sequoia National Park ended up being rewritten and reintroduced. The Barbour bill, named after Representative Henry Barbour of Fresno, eliminated not only the most valuable forest areas that the original bill called for, but also called for half of the existing park containing the most valuable trees to be eliminated, all in return for the addition of a large area of economically worthless high country scenery. The enthusiastic support of the Mather Park Service stood solidly behind the bill; they were in the scenery business, not the forest business.

Greeley went before the House Public Lands Committee and laid out the Forest Service rationale for the Sequoia National Park boundaries which had been drawn to systematically eliminate everything of any possible economic value to any group. "In adjusting those boundaries," he said, "the most important areas of commercial timber have been eliminated from the proposed addition . . . the areas of commercial timber remaining within the area are of negligible extent and of negligible future importance to the forest industries. . . ." He then went on to reassure the committee that all of the possible mineralized areas had also been eliminated as well as all of the "areas where existing use of the range would be disrupted to the injury of local livestock interests."[30] In effect, Greeley had maneuvered himself into position, as chief of the Forest Service, into defining the future course of the national park system, and with the support of the Park Service. The park system would apparently contain scenery without trees with all park areas passing a test of economic worthlessness. Greeley then tried to get the Park Service transferred to the Department of Agriculture, an effort he began in October of 1923.

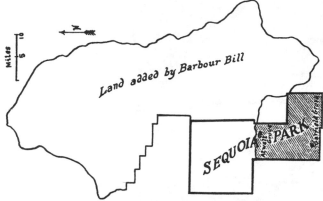

Map showing effect of the Barbour Bill in cutting off the southern half of the present park, also the deep bay in the proposed western boundary which will permit commercial exploitation of timber lands almost in the center of the area added.

Throughout the 1920's, Willard Van Name attacked Park Service Director Mather and Forest Service Chief Greeley's plans to divest parks of their most valuable forests. He desperately attempted to involve the public with his articles, pamphlets, and maps (see above). *Science, December 22, 1922.*

A careful observer of all of these events finally decided to become an activist, a decision that would change the course of American conservation history and would plague William Greeley until the day he died three decades later. Willard Van Name, associate curator of the Department of Invertebrate Zoology at the American Museum of Natural History in New York, moved to protect the national park system's forests from Greeley and Mather.

An eminent scientist, Van Name had access to most of the scientific journals, to the popular national journals of fact and opinion and to the daily newspapers. Shy and retiring, his pen was his flaming sword, a colleague once said of him. He had watched the forest reserves being set aside, the giveaway and fraudulent private acquisition of the Olympic forests, the rise of the Forest Service and its attempts to get control of the parks and its attempts to cut the trees in the parks. He had watched the preservationist battle to create a park service, only to see it now giving away what had been given it to preserve.

When Van Name made the decision to intervene to thwart Greeley's moves to get control of the trees in Sequoia National Park, he implicitly felt that he had no power. At age fifty in 1922, a loner by nature, he had a burning zeal to communicate. Involving the public became his focus and his goal. With his own money, he began producing pamphlets explaining the issues as he saw them. He mailed them nationwide to

Willard G. Van Name.
American Museum of Natural History.

anyone who might be able to influence the outcome. Hundreds of hours of work addressing and mailing faced him each time he wrote one. The pages of *Science* were open to him and he used them often. "The wonderful primeval forests of the Pacific states are disappearing with astonishing rapidity," he charged, "and it is of the highest importance from a scientific as well as from an esthetic and scenic standpoint that at least the few tracts of them that are in the national parks should be preserved."[31] He attacked Mather's 1921 proposal to eliminate the western forests of Yosemite charging that, "if carried out as recommended [they] would eliminate from that park all of its three Sequoia groves and most of its magnificent sugar pine and yellow pine forests."[32] Ever the businessman, Mather responded with a simple economic justification. "The area proposed to be eliminated from the Yosemite is of far more value for grazing and other commercial interests, than it is for purely park purposes."[33]

What galled Van Name most of all was that the Park Service was actively engaged with Greeley and the Forest Service in divesting from protection the remnants of the forests that were already in national parks. To drive his point home, he quoted from a letter received from Assistant Director Cammerer justifying the Park Service's support of the Sequoia National Park bill on the grounds that "the Forest Service has contended that those sections which would be eliminated from the present Sequoia National Park are required for the commercial needs of that section of California."[34] "For thirty-two years [the park] has protected them," sighed Van Name, "but it is to do so no longer."[35] The parks were being given away by the Park Service itself. Van Name's flaming pen summed up the conflict of the Greeley/Mather era: "If we are robbed of money we can go to work and earn more, but if we are robbed of the national parks we lose what neither time, money, labor, or regrets can replace."[36]

Van Name had forced his way into the preservation processes with his typewriter. He began to involve the public in decisions which had before been left to the agencies and Congress. One of Van Name's attackers charged, "He is laboring under the impression that the Forest Service is deliberately scheming to gain control of all timber on the national parks for exploitation, and that the supporters of the Forest Service are its tools or its dupes."[37] Van Name would have accepted the charge happily. That was exactly what he thought. Citizen activism was rising on the horizon and Van Name was soon joined by powerful literary voices.

The technological triumph of the 1920's was the inexpensive automobile. It gave the common man in the West easy access to the forests and parks. The automobile at the same time put him into direct contact with the mile upon mile of rolling, burned-over stump land through which he had to drive to get there. The stark contrast was a jarring reminder to everyone that forestland was not a permanent part of any scene. Outdoor recreation and vanishing wilderness led by the use of the automobile became the concern of many. Aldo Leopold wrote, "we cannot afford to longer ignore the need for action. . . . our larger areas of Wilderness will mostly disappear within the next decade."[38]

As people increasingly were able to get to wilderness the recreational value of forests became a national concern. The National Conference on Outdoor Recreation, sponsored by the Boone and Crockett Club, emerged in 1924 with a Congressional Charter. One of its major goals, *to make the forested lands of the United States available for purposes of outdoor recreation to the fullest extent consistent with national needs for timber production,* posed a threat to the Forest Service, but Greeley was able to co-opt the committee himself. With Greeley's intervention, Assistant Forester Leon Kneipp ran NCOR activity as executive secretary, and Forest Service men occupied key roles throughout its structure. Greeley succeeded in shifting his park boundary adjustment program to an NCOR coordinating committee on national parks and forests. He would be on that committee as would Mather. It was structured so that it would function only in cases of disagreement between the Park Service and the Forest Service. Since Mather was predisposed to giving up the national park forests, Greeley now had a professional group to give credibility to park boundary changes and to the divestiture of forests. The committee was to report to the "President's Committee," consisting of five cabinet officers including the Secretaries of the Interior and Agriculture.

From 1925 on, the conference was presented with boundary adjustments for Mount Rainier, Rocky Mountain, Sequoia, Grand Canyon, Yellowstone, and in a second report, for Yosemite and Crater Lake. Greeley was proud to say that the "report represents complete unanimity on the part of the Forest Service and the Park Service. . . ." But he warned that in all of the park situations involved "there are particular people who in entire sincerity oppose the recommendations of the Committee."[39] Greeley understated the situation.

Willard Van Name burst forth with a thirty-one-page pamphlet in February 1926 called *Hands Off the National Parks,* complete with pictures of the areas to be eliminated, maps and statistics. He quoted from a letter Greeley had written to him earlier, which had said that it was "crystal clear that the strengthening and entrenchment of the National Park idea will be greatly promoted by a careful study of National Park boundaries and the exclusion therefrom of all lands that are not integral or essential parts of units which contain the natural phenomena or utilities the park was created to protect."[40] Greeley's solution was to define national park boundaries by hydrographic divides, to which Van Name sarcastically pointed out that on the basis of the committee's recommendations this was "considered important only in those cases in which valuable timber, reservoir sites or other resources would thereby be juggled out of the parks and opened up to private exploitation."

In *Hands Off the National Parks,* written, paid for, and mailed by Van Name, he took on Greeley and Mather directly, defining the issues clearly, and stirring the public conscience. "The Forest Service has always been a bitter enemy of the National Parks," he said, "and has been the cause of great loss and harm to them, and the main agency in the obstruction that has prevented the enlargement of the park system for so many years. It has always regarded the forests of the National Parks as its natural prey, to be obtained by any and every means that bills slipped through Congress will permit." "These forests are among the most precious possessions of the parks; their hills, valleys and mountains will remain, parks or no parks, but if the magnificent trees that have taken centuries to grow are cut down, dozens of human generations must come and go before they can be restored again. It is to save the forests, more often than for any other reason, that National Parks are needed."[41]

Mather and the Park Service he hit as hard and as directly as he did the Forest Service. " . . . In spite of much fine talk about preserving the natural scenery of the parks, the National Park Service shows little interest in anything but the development of the parks, by means of roads and hotel building, into great money-making enterprises capable of rapidly transporting large numbers of tourists into and out of the parks, and incidentally separating them from their coin. It is very indifferent to the ruin of the scenery by logging or other commercial enterprises as long as this is not conspicuous from the hotel porches or from the viewpoints to which tourists are ordinarily carried by the transportation companies, and as long as the park looks passably well from a speeding automobile. The rest of the park lands the lumbermen, the stockmen, and the power companies seem to be welcome to."[42] He accused the Park Service of not being interested in park expansion and quite willing to turn over to some other bureau "areas which cannot show a value as an asset for profitable tourist exploitation."[43] "Whether the nation wishes the main purpose of the national parks sacrificed for the development of their money making possibilities is another question, but it is one that needs to be settled right away if irreparable damage and loss to the parks are to be halted."[44]

Never losing sight of this goal of public involvement in preservation, Van Name aimed straight at the public policy issues. "What right have the chiefs of the Park Service and Forest Service to get together and trade away the forest lands of the parks? It is a serious matter to give up a single acre of a National Park. It should never be done in secret, without giving the public all the facts connected with the case, telling just what is in the area, who wants it, and why they want it, why it is necessary or advantageous to give it up. The present bureau chiefs merely inform us that they have 'agreed on' certain boundary changes, and assume that what they decide to do or why they do it is *none of the public's business*" (italics are Van Name's).[45]

The group running the National Conference on Outdoor Recreation both in and out of government understood implicitly that an open, public dialog about the issues Van Name raised could lead to an open challenge of the status quo in which each of them benefitted. They settled for name calling and the isolation of Van Name. Charles Sheldon, one of the organizers of the conference, said, "Van Name is a freak and very disturbing—a permanent gnat to Parks and Forest Service."[46] The committee talked it over and decided the best was to ignore "Van Name's outbursts."[47] Nonetheless, he had hit deeply, and the issues of involving the public were not going to go away.

These issues were picked up by H. H. Chapman of the Yale School of Forestry, who tried in 1925 to begin the public policy dialogue that the Forest Service needed to face. He defined the issue precisely:

Shall trees be cut down and used and the forest perpetuated by producing it through forestry methods, or shall the trees be preserved to be enjoyed now? We cannot do both . . .

If a tree or stand is worth more to civilization by leaving it as it is than by cutting, using, and reproducing it, then it should be preserved from the ax.

Who is to determine this? In the final analysis, the public.[48]

Both the Forest Service and the Park Service ignored the public policy issues. Greeley and Mather were in fact attempting to determine, without public involvement, what forests should *not* be preserved. Both were on a collision course with Van Name, and with growing popular sentiment behind him.

Willard Van Name was not the only one who observed Greeley's aggressive attacks on the commercially valuable forests in the parks. Greeley had only been in office four years when the climate inside the Forest Service seemed right for doing what Pacific Northwest Forest Service officials had wanted to do for years—abolish the Mount Olympus National Monument. With rising national interest in outdoor recreation, wilderness preservation, and the quality of life running heavy in the media, it seemed an impossible undertaking to do it by proclamation. And only eight years had passed since the Forest Service had prepared the presidential proclamation which took all of the then commercially valuable timber out of the Mount Olympus National Monument, cutting it in half. No one inside the Forest Service then had questioned the necessity for the elimination because all had accepted that the monument in fact "locked up resources." But the Forest Service's dilemma was apparently solved in the field. Olympic Forest Supervisor Rudo Fromme made plans in 1923 for the complete utilization of all of the timber in the forest, including the timber from every watershed in the Mount Olympus National Monument. He didn't acknowledge the existence of the monument in his first plan. His revised plan of 1924 recognized the monument but included all of its timber within the working circles described. "Removing this timber would in no way conflict with the purposes for which the Monument was created," Fromme said.[49]

Assistant Forester Leon Kneipp promulgated the new official doctrine officially: " . . . the Antiquities Act under which monuments are created does not prohibit a utilization of natural resources but merely the filing of claims or the destruction of antiquities. Forest Management seems to be in perfect liberty to go ahead with its timber plans for the Olympic without fear that the existence of the Monument . . . will ever be an obstacle to the fulfillment of such plans."[50]

Pinchot's 1905 guidelines had trapped the Forest Service in a commercial ideology. Greeley in turn was reinforcing the doctrine at every turn with his focus on the needs of the local mills. The Forest Service counted on the political power of the local communities which were dominated by the mill owners to enable them to prevail in the end. "[When] our timber cutting operations . . . eventually do reach the boundaries [of the monument] and there is economic need for the timber," said Assistant Forester Kneipp, "public sentiment in the communities which are largely dependent upon logging for their livelihood undoubtedly will demand and secure a withdrawal of the monument if it proves to be in conflict with the best use of the timber."[51]

Once the Forest Service had decided that Mount Olympus National Monument did not exist in fact and that its timber was available, the rest of the monument's resources were made available as well. Sixteen hundred sheep began grazing in Lost River Basin, deep inside the monument, in direct competition with the elk for which the monument had supposedly been set aside. Two roads were surveyed and planned — an Elwha/North Fork Quinault road and a Dosewallips/East Fork Quinault road which would have given access to back-country timber.[52] Together, these roads would have chopped the wilderness mass of the Olympic Range into small fragments. A 1916 Forest Service decision that the monument was a game reserve was reversed with a finding that "the Mount Olympus National Monument is not a game reservation and that the Forest Service is not authorized to prohibit hunting and trapping within its boundaries."[53] A strange reversal; protecting elk was the reason for the monument's existence. Even mining was now to be allowed. To have found otherwise would have given the monument a reason for being there in the face of the official denials.

The Forest Service had defined the monument away, but then changed tack in the face of a planned dam in the Elwha River, a dam that would flood part of Mount Olympus National Monument. A proclamation eliminating that area from the monument was prepared by the Forest Service; President Coolidge signed it in 1929.

The Forest Service had assigned the resources contained in a nature sanctuary to commodity production. It happened without a word to the public and without any public involvement — the very practice that Willard Van Name was attacking the Forest Service for in his pamphlets. While this transformation was underway, the drumbeat of wilderness and outdoor recreationists, who were traveling by automobile and seeing mile upon mile of stump lands, beat louder. Recreation was not going to go away and the Forest Service saw the coming crisis. As one Forest Service official said, "recreation interests are a definite menace to the practice of forestry."[54]

Greeley hesitated to admit that logging, grazing, and power devel-

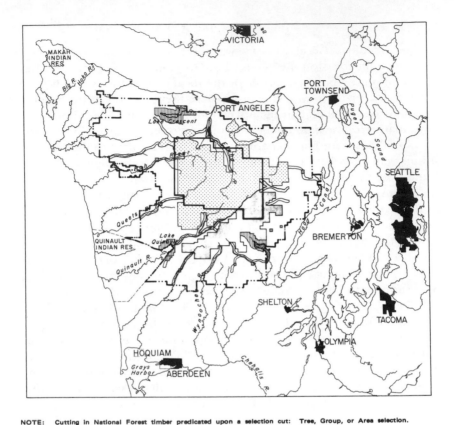

OLYMPIC FOREST RECREATION PLAN 1929 (CLEATOR PLAN)

Willard Van Name discovered in 1932 that the Forest Service's recreation plan had doomed every acre of Mount Olympus National Monument to logging. He launched his effort to create an Olympic National Park on his return to New York.

opment were incompatible with wilderness preservation. That clear-
cutting as practiced in the West was incompatible with every value other
than the maximization of profit was ignored in all the Forest Service's
planning processes. Greeley did respond to the recreationists by establishing a series of administrative "wilderness areas" in 1926, which three
years later became the basis for the Primitive Area regulations of 1929.
It was a public relations move that disguised his real interests; not one
square foot of his wilderness areas was preserved for the future. In fact
the resources so designated were specifically set aside for future economic use: "the establishment of a primitive area ordinarily will not
operate to withdraw timber, forage, or water resources from industrial
use since the utilization of such resources, if properly regulated, will
not be incompatible."[55] The resources being set aside would not have
been utilized at once anyway. The public overlooked the fine print and
believed the Forest Service had changed its ways by the mere fact of
the designations.

The Forest Service came forth with its own plan for recreation in
Olympic National Forest in 1929. Consistent with Greeley's program
of preserving nothing and economically utilizing everything, Olympic's
forest recreation plan, known as the Cleator Plan, had been over four
years in the drafting. Ignoring the existence of Mount Olympus National Monument, it provided for logging the Hoh, the Elwha, and every
acre of the rain forest remnants in every west-side valley. "Timber exploitation will naturally take precedence here," it said. "It is not intended
by these boundaries that timber exploitation . . . is forever and absolutely prohibited." It merely said, of the areas with highest potential
for recreation, that "modifications in ordinary cutting practices will
probably have to be made in order that they should be harmonious
with the scenic and recreational objectives of the acres within."[56] How
recreational values could be preserved with logging roads and clear-
cuts was not addressed. It was another public relations effort anyhow
and everyone in the Forest Service knew, as Assistant Forester Kneipp
had said, that when the mills needed the timber, the communities would
organize to get it. The public had been ignored in the decision that
promised to send every tree of value on the Olympic Peninsula to the
mills.[57] The writings of Willard Van Name, Aldo Leopold, Robert Marshall, and the Boone and Crockett Club were dismissed as the work
of fanatics, out of touch with the reality of jobs and the economic welfare of local communities. Nevertheless, these writings inspired increasing public discontent with what was happening to its forestland.

8 BUREAUCRACIES FAIL

*The Forest Service has no abiding principles of conservation.
It will protect permanently, nothing but bare rocks.*[1]

IRVING BRANT

*. . . As usual, in any deal in which the Park Service has a hand,
the public gets the small end of it.*[2]   WILLARD VAN NAME

D EMANDS FOR AN Olympic National Park to replace Mount Olympus
National Monument appeared in 1926 while the Forest Service
moved to abolish the monument by including its timber in its
cutting plans. The national interest in outdoor recreation and wilderness swept through the Olympic Peninsula chambers of commerce as
it did the rest of the country. The peninsula merchants envisioned real
profits with a national park at their doorstep. Because everyone assumed
that the presence of the monument had "locked up" its resources, the
only question was the kind of development that should take place there.
The Hoquiam Chamber of Commerce's committee looked into the question, and came to the conclusion that "the Olympic Mountains should
be developed strictly as a fishing and mountaineering resort."[3] Caught
up in the wilderness preservation interest of the 1920's, the committee
went on record that any "development should be by trails." Attacking
the Forest Service's moves to build one or more roads through the mountains, it said that not only would a road be open for only a short period
each year but would "not [be] in harmony with the type of development
that such a splendid scenic region should have."[4] But in effect, the Forest

Service had already abolished the monument, and logging roads eventually would be everywhere.

The chambers of commerce believed that the title "national park" would bring more business to the local merchants than "monument" would. With strong agitation for a change in the status of the monument to national park coming from within his home district, Congressman Albert Johnson of Grays Harbor moved to get help from the Park Service in creating a national park. Assistant Director Cammerer dismissed him with "the matter would doubtless come before the Coordinating Committee for study and recommendations" and that no Park Service action would be taken until a bill was introduced that "would bring the matter officially to our attention."[5] In spite of this, Johnson introduced his bill to convert the monument to park status. This was the first Olympic National Park bill that did not authorize timber cutting since the Elk National Park bill of 1904. It called specifically for full preservation under the provisions of the Park Service Act "for the benefit and enjoyment of the people."[6] Forest Service hostility and Park Service lack of interest guaranteed the bill would go nowhere. However, the presence of an Olympic National Park bill finally calling for complete preservation served to illustrate well how deeply interest in preservation had progressed by 1926.

Two years later, in 1928, Madison Grant of the New York Zoological Society, Boone and Crockett Club, and veteran of decades of conservation battles, wrote directly to Mather suggesting an Olympic National Park because "the forests there are magnificent and the Forest Service is considering cutting the trees down in the immediate future."[7] Mather dismissed the suggestion on the grounds that "there is little good reason for transferring its administration to the park service."[8] To reassure the Forest Service, he sent copies of the Grant correspondence to them and received back assurances that the Forest Service was giving "every consideration to a proper development of the recreational resource." The Forest Service did not disclose that every area it had designated for recreation had also been designated for logging. Mather was also told "our present plans call for the building of no highways into the higher sections," but the Forest Service had, in fact, already completed Dosewallips, Elwha and Quinault road surveys.

As letters continued to arrive regularly asking about an Olympic National Park, the Park Service developed a form letter response that included the sentence: "It is a very beautiful region, but thus far it has not been demonstrated that it comes up to the standards set for national parks." Greeley's park standards had become the Park Service's.

Van Name was infuriated by the use of "standards" by the Park Service to deflect what he considered meritorious park proposals — Olympic being number one on his list "because it would probably be possible to include a great deal of fine forest of kinds not at all well represented in any of the present parks."[9] What especially infuriated him was Mather's viewpoint that Mount Olympus, Mount Baker, and Mount Adams "all had to be denied [park status] since their establishment as national parks would at once lower the dignity of position and prestige of Mount Rainier as the noblest glacier bearing peak of the Americas."[10]

"Does the grandeur of the snow fields and glaciers of Mount Rainier depend in the slightest on the act of Congress calling it a National Park?" demanded Van Name. "Will they be a particle less," he asked, "if we have some other beautiful parks? The publication of such indefensible nonsense by the Park Service administration shows its poorly concealed opposition to extending the park system as the public is demanding."[11] "Most of this talk about the danger of lowering the standard of the national parks," Van Name charged, "is poorly disguised anti-park enlargement propaganda."[12]

Van Name's vision for the park system was that of a scientist looking to preserve part of the natural scene that was left. He never let the Park Service, however much he grew to detest it for what it had become, deter him from that vision:

> If we are going to save anything of real nature, scenery, forests, and the larger wild animals, the national parks must do most of it. The policy of limiting national parks to a few spots of extraordinary scenic grandeur no longer meets the requirements of the case if indeed it ever did so. The duty of preserving not only such places but also larger areas of beautiful though less remarkable scenery now devolves upon the national park system, and for this it needs to be greatly extended.[13]
>
> Why should the purposes of the national parks be limited to preserving extraordinary scenic places and to catering to vacationists? Why should they not do some service for the sciences of ecology, zoology, botany, etc., by preserving in their natural conditions some areas that will not be overrun and trampled upon by hordes of tourists? . . . The national parks are the chief hope of retaining any tracts in a natural state.[14]

By 1929 Van Name had had both the Forest Service and the Park Service under attack for nearly a decade, not without some real effect. He had succeeded in bringing the Barbour bill to a halt along with the Sequoia National Park forest elimination it contained. His letters to the newspapers, his pamphlets and his articles had painted both Mather and Greeley as serving the interests of nearly everyone but the public. Greeley's leaving for the West Coast Lumberman's Association the year before did nothing to dispel the cloud of doubt upon him that Van

Name had created. In fact the circumstances of Greeley's departure served to confirm what he had been saying about the Forest Service and the timber industry.

Uncomfortable as he sometimes made the American Museum of Natural History's staff, Van Name nonetheless had a real following there. Finally, however, he involved the museum directly in one of his campaigns. His pamphlet, *A Crisis in Conservation,* was an attack on the Audubon Society, in which he was a life member, for its failure to assist in preventing the extinction of many North American birds. The pamphlet was also signed by Dr. De Witt Miller, who was the museum's curator of birds and vice president of the New Jersey Audubon Society. Miller was prepared to vouch for the truth of every word that Van Name had written. Two other curators at the museum were, respectively, chairman of the board of directors of the Audubon Society and the other its treasurer. Van Name's disclosures had focused heavy criticism directly on them. The pamphlet was scarcely off the press when Dr. Miller was killed in an accident, leaving Van Name as the sole museum staff signature on the pamphlet.[15]

Mather's friends on the museum board moved to muzzle Van Name. Mather and the Park Service always looked bad every time Van Name struck. At age fifty-seven, faced with the loss of his job, Van Name remained uncompromising and defiant. "He assures me that he would rather face expulsion from the staff than to give up his campaign," his department head informed the museum administration.[16] Departmental Curator Roy Miner, working hard to save Van Name, added that "his loss would be a serious blow to the Department, that he has achieved international reputation as a scientist and his published works are much sought after by specialists in his own line." Miner pointed out that "his opponents . . . confine their replies to criticism of Dr. Van Name without specifically answering his questions, the real questions being is he right and does he have the right to express opinions even if he isn't."[17] When Van Name's contract for the next year was given to him to sign, it contained a clause that he should publish nothing that was not first reviewed by an editorial board of the museum.[18] There would be no more pamphlets.

Van Name was not about to be silenced, but he needed help. He concluded that "even a small organization with little money to start with, provided it has the enthusiasm to work hard and the persistence to keep at it, can arouse public opinion and gain support to accomplish things that at first sight would seem impossible."[19]

Charged with the challenge of Van Name's pamphlet, *A Crisis in Conservation,* New York Audubon Society member Rosalie Edge joined the attack on the Audubon Society, meeting in the process Van Name and

Rosalie Edge, 1959.
Carsten Lien.

the others involved. Her campaign to stop the Audubon Society's commercial killing of muskrat in its Rainey Wildlife Sanctuary brought
her and the environmental group she formed with Van Name some
celebrity. When the Audubon Society's president ignored the member's
objections to fur trapping, she launched a proxy fight for votes in the
Audubon Society's elections. As her son Peter Edge tells it:

> The proxy fight was almost surely my mother's idea; it matches so per-
> fectly with her suffrage background. The membership lists were ob-
> tained . . . with the backing (and probably the financial support) of Roger
> Baldwin and the ACLU. This engendered good front-page publicity in
> the *New York Times,* continuing through two proxy contests in successive
> years. My mother's ticket lost on both occasions, but the resulting pub-
> licity and the facts revealed, induced the [society's] directors to force the
> resignation of [President] T. Gilbert Pearson. . . . I make the point of
> Audubon fight, because it laid the foundations for her strength. Won-
> derful publicity! A fine mailing list! And proof that her efforts could in-
> deed move mountains.[20]

A well-educated New York matron from a distinguished background
and fifty-three years old in 1930, Edge was quick-witted and acid-tongued.
She was just what Van Name needed. And most important of all, she
was exactly complementary to Van Name in her approach to other

persons—she liked them. Van Name's distrust had given him an un-canny intuitive capacity to deduce what was occurring from fragmentary data. But he was dour and somber to be around. "Always pessimistic," she said of him later, "he seemed never to get any enjoyment out of his conservation work."[21] Edge was in it for not only excitement and stimulation but for the good that could come from the work. When Van Name proposed to her that his pamphlets be published by a com-mittee, with her as secretary and using her address, she jumped at the chance. "It is so that our lives are changed in one moment," she said. "We get up in the morning unable to see the immensity of the day's decisions; and go to bed at night, our destiny directed in the opposite direction."[22] Thus, the Emergency Conservation Committee emerged from Van Name's need for cover in order to keep his job at the Ameri-can Museum of Natural History. The "small organization with little money, enthusiasm and hard work" that Van Name fantasized about had become reality far sooner than he had imagined.

Fired by their continuing success in attacking the Audubon Society's trapping program, Van Name and Edge turned to wildlife protection. Edge "had a real love for animals and trees [and] for the whole natural condition"[23] which matched Van Name's in intensity. "His zeal for wild-life came indeed from his heart," she said later, "and for this cause he gave without reserve all that he had."[24] Van Name singled out the Bu-reau of Biological Survey as his target in a series of pamphlets begin-ning as soon as ECC was formed. A pamphlet entitled *The United States Biological Survey: Destruction, Not Scientific Investigation and Conservation, Now its Chief Activity* was followed by another, *It's Alive! Kill It!* Both pam-phlets attacked the indiscriminate use of poisons and their affect in the food chains involved. "Would the public approve or enjoy an at-tempt to rid the country of criminals and undesirable citizens by poison-ing the food in the markets and grocery stores?" Van Name asked. "That is the way the wildlife of this country is being treated for reasons that will not bear investigation."[25] Even if these and the pamphlets that fol-lowed were unsigned, their titles everyone knew unmistakenly marked them as having come from Van Name. Another pamphlet, *The United States Bureau of Destruction and Extermination: The Misnamed and Perverted "Biological Survey,"* marked the beginning of the end for the survey.

Van Name's attacks on the U.S. Biological Survey were also attacks on the Mather/Albright regime because Mather had fully embraced the U.S. Biological Survey's program and it had entered the parks at his invitation. Mrs. Edge decided to target part of the Park Service's wildlife-killing program as one of her first projects. Because the pelicans on Yellowstone Lake competed with fishermen from various concession-aire facilities for the trout in the lake, they were labeled "predators" and therefore subject to "controls" by the Park Service. In her pamphlet, *The Slaughter of the Yellowstone Park Pelicans,* she asked, "of what crimes is the pelican accused? . . . It is accused of cutting slightly into the profits of that mighty octopus, the organization of National Park concessionaires, by eating some of the trout by means of which the concessionaires hope to attract fishermen to the park, to spend their money in the hotels, camps, stores and garages conducted by that monopoly." She was learning pamphleteering.

Since the earliest days of the Park Service, the pelicans had been slaughtered as an accommodation to the concessionaires. The actual process was particularly onerous to the ranger force which had to track down the nests, destroy the eggs and club the young to death. When Mrs. Edge began her investigation, the Park Service denied any involvement with decreased pelican populations. But when a seasonal ranger learned of the denials, he removed from a file cabinet the internal documents which described in detail the Park Service's role in the slaughter and mailed them to Mrs. Edge. She printed them verbatim in her pamphlet along with Horace Albright's denial that " . . . no pelicans have been killed in Yellowstone National Park. . . ."[26] The pelican killing program could not stand the light of day. It stopped with the Park Service crying foul because the correspondence with which Mrs. Edge had exposed it had been stolen from its own files. "Yes," she said, "the letters were purloined, but the end justified the means. Needs must when the devil drives."[27]

Even as Mrs. Edge began her career as a pamphleteer in her own right, Willard Van Name's pamphlets descended on her. "Soon with myself as editor and publisher, they were in print and in his breast pocket," she said. "He passed them out to all and sundry, his face illuminated with that smile first famous on the face of the tiger."[28] The pamphlets went out by mail order singly, in dozens and by the hundreds, all free. With each mailing, an addition to the committee's mailing list was made, a mailing list composed of self-selected individuals who had been interested enough in an issue to take the time and energy to write. The power of the committee would, in the end, be its mailing list. Composed as it was of persons who could be triggered to write letters to Congress and to agencies of government, the list represented power, which was recognized at once.[29] Mrs. Edge and Van Name had reached the "societally conscious" group decades before the term itself had been invented.

Irving Brant, a writer and working newspaperman, in preparation of an article for *Forest and Stream* giving an account of the Audubon annual meeting, called on Mrs. Edge for a first-hand account. During the interview, she recruited him to write an Audubon pamphlet which she offered to have ECC distribute. The resulting pamphlet, *Compromised*

Irving Brant, 1974.
Tom Gentle.

Conservation: Can the Audubon Society Explain? printed in October of 1930, brought scholarship, professional writing of clarity and insight along with the jabs that an investigative reporter knows how to deliver. Following soon was *Shotgun Conservation,* in which he charged that "the fundamental trouble with wildlife conservation movements in the United States is that they are chiefly concerned with the conservation of killing privileges." Brant was hooked. He now had a nationwide forum for his own expression — pamphleteering was not much different from what he did for a living. And it offered him the opportunity of getting the changes in attitude and concern for wildlife and nature that he thought were essential.

The Emergency Conservation Committee was now a confederation of three, Brant, Edge, and Van Name. They acted together in the ECC, but each also took separate action at will and each shared carbon copies of all correspondence on important projects going and coming. This was an enormous time commitment in itself because in an era without copy machines, all incoming letters had to be retyped for distribution to the other two. No one would ever have guessed from the volume of their output on extracurricular conservation matters, that two of the three worked at full-time jobs. Brant worked as editorial page editor of the *St. Louis Star Times* and Willard Van Name as an associate curator at the American Museum of Natural History. Even Van Name and Mrs. Edge, who resided in New York, rarely saw each other. They communicated by letter as they did with Brant.[30]

In 1932, just as this working triad emerged as the Emergency Conservation Committee, Madison Grant, on behalf of the Boone and

Crockett Club, asked Willard Van Name to go to the Olympic Peninsula to investigate conditions there. Persistent rumors of the decline
of the Olympic elk had again raised the concern of the Boone and
Crockett Club. Van Name grabbed at the opportunity, plunged ahead
with his investigation, and turned in his report on December 1, 1932.
Using the Forest Service's own printed materials, Van Name correctly
deduced that Mount Olympus National Monument had been implicitly
abolished by the manner in which it was being administered. The area
of the monument that the Forest Service had designated the Snow Peaks
Recreation Area, he charged, "coincides in large part with the supposedly rigidly protected and *inviolate* National Monument, the land
is to be leased for summer homes, summer hotels, and privately conducted resorts, and while 'commercial cases and development are to
be carefully weighed,' no promises [are] made that they will be prohibited."[31] He did not know that all of the valleys of the monument
had actually been included in Forest Service cutting plans. Van Name
attacked the Forest Service's Primitive Areas designation for being "conspicuous for its commercial worthlessness" and asserted that "we cannot for a moment believe that should future conditions make any of
its scanty resources exploitable, or make anyone wish to put a road
through it,"[32] that this would not be done. He never found out that there
were plans afoot to do just that — put a road through it. From the scant-
iest of documentation, he had uncovered the essence of the Forest Service's plans for Olympic. It was almost as if he had read the internal
memoranda of the Forest Service. To make certain no reader of his
report missed the issue, he put in capital letters "NOT ONE OF THE ABOVE
RESERVATIONS SAFEGUARDS ANY OF THE REMAINING STANDS OF BIG TIMBER
THAT ARE STILL LEFT OF THE VAST AREAS THAT ONCE WERE A FEATURE
OF THE OLYMPIC PENINSULA."[33] In one trip Van Name had uncovered
the subterfuge laid down by Chief Forester William Greeley throughout the 1920's.

It was the rain forest areas that Van Name was after. He detailed
the opposition from the Forest Service and the local interests that would
be precipitated by any move to create a park with the large trees included. "This opposition," he said, "*can be faced, fought and overcome.*" In
twenty-five pages, Van Name, in calling for a national park, not only
laid out the minimum area that ought to be included, but presented
a strategy for including some of the timber. He even anticipated the
Park Service's opposition to an Olympic National Park. "Prompt action, not mere discussion and procrastination are needed."[34]

The problem for Van Name was that Madison Grant was not well
when he submitted his report and no one reacted to it. All of his effort to
precipitate an Olympic National Park campaign vanished into thin air.

As bad as the Park Service seemed to be to Van Name, Edge, and Brant, with its pelican killing and other extermination projects, they were in for a shock when they approached Director Albright about trees. Brant wrote to Albright to get support for a campaign to save some of the public forests destined for logging:

> The way virgin timber is being destroyed on the Pacific Coast, with 25,000 board feet wasted to the acre by high rigging and refusal to lumber any-thing less than eighteen inches through, it will be only a few years until the only virgin timber is in the national and state parks. The Park Policy must be expanded to preserve fine stands of all native trees, otherwise doomed. I hope you will fight for such a policy.[35]

Two months earlier, to Brant's dismay, Albright had lain right on the line what the Park Service had become:

> ... We cannot make a move that would be detrimental to the policies and interests of the Forest Service, a sister bureau of the Government.[36]

Brant failed to elicit any interest whatever from Albright in adding trees to the park system. Greeley had succeeded so well that Mather and Al-bright had not only accepted his national park standards concepts but also had accepted that the interests of the Forest Service were the in-terests of the Park Service.

The Emergency Conservation Committee, if it was ever going to suc-ceed in adding forests to parks, would have to defeat not only the For-est Service and the timber industry, but also the Park Service. "The notion that timber of commercial value should be excluded from preser-vation is fundamentally wrong,"[37] said Irving Brant. He and his colleagues in the Emergency Conservation Committee would try to correct the wrong.

Albright's move to stop all further protection of publicly owned old-growth forest with national park status provoked Irving Brant's call to arms to overcome both the Park Service and the Forest Service:

> ... The development of our national parks at the expense of the national forests is demanded by the more fundamental needs of our country — permanent preservation of magnificent primeval forests which cannot be replaced for centuries if once cut down as the Forest Service intends they shall be. . . . [38]

On the eve of the New Deal, American society had evolved to a posi-tion that demanded the inviolability of the national parks from any kind of commercial exploitation. Demands for permanently dedicated areas in the national forests was also underway. Forest policy in a general way was under attack, both inside and outside the forestry profession, for having failed to meet the future needs of the country for timber. In 1933 this rising tide of concern, already underway for a decade and a half, crested with the publication of Robert Marshall's *The People's Forests* and at about the same time, a report of a Congressional investigation of the state of the nation's forests, the Copeland Report.[39] Marshall made a strong case for public ownership of all forests. He used the Forest Service's own statistics to illustrate the magnitude of the forest devastation that had occurred in the preceding thirty years.

Until 1905, Gifford Pinchot had gone repeatedly before Congress and the American public in his long campaign to get the forests transferred to the Department of Agriculture, with a stated expectation that proper administration would produce a break-even situation within five years and profits to the nation thereafter. Not only did this not occur but the Forest Service was now also offering subsidies to private timber owners, whose timber for the most part had been fraudulently obtained from public ownership. "Not only are we losing our forest reserves with no net receipts to show for it," charged Willard Van Name in 1929, "but we are being taxed every year for undergoing the process! Is it not strange that such a state of affairs can continue year after year without publicity or criticism, or without anybody seeming to regard it otherwise than a matter of course?"[40]

Pinchot's belief in the absolute necessity for the government to have control of cutting on private land conflicted with the timber operators' imperative to maximize profits now and let someone else worry about the future. The Forest Service's own statistics supported the validity of Pinchot's position:

Of the 83 million acres of devastated or poorly stocked forest land, 74 million or nine-tenths is privately owned and an appreciable part of the remainder reached this condition before coming into public ownership as a direct result of private operations and ownership.

Of the 850,000 acres devastated each year about 95 percent are in private ownership.

At least 36 million acres of forest are being deteriorated annually, primarily as a result of poor silvicultural practice and unsatisfactory fire protection.

Fully 95 percent of the private cutting is probably made without any conscious regard to the future productivity of the forest.

Private ownership has held four-fifths of our commercial forest land with from 90 percent or even more of the total potential timber growing capacity. As measured by expenditures only about 10 percent of the constructive effort in American forestry is made by it.[41]

There was the rub. With much of the timber gone and with ownership of 80 percent of the forestland having 90 percent of the total growing capacity, private owners were making virtually no contribution to the growing of trees. The timber industry by 1930 was in the process of capturing the remaining timber from the national forests to continue business as usual.

In 1930, the *Scientific Monthly* published Robert Marshall's "The Problem of the Wilderness" in which he expounded on the necessity for an increasingly urbanized society to maintain wilderness. The automobile and rising urbanization had created a demand for the recreational use of wilderness areas which the Forest Service and the timber industry ignored. And while Mather welcomed the automobile to increase park visitation figures, auto owners increasingly attacked Mather for his indiscriminate accommodation of the automobile to develop wild areas of national parks.[42]

The Forest Service, the agent by which forest policy was supposed to be delivered, had become, at age twenty-seven in 1932, little more than an adjunct of the timber industry itself.[43] The service was flawed from its very beginning by the guidelines that Gifford Pinchot had written for it, and it had little concept of the national good apart from the fortunes of the forest-exploiting industries it served.

"The dominant industry" at the local level, said Pinchot, "will be considered first."[44] This set up the Forest Service for accepting, even embracing finally, Greeley's program of cooperation with the timber industry. Greeley also expanded the Pinchot/Graves concept of close ties with the colleges of forestry to include the timber industry. Now the Forest Service, the colleges of forestry, and the timber companies and trade associations represented three component parts to a single political entity. Personnel flowed freely among the three; hundreds of persons served in each during a lifetime career. Public policy goals became subordinate to the principal agency goal: the maximization of profit from the sale of resources on public land. The three comprised a closed network disconnected from mainstream society but strongly committed to the notion that it was right. It prevented all internal criticism of Greeley's subsidy program even though the Forest Service's own statistics annually demonstrated the failure to achieve any major step toward reforestation. The close personal associations in this industry-agency-college combine discouraged faculty members in the forestry schools from raising issues that might get a negative response from the timber operators. With Greeley's departure in 1928 for the West Coast Lumberman's Association, he left behind a Forest Service organization that he personally had put into place, along with an interlocking network of key individuals which he would use for the benefit of the timber industry throughout the rest of his career.

If one evaluates the Forest Service against Pinchot's expectations, the Forest Service might well have to be rated a failure, even while acknowledging its own internal high morale and good management. In practice it was now blind to everything except the needs of the "dominant industries" in its constituency. To all other interests, the Forest Service merely paid lip service, as it did when it set up Primitive Areas which the public believed were dedications but which were really only to be temporarily in place until the resources they contained were needed.

By 1932 the Park Service was sixteen years old and had been under the leadership of Stephen T. Mather for fourteen of those sixteen years. In a sense, he was still in charge through the leadership of his protegé Horace Albright. Mather's schemes continued to drive the Park Service for decades. The *New York Times* recognized the meaning of Albright succeeding to the Park Service directorship. "This means," said the *Times*, "not only that the policies which Mr. Mather developed will be carried on but that their execution is entrusted to a man who played a large part in framing them."[45] Those policies had left the Park Service a management shambles, not knowing what it was, who it was supposed to serve, or what its legal relationship was to mandates of the 1916 Park Service Act. Albright, to his credit, tried to repair some of the damage. He made one of his top priorities "To guarantee the future of the system on a sound permanent basis, where the power and personality of the Director may no longer have to be controlling factors in operating the Service."[46] But Albright, like Mather, had an oddly skewed idea of what a national park should be. Their bear feeding, their elk paddock, the vaudeville shows they both loved, their inclination not to worry about timber cutting as long as it was screened from the public, all demonstrated the shallowness of their views of the parks. It was as if the parks existed for the momentary diversion of the traveling public. Long-fought political battles had produced the preservation concept of the park system in a law that Mather and Albright preferred to ignore. Rather than protect the parks in their complexities, they opted for avoiding conflict and even potential conflict whenever possible. During the crucial early organizational years of the Park Service's history, the agency culture developed norms favoring the extermination of selected wildlife species, garbage feeding of bears, dance halls, and firefalls — harmful, irrelevant productions. These activities, as well as massive road building and countless other destructive actions, obliged the agency to make hypocritical statements about its mandate. By the beginning of the New Deal, the Park Service had known only

the Mather/Albright regimes. The contradictions of their administrations had become deeply imbedded into its organizational culture, and
the Park Service developed a generous toleration for ambiguity. Logging a park forest in an area not frequented by tourists to finance a
purchase in another area was not questioned. Giving monopolies guaranteed profits to the detriment of the public seemed natural. The Park
Service had accepted Greeley's park standard concepts which precluded
making new additions to the park system. The Park Service also accepted Greeley's position that "scenery" belonged in the parks and that
forests, even those forests set aside in the parks before Mather got there,
ought to be under the control of the Forest Service so that they could
be logged. The concept that commercially valuable forests were "not
of park caliber" became accepted within the Park Service and trading
them off for vastly greater acreages of "scenery" with no commercial
value seemed logical and reasonable.

When he took over as director, Albright had established as one of
his top priorities, "finish up the rounding out of the park system." His
proposals were ready in June of 1931, consisting generally of a canyon
here, a small addition to an existing park there. These additions were:

1. Yosemite: Wawona area and Devil's Postpile area.
2. Sequoia: Kings River area, Redwood Canyon area and Mineral King
   area.
3. General Grant Park: Stump area.
4. Cedar Bridges area, Utah.
5. Crater Lake: Diamond Lake.
6. Grand Canyon: Kaibab area and Tusayan area.
7. Grand Teton: Jackson Valley area.

Willard Van Name would have ridiculed the modesty of the requests.
The Forest Service rejected them all out of hand on the grounds that
Congress had not made "a clear cut pronouncement . . . of the quality
standards and social objectives by which the establishment or enlargement of National Parks should be governed."[47] Confronted with a proposal for modest additions to existing parks that did not include giving
up something, the Forest Service upped the ante by invoking Congress.
The Park Service had been immobilized and it had no constituency
to turn to for help.

After sixteen years of existence, the Park Service did not have a constituency beyond the concessionaires and transportation companies,
and it had rejected its natural constituency, the preservationists. The
preservationists were everywhere, in the scientific societies, the outdoor
groups such as the Mountaineers, the Boone and Crockett Club, and
Sierra Club, and in the editorial staffs of the national intellectual press

such as *Harper's, Atlantic Monthly,* and in the eastern newspapers such as the *New York Times.* Willard Van Name had attempted to bring them all together to fight for a greatly expanded park system, to keep forests in the parks, and to keep them undeveloped. Mather and Albright had dismissed Van Name as a "purist." The Park Service had locked out its real constituency and was paralyzed.

At the same time, the Forest Service had become driven by an ideology of raw material production. It had failed to become self-sufficient as promised, had failed to deal with forest destruction and depletion, and had failed to acknowledge the rising social concern about preservation.

A group of citizen activists and two destructively flawed governmental agencies were about to engage in a bitter conflict over public policy. The preservationists would attempt to take publicly owned trees, already assigned by the Forest Service to sawmills, and give them permanent preservation for future generations in the hands of the Park Service. The preservationists would have to wrench them from the Forest Service which desperately wanted to keep the trees on their course to becoming lumber and newsprint. In order to succeed, the preservationists would have to force the trees on the Park Service which did not want them, and which in turn considered itself the best judge of what was and what was not of park caliber.

Willard Van Name had no illusions about what he was going to be up against. "The public should wake up to the serious fact," he said, "that the real agencies that are the chief obstructors of real conservation for our natural scenery, our forests and our wildlife are the government bureaus that we have established."[48] As if to emphasize Van Name's viewpoint, Glenn O. Robinson added later in his study of the Forest Service that, "it seems to be endemic to our bureaucracy that administrators more easily identify with private industry interests than with the public interest."[49]

9 THE BUREAUCRACIES REJECT PRESERVATION

To the United States Forest Service, a tree is something to be cut down. . . . The nobler the tree, the greater the desire to see it laid low. In forestry jargon a tree that has attained its full glory is "ripe," and should be brought to earth just as quickly as possible. No tree that has reached maturity, even if its majesty and beauty would endure for a thousand years, could escape a sentence of death if the Forest Service had its way.[1]

HAROLD L. ICKES

A national park is not created for the purpose of conserving valuable stands of timber. That is the function of the Forest Service.[2]

DAVID H. MADSEN,
NATIONAL PARK SERVICE

WITHIN THREE MONTHS OF TAKING OFFICE, Franklin Roosevelt promulgated a governmental reorganization plan that included the transfer of fifteen national monuments administered by the Forest Service to the Park Service.[3] Neither the Park Service nor the Forest Service had any advance warning that such a proposition was pending. By August the Park Service had notified the Bureau of the Budget, however, that it desired to take over only eight of the fifteen. Mount Olympus National Monument, the largest and most important of those monuments, was not among them. The Forest Service, upon learning from the Bureau of the Budget that the Park Service had rejected taking over the Mount Olympus National Monument, moved to defeat the intent of the Executive Order. It calculated that if the monument were abolished formally there would be nothing for the Park Service to take over if it chose to do so later. Assistant Forester Kneipp asked Regional Forester C. J. Buck for suggestions on how to proceed in abolishing the monument and especially what local reaction might be. "I see no reason," said Olympic Forest Supervisor Plumb, "for continuation of the Mount Olympus National Monument." The way out he proposed was to make it into a federal game reserve with boundaries on hydrographic divides instead of the existing boundaries. But Buck soon changed direction and stopped the plan in its tracks. "A great many people about the Peninsula," he said, "would like to see the withdrawal changed to a national park. Therefore, any agitation of this matter at the present time is very likely to precipitate us into a national park. . . ."[4] Assistant Forester Kneipp answered, "Our best course will be to be diplomatic, polite and patient, with the hope that ultimately things will iron out in a satisfactory way."[5]

In the meantime the Forest Service, through Secretary of Agriculture Henry Wallace, moved to exempt the monuments administered by the Forest Service from the Executive Order. Interior Secretary Ickes settled the whole issue as soon as it hit his desk in November. "I . . . cannot agree," he said, and without discussing it with the Park Service, told Henry Wallace that the Park Service "is prepared to assume jurisdiction at once."[6]

The Park Service was now in the position of having to administer an area that it had insisted for the past eighteen years was not of park caliber. It was in fact still answering inquiries about an Olympic park with a form letter that read, in part, "thus far it has not been demonstrated that it comes up to the standards set for national parks." Nonetheless, the secretary had spoken and the Park Service moved ahead to bring a Park Service presence to the Olympic Peninsula.

By May of 1934, with the issue of the Park Service takeover of the monument now finally resolved, the Park Service itself split into two camps. The Park Service's wildlife division, headquartered in Berkeley, California, wanted the park restored to the size of the original monument.[7] "The forest throughout the elk winter range . . . is magnificent" wrote Ben Thompson from Berkeley, trying to get the Park Service moving, "and would someday be the only thing of its kind left in the country, if it is protected. It is truly of national park caliber."[8]

Conrad Wirth, an Albright appointee now four years on the job, quickly moved to head off Ben Thompson. When Cammerer asked "whether Mt. Olympus was one of our park projects that we are pushing," Wirth went back to the basic Park Service position, quoting from a 1929 memo "that the mountain [Olympus] and surrounding area to a large extent, would duplicate Mt. Rainier National Park, in the same state, we have consistently recommended against its establishment as a national park . . . it is assumed that this proposed park has been disapproved by the Director and shall be carried in the files as such."[9] That was too much even for Cammerer in the environment of the New Deal. He wrote in the margin of Wirth's memo before it was distributed, "any reason why we should not reconsider or restudy?" That was all that was needed. The Park Service was off to restudy the monument even while Wirth and the traditionalists tried and failed to hold to the Mather-Albright line that the Olympics were unworthy.

In the face of the dramatically changed social and governmental climate brought on by the New Deal, the depression, and increasing concern about wilderness and forest recreation, the Forest Service reasserted its previous positions. Its policy statement in the Olympic National Forest's timber management plan for 1934 ignored the forthcoming presence of the Park Service in the monument. The plan even went so far as to include as usual the working circles and cutting blocks which included the timber in the monument.[10] It was as if the plan had been written on the moon, disassociated from every reality. Perhaps Region Six believed it would all go away if no one acknowledged that the Mount Olympus National monument was headed for the preservation the Antiquities Act had required. In a last ditch effort to get monument timber to the mills, Supervisor Plumb announced "it is evident from President Roosevelt's original proclamation creating the Mt. Olympus National Monument that he believed and intended that the preservation of the Roosevelt elk could and should be accomplished, allowing at the same time the use and development of the timber, water and recreational resources of the monument."[11] In the circumstances, it was an incredible statement; the whole issue was preservation.

When the New Deal came to power in 1933, Irving Brant was forty-eight years old and at the height of his career as a newspaperman. He had had a long-term correspondence with FDR dating back to the campaign of 1920. And he had known Henry Wallace back in his hometown of Des Moines, Iowa. Brant also knew personally many of the persons who ended up with appointments in the White House and in the secretaries' offices of both Agriculture and Interior.

He wrote directly to FDR within days of the inauguration explaining that "for some years I have been engaged in several lines of conservation efforts." He went on with great frankness to present his views on the U.S. Biological Survey, the Forest Service, and the Park Service. None of them fared well at Brant's pen. The Forest Service, he said, "thinks of all trees in terms of board feet. It obstructs every effort to preserve scenic areas which contain merchantable trees. It takes a minimum interest in wildlife preservation." After listing specific examples, Brant concluded that "it resorts continually to misrepresentation, as I have found through personal experience."[12]

Brant then leveled his guns at the Park Service which he said "is so completely cowed by the Forest Service that it dares not call its soul its own. It is afraid to push a legitimate park expansion measure in one locality for fear of reprisals in another. It is also handicapped by a concessionaire system which creates a commercial atmosphere in most of the parks and gives the appearance . . . of a compact between the NPS and the concessionaires to bleed the public." After some discussion of the specifics of how the concessionaire system operated to the great disadvantage of the public, he made it clear that expansion of the national park system was a national imperative. Brant warned Roosevelt it would not be easy. "The commercialism of the national parks," he said, "contrasted with the delightful informality of the national forests, makes it difficult to rally public sentiment for the development of the park system."[13]

Brant then wrote in detail to Harold Ickes about the Forest Service's continuing "perversion of the truth" and at the same time began the process of reforming the Park Service. "Somehow the NPS," he said, "just seems to curl up and die when the Forest Service starts its typical work of opposition to national park expansion."[14] With skill and with political acumen, Brant had muscled his way into the highest levels of natural resource policy making. He brought with him detailed knowledge of how things really worked, a provocative, attention-getting writing style, and a passion for the public interest. He had no personal financial stake in his conservation work and his credibility was high. Willard Van Name recognized that he now had a companion in conservation who had everything that he lacked in charm, finesse, and ability to work the system. Willard Van Name tied himself to Brant as did Rosalie Edge. Both Edge and Brant continued to acknowledge that Van Name was the fountainhead of inspiration and perseverance from which the Emergency Conservation Committee had sprung.

As the Park Service began preparations for assuming control of the Mount Olympus National Monument in the spring of 1934, the Emergency Conservation Committee launched its next conservation battle. Willard Van Name turned his 1932 *Report on Forest and Wildlife Protection* into a pamphlet entitled *The Proposed Olympic National Park*. Those in the upper echelons of both the Forest Service and Park Service correctly identified it as the work of Willard Van Name from style alone. Everyone else thought Edge had written it because it was her name that appeared as chairman of the committee. She was still providing the cover Van Name needed to retain his job at the museum. The pamphlet appeared in April of 1934. It was a frontal assault against the economic power of the industry-Forest Service-forestry school triad forged by Greeley. It called for the preservation of the most magnificent of the remaining Pacific Northwest forests and it called for the withdrawal from logging of the most economically valuable forest in the country. Edge was fifty-seven when the pamphlet was finished. Van Name was sixty-two.

Van Name paid for the printing and distribution of the pamphlet. It was mailed initially to the Audubon Society mailing list the ECC had gotten by court order as a fallout from the Audubon trapping scandal earlier. By the use of this list the pamphlet went only to persons who by their Audubon membership had selected themselves as conservationists. Demand for Van Name's pamphlet exploded soon after first mailing. The pamphlets were hardly in the mail when Martin F. Smith, Congressman from Hoquiam, Washington, the Grays Harbor lumber port, wrote to Mrs. Edge complimenting her on " . . . a very fine piece of publicity," he said, "nicely illustrated, well arranged and presented in excellent manner." He asked for a thousand copies which he said he could "place . . . to good advantage."[15] It was not clear to Mrs. Edge whether he intended to place them in the wastebaskets to keep a thousand potential readers from reading them or not. She sent as many as she could spare with the thought that the more people who knew about it the better.

The Proposed Olympic National Park pamphlet triggered the Forest Service's standard response. Arno Cammerer described that Forest Service response in detail to Irving Brant:

> In every case the propaganda and methods employed to block the creation of national parks has been the same. The entire issue, in each case, has been placed on a local economic basis; the local interests have been led to believe that their economic development would be stifled by a national park, and that under the multiple [use] and sustained yield principles of the Forest Service all of the economic potentialities of the area could be industrially developed, while at the same time, the national park qualities of the area would be preserved and maintained—an obvious impossibility.[16]

Realizing that there was a park proposal on the table, the Forest Service began to act out precisely the drama that Cammerer described to Irving Brant. "The timber from the Olympic Peninsula," asserted Regional Forester C. J. Buck, "is essential to maintain . . . the mills of Aberdeen, Port Angeles and Shelton. . . . Withdrawal of large areas of timber from economic usage can materially affect the general business activity of Western

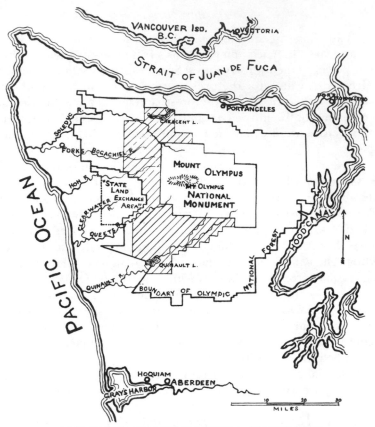

MAP OF THE OLYMPIC PENINSULA, WASHINGTON.

Showing the boundaries of the Olympic National Forest and the present greatly reduced limits of the Mt. Olympus National Monument.

THE MINIMUM AREA THAT SHOULD BE ADDED TO THAT OF THE "MONUMENT" IN ESTABLISHING THE NATIONAL PARK IS SHOWN SHADED WITH OBLIQUE LINES.

A fact that is not generally known by the public is that the Mt. Olympus National Monument is now only about half its original size.

As established by President Theodore Roosevelt in 1909 it would have made a splendid national park in itself. It has been trimmed down in order to eliminate the magnificent primeval forest which was its most unique and one of its grandest features, and to open the region up to lumbering. (Read about this on pages 5 and 16 of this pamphlet.) It is no longer an adequate sanctuary for the elk and other game.

Fortunately it is not too late to make some amends to the nation for this inexcusable act, which was slipped through without warning and with as little publicity as possible. At that time the Olympic Peninsula was little known, and the public in general had no idea what a magnificent region the park system was losing.

Page 2

The threat of job loss forced Willard Van Name to launch the Olympic Park battle anonymously under cover of the Emergency Conservation Committee. He paid the printing and distribution costs of his pamphlet *The Proposed Olympic National Park,* which defined the minimum forest area that needed preservation. Van Name, *The Proposed Olympic National Park.*

Washington. On the other hand," he continued, " . . . regulation of logging operations will preserve areas of scenic or recreational value without injury to either the lumber industry or curtailment in enjoyment of the scenic features involved."[17]

A prominent antagonist to the management philosophy of the Forest Service was Irving Clark, secretary of the Mountaineers, Seattle's leading outdoor organization. He was also known to be bitterly opposed to the Park Service concessionaire and development policies in Mount Rainier National Park. Clark and the Mountaineers had fought the Park Service's policies since the early days of the Mather administration. When the Roosevelt administration came to power, Clark was fighting the Park Service on what was said to be a needless road to Mowich Lake, and on the road being built around the mountain. He viewed it as an assault on wilderness values. Unresolved were plans for a Paradise loop road up Mazama ridge to Panorama Point, and a tramway. Two sites were being examined by the Park Service for possible airplane landing fields at the 6,000-foot level on the mountain.

The Mountaineers had become so disaffected with Park Service administration of Mount Rainier that the previous year they had recommended by resolution that the Park Service be transferred to the Department of Agriculture under the pending Governmental Reorganization Plan. To Clark, Park Service administration was synonymous with the destruction of wilderness. The Forest Service was well aware of Clark's views. It needed his support which justified the detailed seven-page letter he was sent extolling the virtues of Forest Service administration.

Willard Van Name and the ECC needed Clark, too. If they were going to succeed in creating a park on the Olympic Peninsula, there had to be local leadership and a vocal public to prompt Washington's Congressional delegation to support a park bill. Early on, Clark had been identified by Edge and Van Name as the Pacific Northwest collaborator they needed. But Clark's years of dealing with Mount Rainier's issues had convinced him that the Olympics should not go the same way. He balked at supporting an Olympic National Park. When this occurred, Van Name wrote an impassioned appeal on behalf of Park Service administration, never disclosing to Clark that he in fact detested and distrusted the Park Service, too.

"We cannot imagine greater stupidity than for nature lovers to oppose national parks," Van Name told Clark. "If there is a good stand of trees still standing in any national forest it is merely because the Forest Service has not yet gotten around to selling it for lumber. . . ." He then told Clark what he probably did not really believe because he had already failed at it repeatedly, but he needed Clark badly so he said it anyway. "If nature lovers would keep a better watch on the Park

Service much of the ruin could be prevented," he said, "for it is illegal."
He closed his three-page pep talk with the battle cry he had used for
fifteen years in defending the parks from both the Forest Service and the
Park Service. "The National Parks are the best that can be had and if
we fail to work for them and fight for their protection we shall save
nothing at all!"[18]

He won Clark over and Clark, in effect, became the Pacific Northwest component of the Emergency Conservation Committee. In 1934
Clark was fifty-one years old, connected closely to the political scene
and was on a first-name basis with most of the politicians in the Pacific
Northwest. Van Name's instincts about how important Clark could be
would prove to be correct.

Van Name's pamphlet, with its radical proposal to preserve commercial forestland, rapidly became the focal point for discussion of the park
issue for everyone—timber industry and conservationists alike. His map
and boundary recommendations became the measure against which
anyone with a counterproposal would speak.

Almost as quickly as Van Name's pamphlet arrived in Washington
State, the Park Service began work on management recommendations
for an Olympic National Park. The Park Service first attacked Van
Name's pamphlet and reassured the chambers of commerce that the
Park Service had no intention of protecting trees coveted by the timber industry. The Mount Olympus National Monument's newly assigned
custodian, David H. Madsen, delivered a Park Service policy speech
to various groups in numbers of Olympic Peninsula towns in which
he blamed "a certain pamphlet published by the Emergency Conservation Committee of New York" for the "sentiment in opposition to our
activities in this area." He assured the gatherings that "they have no
connection whatsoever with the National Park Service" and that the
Park Service "assumes no responsibility for their statements." He labeled
Van Name's pamphlet as "biased and one sided opinions."[19] "A National
Park is not created for the purpose of conserving valuable stands of
timber" he told them, assigning that task to the Forest Service. "I do
not believe the Federal Government should be even suspected of any
desire to seriously effect the industrial well being of any community
or state by locking up in a National Park a large and important natural
resource." Although he offered it as an additional reassurance, Madsen hit on exactly the issue that Van Name was addressing in his pamphlet calling for an Olympic National Park with adequate forest areas.
"In all the parks that have thus far been created, there is comparatively
little marketable timber. . . ."[20] The Park Service had now in effect
declared war on the Emergency Conservation Committee, the only
group that was fighting to create an Olympic National Park. If there

was ever going to be an Olympic National Park, the timber industry, the Forest Service and now the Park Service would have to be defeated.

The Forest Service also dismissed Van Name's pamphlet as "an appeal to the ultra sentimental and emotional elements." Local Forest Service officials attended all of Madsen's talks but found Park Service ambivalence difficult to read. Assistant Forester Kneipp believed that the Park Service was "quite receptive to the idea of having the entire Olympic Peninsula in a National Park"[21] even in the face of the Park Service denials. Even as the Park Service struggled internally between two camps — a pro Olympic National Park group and "an unworthy of park status group," Kneipp viewed the Park Service as "probably at the zenith of its power and prestige,"[22] a view hardly based on reality but reflective of the Forest Service's New Deal paranoia.

Olympic National Forest Supervisor Plumb, mounting his own speaking program, also attacked the Emergency Conservation Committee for its recommendation to add 300,000 acres containing "approximately 13 billion feet of merchantable timber or 37 percent of the timber stand of the Olympic National Forest and roughly 22 percent of the Olympic peninsula." Plumb was convinced that the statistics would in turn convince anyone of the logic of the Forest Service position. "If this area were tied up in a park, it would mean a loss of $257 million to the peninsula . . . through logging" and he went on to enumerate the losses in school funds, road funds, and the economic calamity that would befall the counties upon the creation of a park. "It must be remembered that forestry is the growing of trees for human use," he said, "and that trees reach maturity the same as any other crop and if not harvested will die and rot. The timber policy of the Forest Service is to maintain continuous production, or sustained yield, on the various watersheds."[23]

Irving Clark, now fighting for a large park, responded, "Another way to express sustained yield is progressive destruction."[24] Clark's position, said Forester Ferdinand Silcox, "makes it strikingly evident that economic factors and the practical consequences of sound principles of forestry have no place in his consideration of the future status of the Olympic National Forest."[25] This was the issue that Van Name was addressing in his pamphlet and around which the Emergency Conservation Committee would attempt to rally the nation behind an Olympic park.

The Forest Service wanted the trees in the Mount Olympus National Monument logged up to the glaciers of Mount Olympus, as long as it was economically feasible to do so, while dedicating these areas to recreation and wilderness, a contradiction that would not bear the light of day. In any case, logging in the monument was illegal under the Antiquities Act. The Forest Service had also issued a mining permit in the monument in violation of the Antiquities Act. The Forest Service policy was, " . . . If the supervisor decided that the granting of a permit to mine would not be incompatible with the purposes of the National Monuments, such a permit may be granted by him."[26] Though protection for elk was the purpose for the Mount Olympus National Monument, the Forest Service's commitment to economic utilization had resulted in the issuance of a permit for 1,600 sheep to forage in the basin of the Lost River, deep inside the monument. The elk were competing with sheep on their summer feeding range as the park battle began.

When the Park Service took over the monument in the summer of 1934, they were stunned by what they found. "We passed through areas which were trampled as a barn yard and smelled worse," said Preston Macy, who became custodian later. "For the Forest Service to have set aside a game preserve and then allow grazing within that area, is to my notion, the height of folly."[27] The Park Service group found that the Forest Service had moved the monument boundary sign seven miles back into the monument on the Elwha River, they assumed to accommodate hunters. The Park Service moved it back to where it should have been.

By the fall of 1934 the much-awaited Park Service report on the monument was ready. Conducted by O. A. Tomlinson, superintendent, and Preston P. Macy, assistant chief ranger, both of Mount Rainier National Park, along with George A. Grant, the Park Service's chief photographer and David H. Madsen, a wildlife expert, the report focused first of all on Van Name's pamphlet. "We disavowed any responsibility for the publication of the pamphlet," they said, priding themselves on the "campaign of education we undertook" which resulted, they estimated, in "a very large majority now in favor" of the Park Service. The boundaries in Van Name's ECC pamphlet incorporated large areas of old-growth forest. Any further consideration of these boundaries was dismissed. " . . . we do not favor the area as proposed by the Emergency Conservation Committee" because it "includes much valuable timber on areas that are not of national park caliber." In the draft report, however, prepared in July without Tomlinson's participation, they were even more frank. Referring to Van Name's pamphlet, they said, "it was proposed to add to the Monument much valuable timber land, and this move was strongly opposed by the lumber interests and the National Park Service." They proposed road building through the Olympics, suggesting a route that "does not traverse the Monument." It ran along the North Fork of the Quinault to Elip Creek and other areas. At the same time the report acknowledged the public call for wilderness. "We agree with what seems to be almost a universal opinion among those familiar with the area that it should remain free from the development of roads. . . ." To recommend a major road construction program while acknowledging the nearly universal public opinion opposed to it was the Mather-Albright legacy.

Timber was the focus of the report. The Park Service committee was able to say without embarrassment that "Some merchantable timber will be included within the proposed addition but the amount is so small as to be of comparatively little importance to the industrial development of this section." The Park Service had defined the chambers of commerce of the logging towns on the Olympic Peninsula as its constituency, just as the Forest Service had. They did not include "areas of outstanding scenic value six miles farther east," they said, because "of reported manganese deposits which might possibly have commercial value." It was a report that could as easily have been written by the Forest Service.[28]

Tomlinson was so pleased that the Park Service was recommending only the addition of 110,000 acres to the existing monument, when all of the preservationists were calling for at least 300,000, that he moved to assuage the fears of the timber industry almost as soon as the report was typed. He sent a confidential copy to the Washington State Planning Council, the industry triad's front organization in the fight to stop a park.[29] Within minutes upon its arrival, it had been reproduced. Every chamber of commerce, timber company, Forest Service employee and forestry professor had a copy within two days. This error in judgment on Tomlinson's part would plague the Park Service for decades.

After the report on Mount Olympus National Monument had wended its way through the various Park Service review committees and had received the official agency imprimatur, Cammerer submitted the new boundaries to Secretary Ickes for review. Ickes approved.

With confidential copies of the Tomlinson committee boundary recommendations now all over the country, Van Name stumbled across what the Park Service was recommending. He dashed from his office in the museum, caught a taxi to Pennsylvania Station and took the first train to Washington, D.C., to see Ickes without an appointment. Van Name was known to Ickes from his letters to the editors and other activities. He also knew him to be an associate of Irving Brant, whom Ickes also knew. Van Name was ushered in immediately. Ickes then heard Van Name's whole story about how the Park Service was under the domination of the Forest Service, afraid of its own shadow, opposed to expansion of the park system, under the control of the concessionaires, and most importantly, how the Park Service's boundary recommendations on Olympic served to illustrate all that Van Name was saying.

Without a moment's hesitation Ickes picked up the phone, called Cammerer and repudiated his approval on the Park Service's recom-

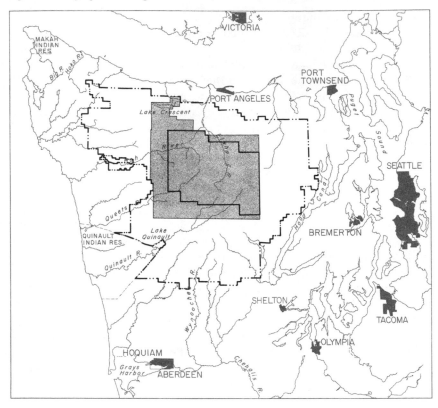

NATIONAL PARK SERVICE PARK PROPOSAL 1934

The Park Service's 1934 "ideal" Olympic National Park was carefully drawn to avoid conflict by excluding all of the rain forest areas and as much other forest as possible. In spite of the Park Service's efforts, the Forest Service responded by trying to regain control of the monument so that its trees could again be included in disrupted cutting plans.

mendation on Olympic. He told Cammerer he would be back with a boundary recommendation himself. Van Name then drew out for Ickes what he then believed an Olympic National Park should be, a modification of his pamphlet boundary that included this time the lower Bogachiel Valley. Ickes turned it all over to his assistant, Henry Slattery, an old pro from Pinchot's days in the Conservation Congress. At Slattery's direction, the Park Service drew up the secretary's Olympic National Park boundary bill with almost the identical boundaries as those in Van Name's pamphlet but now including the Bogachiel. And the Park Service had superimposed on the bill, at Van Name's insistence, a wilderness clause reflecting his distrust of the Park Service.

Sec. 4: The Mount Olympus National Park shall be permanently reserved as a wilderness, and no development of the project or plan for the entertainment of visitors shall be undertaken which will interfere with the preservation intact of unique flora and fauna and the essential primitive natural conditions now prevailing in the area.[30]

The Park Service was stunned. It now had a report about what it believed the Olympic National Park boundary should be, in distribution all over the country as a result of Tomlinson's error, and which now had been repudiated by Secretary Ickes. Instead it was facing an Olympic National Park boundary that it had publicly and repeatedly called ridiculous through its attacks on Van Name's pamphlet. And the situation left an agonizing administrative question about the Park Service's relationship to the Secretary of the Interior. The Park Service still viewed itself as the park experts, but at the same time doubt was emerging about what Secretary Ickes believed.

When word of what had happened got to Tomlinson and Madsen, both sent telegrams to Cammerer. Tomlinson wanted to continue to hold to minimum boundaries for now and add later. Madsen telegraphed that "when the enlarged boundary is published, [the] unfavorable reaction [will] place us in embarrassing position."[31] But the Park Service was no longer in control. Ickes had grabbed that position. Ickes' assistant, Slattery, arranged for Congressman Mon Wallgren, in whose district the Olympic Peninsula lay, to introduce the bill as an administration request bill. The Park Service was galled to learn that Willard Van Name had drawn the boundaries in the bill.

Congressman Wallgren introduced the Ickes/Van Name Olympic National Park bill, HR 7086, on March 28, 1935. The Emergency Conservation Committee had won the first round with the Park Service, the Forest Service, and the timber industry.

The presence of pending Olympic National Park legislation proved to be as embarrassing to the Park Service as its study team knew it would be. With the Park Service's boundary recommendations in circulation, HR 7086 gave the appearance of being an act of Congressman Wallgren in contradiction to the experts. Wallgren responded that "the bill was introduced as recommended by the Park Service here"[32] (Washington, D.C.), which gave the appearance in turn that it was the Park Service that had repudiated its own experts in the field. Only Brant, Edge, Van Name, and the Park Service knew that it was Ickes who had done the repudiating.

The Washington State Planning Council's positions were dominated by Hugo Winkenwerder, dean of the University of Washington Forestry School. He could line up the State Land Commissioner and the

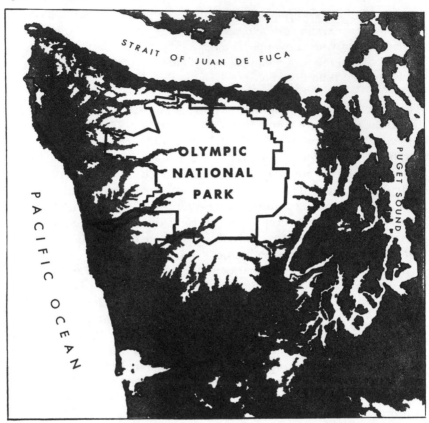

The Emergency Conservation Committee fought to save the remnant sample of lowland forest remaining in the peninsula's west side river valleys. Both the Park Service and the Forest Service fought alongside the timber industry to exclude these valleys from the forthcoming park. The disputed areas appear inside today's park boundaries. *Natural History, September 1954.*

State Supervisor of Forestry to support the positions of Supervisor Plumb of Olympic National Forest and the chamber of commerce representatives. They and other industry-dominated groups had repeatedly recommended the transfer of the monument back to the Forest Service. But once the Wallgren bill was pending, the rising tide of support for it undermined their whole approach. Within a month after HR 7086 appeared, Ben Kizer, chairman of the council, wrote, "If the Planning Council should clamor simply for the present limits for the boundary, its action will at once be taken by the friends of the National Park movement and by all others as one dominated by the timber interests." It was clear to Kizer that to be branded as supporting the interests of the timber industry in the environment of 1935 was to lose all credibility. But the question was already moot; no position the Planning Council would take in relation to the park battle would have any effect on the outcome.

The Wallgren bill launched a widespread and continuing discussion about sustained yield. The timber industry had never had any interest in practicing sustained yield on their own lands and didn't now. Private timber operators wanted the timber to flow to the mills from the public lands as usual. George L. Drake of the Simpson Timber Company said to Director Cammerer, "If these established timber industries . . . are to be maintained, it is necessary that mature timber be made available to them," assuming that the role of public trees was to maintain his company. In the same letter he admitted that " . . . no one to my knowledge, has ever made any statement to the effect that sustained yield was being practiced on private lands."[33] Old-growth trees were viewed by the industry as nothing more than the raw material it needed. Industry spokesman Charles Cowan summed up this position precisely: "The Wallgren Bill fostering the Mount Olympus National Park is," he said, " . . . a sample of the lengths to which misguided and misinformed enthusiasts will go. . . . The so called conservationists want to preserve a raw industrial resource at the expense of the people who live in that area."[34]

The anti-park strategy of the industry triad attempted to convince the public that the forests being targeted for addition to the monument by the Wallgren bill would meet a different fate from that of all of the other forests of Washington State if they remained in Forest Service hands. "This forest would be harvested on a sustained yield basis," Asahel Curtis of the Seattle Chamber of Commerce assured everyone, "and we would not have the logged off land destructed areas so common in logging operations in this state."[35] Curtis believed that sustained yield was a reasonable substitute for preservation. So intense did the issue of sustained yield become that even organizations that had never before uttered a word on forest matters entered the fray. The Seattle Municipal League offered a simple question to the timber industry editorially. "If sustained yield is such a success why not practice it on our present stripped lands and reserve an area for all time by which we can measure our success as horticulturists in big firs, spruce and cedars?"[36]

Even the Park Service took a position on sustained yield. "It will take more than the promises of a 'sustained yield,'" charged Associate Director A. E. Demaray, "to fill the community coffers when the Olympic forest has been chopped down." The Park Service, after having been dragged into the battle by Ickes with a bill that would protect some

of the best remaining rain forests, was now beginning to show propri-
etary interest in the Olympic Peninsula in spite of its opposition to
its own bill. Demaray challenged F. W. Mathias, Hoquiam Chamber of
Commerce head, "Sustained yield has been promised to the Olympic
peninsula for nearly twenty-five years and the yield of the peninsula
has not been sustained. It is hard to understand at this time why the
entire economic stability of the Peninsula should be hitched to the relatively small area of remaining virgin forest involved in the Mt. Olympus
National Park when there are vast areas of the Peninsula over which
the forest has been utterly destroyed and left idle. Why were not these
promises of a sustained yield put into effect long ago? It has been
promised that under the sustained yield program, cut-over forests would
have the same recreational value as the primeval forest; the resources
of the Mt. Olympus area can be utilized for commercial purposes and
still be just as available for recreational use. . . . If this were the case . . .
our economic difficulties would vanish . . . you cannot have your cake
and eat it too. They have seen the destruction of the Pacific Northwest
forests going on at an appalling rate, [and] they have seen the utter
devastation which has resulted."[37]

Never in the history of the Park Service had any official written such
a letter. Usually bland and noncommittal even when its own interests
were at stake, the Park Service was ploughing new fields with Demaray's approach. It was a letter that could well have come from Willard
Van Name himself. Knowing that the letter would be likely disbelieved,
Mathias took the copies he had had made for distribution to a notary
public to be certified as a "true and exact copy" of the original before
he passed it through the industry triad.

Willard Van Name prophetically anticipated how the sustained-yield
dialogue would end. "Of course the lumbermen would not be satisfied
with any real continuous yield plan for the annual cut would be too
small. They want to go through the good timber right away. What do
they care about 40 or 70 years from today?"[38] He continued his attacks
on the Forest Service as well. "The Forest Service will not voluntarily
make the slightest concession for a national park," Van Name charged
far and wide. "It has always been the most bitter and relentless enemy
the parks have had. There is only one way to make it yield: An aroused
public opinion."[39]

As the dialogue about sustained yield increased, the public had before it in the Olympic National Park bill, HR 7086, a real alternative
for the first time to forest devastation. But the Forest Service had its
own plans. Regional Forester Buck sent to the Washington headquarters
a detailed position paper calling for the return of Mount Olympus National Monument to the Forest Service where "it may serve its greatest

economic and social use." Even though everyone outside the Forest Service believed that the monument had preserved what was within its boundaries, it was still Buck's plan to log it and he doggedly clung to the Forest Service's plans to include monument timber in the Forest Service cutting circles. "Handled on a sustained cutting basis," he said, "the timber will yield revenue to commerce and industry far greater than that which the area would yield as a National Park. . . ." "Past experience," he said, "indicates that once a National Park is established within a National Forest area, there is constant agitation to enlarge the park. In this case, such agitation has and would continue to upset the establishment of sustained yield cutting units . . . and would be a primary factor in preventing the stabilization of the lumber industry. . . ."[40]

For a Forest Service administrator to propose to log what was already preserved illustrates the self destructive state into which the Forest Service had sunk. It had become completely insulated from the social currents around it. But as the Forest Service continued to pursue the lost monument, the timber industry and its allies began to accept that there was going to be a park. The timber industry would try to confine the emerging park to the boundaries of the monument, which even they had assumed long ago was preserved by the Antiquities Act. Asahel Curtis of the Seattle Chamber of Commerce told Cammerer to drop HR 7086 because Washington State "sentiment was practically unanimously in favor of a national park with the boundaries same as the present monument." Since HR 7086 had been introduced, he said, "sentiment is opposed to any national park" at all.[41] Cammerer knew better. It was all bluff.

The monument boundaries were generally accepted as the baseline minimum for an Olympic National Park. Defining this baseline as a park boundary was a realistic goal for the timber industry and they grabbed at it. The Forest Service was now alone in its quixotic attempts to commit the monument's timber to logging, especially in view of the fact that the Park Service now administered it. But the Forest Service plunged ahead. It announced that it planned to build the long delayed Dosewallips-Quinault Road through the middle of the Olympic wilderness and the south side of the monument and a road from Sol Duc Hot Springs to Seven Lakes Basin on the north side as well. "These two roads will add to the opportunity to use the area properly," the Forest Service claimed, "and will not measurably detract from the primitive character" of the area. The Wilderness Society, opposed to the core to the development policies of the Park Service, took one look at the Forest Service's plans and embraced Park Service administration.[42] Finally, just a month before the hearings on HR 7086, the Forest Service seemed tacitly to accept that the timber in the monument was never going to be included in its cutting circles. But the presence of both roads would make the inner-area timber economically accessible to the monument boundaries. If there were some delay in establishing a park, many potentially desirable areas for wilderness and national park status could be opened to commercial use.

Just preceding the Forest Service's capitulation on logging the monument, the timber industry took one final fling at getting everything. Using Van Name's pamphleteering approach, the industry produced a multicolored pamphlet which attacked the boundaries of HR 7086 and called for the return of the monument to the Forest Service. It was targeted for Congress and every Senator and Congressman received a copy. However, the effort was wasted because public opinion now favored saving as many old-growth trees from the mills as possible.

Even the timber industry's state ally began to falter. Washington State Planning Council Chairman Kizer told Governor Martin that "In my heart of hearts I should like to see the Monument turned into a national park."[43]

When the hearings got underway on April 23, 1936, the Public Lands Committee room was not big enough to hold the attending crowd. Chairman René L. DeRouen of Louisiana adjourned the meeting to a larger room, delaying the opening. Eighteen of the twenty-one members of the committee were present. Eight to ten was the norm. Cammerer, Demaray, Wirth, and Tomlinson were there among the Park Service group. Assistant Forester Kneipp, looking grim and determined, led a considerable Forest Service group. The Park Service had determined that all but two of the committee members were for the bill.[44]

On the first day, Mon Walgren was the only speaker. Van Name and Edge looked on with pride when Wallgren read as part of his opening statement the editorial that their colleague Irving Brant had put into that very day's edition of the *St. Louis Star-Times*. Brant had sent Wallgren a page proof and specifically requested that he read it. The Congressman then held up a copy of the timber industry's multicolored brochure as an example of the propaganda in which the timber industry was engaging to mislead the public. "You are going to hear a great deal about sustained yield and ripened timber," he said, "Some of these

---

OPPOSITE: As the hearings on the first Olympic National Park bill began in 1936, thirty years of public administration of the national forests for industrial commodity production came under open attack for the first time. Rosalie Edge is at the center of the picture with the Park Service contingent to the right, including Arthur Demaray, Arno Cammerer, Ben Thompson and Fred Overly. William Greeley of the West Coast Lumberman's Association is on the far left with other industry representatives. Robert Marshall is sitting against the wall. *Carsten Lien Olympic Collection.*

HOUSE OF REPRESENTATIVES.
COMMITTEE ON THE PUBLIC LANDS.
MEETING APRIL 23 1936.
FOR HEARING ON H.R.7086 TO ESTABLISH
MOUNT OLYMPUS NATIONAL PARK.

trees certainly ought to be ripe by this time after a thousand years, and it is a strange thing to me that timber ripens so rapidly . . . so soon after a logging road is opened into it."

Congressman John S. McGroarty provided the moment of drama for the day when he got up and announced that he did not want to hear anymore of the "very tiresome talk about logging and lumbermen and all that." "Here is a great forest," he said. "We want to preserve it to the people. I do not want to go on record," he went on, "as doing anything else. Mr. Chairman, I move that the committee report favorably bill HR 7086, and I have got to go."[45] The situation was looking hopeless for the Forest Service and the timber industry. There were committee members who did not even want to hear their testimony.

While Robert Marshall sat in the front row taking it all in, Congressman Martin Smith of Grays Harbor began unintentionally to undermine the timber industry position. He bored the committee with a long iteration of the organizations opposed to the bill. His testimony was perceived as a filibuster and when finally stopped, he protested that his principal arguments were yet to be made.[46]

If there was any lingering doubt in the committee about the timber industry, it vanished with the statement of J. H. Bloedel, president of the Bloedel-Donovan Lumber Mills, a major Olympic timber operator. Bloedel called for the immediate logging of the Bogachiel, Hoh, and other west-side valleys. "I know," he said, "that practically all of this timber is now overripe. I mean that it should be logged to realize anything out of it, inside of the next ten to twenty years." Striking a note of alarm over what would happen if this were not done, Bloedel said, "If it is removed later than this, the trees are apt to be rotten, the limbs will be dead, and it will have not only no commercial value but will lack all the charm of standing green timber, for it will be largely dead timber." Assuring the committee that "there is ample area for enjoyment and recreation" now, Bloedel got right down to brass tacks. "Any further extension of [the monument] boundary lines merely encroaches upon and interferes in the commercial development of this country. . . ."[47]

Rosalie Edge had toured the Olympics in the summer of 1935. She and her son Peter urged the local group in Port Angeles, who were involved in promoting the park, to raise money to get a contingent to the forthcoming hearings. The local group raised $600, enough in 1936 dollars to send four persons by bus the 3,700 miles on the poor roads of the day to Washington. Representing Port Angeles was Chris Morgenroth, a legendary figure since the 1890's when he served as a local ranger; Joseph Johnston, Clallam County prosecuting attorney; and M. J. Schmidt and Major Arthur Vollmer, a retired army man. They would make their appearance on the full-day session. Here is Robert Sterling Yard's eyewitness account of what happened:[48]

It all began with nearly an hour more by Martin Smith [Congressman from Grays Harbor], who took advantage of his being a Congressman to file statement upon statement which were refuted by others, to wave his arms, and to orate till everybody, even the committeemen, looked bored to death. Every witness for the park was cross examined and shouted at till time and again the chairman had to come to their aid. Several of them appealed to the committee to be allowed to conclude their statements. I should say he was on his feet at least half the time. It was like a criminal trial, and believe me, did his side of the controversy no good. The four from Port Angeles made a great showing in spite of interruptions. Morgenroth made a tremendous hit with the committee. His sincerity, great force, answers of fact and refusal to take doubts or denials got all the questioners sitting up straight. Martin Smith's assaults just broke up against his quiet, forceful comebacks. The whole committee was alert and smiling when he got through and one of them said, "Well that's the real stuff, there's a man who's part of it." "Yes," said Morgenroth, "a forest official for many years." He refuted many of Smith's earlier statements and representations. I should say he won the bill right there. But the others in their very different ways, were quite as effective. Johnston and M. J. Schmidt supplemented him, backed him up and came back hard against Martin Smith's attempts to break them down. They also attacked his earlier statements. It was rather stirring to the onlooker, and after lunch Major Vollmer made a forceful finish which Martin Smith could not touch.

The same tactics followed with the other witnesses. Wallgren was often on his feet in defense of his witnesses. The balance of efficiency was all his because of his quieter comebacks and his sticking to the facts. He constantly denied statements of fact and misrepresentations about national park policy. Cammerer did not help him out because he would not get into the wrangling which Smith was constantly forcing, saving his broadsides for a more effective opportunity. . . .

The comic relief came with Mrs. Edge (Rosalie for short) who painted word pictures of the forests. Nobody took her seriously (though after her fashion she was pretty good) except Martin Smith who assailed her so nearly savagely that the chairman remonstrated, "What difference can it possibly make Mr. Smith? . . . " [Smith] tried to show that she hadn't really been in the big timber and did not know what she was talking about. She laughed at him, and that brought him back all the harder. Where did her money come from? Small contributions from fifty cents to twenty-five dollars. And the big contributions? Who made them? There weren't any big contributions. The chairman hammered and remonstrated but Smith got more persistent till the lady held her hand out to him across the table, cupped and asked him for a contribution. There was a roar in which everybody joined in, including Rosalie—except Smith. He was so mad that the laughter grew louder and he said "If you wait for a contribution from me [you will be without funds for a very long time].[49] Still more laughter.

The famous Doctor Van Name also talked for the national park and this time apparently stuck to the truth. But Smith badgered him too. . . . So abrasive had Smith become with his interminable posturing that "several members urged the chairman to hold him down till the hearings are over and then let him come in and talk his head off.[50]

Somebody must have given Congressman Smith from Grays Harbor the word that he was damaging the industry cause because on the morning of April 28, Smith asked only a half dozen mild questions in an ordinary tone of voice. Yard reported that "for the first time we had a normal hearing . . . but in comparison it was dull."[51] By the morning of April 28, Martin Smith was being "choked off so vigorously by the chairman that he stopped in the middle of a sentence" and the members of the committee were laughing at him calling him the counsel for the defense.[52]

Leon Kneipp presented the case for the Forest Service, using all of the economic necessity approaches on which it had depended so successfully in the past. He read back to the Park Service an excerpt from the Macy/Tomlinson small-park boundary report, and when Asahel Curtis testified for the Aberdeen Chamber of Commerce, he put into the record the whole Macy/Tomlinson small-park recommendation. That recommendation would reappear whenever boundaries were discussed for decades to come.

Horace Albright showed up to give testimony against the Forest Service, a startling turnabout from his previous relationships with them. Speaking of the monument reduction of 1915 he said, "We of the Interior Department opposed the reduction strenuously." In fact both Mather and Secretary Lane had endorsed it. Albright was confronted with this question from Congressman James Mott of Oregon: "Is it your contention that the area outside the present boundary of Mount Olympus National Park [sic] is of national park caliber?" Without flinching, Albright said, "Absolutely."[53] This was a reversal of a long-term Park Service policy toward Olympic's forests, a policy Albright had assisted in putting into place. "Does not meet the standards set for national parks" was Park Service policy up to the day the Park Service took over administering Mount Olympus National Monument.

Robert Marshall made a statement on behalf of the Wilderness Society: "The difference between the Forest Service's plan and the Park Service's plan is that the former contemplates throwing open for logging activities 73 billion feet out of 79 billion feet on the peninsula, while the latter contemplates developing 62 billion out of 79 billion feet. The question boils down to whether reducing the commercial development of the Olympic timber from 93 percent of its total volume to 78 percent of its total volume will seriously damage the economic life of the Olympic peninsula."[54] Marshall, a trained forester himself, had identified an important point—the Wallgren bill only reduced the timber producing potential by 15 percent. But the 15 percent allocated to preservation was important to the timber industry to maintain the flow to the mills. The timber industry had no intentions of practicing sustained yield, a fact which Marshall knew well.

Earlier in the same month of April, 1936, the Forest Service's report on the battle over the Taylor Grazing Act, *The Western Range,* had been sent to the Senate. The Forest Service recommended to the dismay of Secretary of the Interior Ickes that it manage all federal grazing land. It was against this backdrop of controversy and hostility that Harold Ickes came to the hearings in person and ended up as the star of the nine-day show. He mocked the Forest Service. "Forest Supervisor Plumb declares," he said, "that 'multiple use has always been the ideal of the Forest Service.' We cannot really understand what Mr. Plumb means by 'use' unless we substitute the expression 'use up.'" Ickes took on all of the jargon phrases of the Forest Service one by one, attacking each in turn with biting humor—unifunctional administration, territorial integrity, selective cutting, sustained yield—they all ended up skewered on Ickes' wit. He also left the committee with an absolutely unmistakable view about where he stood. "I insist," he said, "that it would be a stupid thing for this country to do, an unpardonable thing, to surrender this area to become a laboratory for the working out of a theory of multiple use which inevitably sooner or later, would mean the exhaustion of everything in the area that is capable of being converted into a money profit." He went on to ask the committee, "Why should we subject to the domination of . . . multiple use of one of the most unspoiled scenic areas in our country?" Perhaps never before had any cabinet officer appeared before any Congressional committee with the kind of committed testimony directly hostile to another arm of government that Ickes gave for HR 7086.[55]

Congressman Wallgren and every member of the committee knew, though no one else did, that Ickes testimony was in conflict with the Interior Department report on the bill issued over Ickes signature. When called upon to draft the Interior Department's report on HR 7086, the Park Service secretly began the process of undermining the bill. The Park Service was embarrassed by having its own rejected boundary recommendations in circulation, boundaries so at variance with HR 7086's as to be startling. The Park Service had resolved the incongruity by recommending the elimination of the Bogachiel Valley and adding instead high country scenery in the Dungeness Basin on the dry eastern side of the monument, an area of no commercial value. It was a page out of Mather's book — a way to give national park timber to the Forest Service. Receiving a routine approval at the departmental level, the recommended amendment went to the committee before the hearings but remained unpublished and generally unknown. It was the committee's time bomb.

Congressman Sam Massignale of Oklahoma decided to let the bomb drop on the last day of the hearings. He asked Wallgren about the Bogachiel Valley elimination in the Interior Department's report. Wallgren explained it was being eliminated because of some private land. Not satisfied, Massingale turned to Ickes and asked directly, "Is that agreeable to the Department of Interior that that territory just indicated be lopped off?" Ickes said that he "would rather leave the answer to that question to the Park Service."[56]

Van Name and Edge were stunned. After all the drama of Ickes' statement, he was in effect rejecting HR 7086. It hadn't occurred to them that the Park Service would now reject its own bill but they became suspicious.

So overwhelming was the support for an Olympic National Park in the hearings, so great was the hostility to the Forest Service's approach, and so greedy and antisocial was the timber industry's appearance, that the Public Lands Committee rejected the Park Service's amendment to eliminate the Bogachiel Valley. The committee reported the bill "without amendment with the recommendation that the bill be passed." Pointing out that the trees involved are "subject to the logging practices of the United States Forest Service," the committee added that they are "centuries old and can never be replaced once they are cut down. By giving the area national park status, these trees will be saved from logging and will be made available for the inspiration of the people."[57] Willard Van Name could not have done better if he had written the committee report himself. It was a triumph for the Emergency Conservation Committee and it could all be traced back to Van Name's 1932 report to Madison Grant and the Boone and Crockett Club.

Old pros like Van Name and Edge knew that the Bogachiel bombshell which had been thrown at the hearings had to be a warning signal of activity to which they were not privy. Van Name, upon returning to New York, immediately wrote sarcastically to Ickes that "By a coincidence that area [the Bogachiel] contains by far the finest stand of big timber. . . . Can this nation of 125,000,000 people not acquire a few thousand acres of timberland?" he asked.[58]

Edge immediately wrote to Brant that "I suspect that some amendments to the bill have been agreed upon, that some portion of the proposed boundary has been cut out. I suspect it the more," she said, "because Wallgren does not answer my direct question."[59] Almost poetically, Edge summed up the situation, "The last of the virgin forests are in sight, and the operators press to squeeze the last dollar, to fell the last towering example of forest magnificence at whatever loss to the nation."[60]

The Emergency Conservation Committee was about to make a startling discovery about the Park Service.

10 PRESERVATION HARD IN COMING

Should [the Park Service] not stand up for the needs of the park system, rather than the demands of the lumber interests? Have not the latter enough advocates?[1]

WILLARD VAN NAME

Personally I would like to see the National Park Service return to the principles advocated by Steven T. Mather who believed in limiting the national parks to the major scenic wonders of our nation.[2]

ASAHEL CURTIS,
SEATTLE CHAMBER OF COMMERCE

CONGRESSMAN MARTIN SMITH rushed home to his Grays Harbor constituency as soon as the Olympic National Park hearings were over. In a speech before the Aberdeen Chamber of Commerce, he said that the Olympic National Park was a "certainty whether anyone likes it or not and that the only province of local leaders now is to iron out boundaries or the boundaries may include billions of feet of merchantable timber." He would try to use every available parliamentary maneuver to delay it. Smith believed that had the bill passed the House it would undoubtedly have gone through the Senate without debate. Nonetheless opponents hoped to precipitate a floor fight in which they would attempt to confine the boundaries to the present monument.[3]

In the face of Forest Service, timber industry, and Park Service opposition to the bill, the Emergency Conservation Committee had succeeded in getting Van Name's recommended boundaries in HR 7086

Harold L. Ickes.
National Archives.

through the Public Lands Committee intact. Even in the face of an Interior Department report written by the Park Service that would have
cut out the Bogachiel Valley, they succeeded. Van Name's concept of
aroused public opinion was paying off, as was the sympathy and assistance of key figures in Washington, D.C.

Van Name continued his letter writing, Edge her organizing and
pamphleteering, Irving Brant his self appointed task of gaining support from the highest levels of the Roosevelt administration. By 1936,
Brant had renewed his friendship with Secretary of Agriculture Henry
Wallace, had become a confidant of Interior Secretary Harold Ickes
and had direct access to Roosevelt, who used Brant as a consultant in
conservation matters of all kinds. He also had access to the highest rank-
ing staff persons around all three and he cultivated these as well.

Brant wrote to Ickes in February of 1936: "As I told you when we met
for a moment in Mr. McIntyre's office, I had been talking with the President about the conflict between the National Park Service and Forest
Service, and I now wish to outline to you our conversation and what
preceded it, for whatever it may be worth to you. [McIntyre was the
president's secretary.] Some days earlier, I had made some comment
to Secretary Wallace about the unwillingness of the Forest Service to
let go of any of its lands and he asked me to have lunch with himself

and Mr. Silcox to talk over the Olympus situation . . . the upshot was that Silcox (who seems to have a genuine desire to protect virgin timber) said that if the facts were as I stated he would support a move to have additional areas (he did not say how extensive) permanently protected. But he said he would not sanction the transfer of a single acre to the 'administrative methods' of the Park Service." Brant then discloses in another paragraph what his relationship to Roosevelt had become. "In talking with the President I outlined the matter much as stated above, emphasizing the fact that Silcox agreed to preservation, but said he would not agree to a transfer to the National Park Service. I told the President that I thought this put the action up to him."[4]

Thus Brant provoked the intervention of the president to Forest Service administration. Most significantly he had become the promoter and messenger between the three points of an administrative triangle, even while he earned his living in St. Louis as a newspaperman, far removed from day to day events in Washington.

Two months after the HR 7086 hearings were over, the Forest Service announced the creation of the Olympic Primitive Area as an add-on to Mount Olympus National Monument. It was an effort to delay a vote on the bill and it was an argument to keep the area in the Forest Service domain. Forest Service preservation plans might, they hoped, make a park unnecessary. The Forest Service revised the Cleator recreation plan of 1929, first produced to justify the logging of the monument. Accepting now the boundaries of the monument as the preservation line, they added the parts of their former Snow Peaks Recreation Areas and former Primitive Area which fell outside of the monument boundaries. To give the proposal added weight, the Secretary of Agriculture was designated as the promulgator instead of the chief forester. And to cover up prior plans to log the monument, they added, "The Forest Service plans for the monument contemplated the same sort of simple development and retention of primitive character as it now plans for the adjoining Primitive Area." Forest Service plans to do quite the opposite were already in the public record.

The Primitive Area idea didn't work. Even newspapers hostile to the park made fun of it. "There can be no doubt that the National Forest Service thinks it put a fast one over on the National Park Service," said the *Seattle Times,* "the very obvious purpose of this dedication is to forestall the plan to create Mount Olympus National Park."[5] "Reclassification by official action of the Secretary of Agriculture was apparently intended to give the public impression of great permanence to the arrangement," said the National Park Bulletin to its members, pointing out that if local pressure for economic exploration developed the area would go as other timber stands had in the past.[6] "Any Secretary of

Agriculture or Mr. Wallace himself, if he should change his mind, is empowered by law to abolish the reservation."[7]

The Forest Service included the construction of Dosewallips-Quinault Road and the Sol Duc-High Divide Road in the plan, even in the face of the anti-park group being pro-wilderness. The Wilderness Society pointed out that the construction of the roads would make some of the best timber on the peninsula immediately available.[8] The Forest Service was probably trying to settle the issue on the ground with a few logging contracts close to the monument boundary.

The Forest Service's credibility was beginning to be questioned now, even by its own allies. The Forest Service preservation plan had eliminated the largest trees from preservation. That omission made the Forest Service the subject of ridicule in many national environmental journals and newspapers. And the Forest Service's Primitive Area definition, allowing for economic utilization, seemed a devious use of the language. The Forest Service had no interest in preservation. "Primitive Area" meant logging.

The Forest Service made this clear in its *Report on Olympic Primitive Area:*

> *To inaugurate management of pulp timber on private lands . . . the greatest possible contribution of National Forest Timber is essential.*
>
> Under adequate forest management, the peninsula counties can support, directly and indirectly, including service industries, over 60,000 people; ultimately this dependency could be increased to over 100,000 people.
>
> *To accomplish such an objective, it is essential that the largest possible portion of the National Forest area . . . be managed primarily for timber production . . .* (Forest Service's italics).[9]

The Primitive Area report had stated "Domestic stock has never been grazed in this area, and because of the priority of forage needs for elk, deer and other wild animals, it will never be considered for such domestic use. . . ."[10] This statement was false, and later, during World War II, when the Forest Service received a request to permit the grazing of eighty head of cattle at the headwaters of the Dungeness River in the Primitive Area (a request from its old sheep-herding permittee from monument days, J. L. Keeler), the Forest Service complied. Forest Service Chief Lyle Watts asked the Secretary of Agriculture to give back to the chief control over the Primitive Area. Two days after that was granted, the management plan for the Primitive Area was modified to allow for grazing; Keeler got his permit.[11]

In the summer of 1936, Asahel Curtis, representing the Seattle Chamber of Commerce, appointed himself to keep the west-side forests out of the now virtually certain Olympic National Park. He had also appointed

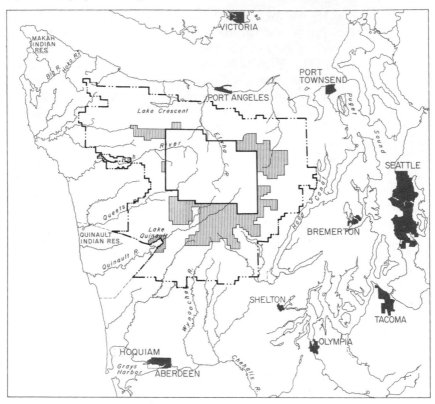

OLYMPIC PRIMITIVE AREA 1937

The Forest Service tried to head off the creation of Olympic National Park by adding primitive areas to the monument. All the large trees were excluded and the rules that allowed for logging and road building in primitive areas were left in place. This Forest Service move convinced even its defenders that it was incapable of preserving anything.

himself to this task almost thirty years earlier when he mounted the campaign on behalf of the timber industry to get Mount Olympus National Monument cut in half, thereby making all its heaviest forests available for logging. His method then was to create an illusion of great hardship resulting from the monument boundaries and of massive opposition to them. Now he undertook the same plan.

As soon as Curtis returned from the Olympic National Park hearings he plunged into the work of letter writing to congressmen, the Park Service, the governor, the Washington State Planning Council, chambers of commerce, and the West Coast Lumberman's Association. Those available by phone, he phoned. He tried to persuade everyone

that the people of the state of Washington were adamantly opposed
to the Wallgren boundary lines but if the boundaries were adjusted
to eliminate the west-side forests, everyone would support a park. He
wrote to Cammerer maintaining that it was he, Curtis, who was really
in touch with the state of Washington. "Should the Wallgren Bill pass
with the boundaries remaining as defined in this bill," he told Cammerer, "there would be deep resentment in the State of Washington."
"I believe that the Park Service would profit by giving consideration
to the thoughts of our people," he went on, "and that they [Park Service personnel] will suffer in the Pacific Northwest if they decline to
do so."[12]

When Curtis was badgering Owen Tomlinson of the Park Service
in person about eliminating the west-side forests from the proposed
boundaries, Tomlinson answered that if boundaries had been left to
representatives of the Forest Service and Park Service "the thing could
have been done without any great difficulty."[13] Curtis was starting to
recognize the irony of the debate. The Forest Service had not conceded
that a square inch of the Olympic forest ought to be a national park,
while the Park Service, which had been adamantly opposed to the Wallgren bill boundaries, was apparently trying to keep the new park out
of commercially valuable forests. In fact, the Park Service was sabotaging its own Olympic National Park bill. The hearings seemed to be a
rousing victory for the Park Service and a rout of the timber industry
and the Forest Service. So complete had been the committee expression for preserving forests that it had even rejected the Park Service-
inspired amendment to eliminate the Bogachiel Valley. Now, however,
the Park Service did exactly what the Forest Service had done. It held
to its prior position that the forests in HR 7086 should not be in the
park, even in the face of the overwhelming display of public support
to the contrary.

Long before the HR 7086 hearings, the Park Service had been at work
on a report to justify getting the boundaries of an Olympic National
Park back to what Tomlinson, Macy, and their committee had recommended in 1934. This second Park Service boundary report was finished
in July of 1936, just two months after the hearings. Its title was: *The Proposed Mount Olympus National Park and Its Probable Effect Upon the Olympic
National Forest and the Economic Interests of the Olympic Peninsula.* It became known as the Horning Report after its author, W. H. Horning,
a professor from Iowa State College who had been hired by the Park
Service to assist in preparing for the HR 7086 hearings and Olympic
National Park issues in general. Still burning from Tomlinson's wide
distribution of the first boundary recommendations, the Park Service
held the report so tightly that no one knew that the Park Service was

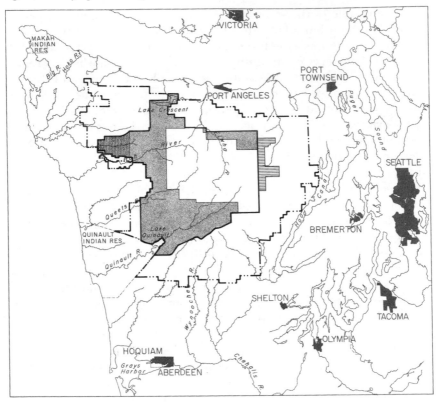

When the Park Service drafted Interior's report on HR 7086 which it opposed, it moved to placate the local timber interests by removing the rain forests of the Bogachiel (marked by vertical lines in the west) and replacing them with the commercially worthless upper Dungeness basin (marked on the east side of the park). Congress rejected the Park Service's move. The map is from the Interior Report on HR 7086, 1936.

working for a small park, even in contradiction to some findings of the report. The Park Service said that its Bogachiel elimination recommendation that had been rejected by the Public Lands Committee was "to alleviate as far as possible the hardships which it is claimed would be sustained by the towns of the Olympic Peninsula if this original bill were enacted into law," though Horning's statistics had established that the forested areas of HR 7086 would provide work for only 172 families on a sustained-yield basis.[14] The battle for a large park seemed to be won in the political arena, yet the Park Service had joined hands with the Forest Service to keep the largest trees out of the park and was, in effect, working on behalf of the timber industry. And it was not only actively working against the Emergency Conservation Committee, it was also working in contradiction to its mandate in law.

Congressman Wallgren's reelection by a three to one margin over his opponent in the fall of 1936 settled the issue of public support. The preservation of trees in an Olympic National Park had been the major issue of the campaign. Nevertheless, Asahel Curtis continued to report that the people of Washington were adamantly opposed to the Wallgren bill's boundaries. The Park Service also ignored Wallgren's reelection and proceeded with their efforts to get the Olympic forests with the largest trees out of the proposed park's boundaries.

The Olympic National Park that Willard Van Name had defined in HR 7086 had failed to come to a vote, and now the Park Service proceeded to take advantage of that failure. The start of a new Congress in January of 1937 required that Wallgren reintroduce the park bill. It was Horning's assigned task to put what was called a "modified Tomlinson boundary" in the bill, a boundary congruent with the original recommendation made by Tomlinson and Macy in 1934.[15]

Horning listed in his report the "General Advantages of the Adjusted Tomlinson line."

1. It will result in less interference with industrial needs for timber, especially at Grays Harbor.
2. It causes much less serious interference with management plans of the Forest Service in several important watersheds on the west side of the National Forest. It leaves sufficient national forest timber in the lower and more accessible portion of each valley on the west side to justify sustained yield management.
3. It interferes much less seriously with practical administrative requirements on the west side of the National Forest.
4. It leaves enough commercial timber on the west side of the national forest to permit the carrying out of sustained yield timber production for all of the pulp and paper mills that *are being proposed and promoted* for the Grays Harbor area (italics mine).[16]

The Park Service was now not only fighting the preservation groups which were working to save a sample of the Pacific Northwest forests, but also had taken on the responsibility of guaranteeing timber for Grays Harbor mills not yet built. It had assigned to commercial use a forest that a Congressional committee had voted to save. The Park Service had done in its July 1936 Horning boundary report what the Forest Service had done in its July 1936 report on *The Olympic Primitive Area,* determine boundaries to placate the demands of the timber industry and rationalize the preservation issues after these demands had been met. In fact the two reports are so much alike they could have come from the same organization. One head-spinning irony remained. The Forest Service, reacting to what it saw as inter-agency warfare, continued to believe that the Park Service was out to take over the whole Olympic Peninsula. The agencies sparred with each other in Congress and in the press, while they both worked on the same goal.

Everyone knew there was going to be a park. The battle had now been reduced to boundaries. The timber-industry controlled Washington State Planning Council was the first to come forth with counter-boundary recommendations. Events had progressed to the point that no one could sit at the bargaining table without that. The Planning Council boundary of 1936, however, was ridiculed because it simply extended Mount Olympus National Monument to include Lake Crescent, accepted the Dosewallips-Quinault Road and then eliminated all the territory in the existing monument south of Anderson Pass through which the road would go. This included some of the most popular and scenic backpacking country, including Heart and Marmot lakes. Hardly anyone believed this proposal had a chance from the day it surfaced in December of 1936. Most ignored it.

The Park Service was going to have another chance at defining boundaries in Wallgren's reintroduced bill.[17] When Wallgren won re-election by huge margins with his support of the large park in HR 7086, the signal to go slow on reductions was sent. But it was not heard by the Park Service. The Park Service took the boundaries in its Horning Report, drawn to accommodate the timber industry, squared them up to run on section lines, modified them here and there, and had Wallgren put them in his new park bill, HR 4724, which was introduced in February of 1937. It eliminated nearly all of the rain forest valleys that the Emergency Conservation Committee had been fighting to include. Ickes approved the new bill.

No one in the Emergency Conservation Committee had any illusions about the Park Service now. Van Name told Brant, when the Park Service was working on HR 4724 boundaries, " . . . I don't trust the Park Service in the slightest degree."[18] William Schulz, an ECC field worker, reassigned from the ECC's battle to save the Yosemite Sugar Pines, was sent to the Olympic Peninsula to see what was going on. There he was apparently misinformed by Tomlinson and Macy. Schulz reported back, "[Tomlinson] is now strongly in favor of the larger park and both he and Preston Macy have cooperated magnificently with me and with all others backing the park. They are real fighters and when we finally get the park, much of the victory can be attributed to them."[19] Ten days later on January 20, 1937, Tomlinson submitted the revised boundaries for Wallgren's reintroduced park bill eliminating 138,000 acres of the

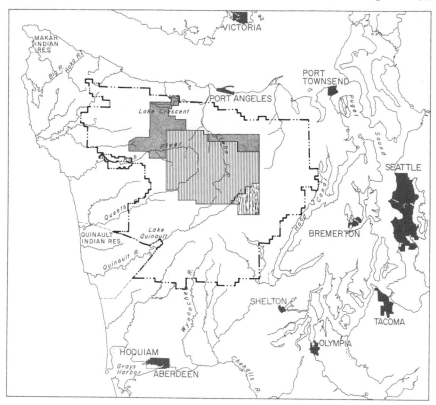

WASHINGTON STATE PLANNING COUNCIL PARK PROPOSAL 1936

The timber industry responded to HR 7086's success in Congress with a proposal to build the Forest Service's long planned Quinault-Dosewallips road. Timber sales next to the monument would then have been possible, making the issues of wilderness preservation moot. But the southeast corner of the monument had to be eliminated to do it.

rain forest area from the previous version. The Park Service had to account for the change. "Congressman Wallgren now desires to pacify the opposition in Jefferson County," said Demaray in explanation of the new boundaries, "and for that reason has requested that certain areas be omitted from the proposed park."[20] Actually, however, the Park Service had led Wallgren into the revised boundaries by presenting Horning and themselves to him as "the park experts."

The new boundaries instantly increased the intensity of the battle. It signified to the timber industry and its allies that more eliminations were possible if their message was intensified.

As the Forest Service prepared for hearings on Wallgren's new bill,

Assistant Forester Leon Kneipp, who had made the Forest Service's last hearing presentation, told Regional Forester Buck, "the graphic and economic data presented by the National Park Service were so far superior to those offered by the Forest Service as to make rather a pathetic comparison." Kneipp disclosed to Buck that if the park pressure was overwhelming, they would present the data necessary to establish that the Mount Olympus National Monument "is in itself sufficient for that purpose without any enlargement of its present boundaries." They would also present data to show that the "monument can best be administered as a part of Olympic National Forest." Economic necessity would win the day and the Forest Service would provide the data to substantiate it.[21]

In December of 1936, Henry S. Graves, now dean of the Yale School of Forestry, answered that argument. Graves was not only one of the Forest Service "founding fathers" who had ascended to the chief forester role when Pinchot was fired in 1910, but he also led it for a crucial decade afterward. It was he who had steered the Forest Service through the timber industry attacks which nearly succeeded in eliminating the Forest Service after Pinchot left. It was he who had orchestrated the Forest Service's elimination of the Mount Olympus National Monument's forests in 1915, leaving only the mountainous core in order to placate the timber industry group led by Asahel Curtis of Seattle.

Graves told the Forest Service he was not only for a park but for the large park as well, in effect admitting that he had been in error in the monument elimination of 1915. And he did not stop there. He went on for three pages of questions and issues that he thought the Forest Service was not facing. "The main body of timber ought not to be cut," Graves said going beyond the park issue, "until we are able to practice a type of silviculture that will satisfy us and satisfy the public." He challenged whether enough was known about Douglas-fir silviculture to practice sustained yield, suggesting that, "No forester can change cold facts of logging economics and finance." Graves then pointed out that "our silviculture in Douglas fir is unsatisfactory and in some places will not be tolerated by the public within a mighty short time." He chided the Forest Service for inadequate programs in recreation and for accepting the overbuilt Grays Harbor mills as meriting support from national forest timber. "The local people still recall the slogan 'Hear Hoquiam Hum,'" Graves said, "the mills did hum and the timber has gone within a short period of my own life."

The former chief told the Forest Service, "you can expect a Park and a big one regardless of what you and I may think of its merits. The general public is on that side. . . . I cannot see why the Forest Service should not recognize the special character of the Olympic problem and ask for legislation to lock up certain portions as primitive areas. It is only by some such device that the public will be assured that the timber will not be opened up by some later administration."[22] But the Forest Service had always refused to have resources allocated by legislation and was not about to change now, Graves or no Graves.

In any event, the Forest Service did nothing. It ignored the challenge from Graves. There is nothing in the archives to suggest his letter was acknowledged. After Robert Marshall and Leon Kneipp initialed it, Graves' letter vanished.

Two months after the arrival of the Graves letter, Chief Forester Silcox laid before Secretary of Agriculture Henry Wallace the stance he was recommending for the department in relation to Wallgren's new bill. First and foremost the Forest Service would show, he said, that public interests were best served by transferring the Mount Olympus National Monument back to the Forest Service. "The Forest Service plan," he said, "provided for preserving in general the primitive character of the area, as opposed to the intensive type of development likely to follow the creation of a national park." If this failed, he recommended that the department then throw its full weight behind the Washington State Planning Council boundaries. Thirdly, Silcox proposed that the final fallback position would be to accept a park with "boundaries which will exclude the merchantable timber resources from the proposed park to the fullest degree. . . ."[23] This was the Park Service's fallback position, too.

Van Name, Edge, and Brant were outraged when they realized that 138,000 acres of west-side forest were gone from HR 4724, the park bill Wallgren introduced in February of 1937. And they were infuriated by the Park Service form letter which went out to all who wrote objecting to it:

> One of Mr. Wallgren's principal aims in eliminating commercially available timber along the west side of the area included in HR 7086 is to alleviate as far as possible the hardships which it is claimed would be sustained by the towns of the Olympic Peninsula if this original bill were enacted into law. The Department of the Interior recommended for similar reasons in last year's hearings on HR 7086 that certain important portions of the same area be excluded. . . .

Here was the signal that the Park Service had eliminated the forests to accommodate the timber industry and that the Bogachiel Valley elimination amendment which surfaced at the hearings had been recommended for the same reason. The letter then went on to make assertions that nearly everyone fighting for a park knew to be untrue:

> Despite assertions to the contrary, this eliminated area does not include the largest and most desirable trees, nor does it include the major portion

of the finest low land forest. . . . It is our firm belief, based upon a careful study of the project during the last three years, that the new bill includes adequate areas of the very finest of the primeval forest of the Olympic Peninsula.[24]

For those close to the Park Service, HR 4724 reeked of Park Service involvement, especially because of the enthusiasm with which they embraced it. But then again it could have been Wallgren that the timber industry had gotten to. The presence of a bill without the west-side forests was an enormous threat to the whole project. With the park momentum running at fever pitch nationwide, it was not unlikely that the bill might sail through the legislative processes and HR 4724 would end up being the park. If the new bill was the work of the Park Service, a wide wedge had to be driven between it and the Secretary of the Interior so that the Park Service position could be undermined at the top. If it was the work of Wallgren, he had to be separated from the Park Service. It also could have been that the Park Service was intimidated by the Forest Service, as Van Name had been saying for more than fifteen years. If it was the work of the Forest Service, the wedge had to be driven between the Forest Service and Secretary Wallace.

Brant wrote to Henry Wallace, "I do not believe that Mr. Silcox would by design eliminate from the protected area the very forests for whose protection the park is to be created." He closed his detailed letter with an arousing personal appeal to their friendship:

I cannot believe that the Department of Agriculture will become a partner in this wanton commercialism, which has not even the sanctity of private ownership to justify it, for the lands and the trees on them *now belong to the nation.* These forests, owned by the people were marked for permanent preservation thirty years ago. They are mature, vigorous, healthy trees which will live for centuries. The original justification for preserving them has been magnified a hundred fold by the disappearance of all comparable stands of timber. Here alone can the wilderness be preserved and I have memories vivid indeed of talks with Forest Service men who said that the Forest Service itself, by its own action, would preserve these forests as a wilderness area. That, evidently, was before the lumbering interests began to run short of timber.

A man has not really lived on earth until he has seen these trees, lifting their crowns 300 feet into the air and at their shaded bases carrying the silence of creation down to our own day. Knowing you as I do, I hope that you will not hold the pen that dooms them to destruction.[25]

Brant was doing everything he could to separate Wallace's power from the Forest Service. He told Ickes that he had written Wallace. "I hope you will take a stand against this emasculation," he said, not knowing that the new park bill, already approved by Ickes, was the work of the Park Service itself. Brant had immediate success in the Secretary of Agriculture's office with his letter. The draft answer to Brant's letter was prepared by the Forest Service; Wallace refused to sign it but sent it instead unsigned to Brant asking for his comment on it. In a five-page, single-spaced reply back to Wallace, Brant tore into each of the Forest Service's arguments and positions. "Merely to apply the Forest Service's estimate to the whole Grays Harbor area," he said, "reduces it to absurdity, but suppose it is correct. In that case ten percent of the cut over lands in the Grays Harbor region will support the entire present population of 17,000, when put on a sustained yield basis, and the entire area will take care of the natural population increase for the next 200 years, without birth control. Why then cut down these virgin forests belonging to the nation. . . ." He closed his answer with another attempt to undermine the Forest Service. "I do not believe that the carrying out of the original Theodore Roosevelt trust is the primary thought of those who are marshaling arguments for Mr. Silcox and for you, to induce you to complete the vandalism of the Northwest timber butchers. I hope you will have nothing to do with a deed which will be execrated by future generations, even if it passes unnoticed by this one which is unlikely."[26]

Whatever effect Brant was having on Wallace, he made J. D. LeCron, assistant to the secretary, and Paul Appleby, also in the secretary's office, increasingly distrustful of the Forest Service. Routine secretarial approvals on Forest Service matters ceased.

The Emergency Conservation Committee decided to fight for the larger national park without attacking the Park Service. As soon as the bill was introduced, they blamed the modifications on the Forest Service. "The power of the Forest Service over the Park Service is clearly demonstrated by the introduction of this new bill of Congressman Wallgren," Rosalie Edge told Ickes.[27] Edge told Assistant Interior Secretary Charles West later, "It is most mortifying to all conservationists that the Park Service, for which we have such affection and respect, is obliged always to submit to any insult offered by the Forest Service and the Department of Agriculture."[28]

Within a month of the introduction of HR 4724, Van Name had gotten a long letter into the *New York Herald Tribune* calling for letters of protest, along with a supportive editorial. Edge had turned out a new pamphlet, *Double Crossing Mount Olympus National Park,* calling for letters of protest. It went by the thousands everywhere but nowhere did it have more effect than in Wallgren's own district. Just six weeks after his revised boundary bill had been introduced, Wallgren wrote asking

Publication No. 63

DOUBLE-CROSSING
the Project for the Proposed

MOUNT OLYMPUS NATIONAL PARK

No Economic Need, But Only Commercial Greed,
the Obstacle to the Mount Olympus Park

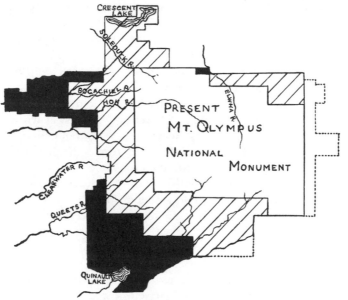

This Map Shows What H. R. Bill 4724 Now Before Congress
Would do to the Proposed Mount Olympus Park

BILL H. R. 4724 WOULD EXCLUDE FROM THE PARK THE
AREAS SHOWN IN SOLID BLACK ON THE MAP, depriving it of
the larger part of its finest forests which are almost exclusively in the
extreme west and southwest parts, and which, if not included, will soon
be destroyed to the last acre. The beautiful region bordering on Lake
Quinault, and also most of the winter range of the Roosevelt Elk, are
in these excluded areas.

As trimmed down by Bill H. R. 4724, the Park would consist of
the present Mt. Olympus National Monument and the obliquely shaded
tracts of the map. The new bill pretends to add as "compensation"
to the nation for its loss of the magnificent forests in the excluded
(black) tracts the small strip on the east side (enclosed by the dotted
line); this land is so devoid of timber, or anything else of value, that
everybody is willing to let the Park have it.

Rosalie Edge began her campaign to defeat the Park Service's move to eliminate the rain
forests from the forthcoming park with her *Double Crossing* pamphlet (March 1937), the
front page of which is reproduced here.

Edge for "as many copies as you can spare that I might distribute them where they can do the most good in the interests of the park." He was offering to distribute materials in opposition to his own bill. Wallgren also disclosed to Edge that he had left the boundaries in his new bill up to the Park Service which had assured him "that the eliminations from the original bill did not seriously reduce the timber area."[29] Later when Mrs. Edge had a chance to see him face to face, he defensively told her, "I'm not a park man. If the park men tell me that's where the boundaries should be, who the hell am I to say they aren't."[30] But now reaction to the new bill had been so hostile that Wallgren abandoned the revised park boundaries and climbed back onto the ECC's bandwagon. "May I say that it is not my intention to compromise in any way . . . I think that your latest pamphlet will help in making the people of my state understand this," he told her.[31]

With the knowledge that the Park Service had given the forest eliminations to Wallgren, Mrs. Edge moved to drive a wedge between Ickes and the Park Service. She gathered up copies of the letters being sent out by the Park Service and sent them to Ickes. "You will note," she said, "that whereas Bill HR 4724 cuts out 138,000 acres of the area included in Bill HR 7086, which you personally defended in your fiery speech in May 1936, Messrs. West, Cammerer, and Demaray pretend that only 14,000 acres are excluded in Mr. Wallgren's new bill. In your opinion are these letters truthful? Should not the letters of public officials contain the bare truth?"[32]

When Ickes sent Edge's letter to Cammerer "for consideration and report," he responded in a manner that caused Ickes to involve himself personally in the Olympic National Park battle. Cammerer, recounting Van Name's intervention on the first bill, said "after his discussion with you . . . you advised us to recommend the larger boundaries to Mr. Wallgren because later adjustments would undoubtedly be necessary." Claiming in effect that the second Wallgren bill represented those adjustments, Cammerer went on desperately trying to explain the letters. Not knowing that Wallgren had been shipped a large supply of Edge's *Double Crossing* pamphlet for personal distribution by him and that he had recommitted to a large park, Cammerer told Ickes that Wallgren "was greatly discouraged and distressed when the Emergency Conservation Committee's pamphlet was issued." "If Mrs. Edge desired to have no Olympic park at all, she could adopt no more effective means of killing the project . . . ," Cammerer told Ickes of the *Double Crossing* pamphlet. "Throughout this project," Cammerer concluded, "our recommendations to you have embodied our best judgment and have been sincerely given. To be libeled by Mrs. Edge as scoundrels and liars because our judgment differs with hers is scarcely justifiable."[33]

Now Ickes began to ask why the Park Service was fighting the groups working for an Olympic National Park instead of those who were opposing it. If something were not drastically wrong, why were the Interior Department, the Park Service and Congress receiving thousands of letters weekly opposing the boundaries that the Park Service, supposedly the park experts, had recommended? Cammerer's defensive memorandum made Ickes realize that the Olympic situation now needed more than he had given it in the past. That was exactly what Van Name, Edge, and Brant had hoped for.

The Park Service dug in. Eliminating the Bogachiel Valley, it said "will exclude a considerable area of commercially available timber for the benefit of the existing timber industries of the peninsula." And of the larger boundaries, "Unnecessary hardship might be inflicted locally, the park would become an impossible administrative unit, park standards would be broken, and in the end there might be no park at all."[34] Following the Forest Service's reconsolidation of position stance in the face of adversity, the Park Service was reasserting the value system handed down to it by the Mather-Albright regime.

While these letters from the Park Service were going out routinely, Harry Slattery, Ickes' personal assistant, returned to the Park Service three of the letters drafted for the Interior Department with a terse note:

> As you know there have been a great many protests against the proposed boundaries of the present Wallgren Bill establishing the Mount Olympus National Park.
>
> The Secretary wants the matter looked into and does not agree that the boundaries proposed by the present Wallgren Bill will be sufficient."[35]

He went on to tell the Park Service that all letters from now on should be noncommittal and that everyone should be advised that "the matter is still under consideration." The Park Service's preferred boundary in HR 4724 had lasted exactly four months. It was the second Park Service boundary to be approved by Ickes only to be repudiated by him later.

There was a hidden flaw in the Park Service's approach. Every boundary recommendation it had made tried to placate the timber industry instead of preserving the natural scene as called for in the 1916 Park Service Act. But the timber industry could never be placated; it wanted all the merchantable timber and it would keep up the pressure to reduce park boundaries.

The Emergency Conservation Committee had again outmaneuvered the Park Service, and while they were doing it, succeeded in blaming HR 4724 on the Forest Service. But Edge, Van Name, and Brant now knew that the Park Service was the enemy, too.

Officials of the Park Service and the Forest Service viewed themselves as miles apart on nearly every issue. Yet they had arrived at a common goal for the commercially valuable forests under consideration for preservation. Each had arrived at this common goal through different routes and each, independent of the other, moved in similar ways to achieve this goal. This alignment was achieved by the Park Service, which began now to go outside its own agency and hire people with personal values diametrically opposed to the values of the 1916 Park Service Act, people who would often flaunt this apparent conflict in values.

Professor W. H. Horning of Iowa State College, on leave to work for the Park Service in the summer of 1935 to prepare data for the forthcoming hearings on the first Wallgren bill, met logging engineer Fred Overly by chance on a Puget Sound ferry. They had met the previous summer when the Crescent Logging Company, through its twenty-eight-year-old employee, Fred Overly, had provided some needed camping equipment for Horning's stay at La Poel Campground on Lake Crescent. When they met on the ferry, Overly was on his way to Glacier National Park as a rookie Park Service ranger. He had recently earned his degree in logging engineering from the University of Washington's College of Forestry. Overly also had Forest Service experience, having worked for Sanford Floe, district ranger at Snider Ranger Station, and for nearly two years he was a saltwater patrolman in the national forests of southeast Alaska.[36] Horning first gave Overly a title, *Former Logging Engineer for the Crescent Logging Company, Port Angeles, Washington.* This, he thought, would lend credibility to the paper he asked Overly to submit on behalf of the Park Service. Overly's paper, *A Study of the Economic Availability of the Timber Included in the Proposed Wallgren Extension of Mount Olympus National Monument,* concluded that as long as larger and less expensive timber was available, only a fraction of what was proposed for the park was economically feasible to log. This, of course, suggested that there was no need for a park. The Forest Service agreed that Horning had done a great job in presenting the Park Service's case.

Overly saw how useful his timber industry ties were to the Park Service. Privy to the most intimate discussions of Park Service planning on Olympic, he uncovered what was not visible to anyone else, that the Park Service opposed the establishment of an Olympic National Park that included the rain forests of the west side. It was heady wine for a twenty-eight-year-old rookie to be hobnobbing with the senior members of his organization. Later he would say of this phase of his career, "as a rookie ranger what I was doing was making policy for the Park Service and it has been rather difficult for me to conform since."[37]

From the very beginnings of his Park Service career, Overly was obsessed with logging—it was his education and he saw it as his mission.

Fred Overly, 1957.
University of Washington.

He was pleased to learn that the Park Service believed that most of the west-side trees should be allocated to logging. In the summer of 1936, following the park hearings, Overly was assigned to represent the Park Service on a fourteen-day Trail Riders of the Wilderness trip through the existing Mount Olympus National Monument and Olympic National Forest sponsored by the American Forestry Association. It drew an important group including several Forest Service senior officials. In his report of the trip, quoting a conversation with Paul Logan of the Forest Service, Overly said " . . . while we were riding through a fine stand of Douglas fir on the Elwha River, Logan turned in his saddle and called back to me, 'What's the Park Service going to do with all this timber?' I replied, 'We'll log it all . . . ',"[38] a strange response from a Park Service official in any circumstance.

Overly's presence inside the Park Service was useful to the timber industry. Just four days after the introduction of Wallgren's revised park bill, Petrus Pearson, general manager of the Crescent Logging Company, Overly's former employer, asked Overly to come to his office to talk over the new park boundaries with him. He had two concerns with which he wanted Overly's help. His Piedmont Camp, part of the Port Angeles and Western Railroad along Lake Crescent and part of his Soleduck logging operations, were in the new park boundaries. He knew that restrictions might be placed on the operation of the company railroad and he knew that 100 million board feet of Forest Service timber was going to end up in the park—timber that he wanted to cut while the railroad extended into the area. Pearson wanted to work out an exchange and wanted to make sure the Park Service would not object.[39] With confidential memos in behalf of Pearson's position, Overly succeeded in getting the Park Service to agree to the exchange when it had been worked out with the Forest Service.

When Overly, just after this event, was detailed to Washington, D.C., to draft the Interior Department report on HR 4724, he wrote into the departmental report a recommendation that the railroad tracks be made the park boundary in order to accommodate the Crescent Logging Company. The whole northern slope of the Lake Crescent basin would thereby be eliminated from the park. Overly wrote into the report:

> This proposed amendment eliminates approximately 2000 acres from the proposed park. The purpose of the change is to exclude from the park the tracks of the former United States Spruce Production Corporation railroad, which tracks parallel the north shore of Lake Crescent for a distance of eight miles. A commercial development of this character is considered an undesirable feature to include within the boundary of a national park.[40]

The Park Service approved the amendment in spite of the fact that the railroad was over $700,000 in default on its purchase contract to the government and was expected to go bankrupt imminently rather than pay it. At that point, the roadbed would have reverted immediately to government ownership and the park with it, making Overly's move to sacrifice the Lake Crescent North Slope even more meaningless than it was. The 2,000 critical acres of forested hillside surrounding Lake Crescent went out of the proposed park boundaries without a question being raised. Overly was correct, he was making policy for the Park Service. The fact that he could do it from his entry-level position at all is stark testimony to the nearly nonexistent preservationist value structure the Park Service was left with after the early administration of Mather and Albright.

While Overly was promoting logging interests in the Park Service, Chief Forester Ferdinand Silcox, who had worked against the establishment of Olympic National Park and then to reduce park boundaries, seemed to have a sudden change of heart. Painfully aware that the Forest Service he had inherited from the years of William Greeley's leadership allowed only for timber production, Silcox moved to reform the Forest Service from within. The Henry Graves letter seemed to have some effect after all. Silcox decided to disarm the preservationists by appointing Robert Marshall as chief of the Division of Recreation and Lands. Marshall, at thirty-seven years of age, was a well-known forester with a Ph.D. in plant physiology, the millionaire author of *The People's Forests,* and founder and underwriter of the Wilderness Society. He was a bright, articulate advocate for an Olympic National Park. He had been a thorn in the Forest Service's side for years. Marshall's was a dramatic appointment.

Marshall had not been on the job a month when he challenged, in much the same manner that Henry Graves had, nearly all of the premises underlying the Forest Service's position on Olympic and much of the assumed factual basis on which they were proceeding. He was at a level in the organization where he could challenge whatever he wanted to challenge and may have had a mandate from the chief to do so. No one believed for a minute that he shared any of the Forest Service's values, but there he was in their midst. Nonetheless, on a crash basis, Marshall was attempting to save the Olympic forests for the Forest Service. The problem for him was that the Forest Service's value system did not allow for preservation and yet legislatively mandated preservation was the only possible way for the Forest Service to retain control. It was hard for anyone to believe he was not working for a park, which made him suspect. In fact, he was working for the preservation of trees in a permanently dedicated national forest wilderness.

Marshall began the challenge to his colleagues with a six-point memorandum which he labeled *Reasons Why I Feel an Area Approximately the Size of the Proposed Mt. Olympus National Park, or Larger, Should be Reserved from Cutting.* Marshall told the Forest Service:

1. The forests of the Olympics constitute the last opportunity in this country, and almost in the world, of setting aside a really large expanse of big timber. By big timber I mean not trees two and three and four feet through, but the stupendous stands which are found only along the West Coast of North America, which contain many specimens 8, 10, and 12 feet in diameter with a few trees even larger than that.
2. Any sort of cutting in this big timber will destroy its highest aesthetic values. Even the most perfect forestry practice that could be imagined would remove the largest trees which are the very ones which are most appealing from a standpoint of beauty.
3. The way to bring sustained yield to the Olympic peninsula is through regulation of private cutting or through public acquisition of private timber, not through failure to recognize major aesthetic values.
4. If the general policy were adopted that every resource of the nation

should be used for maximum immediate employment, then all parks and special reserves would have to be abandoned.

5. A large percentage, if not all, of the employment lost would be made up of those who would be required to help handle the large tourist trade which would come to the Olympic peninsula.

6. The employment figures are theoretical, it has not yet been demonstrated that sustained-yield forestry can be practiced in this big timber. On the other hand, the cutting of this area will ruin forever the superlative beauty of the last extensive stand of the most magnificent timber the world will ever see.[41]

While the Forest Service was reeling from that memorandum, he fired off another when the Forest Service's draft of the Agriculture Department report on Wallgren's new park bill circulated internally, an eight-page attack which he entitled *Dissenting Opinion on the Forest Service's Report on the Proposed Mt. Olympus National Park Bill.*

His colleagues at the Forest Service tried to isolate him from the management processes and to treat him as an aberration, which of course he was. And without dealing with the issues Marshall raised, many of which Henry Graves had raised a few months earlier, the Forest Service reconsolidated itself around its original priorities, now at this stage only a pipe dream with no possible chance of achievement. Here they are:

1. Management by the Forest Service of the monument and established primitive areas. "This conclusion is justified by the facts and insures a balanced utilization of the resources . . . from the standpoint of recreation and timber production."

2. If one is not achievable then "establishment of the monument as a national park without any addition whatever."

3. Rejection of the Silcox plan to support the minimal boundaries of the Washington State Planning Council park as a fallback position. "This would lock up the additional two billion feet of timber on the Hoh and Bogachiel which are not considered justified."[42]

The Forest Service now had a preservationist deep inside its structure, put there to raise the issues that needed rethinking if the Forest Service were to retain its freedom from legislative fiat. It rejected him. The Park Service had invited a logger into its midst, had openly identified him as such, and had maneuvered him into a position where he could take part in agency policy making regarding the trees it was obliged by law to preserve. In the Forest Service case, the existing value system was so strong that anyone in the organization showing deviancy from it was shunned. The Park Service's value system was so weak and ambiguously defined that it could embrace anything, however conflicting it might be with the statutorily defined preservation purposes under which it was established. Both responses were dysfunctional to the needs of each agency and both agencies would later pay for their inability to deal with the value conflicts churning deep inside their respective organizations.

11 THE PRESIDENT MOVES IN

The position of the Park Service seems to me weak and to subordinate its duty to serve the interests of the American people to local and Forest Service interest.[1]   WILLARD VAN NAME

Our action in supporting the present Wallgren bill is based upon our conviction that the area provided in the bill includes adequate samples of the finest virgin forests on the Olympic Peninsula . . . that sufficient support to put across the larger project cannot be secured.[2]   ARNO B. CAMMERER, DIRECTOR, NATIONAL PARK SERVICE

WHILE THE PARK SERVICE'S BOUNDARIES in HR 4724 were being rejected by Ickes, and Ickes was beginning to question the Park Service's handling of the whole Olympic battle, the Forest Service was struggling with Secretary of Agriculture Henry Wallace. Never having had anything questioned at the secretarial level before, the Forest Service viewed itself as virtually autonomous. However when they submitted their report on HR 4724 for Wallace's signature in the spring of 1937, Paul Appleby, Wallace's assistant, rejected it out of hand as controversial and unacceptable.

The Forest Service report called for the Forest Service's getting Mount Olympus National Monument back, a goal now considered bizarre even by their own secretary's office. It reasserted the compatibility of recreational values with timber cutting, a position that Robert Marshall had failed to get the Forest Service to reexamine. And it cited the economic problems that would follow "the proposed withdrawal from industrial utilization of a substantial part of the available timber supply. . . ."[3]

Wallace finally approved a long argumentative discourse justifying continued Forest Service administration but with the proviso that "if, however, the Congress is convinced that a national park should be established in the Olympic Range, more suitable boundaries than those now described in HR 4724 should be adopted. . . . " The Secretaries of Agriculture and Interior had now, on the record, come to the same conclusion — that the boundaries of HR 4724 were wrong for a national park. The Forest Service also introduced in the report the element of delay: " . . . there seems to be no need to hasten a decision" they wrote, assuring the Public Lands Committee that no timber sales were contemplated.[4]

Wallace's Secretarial Assistant, James LeCron, through whom nearly every Forest Service matter flowed to the secretary, was in constant touch with Irving Brant and William Schulz of the Emergency Conservation Committee and also with Robert Marshall. Associate Chief Carter reported that on Olympic matters, LeCron reflected the views of those three rather than those of the Forest Service. "He seemed to think," said Carter, "that in the proposed exchange of letters with Brant, the Forest Service had all the worst of the argument. He said he thought there were several serious holes" in the departmental report on the second Wallgren bill.[5] LeCron had asked Marshall to prepare a memo on his views of the Olympic situation for the secretary, a license by which the Forest Service's own employee could now undermine at the top the official position of the agency he supposedly served.

Carter identified the issues the Forest Service now had to deal with in relation to their own secretary:

1. The use which we propose of the Olympus area represents a local point of view, whereas the park proposal represents a national point of view.
2. That there is something wrong, almost sinister, in the point of view that would allow the cutting of timber rather than the use of virgin forest for recreation alone.
3. The implication of Marshall's point of view that the only real possibility of recreation is in virgin forests rather than in managed forests.[6]

There was no way that any of these issues could be dealt with without changing the fundamental nature of the Forest Service itself. It was not surprising, therefore, that no one except Robert Marshall made an effort to deal with any of them.

The difficulty that the Forest Service was now having with the Secretary of Agriculture's office was exactly what Irving Brant had set out to accomplish. And Van Name, Edge, and Brant had succeeded by the summer of 1937 in driving the same wedge of doubt and distrust between Secretary Ickes and the Park Service. The deeper those two wedges were driven the greater the potential for success for the Emergency Conservation Committee in getting the park they wanted.

Confusion and chaos had resulted from Wallgren's introduction of the Park Service's new bill in February of 1937. The Park Service said that eliminating the rain forests was the best that could be hoped for; holding out for more forest would inevitably doom an Olympic National Park. Just not politically realistic, the Park Service said. A number of important preservationist groups believed the Park Service and embraced the new boundaries as the only hope for a park. Among these were the Mountaineers and the Northwest Conservation League in Seattle. Rosalie Edge and her *Double Cross* pamphlet were viewed as visionary and extreme even by some of the staunchest park supporters. Edge kept plugging away in spite of the problems, mailing more pamphlets and generating more letters attacking the new boundaries. She wrote long and earnest letters to those who were now supporting HR 4724 to get them to work for its defeat. "I think you have misunderstood Mr. Macy," Edge with great restraint told Elvin Carney, the president of the Mountaineers. "A *fine forest* may be preserved in the Bogachiel and Hoh Valleys — but the *best* has been left out of the proposed boundaries."[7] In the middle of all of her desperate work to wipe out the support for the bill that the Park Service was generating locally, the Public Lands Committee favorably reported the bill as it stood. What the ECC feared most was now happening. The Park Service's park bill without the rain forests was headed for a floor vote in the House. And even its worst enemy, Congressman Martin Smith of Grays Harbor, was predicting it would sail through the Senate once it cleared the House.

The Park Service was working hard to attract support for the smaller boundaries in HR 4724 from local groups; the Emergency Conservation Committee was imploring the same groups to attack the bill. The Forest Service was still clinging to a non-yield position on Mount Olympus National Monument; the timber industry supported the Washington State Planning Council's small park. The council's small park would be the Forest Service's fallback position — or perhaps it wouldn't. The Forest Service in Washington and on the Olympic Peninsula could not agree.

In the midst of this chaos, President Roosevelt suddenly decided to act on Irving Brant's urging of nearly a year before and visit the Olympic Peninsula to see for himself what was being talked about. Brant had been feeding Olympic timber data to Roosevelt for over a year as it was developed by the Park Service's W. H. Horning, so Roosevelt had technical information at his fingertips. When Brant learned of the trip, he wrote a detailed memorandum for his use and sent it to Mrs. John Boettiger, the president's daughter in Seattle, where her husband was publisher of Hearst's *Seattle Post-Intelligencer*. He asked her to hand it to Roosevelt when he arrived; she did.

Brant knew that the Forest Service would be running the show in any presidential visit to the Olympic Peninsula. He reminded the president that the year before "when you told me you wanted to visit the area, I made the remark that if you had the same experience Secretary Wallace did, local Forest Service officials would see to it that you saw nobody who wanted a real park." Brant then suggested that Roosevelt include Preston Macy, custodian of Mount Olympus National Monument who, unbeknownst to Brant, was working hard to gain local support for the smaller boundaries of HR 4724.

Brant, to separate Congressman Wallgren from the Park Service, told the president that Wallgren "claimed he followed the wishes of the Interior Department, but the attitude of Secretary Ickes does not support that claim." Both statements were true. Brant did erroneously report to Roosevelt, however, that neither Ickes nor Wallace had submitted reports on HR 4724 when in fact Wallace had—Wallace was opposed. Ickes' report, drafted by the Park Service, favored the bill but it had remained unsigned and had not yet been forwarded to the House.

Brant then attacked the Forest Service. The Forest Service claimed, based on timber surveys, that "it would be possible to sustain 6,630 persons on the crop yields of lumber in the area of the reduced Wallgren bill. . . . " "If those figures were correct," Brant told the president, "it would be possible to sustain over 200,000 persons on the cut-over lands of the Olympic peninsula, so why cut down the last virgin rainforest of the Northwest to get more cut over land to reforest?"[8]

So that Roosevelt could have everything reduced to its simplest possible terms, Brant concluded with an attack on the reduced Wallgren bill boundaries courtesy of the Park Service. "In general, the lower the slope the larger the trees," he said. "The farther the park is pushed up the mountains, the smaller the trees. It can't be a real park unless it takes in the areas the Forest Service is trying to keep out and unless these areas are brought in there will no protection for the winter range of the Roosevelt elk herd."[9]

Armed with Brant's memorandum, Roosevelt began his Olympic Peninsula tour by passing word to the Forest Service that he wanted representatives from the Park Service present. The Forest Service had not invited any Park Service staff or any local Olympic National Park advocate to take part in the reception of the president. Faced with this situation, Tomlinson had given up the idea of going over to the Olympic

Preston P. Macy.
NPS Courier February 1982.

Peninsula. "I did not want the Forest Service," he said, "to think that I or any Park Service representative was trying to butt in on their show." On the morning of September 30, however, Regional Forester C. J. Buck called Tomlinson at his home at six o'clock in the morning to tell him that "the President wants to see you at Lake Crescent this evening at 6:00 p.m." When Tomlinson got to Port Angeles he found that Macy had never been contacted. In a chance meeting with Buck in the Port Angeles Federal Building, Tomlinson said he was bringing Macy along. Brant had succeeded in causing the Forest Service to lose control of the presidential visit, although it would be months before Tomlinson and Macy learned about that.

Roosevelt's plans, upon arriving in Seattle, were to take the navy destroyer, USS *Phelps,* to Victoria, B.C., for one of his famous good neighbor trips on Thursday, September 30, 1937. Late in the afternoon he planned to cross the eighteen-mile-wide Strait of Juan de Fuca to Port Angeles, directly across the strait to the south from Victoria. Never in Port Angeles history, before or since, had such an exciting event swept through any small mill town at the edge of any forest. Here it was, happening in Port Angeles, the least likely place of all for a presidential visit.

The day before the president's arrival, three high school boys and four men headed for Barnes Creek armed with special permission from the State Game Department to let them catch fish for the presidential table. They brought in 201 large native brook trout interspersed with some fine rainbow and eastern brooks which would appear on the breakfast menu at the Lake Crescent Tavern (now Lodge) where the president was to stay. The women of Lake Crescent picked wild black-berries and blueberries for the pies which would appear on the dinner menu. The Forest Service had attended to every detail with the organizational skills for which it was well known. The Forest Service shield appeared on the menus of every meal where the president would stop.

On the day Roosevelt was to arrive, schoolchildren poured into town. By early afternoon 3,000 of them had arrived and were milling about in front of the courthouse. Ten thousand other residents lined the streets where the motorcade would run. Rain poured all morning but in early afternoon let up and finally stopped at three o'clock in the afternoon. To go with the street decorations which festooned the town, there was a gathering of bands. The Port Angeles band was stationed at First and Laurel streets, the army band from Fort Worden hailed the chief at First and Lincoln while the Boy Scout Drum and Bugle Corps waited with Port Angeles' Roosevelt High School Band at the courthouse. As the afternoon wore on the whole town stood poised and waiting.

Finally the tension and boredom were broken by the beginning shot of the twenty-one-gun salute fired by the Coast Guard cutter Ingham, which echoed first off the Ennis Creek hills and then off the Morse Creek hills. Everyone knew when the salute began that Roosevelt was inside Port Angeles harbor. The sun broke through as Roosevelt disembarked to the huge yellow Packard open car that had been provided for him. Rows of green-uniformed Forest Service men brought from all over the region stood at attention on the dock.

When he drove up Lincoln Street and stopped in front of the courthouse, the 3,000 assembled schoolchildren and the drum and bugle corps of Troop 474 broke into their salute, the crowd silenced and the Roosevelt High School band began the Star-Spangled Banner; the courthouse clock banged out six o'clock. As Roosevelt sat bare-headed in his open car waiting patiently for the ritual to end, his eyes caught the huge sign hung across the whole front of the courthouse by the local park activists. It read: "Please Mr. President, we children need your help. Give us our Olympic National Park." When Mayor Ralph E. Davis, who had ridden with the president from the dock, finished his introduction, Roosevelt seized the moment as he had countless times before in similar circumstances. Speaking extemporaneously, he told the citizens of Port Angeles and the whole country by way of the wire service reports:

> Mr. Mayor and my friends of Port Angeles, that sign on the schoolhouse
> is the appealingest appeal that I have seen in all my travels. I am inclined

In 1937, Roosevelt told the 3,000 schoolchildren assembled in front of the Clallam County Court House (upper right), "You can count on my help in getting that national park." It was a crucial move. *Bert Kellogg Collection.*

to think it counts more to have the children want that park than all the rest of us put together.

So you boys and girls, I think you can count on my help in getting that national park, not only because we need it for us old people and you young people but for a whole lot of young people who are going to come along in the next hundred years of America.

I hope you will pray for a good day tomorrow so I can see the rest of the Peninsula.[10]

The Forest Service had organized the tour magnificently so far, but it was learning fast that it simply could not control everything. As soon as Roosevelt had finished his simple words, the presidential entourage proceeded towards Lake Crescent where Roosevelt, armed with Irving Brant's memo, would move to get the Olympic National Park proposal out of the mess that had been created by the Park Service's latest bill.

When Tomlinson and Macy were nearly finished with their dinner, James Roosevelt, the president's son, who was acting as his secretary, walked over to their table and told them the president wanted to see them. When they entered, J. D. Ross of Seattle City Light was in a discussion with Roosevelt which immediately ended in order to welcome

Macy and Tomlinson. Park Service representatives were now in discussion alone with the president before any Forest Service men had been contacted, a fact which did not go unobserved. It was a risky move for Brant to have them there, but he did believe on the basis of his and Schulz's contacts with them both, that they were for the large park. In fact, they had virtually orchestrated the rain forest elimination boundaries of HR 4724 from their positions on the ground in the Pacific Northwest, as well as the Park Service's even smaller earlier boundary recommendation.

For approximately forty-five minutes, Tomlinson and Macy were confronted with detailed questions about Mount Olympus National Monument, the Washington State Planning Council proposal, why the Bogachiel Valley had been excluded from the Wallgren bill, and about manganese deposits. Virtually everything was from material that Brant had prepared for him and FDR refuted several of the Park Service's prior positions including their Bogachiel stance and allowing the alleged presence of manganese to set boundaries.

Then James Roosevelt brought in Regional Forester Buck, who had several maps, and a few minutes later Congressman Wallgren entered. Primed with both the material from Brant and from the many face to face discussions they had had, Roosevelt went to work on Buck. "You are not allowing a large enough National Park," he told Buck, "I am thinking 50 years ahead when this state will have a large population and will need extensive areas for recreational purposes."

Then Senators Bone and Schwellenbach and, a little later, Congressman Martin Smith of Hoquiam, were brought in and joined the discussion. Still working away at Regional Forester Buck, Roosevelt told him that the Forest Service was not preserving enough timber, to which Buck responded that the type map showed some Douglas fir in the present monument. Macy saw his chance and pointed out that "correct Forest Service type maps show only about 16,000 acres" of fir, implying that incorrect data were being presented. The president at this point told Buck, "Your map shows that fully 80% of the present Monument contains only Alpine fir and barren country. We must have more large timber. . . ."

When Wallgren tried to defend the east-side boundaries of his bill as being drawn to exclude manganese deposits, Roosevelt responded that "the mineral can be imported for a third or less than the cost of producing, and that it should be given no consideration in drawing the park boundaries." With all the key legislators and bureaucrats present, he let them know that the government could purchase the private timber holdings in the Bogachiel Valley. When Congressman Smith mentioned the loss of payrolls, Roosevelt responded that "five billion feet of timber is but a drop in the bucket compared to the 119 or 120 billion feet already logged on the peninsula and that there need be no worry over the comparatively small amount reserved, which is far more valuable for its recreational use than for lumber." It was Brant speaking with Roosevelt's tongue.

After beating back all the objections with facts, persuasion, charm, and raw power, everyone present knew there was going to be a large park. Everyone also knew he would support it in one way or another, regardless of whatever private reservations he held. Roosevelt's performance was an Emergency Conservation Committee triumph over the Forest Service, the Park Service and the timber industry.

Then disaster struck. What Roosevelt had so skillfully resolved in favor of the large park that Brant, Edge, and Van Name had been working for, he not only undid but he also unwittingly left confusion behind in the wake of the undoing. Roosevelt told this warring assemblage of bureaucrats and politicians that there was nothing particularly beautiful about dead trees. In Yellowstone Park, he said, there were fifty thousand acres of bug-killed lodgepole pine that should be salvaged, but that the law at present prevented this from being done. After some discussion, mostly a Roosevelt monologue, he reiterated the desirability of utilizing dead and dying timber, and indicated that it should be cut regardless of its location whether in parks or forests. Going on expressing his views about overlap in function as between the U.S. Biological Survey, the Park Service, and the Forest Service, he left the distinct impression that he was calling for the Forest Service to handle the forestry work in parks and forests, the Park Service to handle the recreational activities in both, and the U.S. Biological Survey to serve both. When the meeting broke up about 10:30 in the evening and the group made their individual ways from the presidential cottage through the torrential downpour, they all knew there would be a large park, but perhaps one in which logging would take place.[11]

The cloudburst that had been underway all night long suddenly stopped at 6:45 in the morning; some said it was divine intervention because now the president's motorcade could proceed around the Olympic loop highway as planned. Roosevelt was scheduled to have breakfast at 8:30 and to the delight of those who had done the fishing, he ordered the trout from the special Forest Service menu. The Forest Service had also assembled the longest logging train in Clallam County history and timed its arrival at Lake Crescent during Roosevelt's breakfast. As he ate, the train wended its way around the curves of the lakeshore opposite the windows of the lodge dining room. Sunshine began to peek through the clouds and shimmer on the lake. It was a spectacle to remember.[12]

Port Angeles Evening News

PRESIDENT HONORS CITY WITH VISIT

Favors Creation Of Olympic National Park

High Rigger Shakes Hand Of President

BET YOUR SHIRT ON IT, THERE'LL BE A PARK
By WILLIAM D. WELSH
"The Rarebitter"

ON "GOOD NEIGHBOR" TRIP

Executive Pauses To Greet School Children At County Court House

Sen. Bone Takes Strong Stand In Behalf Of Park

Port Angeles Almost Missed Chance To See Chief Executive

SIDELIGHTS OF VISIT

Tacoma Ready For President

Every detail of FDR's visit to Port Angeles was reported there. *Port Angeles Evening News, October 1, 1937.*

Roosevelt asked Tomlinson to ride with him on the tour. When he got to the car, Buck was already there. Roosevelt spent most of the time asking technical forestry questions of Buck. Tomlinson said later that "the President . . . showed a thorough understanding of forestry matters," which Roosevelt could attribute to his involvement with Irving Brant but which no one else knew.[13] Problems befell the Forest Service at the fire-fighting demonstration at Snider Ranger Station when a fire pump, crucial to the demonstration, failed to function "although baited and begged with tears in the eyes," former Forest Supervisor Rudo Fromme said later. Buck finally jumped out of the car, grabbed Fromme and told him to "Get over to the President's window and tell him what's going on . . . he's getting impatient." When Fromme got to the president he found that he was focused on Lake Quinault Lodge where they were scheduled to have lunch. "Do they serve pretty good eats?" Roosevelt asked.[14]

After a salmon lunch at Quinault Lodge, Buck had arranged for Governor Martin and Congressman Martin Smith to ride to Tacoma with the president. Both were adamantly anti-park and pro-timber industry and could counter with an economic viewpoint any of the pro-park viewpoints which might have gotten to the president. In the meantime, Buck and Forest Supervisor Bruckart, in an effort to save the Forest Service some embarrassment, had ordered the boundary sign at the southern end of the forest moved. They did not want the president to identify the Forest Service with the two miles of logged-out desolation inside the forest boundary. Here was a sea of burned stumps without a seedling in sight. Most of it was Forest Service land.

Buck had the boundary sign moved to the edge of the old-growth forest two miles to the north. The sign, twelve by fifteen feet square, contained the Forest Service shield and the word "Farewell." John Boettiger, the president's son-in-law, was taken in completely. In the *Seattle Post-Intelligencer* the next day, Boettiger wrote: "Soon the limits of the National Forest were reached and with dramatic suddenness the scenery changed. Instead of the road being a narrow ribbon clefting the tall trees there was barren desolation on both sides of the road for miles. Here a ruthless job of logging had been done, the land having been stripped altogether of its big trees, and then abandoned to fires which have left it just hill after hill of charred stocks and stumps."

The seasonal employees who had carried out the sign work were bothered about the sign moving when they did it, but when they read Boettiger's account in the paper they were outraged. They had been made party to a scam in which the president's party had been taken in. Just as a seasonal employee had exposed the Park Service when it lied about the pelican killings on Yellowstone Lake, a seasonal employee would now expose the Forest Service. One of the seasonal work crew that had done the sign moving work sent an anonymous, detailed letter to Roosevelt explaining what had happened and citing Boettiger's article as proof that the party had been taken in. "I know how little value is attached to an unsigned letter but with my job—little though it is—involved, I can't afford to lose it by attaching my name."[15] When a copy of the letter was sent to Tomlinson by Boettiger, Tomlinson confirmed it for him. "I saw the large 'Farewell' sign," he said, "and the

two men riding with me laughingly remarked that the Forest boundary had been moved for the occasion." Tomlinson then sent copies
throughout the Park Service to the merriment of all. There was, however, nothing about the incident to give the Forest Service anything
but agony. Buck's attempts to avoid the sign-moving issue only created more doubt. In the end Silcox ended up chastising Buck for all
the misinformation. "There is a direct conflict between the statement
in your letter that the boundary south of the 'Farewell' sign was plainly
marked," Silcox said, "and the assertion in the anonymous letter
that . . . the boundary sign had been removed. . . . I think we will let the
matter drop. I hope we will not be pressed further because, as I say,
I think we are substantially short of being in a wholly defensible position."[16] Everything about this logged-off land had been made more sensitive for the Forest Service because of the attitude of the president.
At one point south of Lake Quinault, he had turned to those riding
with him and said, "I hope the son-of-a-bitch who logged that is roast-
ing in hell."[17]

The frustrating evening in Roosevelt's Lake Crescent cottage, where
Clarence Buck contradicted Brant's arguments, and the sign incident
that had infuriated Roosevelt's son-in-law, John Boettiger, was too much
for Buck to overcome. Roosevelt personally ordered Henry Wallace to
transfer Regional Forester Buck out of the Pacific Northwest. Wallace
took no action on the order assuming it would all blow over. Later when
Irving Brant was sitting in the president's office dealing with Olympic
matters, it came to a head. Here is how Brant described what happened:

> . . . FDR told me that he wanted the Forest Service to prepare a report
> for him on a certain phase of the economic questions involved, and asked
> me whether I thought they could be relied on to do the work fairly. I
> said that he could rely on Chief Forester Silcox, but I didn't know what
> would happen if it was turned over to Regional Forester _____. [Brant
> could not recall Buck's name] He said: "Is that the man who was there
> when I visited the peninsula?" I told him yes. He picked up the telephone
> receiver and asked for Secretary Wallace (who, I should remark was
> genuinely friendly to the Olympic National Park at all times).
>
> "Henry," he said, "what happened to that fellow at the Portland Office
> of the Forest Service, the one I told you to transfer?" (a pause).
> "You didn't?"
> A long pause at the White House end.
> "Well, I want it done."
> The Regional Forester was transferred to Washington, where, I should
> add, he did not let his antipathy to the park interfere with duties after-
> wards assigned to him in connection with its enlargement.[18]

The Olympic battle by now was scarring the Forest Service. Not long after his Olympic Peninsula trip, Roosevelt told Harold Ickes that eight out of ten of the foresters were hand in glove with the lumber interests. "I think there is developing in the President's mind a good deal of a question," Ickes said, "about the Forest Service as it has been operating in Agriculture."[19]

Ickes' role in the park battle up to the presidential visit had been ambiguous at best. He had let the Park Service lead him into approving the very small addition to Mount Olympus National Monument in 1934 which he later repudiated. The Park Service had induced him to recommend an amendment eliminating the Bogachiel Valley from the first Wallgren bill which was repudiated by the Public Lands Committee. The Park Service then had gotten him to approve the elimination of the rain forests in the pending Wallgren bill, HR 4724. He ended up repudiating that without offering direction or leadership about what the boundaries should be, which left the Park Service free to continue lobbying for the boundaries it wanted.

After the president's Olympic Peninsula trip, however, Ickes plunged into the fray. The Park Service had been so successful in eroding support for the larger park among the park supporters with its line "that if they don't work quickly for this bill they'll get nothing" that Irving Brant confronted Ickes directly about what park supporters were saying. "They seem to believe that in taking this view they are reflecting the opinion of the National Park Service."[20] Ickes rejected the Park Service's draft answer and wrote his own answer to Brant and circulated copies throughout the Park Service. Ickes told Brant that he "thoroughly approved a larger area for the park" and that Brant could count on his full support. So that the Park Service would get a clear message about his position on Olympic National Park, he went on: "Anything you can do to break up the sinister combination of despoilers who have conspired to thwart this splendid conservation project, and whittle it down for their own selfish ends will be regarded as a distinguished public service."[21] For two pages he went on, mouthing back to Brant Brant's own position on forests, preservation, and what the public interest in the matter was that the administration intended to defend. Brant did not need to hear any of it but the Park Service did. And they had a hard time with it.

The president of the United States had proclaimed himself in favor of a very large park, and the Secretary of the Interior had endorsed the idea. But even in the face of this formidable power over them, the Park Service tried yet again to undermine the emerging park. Horning proposed that by encouraging the big park enthusiasts to amend the present Wallgren bill instead of submitting a new bill, "a lot of opposition to the extremely large area will be encountered despite the wishes of the President." The boundaries of the present bill might then be the acceptable compromise, he deduced.[22] The Park Service was now working to build up opposition to enlarged park boundaries.

Ickes fast discovered that he had a major problem on his hands with the Park Service and its attempts to undermine the large park. The Park Service wrote its now familiar argument—that the boundaries of HR 4724 were all that could be expected politically—into the draft letters being sent back to the secretary's office as well as those sent directly. When Ickes read a pile of these drafts one day he realized that none of his messages about support for a large park sent to the Park Service since the president's Olympic trip had had any effect. He then moved fast to send the message as directly and forcefully as possible to Arthur Demaray who was acting director in Cammerer's absence:

> I don't seem to be able to get over the point about this Olympic National Park. I would not be willing merely to go along on what the local people might offer in the way of a park. I would not necessarily be willing to accept the Wallgren Bill. As you know, this was my position at the last session of the Congress. Can't the Park Service write a letter in this matter that isn't defeatist, or will it be necessary for me to write it myself?[23]

The Park Service continued to undermine the Olympic project with silence and withdrawal. Irving Clark finally wrote directly to Ickes in absolute exasperation. " . . . I would like to inquire," Clark asked Ickes, "why it is that the National Park Service staff in Washington is not pushing it more vigorously. . . . It seemed to us that the National Park Service office in Washington might at least offer a little more encouragement to the friends of the Park, and give more sign of active interest in support of the project."[24]

Ickes gave up on the Park Service, took the Olympic National Park project over personally and in so doing turned it over to Irving Brant.

Meanwhile, no sooner had President Roosevelt departed from the Olympic Peninsula than the timber industry swung into action. Roosevelt had provided everything the timber industry needed to take a whole new approach to the emerging park. The industry interpreted his talk about salvaging dead trees in the parks and his meanderings about agency overlap as a call for commercial utilization. Former Chief Forester William Greeley, for nine years head of the West Coast Lumberman's Association, stepped forth to orchestrate the response of the Washington State Planning Council. They had painted themselves into a corner with their meager park proposal, which called for the elimination of some 33,000 acres from the existing Mount Olympus National Monument, and jumped at the chance to get out of it. Greeley proposed a core park with about the same boundaries as their existing proposal to be surrounded by area "where timber could be utilized under such methods as would preserve scenic and recreation values . . . to be determined by the Forest Service."[25] It was the one straw the timber industry had to grasp.

The industry now began calling in all its chits. One of the ties it had was to the National Parks Association, with its interlocking directorate with the American Forestry Association. Keeping the largest of the trees out of the park was the timber industry's goal, a goal shared now with both the Park Service and the Forest Service. William Wharton, president of the National Parks Association, joined the park battle on behalf of the Park Service when it became clear that the Park Service's boundaries in HR 4724 were about to be exceeded. By year's end, the National Parks Association came out for the timber industry. "A large area of commercially valuable forest badly needed by the industries of the Peninsula is found in the Lake Quinault section as well as along the lower Hoh and Bogachiel Rivers. To insist on the inclusion of these lands within the proposed park very possibly might have had effects on the economic life of the people." The NPA challenged the forests in the original bill as "lacking in national park caliber." Their whole position could have been written by Greeley himself. The NPA took up Fred Overly's efforts on behalf of the Crescent Logging Company to get the boundaries on Lake Crescent changed to the railroad tracks, eliminating the tracks as well as the whole hillside to the north surrounding the lake.[26] Ickes and Brant would never forgive this move by NPA, a move which had come straight from the Park Service itself, a fact which they did not at first know.[27]

By year's end the Forest Service had been silenced by Roosevelt's Olympic Peninsula visit and his public statements in support of a large park. Ickes in turn had taken direct control of the park project and had responded to the Park Service's reluctance to proceed by issuing a report on HR 4724 that called for its amendment to add the forests of the Bogachiel, the Hoh, the Elwha, the Quinault, the Skokomish, and the upper Dungeness as well as a coastal strip that Roosevelt wanted. The Park Service withdrew in sullen defeat with Ickes' boundaries now before Congress. The secretary's office in the Department of Agriculture had Silcox under tight control and he was now cooperating fully to produce whatever park the administration wanted without further reference to Region Six.

Everything that had so far happened to create a park could be attributed to the actions of the Emergency Conservation Committee, which was now itself in shambles. The collegial relationship of dedication, communication, and trust that Brant, Van Name, and Edge had

shared from its beginnings had been torn apart by the abrasive personalities and petty infighting of Edge and Van Name. It all began when
Van Name became furious at Edge towards the end of 1936 for what
he believed was the withholding of information from him. He told Brant
that " . . . I cannot have further dealings with her. My many years of
effort to build up the ECC," he said, "have been defeated by her temper and stupendous egotism. I believe that she has times when she does
not fully realize what she is doing." Brant had managed to hold everything together for a while. "I have concluded that most people who do
things worthwhile," he told Van Name, "have both temper and egotism,
but that achievement is aided by keeping that under control."[28]

"Poor Mrs. Edge is certainly getting worse and worse," Van Name
confided to Brant a year later. "I fear a sad fate is coming upon her.
She is certainly not competent to head an important conservation organization in her present mental condition."[29] Van Name remained as
committed as ever, as did Edge, each working away on all of their
projects. But when the time came for Van Name to come up with the
money out of his own pocket to send William Schulz to Seattle to work
as a community organizer and local contact man for the ECC as he had
guaranteed he would, he asked Brant to handle the money so he would
not have to have contact with Mrs. Edge. With tongue in check, Brant
told Edge that "I have received an anonymous contribution . . . for the
employment of Mr. Schulz on the Olympic Peninsula" and went on to
explain that he would remit to Schulz.[30] Brant was stunned when Edge
wrote removing the ECC from any further involvement. Brant explained
that "the impression I got was that he had concluded that it would be
good for his nervous system not to have direct dealings with you."[31]

To Schulz's anguish, Mrs. Edge refused to allow him to have any further identity with the ECC, an identity which would have given him
much greater influence and many organizational advantages in promoting the park. She became obsessed with Van Name, who had only
wanted to avoid having contact with her. "There is no disagreement
between Dr. Van Name and myself," she told Brant. "I have treated him
with all the gentleness and forbearance that one would use towards a
sick child. He has a complex about me. The situation is distressing and
embarrassing, and I dislike discussing it even with you." Always ready
to attack Van Name's stability, she went on to tell Brant that " . . . old
friends of calm judgment exacted a promise from me that I would not
see him alone."[32]

Brant then prepared Schulz to go to the Pacific Northwest to build
for the final push to get a large park bill passed with full support from
Washington's Congressional delegation. He was forced to disclose all
of what was going on to Schulz to account for the fact that Schulz could

not conduct the campaign under the auspices of the ECC. "I have no interest, other than of regret, in the Van Name-Edge impasse," he told Schulz. "The only question in my mind is how to make the campaign effective."[33]

But as autumn wore on Edge seemed to lose heart. "I love my ECC and I love conservation work," she told Brant, "but the whole committee was started for Van Name and belonged to him. Now that he hates it and has knifed it, why should I go on?" She went on to tell Brant, "I have a revulsion of feeling about myself. I no longer see myself as big and magnanimous, enduring all things, etc., etc. I only see myself as ridiculous to have endured all I have gone through. I think I should dissolve the ECC and that New Year's Day, 1938, is the time to do it."[34]

In order to get the Olympic National Park project to where it was, the ECC triad of Van Name, Brant, and Edge had successfully defeated the timber industry, the Park Service, and the Forest Service on their own home bases. Would it now defeat itself as well?

12 AN OLYMPIC NATIONAL PARK PASSES

I do not for a moment admit that Governor Martin of Washington represents a majority of the citizens of that state. But even if he did, how about the millions of citizens of the forty-seven other states that have an equal ownership in these trees?[1]

WILLARD VAN NAME

. . . the miserably weak and craven Park Service . . . would be perfectly satisfied with a park without any of the worthwhile features.[2]

WILLARD VAN NAME

N O MATTER HOW DESTRUCTIVE Edge's behavior became toward Van Name, Brant refused to acknowledge it. He went on with the Olympic National Park efforts, never taking his eyes off of their mutual goal, the saving of the west-side rain forests. With no response from Brant for any of her outbursts, Edge told Brant " . . . you haven't given me the help I need in deciding whether the ECC shall go on. Meantime, very strong pressure has been brought on me that the committee is too vital to die a natural death, and that if I kill it, it is murder."[3] With that declaration, Edge dropped the outbursts against Van Name but stubbornly clung to her insistence that Schulz's community support work in the Pacific Northwest not be identified with the ECC.

Meanwhile the Park Service continued to work to head off the establishment of a large park. Tomlinson, Macy, and Overly sent a joint memorandum to Cammerer defining what the proper priorities were for areas to be included in the new park bill of 1938.[4] The Bogachiel Valley was placed seventeenth of eighteen priorities. Only the rain forests of the Queets and Quinault valleys were placed lower, the very forests that the ECC had put first. Brant and his cohorts never knew of this recommendation but they certainly uncovered the Park Service attitudes that went with it. Brant wrote Ickes that "the Park Service shows no spirit . . . and if they are not held to the line, they will go back to the boundaries of the second Wallgren bill," which, "according to an informant, were first suggested by the Park Service."[5] Edge charged the Park Service with indifference to the whole project. Schulz, working hard in Seattle to organize local support for a park, agreed. "I am much troubled," he told Brant, "at various evidences of pussyfooting and perhaps double dealing within the Park Service."[6] They were reassured when Ickes asserted, "I will not make any concessions. . . ." He then naively added, " . . . the Park Service, I am sure, would stand up straight and as to the limits of the park, it knows my position."[7]

As the Park Service became convinced a park bill was certain to pass soon, it reverted to the developmental policies of Mather. The Park Service had gotten Wallgren to eliminate Van Name's wilderness clause on the grounds that the 1916 Park Service Act made it unnecessary. Tomlinson then informed a group of key Pacific Northwest conservation activists that the first thing the Park Service should do when the bill passed was to reconstruct the road to Deer Park and connect it with a road to Obstruction Point. Then there would be a loop that could connect to a high standard road to be built later, he told them. He also proposed another road to connect Olympic Hot Springs on the Elwha with Sol Duc Hot Springs on the Soleduck "in order to provide access to some of the country."[8]

Ickes believed that because he had transmitted his preservation and wilderness position with clarity and forcefulness that the Park Service was with him. He did not understand that the power of an organization's culture could override a secretary's policies. The conservationists did, however, understand the Park Service's administration of Mount Rainier, which had appalled them for twenty years. Now the hated administration of Mount Rainier was reappearing in the Olympic Mountains. In any event, with Ickes now personally directing the Olympic National Park project, the Park Service had to support visibly what Ickes wanted, whatever they really believed, just as the Forest Service now had to do what the Secretary of Agriculture's office directed.

Irving Brant's twenty-two-page ECC pamphlet, *The Olympic Forests For a National Park*, was mailed in January of 1938. In short order, Rosalie Edge had distributed 11,000 of them nationwide. Orders poured in for more. Most of *The Olympic Forests* was devoted to an attack on the Forest

Service, its pro-timber industry position, its integrity, and the truthful-
ness of its figures. Analyzing the Forest Service's figures, Brant pointed
out that "it appears that the entire Olympic Peninsula would give employment to 237,858 persons in pulp, paper and rayon, and to a grand
total of 1,000,000 persons in lumber. . . . Add their dependents and you
have a population of 4,000,000 on the Olympic Peninsula, all living
on the products and by-products of sustained-yield lumbering." Brant's
attack was devastating. Representative Joseph Guffey of Pennsylvania
entered the text of the pamphlet into the Congressional Record.

Silcox was attacked by the Secretary's office as soon as Brant's pamphlet came out. Paul Appleby, special assistant to the secretary, not only
told Silcox that "Irving Brant is a friend for whom we have much regard"
but also went on to support Brant against the Forest Service. "It seems
to me," Appleby told Silcox, "that this pamphlet puts the Forest Service in an embarrassing situation, and really a situation that it earned
for itself. I wonder if you don't agree with me."[9]

The president's visit to the Olympic Peninsula and his public decla-
rations for a very large park had demoralized the Forest Service. The
will to fight was gone. "Our position has not found much support in
the Secretary's office," Assistant Chief Christopher Granger told the
Washington staff. Their Olympic National Park effort "has not the approval of the President, is not supported by the Senators from Washington, and it seems idle for us to carry that campaign further."[10] Now
the efforts of Henry S. Graves and Robert Marshall were felt. Both had
called for statutory dedication of an Olympic wilderness as the only
way by which the Forest Service could expect to keep from losing a
major part of the Olympic forest to the Park Service. With the park
bill about to pass, the Forest Service grasped at this straw.

Regional Forester Clarence Buck produced the first draft of *The Olympic Forest Wilderness Bill,* which prohibited the cutting of timber, the
building of roads, the entry of mining claims, the grazing of livestock,
and the construction of dams. Just four years earlier, this same Regional
Forester Buck fought to log the monument. Appleby suggested that the
imminent loss of a significant territory necessitated legislation to keep
the forest under Forest Service administration. Change was not about
to happen easily, however, even though it was Buck, arch enemy of the
park, who had responded to Appleby's challenge.[11]

Support for Buck's Olympic wilderness bill would separate the Forest Service from the timber industry and its allies, an event that was
inconceivable to many foresters. And there were sharp disagreements
in the Forest Service itself. Disagreements so sharp in fact that the Forest Service broke into two warring camps. The dominant traditional
reaction to Buck's Olympic wilderness bill held that "If such resource

development is to be forever prohibited by law, regulation or what-not, it no longer belongs in the National Forest . . . no objection should be made to designation of the areas as a national park."[12] A smaller, less powerful but articulate group moved to embrace anything that would keep the Olympic Forest under Forest Service control. In the face of the wisdom of resource exploitation reasserted by the dominant agency position, they rationalized, "The preservation of timber is a biological problem for which the Department of Agriculture is much better equipped than any other department of the Federal Government, including Interior."[13]

Associate Regional Forester F. A. Brundage split from his superior, Buck, over it. Reiterating all of the classic Forest Service values, Brundage charged that Region Six relationships were going to be severely strained by the bill and that they would be accused of bad faith. Including west-side forests in the bill, he told Buck, "makes our previous position that these areas are unsuited for recreation or inspirational purposes . . . rather ridiculous." Brundage attacked Buck for selling out, saying "The Forest Service would be open to the accusation of reversing its position in a last ditch effort to retain jurisdiction of the area."[14] Brundage was right. Strengthened by Special Assistant Appleby's urgings, Buck was now willing to make any move necessary to keep Olympic as Forest Service territory. Brundage wanted to stand resolutely with traditional Forest Service values, even if this meant losing the Olympic Forests to the Park Service. Both gathered significant support for their positions.

Silcox settled the issue for both factions after he returned from a meeting in Roosevelt's office in February of 1938. The president's approval of national park status was so evident, he said, that every other kind of reservation was out.[15] With that Buck's bill vanished.

Torn by dissension from within his own staff, attacked from the outside by Brant and the ECC, provoked by the Secretary of Agriculture's office and at odds with the president, Silcox prepared a fifteen-page memorandum for Secretary Wallace defending the Forest Service against Brant's charges. When he found no one was interested, Silcox simply walked away. He decided that all of the power was on the side of the conservationists and he would support any boundary proposals from then on, however outrageous he thought them to be. Brant erroneously believed that Silcox had been won over: in fact, he had been defeated. The following year, he would be dead of a heart attack. Some would say that the Olympic situation contributed mightily to it.

While the Forest Service was grappling with statutory preservation for the first time and the Park Service was still slyly working to keep rain forest areas out of the park, the timber industry jumped into the park battle directly and took the lead. John B. Woods of the National Lumber Manufacturers Association and William Greeley of the West Coast Lumberman's Association took over direction of the opposition as the Forest Service withdrew. Silcox went so far as to give formal notice of its withdrawal: "The Forest Service has gone about as far as it can. . . . The matter now rests with Congress. . . ."[16] Woods and Greeley treated the Washington State Planning Council as if it were a timber industry committee of which they were in charge. In fact, that was how it was. The council had always followed the direction given it by the timber industry, and the governor had always done what the council asked him to do. Thus the stage was set for the final showdown in the spring of 1938.

By this time in the battle, the timber industry had no credibility and had been successfully tarred with the brush of greed and devastation. Even the largest of the woodworkers' unions in Grays Harbor was supporting a large park. William Greeley and John Woods fought on nonetheless. The strategy they orchestrated for the Washington State Planning Council was to call for a commission to recommend boundaries and to use Roosevelt's loose remarks at Lake Crescent as a mandate to proceed with a plan for logging the west-side forests of the proposed park. They moved Governor Clarence Martin to the forefront as the spokesman for the people of Washington State.

In short order, the commission idea had to be abandoned because the boundary battle had already been won on the turf of public opinion. Greeley and Woods had the governor, however, and they could give him a plan with proposed boundaries which would protect the interests of "the people of Washington" as an alternative to the economic havoc that they claimed Wallgren's bill would create.

Ickes took it upon himself to talk to Wallgren about expanding the boundaries of his second bill to include the west-side forests.[17] Wallgren agreed and the final park thrust was underway, with Brant working with Wallgren on a new bill. President Roosevelt put park enemy Martin Smith of Hoquiam in charge of contacting Washington's two senators, along with Wallgren, Silcox, and Cammerer, for a meeting with him on final boundaries. They gathered in Roosevelt's office at 11:30 in the morning on February 8, 1938. Roosevelt wanted all the wilderness areas that the Forest Service had set up around the boundaries of Mount Olympus National Monument included to prevent any future Secretary of Agriculture from cutting. Additionally, he wanted those areas deemed necessary by the assembled group added along with corridors to the sea along two rivers. The group decided to meet the following Saturday to achieve what Roosevelt wanted.[18]

Roosevelt did not want that group alone to have control of boundary decisions. Irving Brant appeared at the Saturday boundary meeting at Roosevelt's request and was viewed as his representative. Silcox brought Regional Forester Buck along and Cammerer brought a couple of Park Service staff. Wallgren and Smith completed the group.

It was a frustrating, even agonizing meeting for Brant. "Wallgren was running backward all the time," he said. "He would have given in to Smith on every point. . . ." Smith insisted that the rain forests of the Quects and Quinault be eliminated and they were, with the support of Wallgren and to the anguish of Brant. "The meeting was greatly aided by the attitude of Silcox, who was very friendly to the park," Brant said,[19] viewing his acquiescence as support. Buck, however, accurately reflected what had happened. "The Park proponents were given practically a free hand by the Forest Service. . . ." Knowing that the boundaries that emerged would be considered preposterous by the Region Six staff, Buck warned them after the meeting that "since the line was drawn in the presence of the Chief of the Forest Service and under the direction of the President any protests made will come solely from the economic interests, presumably concerned."[20] The Forest Service was now completely silenced, with Buck himself leading the silence. Silcox led the acquiescence in any boundaries that ever would be proposed from then on.

What emerged from this meeting was a proposed park of nearly one million acres with corridors in the Hoh and Bogachiel valleys all the way to the ocean. It was a short-lived boundary, however. The Port Angeles Chamber of Commerce sent Chris Morgenroth and Mike Schmitt to Washington, D.C., by plane immediately. Both had testified in favor of the park at the 1936 hearings. Based on their views, FDR agreed to the elimination of the corridors on the Hoh and Bogachiel rivers but insisted on retaining the coastal strip. It was agreed that the corridors could be added later when acquired. "If the present bill is approved," declared Tomlinson privately, "it will not only be more than we bargained for, but it will be a headache from an administration standpoint."[21] The Park Service now could do nothing more to stop the park they did not want.

Instead of trying to introduce the new boundaries as an amendment to his Park Service-inspired second bill, Wallgren decided to start fresh. HR 10024 burst forth on March 25, 1938, with huge boundaries that signaled vast and growing support for preserving trees and wilderness on the Olympic Peninsula.

It was now time for Greeley of the West Coast Lumberman's Association and Woods of the National Lumber Manufacturers Association to make their last move and they needed to hurry. They worked carefully through the Washington State Planning Council and the other

Latest Information on the Olympic Park Bills:

H. R. 10024, submitted March 25th, 1938, to replace the Second Wallgren Bill, H. R. 4724.

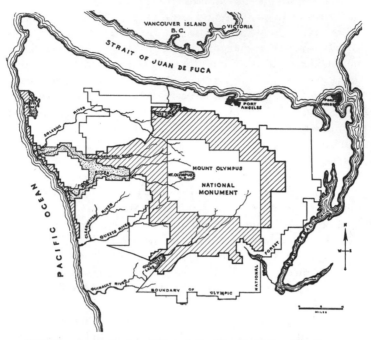

This map shows the boundaries of the Olympic National Park, as proposed in a series of conferences between President Roosevelt, Congressman Wallgren, and the Directors of the National Park Service, and the U. S. Forest Service. They are embodied in Bill H. R. 10024, submitted to Congress by Mr. Wallgren on March 25th, 1938.

If Congress enacts this new bill, a national park will be established immediately, consisting of two detached sections. The main section is substantially the area covered by the first Wallgren Bill, H. R. 7086, before it was emasculated by the Second Wallgren Bill, which Mr. Wallgren himself never liked, and which he now proposes to discard. Also, in the park, but detached, is a long strip of seacoast.

Between these two areas, shown in dotted lines, are corridors down the Hoh and Bogachiel Rivers, connecting the two portions of the Park. These lands are privately owned. The bill authorizes the President to place them in the park when, as, and if they should be acquired by gift, purchase, or otherwise.

Please write at once to your Senators and Congressmen approving the creation of the Olympic National Park, and urging that they vote for H. R. 10024. Such letters are very important for they show the government that the people of the U. S. wholeheartedly desire the Park. With such assurance, Congress can act to save the forests from destruction, and the elk from extermination.

EMERGENCY CONSERVATION COMMITTEE

734 Lexington Avenue, New York, N. Y.

Rosalie Edge happily announced the defeat of the Park Service's attempts to create a small park (H.R. 4724) with this broadside, which was mailed to everyone on the ECC mailing list. *ECC broadside on HR 10024.*

agencies of the state of Washington. They pushed hard for a commission of local people to be appointed "so that the balance of power will not rest with eastern enthusiasts." They got the University of Washington Board of Regents along with other groups to demand a commission. Woods even believed, at that late final hour, that the commission "could be broadened to include the question of whether the park was necessary."[22] For them, everything was lost, but they fought on because they were paid handsomely to do so. Holding up the bill now became the focal point of their strategy. " . . . to get the Governor and some labor leaders to make known definitely and forcefully the state's objection to this matter is the best possible way of holding it up," Woods declared to Greeley. They accepted that the bill was going to sail through the House but when it reached the Senate, they would urge the appointment of a Senate committee to investigate.[23]

Greeley, whose office was in Seattle, joined Woods in Washington, D.C., and called on each member of the Washington State Congressional delegation. Greeley then went directly to Washington's Governor Martin with an approach to head off the park. Send specific recommendations to the president, Greeley told him, because the delegation viewed the president as the key. "As Governor," Greeley said, "you can positively and aggressively focus opinion in the state behind a National Park of reasonable proportions. . . ."

On March 31, Governor Martin, whose every move was now orchestrated by the timber industry, presented Roosevelt with the park plan prepared by Greeley. He presented it as his own, as if speaking for the people of the state of Washington. This demonstrated how completely out of touch with the reality of the situation both he and Greeley were in the spring of 1938. Calling for a park of 450,000 acres containing no commercially valuable timber, with a road up the Dosewallips and down the Quinault, Greeley's plan ignored the public dialogue about forest policy and wilderness that had been underway for nearly five years. Governor Martin's proposed bill, *The Olympic National Park and Forest Demonstration Area,* simply preserved the mountain core while leaving the rest under the Forest Service for cutting.

Congressman Martin Smith, over Wallgren's vehement objections, got the Public Lands Committee to extend the courtesy of a private hearing to the governor. Governor Martin, Ben Kizer of the Planning Council, and Peter E. Terzick, an editor of the official organ of the lumber and sawmill workers, appeared to testify in accordance with the original strategy laid out by Greeley. The Public Lands Committee heard their story patiently and courteously.

Governor Martin and Kizer went to see Roosevelt following the Public Lands Committee hearings. When they arrived for their noontime appointment, they found Congressman Martin Smith, Mon Wallgren, and Senators Bone and Schwellenbach also present. Roosevelt again dominated the meeting from the start. He told the assembled group (he claimed later) that he wanted the House to pass a bill providing for as large a park as possible. Then, when the bill got to the Senate, if the area was whittled down, he wanted an amendment put on which would give him the right to add to the park by proclamation. Wallgren ran straight from the White House to Ickes' office. He told Ickes the people of the state of Washington were for the larger park and that Martin was a reactionary who did not represent public sentiment towards the park at all.[24] Congressman Smith rushed back to his office to let the Washington State Planning Council know that Roosevelt wanted the reduced compromise boundaries of HR 4724 brought to the House, passed, and sent to the Senate. "In the Senate," Smith said, "the suggestions of the President for a national park of approximately the area of the present monument . . . and with selective logging to be permitted in the outside area in the National Forest will be incorporated as amendments." Any extensions by proclamation, he said, would have to be by joint action of the federal and state governments.[25] It was a momentary triumph for Smith, the governor and for Greeley. There was no way the state would agree to additions by proclamation.

Roosevelt had apparently deliberately confused the scene as a strategy to deal with the timber industry and its strong influence over the Senate. Governor Martin returned to Seattle openly discussing his "deal" with the president for a small park. The *Seattle Post-Intelligencer* swung over to the timber industry position promoted by the governor. The *Seattle Times,* strongly opposed to the larger park all along, joined the *Post-Intelligencer.* Demoralized, Edge told Brant that "Schulz longs to deny that the President yielded to Governor Martin—but how can he?"[26]

A week later, the House Public Lands Committee voted unanimous approval of Wallgren's new bill with the huge boundaries, completely ignoring the governor and the timber industry position. At Wallgren's request, his bill was amended to eliminate the Hoh and Bogachiel corridors and 33,000 acres from the lower Bogachiel Valley. The Crown Zellerbach Corporation had put so much pressure on him that he yielded. Their ownership of the one-mile-wide strip in the valley gave them virtual control over the land eliminated. Brant told Roosevelt of this and reminded him that the eliminated area contained the finest stand of Douglas fir, the most unspoiled wilderness and one of the chief migration routes of the elk herd. "The elimination," Brant said, "practically ruins the bill."[27]

In spite of the problems, the amended park bill appeared on the House calendar for a vote on May 16, 1938. Congressmen Edward Eicher

*"Well, I still claim it was
a good site for a sawmill when we moved here."*

Rosalie Edge considered her use of this cartoon from *The New Yorker* a critical element in the ECC Olympic campaign. "It expresses the reality that most everyone has experienced with his own eyes and gets him in touch with his feelings about it," she said. It was first used in Irving Brant's ECC pamphlet, *The Olympic Forests For A National Park*, which was distributed to each House member from the floor just before the Olympic park vote. No Congressman had time to read the pamphlet but each had time to see the cartoon and the map. The vote was unanimous for the park bill. Edge used the cartoon with similar result when fighting the Park Service's attempts in 1947 to eliminate from the park the west side rain forests. *New Yorker, unknown date, ECC files.*

of Iowa and John Cochran of Missouri began rallying groups of supporters as soon as the House convened. Eicher passed dozens of Brant's *Olympic Forests for a National Park* pamphlets to members on the floor. They had no time to read them but the maps and cartoon from *The New Yorker* told the whole story. When the vote came, the bill passed under a suspension of the rules requiring a two-thirds vote and without amendments. It was an overwhelming victory. The park was on its way.

Meanwhile, much misinformation about the new park was being circulated by the timber industry, its newspaper allies and the Washington State Planning Council. They said that 200,000 acres of state school land would be bottled up, that wealth from manganese was now un-available, and that $20 million would be immediately lost to the state. The newspapers reported these claims all as fast as they came off the press releases of every anti-park group in the state. At Brant's urging, Ickes sent a recorded speech to radio stations in Seattle and Spokane to be aired the day after the bill passed the House.

His speech recounted the wide support the park enjoyed through-out the state and tore into the repression of free speech at the Univer-sity of Washington on the Olympic National Park issue because of "Grays Harbor lumber people objecting." (The publisher of the Grays Harbor newspaper, a university regent, and the dean of the Forestry School were both vehement in their anti-park viewpoints.) Ickes pointed out that all the newspaper editors were for the park "but not for a real park. They are for the same kind of a park that the lumber interests are for." In the biting prose for which he was famous, Ickes took on Governor Martin on his own home turf. He charged that Martin made it appear that President Roosevelt was abandoning his wish for a large park. Ickes presented the governor of Washington as a liar. "President Roosevelt told me personally, after his meeting with Governor Martin," Ickes said, "that he wanted the largest park it was possible to get." He closed his speech with: "The President does not want a small park. The Department of Interior does not want a small park, and I am sure that the people of Washington want a park that will rank with other great parks and be a credit to a great state."

For a Secretary of the Interior, the speech was a bold move. It caused a sensation. It brought the state of Washington's Congressional delega-tion together, emasculated what was left of timber industry influence, and made the prospect of a large Olympic National Park imminent. No one but Ickes knew that every word of the speech had been written by Irving Brant.

After Ickes' speech, the park battle seemed to drop into a period of watchful waiting. The bill, now in the Senate processes, seemed to go nowhere. However, Governor Martin's and Congressman Smith's deliberate misstatements had fouled up Brant's strategic dealing with Washington's two state senators. The senators were afraid if they sup-ported any bill fixing the size of the park, hostile newspapers would accuse them of double-crossing the governor. At the same time, by mis-representing what Roosevelt had said, the governor and the newspapers made it difficult for Roosevelt to add to the park by proclamation.

Brant decided to change the strategy and correct the omissions in HR 10024. He proposed to Roosevelt that the Senate pass a skeletonized park bill which would meet the needs of the senators who feared "op-ponents might claim that you had been given discretionary power to

add to a park which in their view is already too large." Brant told
Roosevelt, "I can see other advantages to the skeletonized bill. It would
make use of the discretionary power imperative, thus preventing appeals to you not to exercise the power granted. And it would enable
you to reopen the matter of the Queets and Quinault areas, where the
boundaries defined in HR 10024 are inadequate."[28]

After submitting the amendment authorizing the president to add
to the park by proclamation, Brant discovered that Regional Forester
Clarence Buck had prepared an amendment at Senator Bone's request,
which Bone had sent on to Roosevelt as part of the Senate's Olympic
National Park bill package. Buck had not given up. He jumped at the
opportunity given him to nullify the whole park bill by amendment.
He had added the following to the proclamation amendment:

> Provided, that the timber resources on all lands so set aside by Executive
> Order may be made available for industrial and commercial use under
> such principles of selective logging and sustained yield management as
> may be necessary to maintain a forest cover and the productivity of said
> lands, the control and supervision of such timber cutting operations to
> be exercised by the Forest Service of the Department of Agriculture, un-
> der such rules and regulations as the President may prescribe.

To Brant's horror, Roosevelt seemingly accepted the whole package,
including Buck's amendment. The amendment forever prevented the
president from being involved in the preservation of the Olympic forests. If he did not add them to the park, they would be cut. If he did
add them, they would also be cut. Brant rushed to his typewriter and
pounded out two hard-hitting pages attacking every nuance of Buck's
amendment. "In adding areas to the park," he told Roosevelt, "you would
have no power under this amendment to protect scenic areas from lumbering. . . . It says the timber resources on *all lands* added by proclamation may be lumbered. With the defined areas cut down in size in the
amended bill, practically all of the really fine trees will have to be added by proclamation."[29]

Bone backed away after Brant's intervention and the amendment
disappeared from consideration in the White House. What was ominous
to Brant was the incredible power of the timber industry, still operating powerfully behind the scenes.

Having the Park Service's HR 4724 boundaries reappear, even with
the president having the power to add forest later, made both Van Name
and Edge uneasy. "It seems dreadful to go back . . . " Edge said, because
it meant as soon as the bill passed they had to start the campaign all
over again "in order to properly encourage the President to make the

transfer. . . ." She told Brant, "it seems to me that I can never again go into another park campaign."[30]

On Saturday, June 11, the Senate Committee on Public Lands and Surveys reported favorably on HR 10024 with the boundaries of HR 4724 and with the proclamation clause drafted by Brant exactly as Brant had strategized. The bill passed the Senate on Monday with amendments that restored the boundaries of HR 4724 and with power to the president to add forests by proclamation. The bill was sent back to the House on Tuesday for a vote on the amendments the following day. Brant then discovered that the Senate was going to adjourn the next day before it was possible to get the park bill back from the House. The park bill was doomed. Brant again, however, was able to rescue the park, this time with the railroad unemployment bill which had passed the House the day before. In a note to Roosevelt, which he got White House staffer, Tom Corcoran, to agree to hand deliver to him, Brant listed all the political reasons why the railroad bill needed to pass before the end of the session. "I believe there are distinct advantages to passage of this bill," he told Roosevelt, "which I am told would go through instantly if you gave the word."[31] When Roosevelt read Brant's letter, he picked up the phone; the Senate leadership responded by holding the Senate in session. The Olympic bill would now have time to return from the House, with time enough to pass the Senate. Brant claimed afterward he did not see the connection between the two bills at the time but the record itself suggests otherwise.

Wednesday afternoon, June 15, René DeRouen of the Public Lands Committee called the bill up for action. Under the rules, unanimous consent was required or the bill had to go to conference, a situation everyone was desperate to avoid. Republican leader Bertrand Snell objected, primed by Congressman Martin Smith of Hoquiam, forcing it to conference. Brant, though, had a hand in appointing the conferees. "DeRouen and I went over the list of Senators," Brant said later, "as I knew who were friendly. . . ." Then they found that the House was going to recess without an evening session, so the conference report had nowhere to go. "DeRouen consulted the House leaders and came back saying he had a scheme that must be kept quiet," Brant said. "He would ask unanimous consent to file a conference report up to midnight. He said that only a few old timers knew that this would give the report privileged status and he could call it up anytime and get it adopted by majority vote, instead of having to suspend the rules and get a two-thirds majority. He got this permission."[32]

When the conferees met at 7:00 in the evening, with Brant sitting outside the door to orchestrate the processes, "Senator Key Pittman objected to the plan of taking the House bill, and suggested sticking to the Senate bill, with an amendment limiting the total size of the park to 898,282 acres, and providing that the President should wait twelve months before adding land by proclamation." DeRouen came out to tell Brant about it. "I said I thought Pittman's plan was all right," Brant said, "provided there was a free choice of areas to be added. . . ." The conferees cut the twelve-month delay to eight when Brant pointed out that the Park Service needed to know what land would be inside the park to establish campgrounds for the next season. "The main problem had been to make it possible to restore the Bogachiel without having the whole bill thrown out on a point of order that the conference report created a park bigger than would be established under either House or Senate bill. I had suggested," Brant went on, "that they meet this difficulty by adding the Bogachiel to the House bill and taking the seashore strip out. . . ."

On Thursday, June 16, the House met at 10:00 o'clock in the morning and promptly agreed to the conference report. But shortly after noon, Senator Bone discovered that the clerk who wrote up the conference report had used the words "to be added to" instead of the word "of," which meant that the president could add an additional 898,282 acres to the park, doubling its size. "It would have wrecked Bone politically," Brant believed. A concurrent resolution was offered to correct the error. The Senate adopted it quickly but it also had to pass the House or the bill was dead.

Here is what Brant had to say of the final moments before Congress adjourned:

> In the House, unless the resolution was agreed to unanimously, it would have to get a two-thirds majority under suspension of the rules, and since the bill still had the clause in it that Snell was fighting (proclamation power), it was serious danger. Luckily, nobody except Wallgren, DeRouen, Speaker Bankhead and Majority Leader Rayburn knew about it. I saw DeRouen walk over and shake hands cordially with Snell, saying goodbye and a pleasant summer, old pal. Martin Smith thought it was all over and wasn't there. My wife and I were in one gallery; Tomlinson and Overly in another. The House had recessed for four hours and it was getting late. Controversial stuff came on, and the House voted down an appropriation for Tahoe National Park with apparent relish. Then it became evident (from Wallgren's movements) that Rayburn had sandwiched the Olympic resolution in with some unanimous stuff to which nobody was paying any attention. Wallgren finally moved to take up Senate Concurrent Resolution 42, the clerk read it (Wallgren said afterwards that at this point everybody on the floor seemed to be turning to look at him) and the instant the reading stopped, Bankhead said: 'Without objection the

Senate Resolution is concurred in and a motion to reconsider laid on the table.' Bang! That was over. Tomlinson and Overly and my wife and I all jumped up at the same moment, I let out a yip, and we left before anybody called the police.

Read the Record and you'd think nothing at all occurred, but DeRouen and Wallgren practically put in two solid days getting the bill through. . . . Nobody except Smith favored the timber interests.[33]

Both Van Name and Edge stood in awe of Brant. "You are the master strategist," Edge told him. There would have been no park without Brant, who had a move to make for every impediment that emerged. In an understatement, Brant said, "my own work on the park bill consisted chiefly of pulling things out of the way of it."[34] In fact, he had orchestrated nearly every governmental move from the beginning, four years earlier.

To Rosalie Edge had fallen the task of organizing the coalition of scientific societies, museums, academicians, environmental organizations, and media through her pamphleteering. Her work had produced a powerful, responsive political force with the ECC at its center. When the Olympic National Park bill finally passed, Edge informed her coalition with some chagrin that "only two organizations whose cooperation we sought . . . failed to help us—The National Association of Audubon Societies and the National Parks Association. We do not think that the Audubon Association was actually opposed to the Olympic Park—but it was lethargic and indifferent. The National Parks Association was opposed to the park. Its President, Mr. William Wharton, even telegraphed President Roosevelt, urging him to veto the bill. It is significant that Mr. Wharton represents the American Forestry Association on the Board of the National Parks Association; Mr. Wharton is also first Vice President of the Audubon Association." After criticizing Wharton, Edge renewed the call to battle: "the forests of the Hoh and the Bogachiel must be saved, and we are confident they will be saved."[35]

But Olympic National Park remained unfinished and without the west-side rain forests and the magnificent Bogachiel Valley that had been fought over for so long. And Brant innocently triggered the Van Name-Edge battle anew when he told Van Name after the Olympic National Park bill finally passed, "your name ought to be carved on the biggest tree in the park." When Edge read that in the carbon copy Brant sent to her, she responded with a two-page attack on Van Name.[36] Brant refused to acknowledge having seen it.

It had been nearly fifty years since the first Olympic National Park proposals had been made in 1890, and thirty-four years since the first park bill had appeared in 1904. In that period, the timber industry had put everything it had into the park battle and had lost massively. But it almost won by default in the end. The following year, war broke out in Europe and Congress became obsessed with defense. It is entirely likely that the moment the Olympic National Park bill passed was truly its final opportunity, the last moments of the last war-free Congress.

13 A FOREST PRESERVED— AT LAST

It is the intention to keep this park, so far as possible, in a wilderness area. It is truly a wonderland of nature and is more than I can understand how people who pretend to be interested in conservation could be opposed to its creation as a natural park.[1] HAROLD L. ICKES

Certainly no wilderness lover could selfishly demand that the national parks be kept only for those who are physically able to travel on them on foot or horseback, for they are definitely set aside for the benefit and enjoyment of all.[2]

ARNO B. CAMMERER,
DIRECTOR, NATIONAL PARK SERVICE

HANGING HEAVILY OVER ALL THAT HAD TRANSPIRED in getting the park bill passed was that the Park Service had eliminated Van Name's wilderness clause from HR 4724 at the same time it eliminated the rain forests included in the first bill. The Park Service claimed a wilderness clause was not necessary because the 1916 Park Service Act already required that the parks be administered as wilderness. The wilderness clause had simply gotten lost in the battle over trees and boundaries and somehow the bill had passed without it. Suspicion of the Park Service ran high as the local chambers of commerce began announcing plans for a "developed" Olympic park. Ickes took action.

Ickes tackled the Park Service's development bias with a vengeance. In his Seattle speech at the celebration banquet held for the passing of the park bill, he publicly committed the Park Service to wilderness administration before it even had a chance to react. "KEEP OLYMPIC PARK A WILDERNESS, ICKES URGES IN TALK HERE," read the banner headline in the *Seattle Post-Intelligencer* the next day. Irving Brant had again written every word of the speech, a fact which he shared with no one, not even Rosalie Edge.

At Brant's suggestion, Ickes then moved to take away the Park Service's freedom to overdevelop the parks. Brant drafted for Ickes the first bill ever introduced in Congress to authorize Congressionally protected wilderness. Areas so defined as "wilderness" in national parks would be off limits to further development and out of the Park Service's control:

> *A bill to authorize the setting apart and preservation of wilderness areas in national parks and monuments* . . . That in order to preserve perpetually for the benefit and inspiration of the people of the United States the primitive conditions existing within national parks and national monuments, the President may, by proclamation, upon the recommendation of the Secretary of the Interior, set apart tracts of land within national parks and national monuments as wilderness areas when he determines that it would be in the public interest to do so. No hotels, permanent camps, highways, roads, truck trails or other similar physical improvements shall be constructed within such wilderness areas. Nothing in this act shall be construed as prohibiting the erection of foot and horse trails, simple trailside shelters . . . [3]

"If this bill is enacted into law," Ickes said, "it will be possible to protect the great wilderness of the newly established Olympic National Park from unwise road construction, and from hotels which might better be operated in nearly local communities."[4] Ickes' statement, along with the bill, summarized how much faith he had in the Park Service's capacity to administer the park as wilderness after he was gone from office. With Congress increasingly occupied with defense, however, the bill vanished before hearings could be held.

Ickes' moves against the Park Service subtly continued. He cherished the direct communications from the field he had received from William Schulz, operating in Seattle on Van Name's money as the *de facto* ECC field representative. Bypassing the Park Service to get information proved to be so useful that as soon as the Olympic National Park bill passed, Ickes put Schulz on the Interior Department payroll as field representative and moved him to California to begin work on the ECC's

When Harold Ickes visited the Hoh after the park bill passed in 1938, he ordered the Park Service to keep the road-ending where it was. Park official O.A. Tomlinson marked the occasion with a picture. *O.A. Tomlinson papers.*

Kings Canyon and Redwood Mountain projects. The Park Service was required to provide Schulz with office space even though they could never be certain what he was reporting to Ickes or Brant, or what Ickes was saying to him. Ickes' appointment of Schulz illustrated his general distrust of the Park Service after what he had seen during the Olympic National Park fight.

The ink from Roosevelt's pen was scarcely dry on the Olympic National Park bill when anti-park forces took the initiative to head off west-side forests being added to the park. On his return from Alaska Ickes was cornered by John Boettiger, the president's son-in-law, for a private meeting with the Washington State Planning Council in Seattle. They wanted Ickes to submit to the president the extensions they had agreed to. Ickes flatly refused. Schulz, in Seattle at the time, found out about the meeting and told Boettiger's secretary that Ickes was expecting him to attend. He did, and his presence was felt. Ickes virtually turned the meeting over to Schulz to counter timber-industry arguments of the Washington State Planning Council. Ickes seemed to relish the fight, Schulz said later, and was absolutely adamant to their fervent pleas.[5]

When Ickes returned to Washington, D.C., he received a request from Ben Kizer of the Planning Council to appoint a Park Service representative to meet with their executive secretary to make a joint boundary recommendation. Ickes appointed Regional Director Frank Kittredge and told him the minimum boundaries he should agree to were the boundaries Brant had already gotten Tomlinson to agree to. This didn't work and as soon as the joint Kittredge/Planning Council report was seen by the secretary, he rejected it.

All credible power to make recommendations was held by Irving Brant, now a full-time but temporary consultant to Ickes and Roosevelt. Brant, the citizen activist conservationist, was in position to define what the president would add to the park. His report was ready at the end of 1938. When Roosevelt read it, he forced both Ickes and Brant to rethink the whole thing. "I am disturbed," Roosevelt said, "by three matters which we cannot accomplish under the recent Olympic National Park Bill. The first of these relates to the preservation of the Pacific shoreline." Roosevelt wanted that accomplished along with acquisition of strips connecting the park to the coastal strip. He also wanted to buy the timber on the Quinault Indian Reservation from the Indians. "I think we should have legislation for the preservation of all the remaining timber in the Quinault River Valley," he said.[6]

Ickes immediately went to work. Public Works Administration Project 723 was launched with $1,700,000 to acquire a wilderness coast and river strip. To leave room for the later addition of this new area to the park, Brant revised his report to eliminate three critical miles on the Dosewallips and the whole of the Upper Dungeness Valley. In the end, they agreed this was not the time for more legislation. The Quinault forest that Roosevelt so wanted to preserve ended up in the Grays Harbor sawmills.

In December of 1939, Roosevelt wanted the additions to the park to move forward. The required consultation with the governor of Washington and the Departments of Agriculture and Interior was scheduled for December 9 in Roosevelt's office. Irving Brant prepared a sixteen-page memorandum of objections that the state might come up with and the underlying basis for them. "The Port Angeles Chamber of Commerce," he said, "reflects the position of its chief industrial company, Crown-Zellerbach, which desired to lumber the large Sitka Spruce of Bogachiel and Hoh valleys so as to postpone the transition from natural to chemical whitener in its print paper." This he had learned from the Port Angeles mill manager himself. Brant prepared Ickes and Roosevelt well for the confrontation ahead in the meeting.

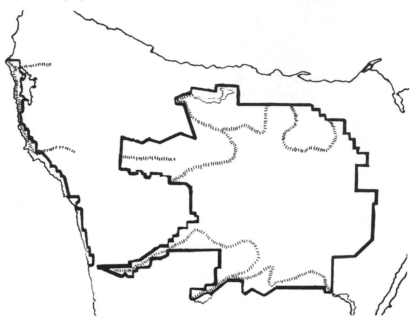

When Secretary Ickes' 1939 park wilderness bill vanished with the start of World War II, the Park Service began attacking the concept of wilderness in Olympic National Park with a series of road proposals (note hatch marks, above). All but one were loop roads which would have diverted traffic off of US 101 and into the park. The coastal strip road was funded in the Mission 66 program but defeated in the end by citizen protest.

At the meeting in the president's office were Roosevelt, Ickes, Wallace, Chief Forester Silcox, Director Cammerer, Governor Martin, aides Ben Kizer and George Yantis, Ranger Fred Overly of Olympic National Park, Irving Brant, and Irving Clark of the Wilderness Society and the Mountaineers. As the meeting began, Yantis' first sentence contained the word "manganese." Roosevelt turned to Governor Martin and said, "Now, Clarence, you know and I know that there is nothing to this manganese business. I don't want to hear another word about it."[7] Brant's memo had dealt with all the manganese issues.

Yantis and Kizer then brought out maps showing that on the basis of the rainfall in the Bogachiel Valley, twelve miles of rain forest was already preserved. Brant pointed out it was heavy rainfall at low altitude in a moderate climate that produced the rain forest and none of the Bogachiel forest was then in the park. The state wanted the timber to justify building a railroad to harvest more timber. Brant asked, "Why, then, sacrifice to subsidize a railroad whose only required use would be to destroy the scenic forest itself?" Finally, when beaten down on

economic issues, Kizer and Yantis began to belittle the scenic importance of the areas. Several times, Roosevelt turned to Martin and cited
the Forest Service surveys that showed that the western valleys were
not essential to the Olympic Peninsula's economy.

At the conclusion of the meeting, Roosevelt asked Kizer and Yantis
to remain in Washington for a conference the next day with Silcox,
Cammerer and Brant. Overly, Ben Thompson and Demaray of the Park
Service joined this group. Kizer and Yantis worked every possible delay
to keep the Bogachiel and Hoh additions out of the park. They insisted
that Roosevelt expected a thorough report on sustained-yield logging
which Silcox in turn insisted would take some time to prepare. They
then proposed that all but the west-side forest additions be made, with
an announcement that a study was in progress for these forests. Unable
to get agreement to anything they proposed, Kizer and Yantis accused
Brant in their report of asserting that Roosevelt was committed to
adding all of the disputed areas to the park, which simply was untrue.

When E. K. Burlew, acting as secretary in Ickes' absence, saw this
charge by Kizer and Yantis in their report, he called everyone who had
been at the meeting and established what had happened from notes
taken by Demaray and corroborated by others. He then sent a letter
to Roosevelt by special messenger. "I am writing you this letter," he said,
"to assure you that no one in the National Park Service was so indiscreet
as to attempt to commit you in advance on a question which you must
finally decide."[8] The final chicanery to keep the Bogachiel and Hoh areas
out of the park was headed off. It was a move by desperate men who
for all their efforts were going to receive no concessions at all and were
being forced to return to Washington State in defeat, as they saw it,
by the high-handed methods of the Roosevelt administration.

Irving Brant then wrote the formal Interior Department boundary
recommendation, laying to rest a half century of fighting to keep the
best of the Olympic Peninsula's remaining forests out of a national park.
Of the forested Bogachiel, Hoh, and Queets valleys, placed last by the
Park Service in its priorities, Roosevelt was told "that these three are
by far the most beautiful and most essential to the park of all the recommended additions."[9] The rejection of the Park Service's views was now
complete.

All that now remained to meet statutory obligations was the recommendation of Henry Wallace. On December 13, 1939, Silcox completed
the dictation of the Department of Agriculture's report and immediately suffered a massive heart attack. He signed the report on his
deathbed, signing away the cream of the Forest Service's coveted Olympic forests, an act to which he was vehemently opposed but completely
reconciled to. Even with all of the additions being proposed for preser-

vation, there would remain an opportunity to expand pulp mill operations by 30 percent, Silcox had said, without considering volume added
by new growth.[10]

Both Ickes and Brant were jarred by Silcox's death. Both had grown
to respect and even admire him. It was Silcox who had taken the brunt
of Brant's bitter mockery of the Forest Service and had been forced
time and again to defend the Forest Service against Brant's attacks. Brant
told Van Name, "Why do the best men have to die? He was worth all
the rest of the Forest Service staff put together."[11] Ickes said he "felt
a personal sense of loss . . . he had a fine and broad and understanding outlook on social and economic questions."[12]

Ickes and Brant met with Roosevelt on Christmas eve, 1939, and
reviewed everything, including pictures of the Bogachiel Valley. Roosevelt ordered a letter prepared for Governor Martin informing him that
all the forests he had contested would be added to the park. The task
of writing the letter to Governor Martin fell to Irving Brant. Roosevelt
told Ickes and Brant that he would sign the proclamation before the
first of the year.[13] Every acre that Brant recommended was going into
the park. No one in the governor's office ever knew that it was Brant
who had written Roosevelt's letter to the governor in justifying the
preservation of the trees of the Hoh and the Bogachiel that the governor so desperately wanted for the mills of the Olympic Peninsula.

The timber industry fought on to prevent the president from adding the west-side forests. Working through Thomas T. Aldwell of the
Port Angeles Chamber of Commerce, they presented the case for local
citizens' rights to "their" timber. As Clallam County auditor at the turn
of the century, Aldwell had been a key player in constructing the subterfuge that led to the private acquisition of three-fourths of the timber in the Olympic Forest Reserve. For more than four decades, he had
fought doggedly for the interests of the timber industry. Even though
he had never been their employee, the Crown Zellerbach Corporation
rewarded Aldwell with its fifteen-year service pin for his efforts. Aldwell was delighted: "It will always be considered as one of my most
valued possessions, as indicating your appreciation on behalf of your
company of any service I may have been able to perform," he told J. D.
Zellerbach. Aldwell went on to assure his continuing loyalty. "My own
and our community's best efforts," he pledged, "should and always will
be put forth to advance the best interests of the company."[14]

With Tom Aldwell pledging openly to lead Port Angeles in advancing
the interests of the Crown Zellerbach Corporation, Roosevelt proclaimed
on January 2, 1940, that 187,411 acres of the forests of the Bogachiel,
Calawah, Hoh, Queets, Quinault, and Elwha valleys were now safe from
logging. Trees that Crown Zellerbach had included in its future profit-

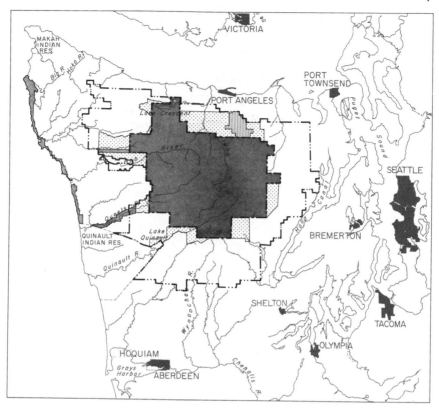

OLYMPIC NATIONAL PARK—PRESIDENTIAL ADDITIONS OF 1940, 1943, AND 1953
To insure the Olympic Park Bill would pass the Senate, Roosevelt and Brant concocted a plan to cut the park bill back to the Park Service's HR 4724 boundaries, with authorization for the President to add the rain forests by proclamation later.

making plans had slipped away from its reach for the moment. Remaining in the proclamation were 62,881 acres for adding later: the Queets Corridor, the Ocean Strip, and the nine-mile-long Bogachiel Valley exchange strip. The task that had begun fifty years earlier was now nearly complete. "The magnificent western valleys, with their gigantic trees and beautiful rain forest growth," Brant said, "had been made a perpetual treasureland for the whole American people."[15]

Roosevelt's proclamation appeared to be a stunning victory for the Park Service. Olympic was now the third largest in the whole park system, made so by the territory the Forest Service had most wanted to keep. In reality, the park as it now stood was a defeat for the Park Service. Ickes had rejected the Park Service again by accepting Irving

Brant's boundary. Defeat permeated the inner being of the Park Service at the same time that every environmental organization in the country basked in the triumph of victory.

Although Ickes never admitted to Brant, Edge, or Van Name that anything was wrong at the Park Service, he knew better. Everything wrong with the Park Service Ickes began to blame on Cammerer and his leadership, instead of seeing Cammerer as the embodiment of what was wrong throughout the whole structure of the Park Service. In March of 1939, Ickes wrote in his diary about a meeting with Cammerer: "As usual, he sat by my desk vigorously chewing gum in an open mouthed manner," Ickes said. "I asked him who was responsible for his bureau and when he acknowledged that he was, I told him the facts seem to prove what I charged him with some time ago, namely that he is in total ignorance of what goes on in the Park Service." Ickes concluded that the Park Service had "become too stereotyped and there are too many incompetent people down there . . . I will probably do considerable shaking up in the Park Service."[16]

By September, while Brant was bringing his Olympic National Park boundary recommendations to final conclusion, Ickes decided to fire Cammerer and replace him. Robert Moses of New York was the kind of strong forceful leadership Ickes thought the Park Service needed. However, Roosevelt did not like Moses, telling Ickes that "he would get things done. And in getting things done he would run over any body or any law. He pays absolutely no attention to the law. You would get awake in the middle of every night and wonder what Bob Moses was doing and how he was doing it."[17] Ickes continued to fret about the nature of the Park Service. "No doubt remains in my mind," he said, "that the Park Service needs new blood and a strong man."[18] Two days before the 1940 Olympic National Park proclamation, Ickes again went to Roosevelt and told him that he "still would like to have Bob Moses as head of the Park Service." Ickes reported, "In instant response to my suggestion the President said: 'Well I wouldn't.'" That ended the Moses effort. Ickes lamented that "a year of vigorous administration by someone other than a bureaucrat would do the parks a lot of good."[19]

Six months later, Cammerer resigned for reasons of health and Ickes moved him to a regional directorship. Ickes was diplomatic and Cammerer left with dignity. In accepting his resignation on June 19, 1940, Ickes announced:

> Arno Cammerer's services to the government for the past seven years as Director of the National Park Service have been outstanding. He has sacrificed his own health in his devotion to duty during this period of great expansion of our country's park facilities . . . It is with pleasure that

I announce that he will continue in the National Park Service in a responsible position.[20]

Within months, Cammerer would be dead of a heart attack. No one knew that he had been fired.

The adding of the Olympic rain forests in January of 1940, followed by the removal of Cammerer and the appointment of Newton B. Drury, was a turning point in the history of the Park Service. It would now face grave new stresses.

The timber industry had always controlled the Pacific Northwest. It made certain that the right state legislators got elected, that the Congressional delegations voted what the industry wanted and that administrative agencies like the Forest Service were allies. Before the park battle began, there was public discontent over the miles of burned and unrestored stump land that the timber industry had left as the forest heritage of the Pacific Northwest. After the park battle was over, discontent focused on concepts of the timber industry's greed. William Greeley's lumberman's organization took a public opinion poll to find out what Americans thought of lumbermen immediately after the park battle. What he found was no surprise. "[It] showed that Americans generally had a very low opinion of lumbermen," he said. "They were almost in the class of public enemy number one."[21]

Fifteen years before the Olympic National Park battle began, H. H. Chapman, writing to the forestry profession from his position at Yale, made a classic statement: "The short sighted policy of utter destruction of private forest property," he said, "like the placer gold mining of the west, may have to be terminated in the public interest. . . ." The "may" had been changed to "must" by the public dialogue that had later occurred in the Olympic National Park struggle. Chapman had also stated what now was accepted as fact about the attitudes of lumbermen. "Lumbermen . . . are not interested in what becomes of the land as *forest land* after cutting," he said. "Most of them will admit this and justify it. Many are interested in forestry, provided they themselves do not have to practice it."[22]

As the public at large had finally come to agree with Chapman's statements, the Forest Service reported that in one Olympic Peninsula county alone, the lands logged before 1920 were restocked better than those logged since. "Because of the large scale of several of the logging operations in the county during the last two decades," the report said, "clear cut areas of 20,000 acres or more in extent with practically no seed trees have resulted." The report charged that 63 percent of the areas logged were completely unstocked, 24 percent were poorly stocked and only on 13 percent were the cut-over lands adequately restocked.[23]

Here was corroboration from the Forest Service itself that the timber industry's liquidation logging policies were its mainstay, not the elusive sustained-yield policy.

The sustained-yield talk that the industry used to justify continued cutting was dismissed by Irving Clark. He said, "sustained yield is progressive destruction."[24] This became the battle cry of pro-park forces for which the timber industry had no answer. After the Olympic National Park battle, the industry would never again have the public on its side.

Thanks to the Emergency Conservation Committee, the public had been directly mobilized for the first time as a political force in public resource allocation. To curb that power was going to be essential to the timber industry's future. Just days before Roosevelt's 1940 Olympic National Park proclamation, Senator Key Pittman disclosed the industry's answer to public involvement. He introduced a bill requiring the consent of a state's legislature before any new national park or addition could be made.[25] New national parks would be much more difficult to achieve, if not impossible, if the bill had passed. It went nowhere.

Before the park battle began, the Forest Service was viewed as a governmental conservation organization, a viewpoint remaining from the massive publicity of the Pinchot-Graves era. When the marriage between the timber industry and Greeley's Forest Service was consummated in the 1920's, that image was still little changed in the public's mind. As fallout from the Olympic National Park battle, the Forest Service ended up affixed in the public mind as nothing more than a front for the timber industry, and it has never asserted a public position counter to this view.

The Forest Service began with an assumption that every economically merchantable tree on the Olympic Peninsula would eventually be cut, even those in the supposedly inviolate Mount Olympus National Monument. After it had lost that battle, it accepted the inviolability of the monument and pretended that it had never thought otherwise. Later, the Forest Service established "primitive areas," but only where the timber had no foreseeable economic value and under rules that allowed timber cutting when necessary. Finally, when it was already defeated, one group within the Forest Service supported Graves' and Marshall's concept of legislatively preserved wilderness, under Forest Service administration but removed from their control.

The most obvious reasons for the Forest Service loss in the Olympic Park battle were lack of support from the Secretary of Agriculture and the president, and the lack of an immediate need for the timber. But another reason was the Forest Service's inability to respond to the questions and accusations being made by the public. It never responded to the simple five-word declaration of Irving Clark—"sustained yield is progressive destruction." Irving Clark also charged, "The only timber the Forest Service wants to save is timber the loggers don't want."[26] Most of the Forest Service's economic-necessity arguments could be brushed aside with a commonly held public viewpoint: "Why destroy trees which have spent hundreds of years in growing and which can never be replaced, to extend a profit period which at best can last but a few years?"[27] The question, still one of vital public policy, was answered by the public via the Congressional vote for Olympic National Park. The Forest Service had been maimed early on by Gifford Pinchot, who had thoroughly indoctrinated its personnel into believing that

> The first principle of conservation is development, the use of the natural resources now existing on this continent for the benefit of the people who live here now.[28]

Clarence Buck, Regional Forester of Region Six, had so vigorously attempted to act out this principle administratively, that he ended up being removed from office by the president of the United States himself.

Consequently, at the end of the park battle, the Forest Service had no credibility, either in its own secretary's office or at the White House. Roosevelt told Ickes "that eight out of ten of the foresters were hand in glove with the lumber interests."[29] The Forest Service was forced by these circumstances to approve without comment any boundaries that Roosevelt and Ickes wanted.

Ironically, as the Forest Service's troubles increased, Chief Forester Silcox's stature rose. Silcox escaped attacks during the park campaign because he had engaged in an internal battle to move the Forest Service away from the marriage with the timber industry that Greeley had introduced. Silcox even wanted to stop contract logging and have it done by the Forest Service. He brought Robert Marshall in to reform its politically untenable relationships. But with Silcox's death, all reform was swept away and Robert Marshall had died of a heart attack a month before Silcox died. A few months later, Irving Brant told Schulz, " . . . since Silcox died the Forest Service has been rolling downhill very rapidly. The pro-lumbermen elements seem to be once more on top. . . ."[30]

The direct involvement of the public in resource allocation, which began with the Olympic campaign, was as troublesome for the Forest Service as it was for the timber industry. The timber industry's answer had been to force park advocates to fight a second legislative battle in state legislatures, where the timber industry had control. The Forest Service looked nostalgically back to the 1920's, when it controlled the national park agenda through the National Conference on Outdoor

Recreation which Greeley had foisted on a weak and willing Park Service. This coordinating committee had cut the public out of crucial park decisions. But now, with the Emergency Conservation Committee working hard to build citizen support for Kings Canyon and Redwood Mountain in California, it was clear that the Forest Service would again lose more territory and have more timber taken out of production.

Just six months after the Olympic National Park bill was signed, the Forest Service made its move to save its diminishing empire from future Olympic type confrontations. Henry Wallace proposed to President Roosevelt that he appoint four members to a committee, two from a list submitted by him, two from a list submitted by Ickes. The four would then choose a fifth to be chairman. This committee would examine a list of all the national forest areas that the Park Service believed should be made into parks and then get the Forest Service's response to that list. "From this investigation," Wallace told Roosevelt, "it would be possible to reach an impartial conclusion much more basically sound than any derived from present procedures."[31] The "present procedures" were public involvement and the support that preservation groups could generate. The Forest Service knew after the Olympic fight that it would lose again in a confrontation with the public, as indeed it did. Roosevelt would have nothing to do with such a committee.

World War II was now at hand. It would give the Park Service, the timber industry, and the Forest Service new opportunities.

14 WWII– GET THE TREES OUT, AND NOW!

The Olympic Peninsula National Park should do its part towards victory by giving up certain of its fine grade, old growth timber to the war effort. The principle of the draft should extend from our boys to our resources. Nothing is too sacred to do its share.[1]
W. B. GREELEY

You cannot place the value of beauty or recreation above the value of victory and no rules should stand in the way of cutting this timber for war purposes.[2]
REP. FRED NORMAN

The phrase "nothing being too sacred etc." is just a lot of hooey. These are the lumber barons of Washington — they practically rule this state. [Not] one of them has the welfare of our country at heart. . . . Mr. Norman is their representative and the victory of their pocketbooks is all that matters.[3]
ANDREA S. LANNING,
TO SECRETARY OF INTERIOR, JUNE 24, 1943

IRVING BRANT WAS EXACTLY THE MAN Ickes was looking for to take over direction of the Park Service: aggressive, committed to preservation, politically astute and able to entice both the public and Congress. But Brant knew his limitations; he was a writer, not an administrator.[4] He declined repeated offers.

To find a strong, dedicated preservationist, Ickes turned to Newton B. Drury, whose role in the Save the Redwoods League seemed ample

Secretary Ickes believed his appointment of Newton B. Drury in 1940 would take care of the Park Service's problems. He took the time to stand beside Drury as he took the oath from Interior's Chief Clerk, Floyd Dotson. Later, Ickes called Drury "a gutless pygmy" and worked until the day he died to discredit him. *National Park Service.*

evidence of his commitment to saving trees. Irving Brant delighted in Drury's appointment. "Anyway," he told Rosalie Edge, "he will be a real head. And Cam was just a friendly figurehead. Demaray has been the real head of the Park Service for years . . . while Ickes has been the policy maker."[5] Drury was a man who had been engaged in saving trees in California. Ickes presumed he would continue that focus in his role as director. The only ominous note to Drury's appointment was struck by William Schulz, who warned Brant that Drury has "very strong pro-Forest Service leanings" and would not champion the creation of Kings Canyon National Park, which clearly was centered on the saving of trees.[6]

Drury inherited forests under attack by the timber industry the moment he took office. The Hoquiam Chamber of Commerce had just adopted a resolution calling for immediate restoration of the Mount Olympus National Monument boundaries of 1930.[7] The Polson Logging Company was demanding to continue cutting on the lands in the Queets Valley being acquired for the Olympic Park corridor. William Greeley of the West Coast Lumberman's Association was trying under the guise of war preparation and patriotism to win back the trees that had been lost to the park in the just-concluded park battle. And the local Park Service administration was studying what park resources might be contributed to the emerging war effort. Drury's "pro-Forest Service leanings" would now be tested to the maximum. Could Drury cope with both the extreme pressures from the timber industry and the internal pressures from his own organization, as Harold Ickes had so far been able to do?

Ickes then committed a fundamental error in the Park Service's management of Olympic National Park. He left in place to administer the Olympic forests the same local Park Service crew that had been persistently working to keep the bitterly won rain forests out of the park. There was Owen Tomlinson, the senior Pacific Northwest park official, Superintendent Preston Macy, now an established resident of Port Angeles with close ties to its chamber of commerce, and Assistant Superintendent Fred Overly, a logging engineer with close ties to the timber industry.

The onset of World War II meant that the overbuilt lumber mills of Grays Harbor might be able to forestall imminent closure caused by the nearly total depletion of the old-growth timber supplies. Former Chief Forester, William Greeley, now head of the mill owners' organization, began orchestrating a direct campaign to keep the mills running.

When the park was created, the mills' demands for logs became mingled with the government's acquisition of the Queets Corridor. From the very start of this acquisition process, F. A. Polson of the Polson Logging Company created many problems during the Interior Department's attempt to acquire those lands. He wanted the timber on those lands. Ickes and the Interior Department staff tried desperately to get agreements for selective logging, but Polson was not interested. Polson wanted to trade logged-off land, which was only a tax burden to him, for timber on his own land and on lands already acquired by the Park Service for either the corridor or strip. Regional Director Frank Kittredge produced pictures of the logging that Polson had done in the Soleduck Valley. He told Drury, "I am afraid that they won't leave the Queets strip where they propose to take out the spruce, in much better condition if they were allowed to go ahead under the terms of the absurd agreement which they proposed."[8]

In the end, nearly all of the lands of the Polson and the Merrill and Ring logging companies' within the Queets Corridor were omitted from the Park Service's land acquisition process so as not to interfere with Polson's logging plans. Polson got everything he set out to get: 1,300 acres of the finest spruce forest destined for the park went to the mills in Grays Harbor.

Before long, the acquisition program for the primeval forests of the Queets Valley and the Ocean Strip had become completely distorted.

When the lands of the Queets Corridor settlers were acquired for the park in 1940, the settlers were for the most part satisfied with the settlement—market value and lifetime tenure if desired. Most left at once. The peninsula's chambers of commerce organized a protest by settlers in the Hoh and Clearwater Valleys. Here so-called Iron Man of the Hoh, John Huelsdonk, whose ranch was at least 15 miles from the Queets and not affected at all, stands beside one of the professionally prepared signs provided to the "Queets Settlers." *Bert Kellogg Collection.*

When the project began to run low on money, the Park Service operated on a presumption that no more money was available. Park Service negotiators began making stipulation agreements with the timber owners whereby land acquired for park purposes was acquired subject to logging. This put the Park Service directly in the logging business. The Park Service found that in their stipulation agreements they would have to forget about selective cutting of spruce—there simply was not enough of it for the logger to log profitably. Now the Park Service would be doing what had been the subject of national debate for the seven preceding years: clear-cutting the forest that it was supposed to save.

From the moment that Assistant Superintendent Fred Overly entered the Park Service, he had been identified as "logging engineer" to lend credibility to his timber reports, several of which he authored before 1940. After the 1940 addition of the west-side forests, he went to work producing his report, *Estimate of Timber Volumes in Olympic National Park.* Oddly, no one in the Park Service ever considered doing a study on preservation. The continuing focus on timber volumes and where commercial timber was located in the park reflected the Park Service's values. When Overly finished his study in October of 1940, while Greeley's "Get timber out of the park" campaign was building up steam, he was requested by Acting Director Hillory A. Tolson to prepare a detailed report on all the commercial species in Olympic National Park, Queets Corridor and Ocean Strip. Hearing that a detailed timber analysis was underway meant to Greeley that the Park Service was preparing to yield to his pressure and that by increasing the crescendo of the anti-park rhetoric, the yield would be much larger.

Jointly with Associate Forester Jack B. Dodd, Overly finished the Queets Corridor Timber Volume study in February of 1941.[9] Greeley could hardly have gotten more if the West Coast Lumberman's Association itself had done the study. Overly and Dodd concluded, "we do not believe it would be objectionable to permit commercial utilization of spruce, and for that matter, other timber" in the Queets Corridor.[10] Overly outlined a plan by which the Hoh and Bogachiel valleys could be systematically logged. "It would constitute an orderly retreat," he said, "and would contribute to the supply of spruce lumber." The Hoh Valley would go first. "The road is suitable for hauling logs, is already in existence at no cost to the logger and the spruce timber is adjacent to the road," Overly pointed out. "Logging operations could be started in this area with a minimum of delay."[11] Just sixteen months had gone by since the Interior Department recommendation to add the Bogachiel, Hoh, and Queets valleys to the park had gone to Roosevelt with Ickes' comment that "these three [areas] are by far the most beautiful and most essential to the park of all the recommended additions."[12]

Again, without Ickes' knowledge, the local Park Service administration was attempting to destroy what the preservationists had fought for more than fifty years to achieve. Drury understood the danger for him when he read Overly's report on May 7. He immediately directed that "when this report is copied, any implication that we have proposed, or assumed, cutting of spruce in the park should be eliminated."[13] The problem for Forester John Coffman, to whom he gave the order, was that the very existence of the report stood as stark testimony that the Park Service was fully prepared to yield. Many lumbermen probably knew much of what was in the report because they had supplied much of the data that went into it, and they associated daily with Overly at the Elks Club in Port Angeles.

With the Polson Logging Company clear-cutting the tracts the Park Service wanted on the Queets Corridor, the Park Service could maintain a stance of cooperation with the war effort. As Greeley ran from agency to agency and meeting to meeting to pressure for an unlimited flow of logs, two disquieting facts in Overly's report were ignored. One was that the Grays Harbor mill owners had far more capacity than was

OLYMPIC·NATIONAL·PARK

NOTICE

THIS ROAD WAS BUILT BY MAYR BROS. LOGGING CO.
TO REMOVE TIMBER PURCHASED FROM THE STATE.
SPORTSMEN USING THIS ROAD DO SO THROUGH THE CO-
OPERATIVE EFFORTS OF LOGGERS. LET US RESPECT
THEIR PERSONAL SAFETY, RIGHTS, PROPERTY,
MATERIALS, AND EQUIPMENT. WATCH FOR LOGGING
TRUCKS AND DRIVE CAREFULLY.
FLOYD DICKINSON - PARK RANGER

The Park Service subverted attempts to preserve trees in the Queets corridor by letting property owners cut the old-growth trees with 15- and 20-year cutting rights. The corridor became a vast Park-Service–supervised logging show. This sign was posted in 1948. *Carsten Lien.*

being used. This excess capacity had nothing to do with war but remained a driving force. Overly openly attributed the exclusion of the Polson lands from the acquisition program in the Queets Corridor to this fact alone.[14] The second was that all of the spruce production was going to France and Great Britain. The unanswered question was, where were the domestic consumers of spruce?

After the United States entered the war in December of 1941, the War Production Board staffed its lumber division with the very timber industry and Forest Service personnel who had fought the creation of the park throughout the 1930's. F. H. Brundage moved from Region Six of the Forest Service to assume the role of Western Log and Lumber Administrator, reporting to a whole cadre of timber industry executives who headed the lumber division itself. William Greeley now had a powerful governmental agency behind him. It took Greeley only a month after the United States entered the war to launch his governmental campaign against the park. "For immediate help," he told Donald Nelson, director of the War Production Board, "we wish to ask your assistance in obtaining a moderate supply of spruce logs from the Hoh, Queets and Quinault watersheds . . . recently placed in the Olympic

National Park." This he said was to meet the deficit in production of airplane grades of Sitka spruce.[15]

Greeley was creating the illusion of hardship and shortage. Spruce had never been on the critical list of materials and was not expected to be. Greeley told Superintendent Preston Macy that "the construction of American planes is turning more largely to wood; and airplane grades of both Douglas fir and Sitka spruce have become one of the most essential war materials."[16] Three days later, Owen Tomlinson had a long talk with Senator Wallgren, who had just completed a Senate subcommittee tour of all the large aircraft plants in the country. Wallgren reported to Tomlinson that there was no wood being used in any of these plants, "no Sitka spruce or Douglas fir, so far as he knows — and he has never heard a word about any shortage of wood holding up production of aircraft."[17] In reality, except for a few trainers, all American aircraft production was in aluminum by 1940. Greeley had set out again to create the subterfuge necessary to obtain profits for the mill owners.

Greeley's predecessor as chief of the Forest Service, Henry S. Graves, moved to stop him in his tracks. Graves occupied a unique position at that moment. It was he who had engineered the removal of the forests from the Mount Olympus National Monument to accommodate the timber industry in 1915 during World War I. Eighteen months before the park bill had passed in 1938, Graves had come out solidly for preserving all of the west-side forests in a national park. To the anguish of the Forest Service at the time, he had even attacked the premises on which the Forest Service was operating its logging program in the Olympics. It was Graves' men in the Forest Service who had derisively labeled as "Greelyism" the marriage of the Forest Service to the timber industry in the 1920's. Graves saw a repeat of the same kind of campaign that the industry had mounted in World War I, to which he had yielded.

Graves wrote directly to Drury giving him, he hoped, the tools that he needed to dismiss claims that the spruce in Olympic National Park was needed. He cited the data from the Forest Service's latest studies, "the results of a very careful forest survey of the region," he said. The total volume of large Sitka spruce in Olympic National Park represented only one percent of what was then available in Washington and Oregon. Another report cited the volume available in the Tongass Forest of Alaska. "From the foregoing it is clear that there is no real necessity to open the Mount Olympus National Park to cutting timber," he told Drury. "I am opposed to any such movement advanced under the guise of national defense."[18] The single most powerful tool that Drury was given to defend Olympic National Park—irrefutable data from the Forest Service's own published reports—was ignored by Drury and the Park Service. No one in the Park Service, including Drury, mentioned the existence of Graves' data as the fight progressed.

The pressure inside the Park Service to begin logging Olympic National Park continually fed the external pressures. Each Park Service timber report, available to the whole logging community, not only gave credibility to the shortage myth but also transmitted the readiness of the Park Service to yield if only a little more pressure were applied. The only question that remained inside the Park Service by November of 1942 was where in Olympic National Park the logging would begin first. That was resolved by Assistant Forester Reino Sarlin's report, *The Availability of Vital Woods which can be Contributed to War Needs by the National Park Service Within the Olympic Peninsula*. The title itself suggests the eagerness with which the Park Service was moving ahead to contribute its resources. But the content left no doubt. Sarlin, in putting the finishing touches to the plan, said:

> The one area within the Park which could best be sacrificed, is the Bogachiel section. Here is contained nothing that cannot better be emulated in some other Park area. Overly, in his report, has assigned a high priority for logging within this area, second only to the North Fork of the Quinault. With this thought most officials have agreed.[19]
>
> The Hoh River area will presumably furnish the first spruce to be taken from inside the park proper. This seems likely because of its accessibility, and because of the high grades that are coming out of the adjacent State ownerships.[20]

Sarlin also disclosed in his report that Regional Director Tomlinson, Superintendent Macy and Regional Forester Sanford had all agreed to try to get the War Production Board to allocate money for the construction of a road up the Bogachiel Valley, "said road to tap not only park timber but that timber within the private corridor as well."[21] The "private corridor" timber by this time had been acquired by the Forest Service and was in public ownership awaiting addition to the park.

Ickes didn't know the Park Service had prepared for the immediate logging of his beloved rain forests. The information he got from the Park Service, however, convinced him of the necessity to log the Queets Corridor. On December 21, 1942, he asked for presidential authorization to sell spruce and Douglas fir from the primeval forests of the Queets. On Christmas Eve, Roosevelt approved it and by December 30, the logging process was underway. It was a triumph for Greeley.

Rosalie Edge received the Park Service press release about the Queets Corridor logging decision with anger. "Now the most glorious of its trees are to be cut, leaving a mere screen to preserve the beauty of the proposed parkway through the corridor—'so far as possible.' So far as possible! It is not possible." She had watched the Park Service yield to the demands of the timber industry many times in the park boundary battle. Relying on nothing but instinct, she informed her pamphlet-reading public, "We remember how stubbornly the lumber interests fought against saving any part of the Olympic Forest. We believe that they have now with more avarice than patriotism, taken advantage of the opportunity offered by war to bring undue pressure on the Park Service."[22]

Greeley scheduled a meeting with Drury on January 18, 1943, in the Chicago office where the Park Service had been moved for the duration of the war. He told Drury that the time had come for the Park Service to begin contributing to the war. He laid out the statistics on demand versus availability which actually related to the overcapacity of the Grays Harbor mills and not to the war. In a carefully coordinated move two days later, F. H. Brundage, now of the War Production Board, reported to Ickes: "I recommend that the National Park Service make the high quality Douglas fir timber on the designated Hoh River area and Bogachiel River within the boundaries of the Olympic National Park available for cutting at an early date. . . ."[23] He must have had a copy of Sarlin's Park Service report on the availability of park timber in hand.

Drury wrote to Ickes the following day: "It is recommended that if called upon by the War Production Board to do so, you approve the logging of 15 million feet of selected spruce in the 1940 Hoh Extension of Olympic National Park." To insure the maximum profit to the logger involved, he recommended "that in view of the doubtful value of the lands for park purposes after selective logging the logger be able to utilize all species in accordance with the logging practices . . . on nearby lands of similar character." This would, if accepted, guarantee utter devastation in clear-cuts. As if to convince Ickes that Greeley was a legitimate source for his recommendation, he told Ickes, "I am convinced that Col. Greeley's judgment in this matter is dispassionate and based upon as complete a knowledge of the facts of a complicated situation as it is possible to obtain; and that he shares our regret that the needs of war compel the invasion of the Olympic National Park by logging."[24]

Drury hand-carried the memo to Washington, D.C., where he got a taste of Ickes' attitudes, lost his nerve, and ordered the memo be retained in the files unsigned for use later on. Strangely, just before Drury had prepared his memo requesting that Ickes start the logging of the park proper, the University of Washington had offered 78 million board feet for sale on its Queets Corridor tracts and had received no bids at all.[25] Drury proceeded ahead with the proposed logging of the park despite the proven lack of immediate demand. Ironically, at the very moment of Drury's memo, the first raft of spruce arrived from Alaska, another factor which did not deter him at all.[26] The timber industry position began to become unhinged. Congressman Fred Norman of Grays Harbor admitted that the mills wanted Douglas fir, not spruce.[27] Greeley still pressed on, even knowing that spruce had never been put on the critical materials list by the War Production Board.

Desperate to head off the invasion of the park, Irving Brant gave Ickes four strategy moves. Brant suggested that consideration be given to the effect of the Canadian embargo on the export of logs to the United States. By then, it was common knowledge that the spruce was going to Great Britain, so the Canadian embargo seemed uncalled for. Ickes told Roosevelt "that it would be inadvisable to initiate action which would authorize the cutting of timber in the Olympic National Park until this Canadian embargo question is disposed of or until every other source of aircraft timber supply has been exhausted."[28] With Roosevelt's support of Brant's suggestion, Ickes now could keep the War Production Board and the timber industry at bay.

With Roosevelt, Ickes, Brant and Irving Clark now desperately working against having the Park Service yield timber from the park, the Park Service itself was attempting to do that very thing. Nearly a year earlier, Greeley had written to F. W. Mathias of the Hoquiam Chamber of Commerce, "I think Mr. Drury believes that the boundary for the Olympic National Park was placed too far to the west. It is my impression that he would be willing to restudy this Park boundary and to concur in recommendations to Congress for eliminating a portion of the westside areas. . . ."[29] It was widely known around Port Angeles that the Park Service wanted the Bogachiel Valley out of the park. The Port Angeles Chamber of Commerce decided to take a run at getting it out, demanding that everything west of the line between Ranges Nine and Ten be eliminated. When Washington Congressman Henry Jackson asked local political activist Harry Henson for a report on the situation from Port Angeles, Henson confirmed that "Park officials would not object strenuously to the removal of park lands west of the line between ranges 10 and 11," on the Bogachiel and Hoh. This was the exact position the Park Service had taken to get the Bogachiel Valley out of the park by amending HR 7086 seven years earlier.[30]

Greeley succeeded in getting resolutions calling for the logging of Olympic National Park from virtually every chamber of commerce in western Washington. When the Seattle Chamber of Commerce de-

SO THAT ALL MAY KNOW-

The Serious Situation Now Facing Port Angeles War Industry and Postwar Employment

☆ ☆ ☆

WHAT OTHERS THINK

Departments of government and individuals of authority having been apprised of the critical nature of this shortage of timber are unanimous in their desire to assist. Foremost among our supporters has been Governor Arthur B. Langlie. Here are some comments from letters and editorials.

From T. S. Goodyear, State of Washington Department of Conservation and Development:

"The attitude of this department has not changed since the original extension of the Park, at which time we fought desperately to have some of the over-ripe merchantable timber areas eliminated."

From Lyle F. Watts, Chief, United States Forest Service, Washington, D. C.:

"This response in no sense minimizes the great importance of the problems we are facing in supplying our requirements of forest products for war purposes, nor the importance of maintaining and improving the economy of Port Angeles. We shall continue to do all we can toward helping to solve these problems."

From George F. Yantis, National Resources Planning Board:

"Thanks for your letter of the 5th. My interest and views in this matter are in accordance with yours . . . If opportunity presents itself, I shall do what I can. I will also take the matter up with Mr. Delano, chairman, who, I think, shares the views I have."

From H. E. Holman, Chief, Lumber Production Section, War Production Board, Washington, D. C.

". . . Operators depending upon Peninsula timber are facing something of a problem and during the post war days will experience additional difficulties unless some practical plan can be developed and applied in the very near future . . . We will bring your request to the attention of the various agencies here . . . who have been looking into this problem . . ."

EDITORIALS

(In Part)

Seattle Post Intelligencer—"Timber Problems on the Peninsula."

". . . Recently, under the impetus of war demands, heightened by the fact that Northwest timber is again being used in large quantities for airplanes, it has developed that the timber resources immediately available to Port Angeles mills are insufficient to maintain production. The Port Angeles Chamber of Commerce accordingly instituted a movement for the return to the United States forest service of timbered areas now included within the park boundaries, containing about three billion feet of merchantable timber, to be handled by the forest service on a sustained yield basis, so that mills of the area would be able to meet war demands and maintain production and employment in the post war period.

"This appeals to us as a perfectly reasonable request, in view of the changed conditions, and especially in view of the broad-minded attitude previously displayed by the Port Angeles chamber in connection with the whole park controversy.

"The immediate object should be to enable Port Angeles mills to get the timber they need to meet war requirements."

Seattle Times—"None to See Trees' Beauty if Fringed by Ghost Towns."

"In a time when national demands, based on unquestionable national needs, is for more and more production of essentials, the major industry of a great section of the State of Washington is arbitrarily bound by limitations. Its production at best is sporadic; for the most part it can barely mark time. We allude to the combined lumbering, plywood and pulp industry of the Olympic Peninsula. . . .

"The timbered resources of the Olympic Peninsula have been made untouchable by man. Not even the oldest and totteriest tree may be taken. The industries of the Peninsula falter and languish. Every community suffers accordingly.

"There is plenty of room on the peninsula for a good-sized park. There is over-abundant timber for industrial use; and future abundance to be made certain by wise administration."

Seattle Star—"Correct This Error"

"We're writing this one to the Washington delegation in congress, all eight members of it. The northwest sector of the state you represent is in trouble; trouble brought on by our government itself. As you well know, a huge hunk of the Olympic Peninsula was taken from the tax rolls, put into the Olympic National Park. Far more acreage than was necessary went into that tract. That peninsula will be denuded of industry unless there is a change pretty soon. Lumber mill after lumber mill will pack up and go elsewhere. Nearly a million acres are now included in the park. Not more than 450,000 are necessary to the maintaining of the finest such park in the land. The rest, gentlemen, should be returned to the U. S. Forest Service, to be turned into sustained yield logging."

Every home owner and wage earner in this vicinity is affected by the fact that because of the large timber area which is at present locked within the boundaries of the Olympic National Park, there is not sufficient timber available to supply the wood industries of the peninsula. These industries are the lifeblood of our community.

Within the 855,000 acres of the Park, (including the 20,000 acres of the Morse Creek Watershed) and the Queets and Ocean Beach Corridors which are to be added (making the Park almost 900,000 acres in size) there are about 21 billion feet of timber

Investigation reveals that there is imminent danger to our industrial existence. The Rayonier Mill is able to operate only 20% of their fir capacity; The Crescent Logging Co. Mill at Carlsborg has a timber supply for not to exceed two years; The Peninsula Plywood Mill has permanently closed down one shift, has depended greatly on timber from Oregon and has already acquired a millsite there; Olympic Shipbuilders are hampered—all because of shortage of fir timber.

In Full accord with the preservation of the natural beauty of the Park but cognizant of the interests of our fellow citizens whose very existence depends on timber, the Port Angeles Chamber of Commerce has passed the following resolution and sent it to the proper authorities.

Resolutions: **By Port Angeles Chamber of Commerce, April 12, 1943.**

WHEREAS, Congress authorized the President of the United States to increase the Olympic National Park to 898,292 acres, and

WHEREAS, the original request of the local sponsors of the Park and the representatives of the Park Service was for a Park taking in approximately 400,000 acres, including the Olympic National Monument, with its boundaries squared up, and

WHEREAS, the Olympic National Park contains over 17 billion feet of timber including on the west side large quantities of Fir, Spruce and Hemlock timber vitally needed for our war industries, and

WHEREAS, the area west of the boundary line between Ranges nine (9) and ten (10) west of Willamette Meridian was outside of the originally contemplated Park boundaries and contains a comparatively small amount of high mountainous or scenic country,

NOW THEREFORE BE IT RESOLVED by the Port Angeles Chamber of Commerce that the President of the United States be requested to eliminate from the Olympic National Park area and restore to the United States Forest Service, to be logged on their **sustained yield plan** now in effect, the area west of the boundary line between Ranger nine (9) and ten (10) west of Willamette Meridian and north of the Township line between Township 27 north and Township 26 north,

(Signed)
Thos. T. Aldwell, Chairman Industrial Committee, Port Angeles Chamber of Commerce.

—★—

After a full and careful investigation of the problem, the Seattle Chamber of Commerce, before a full committee of the State Development League and Board of Trustees, adopted the following:

Resolution re controlled logging in areas now in Olympic National Park, approved by the Board of Trustees of the Seattle Chamber of Commerce, June 1, 1943.

The Board of Trustees of the Seattle Chamber of Commerce urges members of the Washington delegation in Congress to seek the passage of an Act which will allow the cutting of mature timber through transfer to the Olympic National Forest of timbered areas not essential for Park purposes, but now needed for war uses and which will be urgently needed in post-war reconstruction, and still preserve the scenic beauty and recreational and museum features of the Olympic National Park for generations to come.

Processors of forest products on Puget Sound and Grays Harbor have been forced to draw on timber supplies from as far south as Roseburg, Oregon, to keep their mills running to fulfill war orders. Many veneer plants have been forced to reduce production because of a shortage of veneer logs, and at least one plant has bought a site in another state and has definitely planned to change its location to a point where suitable timber can be obtained unless some timber is made available locally. In order to supply war needs, the United States Forest Service is putting timber on the market in the Puget Sound area at a rate far in excess of the sustained yield capacity on the more accessible units of the national forests.

An Olympic National Park proposal was made in 1934 by the National Park Service. This preliminary report was made to the Director of the National Parks on October 5, 1934 with a recommendation of an addition of about 110,000 acres to the Mt. Olympus National Monument. Later the Washington State Planning Council made a study and recommended that an area of about 110,000 acres be added to the Mt. Olympus National Monument, making a total of roughly 450,000 acres, with an estimated stand of old-growth merchantable timber of approximately five billion board feet. Since that time the area of the Park has been expanded to about one million acres, **including the corridors.** The stand of timber in the Park area has been estimated at 21 billion feet.

With the many thousands of acres of typical Western Washington forests already preserved in Rainier National Park and other public reservations, the preservation of five billion feet of additional timber on 450,000 acres in the Olympic National Park would seem to be ample for national park purposes, in view of the fact that timber is now preserved along scenic highways and recreational areas in the National Forests.

Within the present boundaries of the Olympic National Park is to be found the highest quality timber in the United States. It is urgently needed for construction of airplanes and in many other war uses. Cutting on the west slope of the Olympics could be carried on without impairing the scenic or recreational values because of the luxuriant growth which prevents diversion of sightseers from the regular roads or trails.

Large old-growth spruce, so valuable in airplane construction, is found along the river bottoms. Most of the timber on the western slope of the Olympic Mountains is mature or overmature and is decaying faster than it is growing. Unless these trees are harvested during the next few decades there will be a great and needless economic loss of the nation's finest timber resources.

—★—

An important phase of this situation is, the National Forest Service gives to the adjacent counties on the Peninsula 25% of the proceeds of all timber sales. On 4 billion feet alone at $5.00 per thousand feet this amounts to $5,000,000 for maintenance by counties of roads and schools.

—★—

NOTE: The "Sustained Yield Plan" mentioned in the Resolutions has been in operation in Sweden for centuries and successfully maintains the necessary growth of forests, perpetually.

Proof of the need is indicated by the following facts: THE U. S. FOREST SERVICE REPORT SHOWS THAT IN CLALLAM COUNTY THE ANNUAL GROWTH OF ALL FIR TIMBER ON PRIVATE, STATE, COUNTY, INDIAN AND NATIONAL FOREST LAND IS ONLY 44,405,000 FEET PER YEAR. PORT ANGELES MILLS ALONE USE OVER 126,000,000 FEET ANNUALLY.

Published for the Information of all by

THE PORT ANGELES CHAMBER OF COMMERCE

In 1943, Rayonier, Crown Zellerbach, and other Port Angeles mill operators increased their attacks on the park, demanding the heavy rain forests of the Bogachiel, Calawah, Hoh and Soleduck, including Fairholm Hill, be made available to them. *Port Angeles Evening News, June 30, 1943.*

manded the logging of the park, every Seattle newspaper agreed. The *Seattle Times* told its readers, "Trees needed to fill war orders are decaying faster than they are growing in the Olympic National Park, and great loss will result unless they are harvested. . . ."[31] The *Seattle Post-Intelligencer* wanted the Port Angeles mills to have what they wanted: "Getting the timber that Port Angeles mills ask right now, for the war effort, ought to be the objective," it said.[32] Now Drury picked up the pace of his pressure to get Ickes to yield.

On June 21, 1943, Drury sent a memorandum to Ickes similar to the one he had tried six months earlier. This time, however, his views completely reflected Greeley's. Drury recommended "that the Department show its willingness to sacrifice in 1943, as shown to be needed, the forest area contained in the 1940 western additions to Olympic National Park totalling 77,045 acres with a stand of 246,867,000 feet of Sitka spruce."[33] Here was the director of the Park Service, personally selected by Harold Ickes, working actively for the timber industry. Ickes sent the memo back to Drury, "not approved."

A week and a half later, on July 3, Drury tried again, this time through Assistant Secretary Oscar Chapman, recommending that only the Hoh and Bogachiel valleys be logged. When Drury's memo was passed on to Ickes with Chapman's recommendation for approval, Ickes wrote back, "I still do not think that we ought to be called upon to supply Sitka spruce from our lands reserved for park or recreational purposes while there is plenty of spruce in British Columbia."[34]

Ickes was doggedly using his position as secretary to keep the timber-industry-controlled War Production Board from being the vehicle used to get Olympic timber. Just after Ickes sent another "not approved" back to Chapman and Drury, he sent a letter to Donald Nelson, chairman of the War Production Board, outlining seven steps that could be taken immediately to alleviate the shortage of spruce. "I urge that the War Production Board," he said, "give immediate consideration to the following alternatives, which I believe should be exhausted before the forests of Olympic National Park are cut."[35] Now Ickes could ask for evidence that each of the seven steps had been exhausted before yielding further.

On the day Ickes sent his memo to Nelson, Congressman Henry Jackson opened hearings in Seattle on the lumber shortage problem. The timber industry ran the show. Almost every witness called for the logging of the park. The Washington State Planning Council called not only for the elimination of the forests which had been added to the park but also presented a map of their original recommendation as the proper boundary—a recommendation that even eliminated a part of the original Mount Olympus National Monument, everything south of Anderson Pass. The hearings brought into the open the fact that there was no shortage of timber. The shortage was of manpower to get available timber to the mills, caused in turn by low pay and the draft. Even Greeley's own testimony contradicted what he had argued about timber shortage. He said that in Oregon and Washington, 1,064 mills were in operation and that production was off only 15 percent.[36]

PROPOSED OLYMPIC NATIONAL PARK ADDITIONS

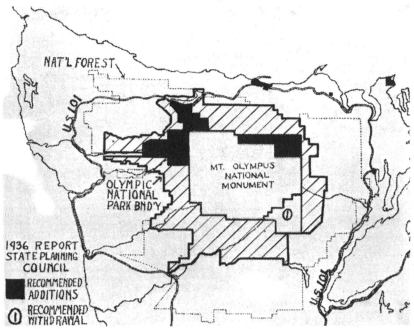

RENEWING its protest against the enlarged boundaries of Olympic National Park, the Washington State Planning Council submitted the above picture to the Small Business sub-committee of the House of Representatives as its recommendation of a means of securing additional timber to supply the nation's war-caused lumber diet and, at the same time, retain needed recreational facilities. The shaded portion of the above picture shows the boundaries of the park as set by Congress in 1938. Solid black are the portions which the Planning Council recommendation would add to the original Mount Olympus National Monument.

Speaking for the timber industry and the Seattle Chamber of Commerce in 1943, C.S. Cowan said, "the time has come to throw aside subterfuge and come out with the real issue, which is to put those park boundaries where they belong . . .", i.e., the industry proposed boundaries of 1936. The "additions" are falsely labeled; the park would have been decimated. *Map and caption from Daily Olympian, July 20, 1943.*

The newspapers covered the hearings routinely. The shortage of manpower shared the spotlight with logging the park. But Congressman Jackson's preparation for the hearings had disclosed the real reason for the increased pressure to log the park: the end of the war was in sight. Instead of this alleviating pressure on the park, the timber industry increased the pressure. The high wartime corporate taxes on profits had been the driving force behind the park logging thrust. Here is how it was explained to Congressman Jackson:

> They [timber interests] are holding large acreages bought at low stump-
> age prices which if logged would show considerable profit on which they
> would be taxable during a period of high tax structure. On the other
> hand, if they can now purchase the timber in question at a higher figure
> and log the same, they would naturally not show as high a profit in the
> prevailing market and would not be subject to such a relatively high tax.
> They are concerned with retaining their low priced stumpage areas until
> a time when the tax structure would not be detrimental to other earnings.[37]

This information, gathered from the streets of Port Angeles by Postmaster Emerson Lawrence, was in the hands of Congressman Jackson
before the hearings but it never surfaced. This war-tax situation had
driven the industry's efforts from the very beginning and the old-growth
forests of the Queets, acquired to be preserved for the park, had been
sent to the Grays Harbor mills to maximize logger profits.

Two weeks from the time Ickes had sent his memo challenging chairman Donald Nelson of the WPB with his seven alternatives to logging
the park, the lumber division of the WPB had prepared an answer for
Ickes. Timber-industry executives ran the lumber division of the WPB.
They were undoubtedly aware of the underlying tax situation. They
moved Nelson into a direct confrontation with Ickes, even in the face
of the just-concluded hearings that established that there was no timber shortage. "The War Production Board sees no possibility of meeting future aircraft spruce lumber requirements," Nelson told Ickes,
"without drawing upon some of the resources of the Olympic National
Park." He then laid out the method by which the park would be logged:
transfer the forest lands to the Reconstruction Finance Corporation.
This required that spruce and Douglas fir be declared a critical material, which had never been done. The WPB's lumber division had an
easy solution to this problem. "On receipt of your agreement with this
program," they had Nelson tell Ickes, "I am prepared to ask the President to define Sitka spruce and Douglas fir as critical and strategic
materials."[38]

Before Ickes got a chance to react, the whole of pro-logging effort
exploded in disarray. On September 3, Drew Pearson's syndicated
"Washington Merry-go-round" column dropped a bomb that ended the
battle:

> However, here is one fact which Ickes so far has not mentioned to Don
> Nelson. Nelson may not know it, but a vigorous battle has raged inside
> his own Lumber Division regarding the use of Sitka spruce for mosquito
> bombers. Charges have been made that this played into the hands of one
> big company—Weyerhaeuser.

Weyerhaeuser is the biggest lumber company on the West Coast and dominates the supply of Sitka spruce. Strangely enough a former employee of Weyerhaeuser, J. Philip Boyd, is now head of Donald Nelson's WPB Lumber Division.

When the question came up of making mosquito bombers out of Sitka spruce, several lumber advisors inside the WPB, knowing it was not plentiful, recommended that Southern yellow poplar was as good or better. The scheduling unit at Dayton, Ohio, classified yellow poplar as equal to Sitka spruce for 'aero specifications,' while W. D. Connor, former acting chief of WPB's Lumber Division also recommended yellow poplar.

This brought an immediate protest from Boyd, whose former company, Weyerhaeuser, controls most of the rival lumber to yellow poplar. Boyd, then chairman of the lumber advisory committee, promptly wrote an opinion to the Army-Navy Munitions Board protesting the use of any wood except Sitka spruce. His opinion was labeled by one WPB lumber expert, Nathaniel Dykc, as 'misleading, biased and unfair.'

. . . And Boyd, who demanded that mosquito bombers be made of the wood which his old company largely controls, is now advising D. Nelson in his demands on Secretary Ickes that the Olympic National Park be opened . . . for more Sitka spruce.[39]

Greeley's plans went up in smoke with Pearson's disclosure. The fact that Canada was getting 40 percent recovery of airplane stock from each log, compared to 10 percent recovery in the United States, suggested to many that the WPB was deliberately attempting to create a shortage by setting specifications that created this illusion. This especially seemed true when the British happily accepted the Canadian spruce lumber for the mosquito bombers and used it as freely as the American lumber without reference to the specification difference. Ten percent recovery meant that only 10 percent of each log was actually used in the manufacture of airplane lumber.

While Ickes was working to break Canada's embargo on logs to the U.S., the timber industry supported it, thereby keeping prices high and pressure on the park. J. H. Bloedel, chairman of the Bloedel Donovan Lumber Company, in defending Canada's embargo while trying to get Olympic National Park timber, said "she [Canada] would only be robbing her own supply should she permit export of [Sitka spruce and Douglas fir]."[40]

Eleven days after Pearson's column appeared, Ickes answered Nelson in a six-page memorandum. Sensing that the wound to Nelson's position on Olympic logging was mortal, Ickes said, "Conservation groups throughout the nation are already making protest against your

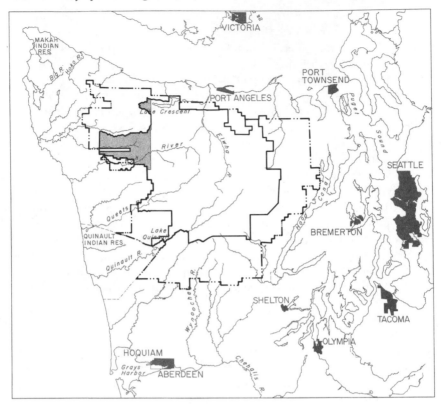

PORT ANGELES CHAMBER OF COMMERCE PROPOSED ELIMINATION 1943

In 1943, the Port Angeles mill operators demanded that the Park Service give up timber for logging on Fairholm Hill, and in the Soleduck, Bogachiel, Calawah and Hoh Valleys (the shaded areas of the map). The Park Service responded by forming a park boundary study committee, which it hid from the environmental groups that had fought the long political battle to preserve the park's forests.

proposal, and we owe it to them to show that we have explored all other possibilities before we undo, even in part, that splendid conservation accomplishment." He then proposed six more pages of hurdles for Nelson to overcome before he would consider logging the park.[41]

The Drew Pearson column and the other disclosures about the timber industry had left Greeley and his "log the park" program high and dry. On September 23, 1943, Nelson informed Ickes, "Spruce production for the immediate future is not dependent on the availability of stands in the Olympic National Park."[42] Not even two months had gone by since he had produced statistics proving the dire necessity for logging

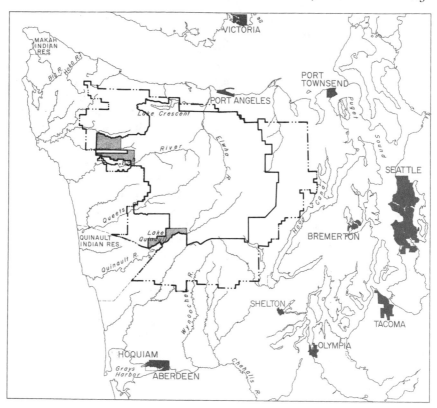

NATIONAL PARK SERVICE FOREST ELIMINATION PROPOSAL 1943
Olympic Park Superintendent Preston Macy was chairman of an internal Park Service
committee that decided that the Port Angeles mill owners should get most of what they
were demanding and that over 15,000 acres of the Quinault should be removed from
the park as well. The Quinault trees would have served the mills of Grays Harbor.

the park immediately. Greeley's Sitka spruce caper was over. There was
so little need for spruce that the Alaskan spruce program was cancelled
three months later.

Ickes had stood alone against the Park Service. He stood alone against
the timber industry and the War Production Board which it controlled.
Finally, he had to stand alone against his own assistant secretary, who
had been won over to the necessity for logging the park. The saving
of the Olympic forests belongs to Ickes alone.

When the spruce battle was over, Drury asked for a boundary study.
Every Olympic boundary recommendation made by the Park Service
for nearly ten years had been rejected. The boundaries given the Park

Service to administer were now under constant timber industry attack, signifying to them that they were correct in their judgment to leave the rain forests out. At the same time, it never occurred to the Park Service that it was causing the ongoing attacks by the way it was administering the park. Superintendent Preston Macy, designated to take charge of the study, was told by the Park Service's Washington office what his task was to be: "Regardless of the spruce demand," he was told, "the Service may decide to effect certain adjustments so as to mold the boundaries nearer to our hearts desire. . . ."[43]

Macy delivered the Park Service's "hearts desire" boundary recommendation a month later, the same day that Nelson threw in the WPB's towel in its fight with Ickes. The Park Service's boundary recommendations would divest what conservationists had worked for more than half a century to protect, a real sample of old-growth Pacific Northwest forest. The Bogachiel, the Hoh, and the Quinault valleys had been put up for grabs. Macy told Drury, "we feel the 'elimination boundary' which we are suggesting will be an actual improvement, as to administration and protection, over the present park boundaries. . . ."[44]

Drury's Park Service may have lost to Ickes in its battle to log the park but Ickes now had another smoldering bomb under his nose, placed there by a director personally chosen by him for what he believed to be his preservationist instincts. The Park Service recommendation was an enticement to the timber industry. To make certain that the timber industry would know what they were going to receive, the Park Service even calculated the millions of board feet of each species in each of the three units recommended for elimination.

It had taken the timber industry only three and a half years to get to this first important step on the way towards what had always been the industry's goal—Olympic's trees headed for the mills. The timber industry now had a recommendation from the Park Service itself that affirmed what the Forest Service and the timber industry had said all along—that the park's west-side forests were simply not worthy of preservation.

A month after getting Macy's recommendations and ignoring the fact that he had repeatedly asked Ickes to log the park, Drury told Brant in a paroxysm of hypocrisy and double dealing:

> Since you have understood and supported our position opposing the logging of Sitka spruce within the Olympic National Park for war aircraft needs . . . I am glad to be able to tell you that the War Production Board . . . has indicated that such logging is not at this time necessary. . . . Your great interest in the preservation of the park against inroads through logging is most sincerely appreciated.[45]

Because of the war effort, Irving Brant and his preservationist colleagues in the ECC were oblivious to the fact that even the Park Service was now working at dooming to the logger's axe the very trees that preservationists had fought for and won after so many decades of effort. And for no better stated reason than "to mold the boundaries nearer to our heart's desire."

15 THE PARK SERVICE GOES DOWN IN FLAMES

We have a moral right to have a portion of this area transferred back to the United States Forest Service where it can be logged.[1]

THOMAS T. ALDWELL,
PORT ANGELES CHAMBER OF COMMERCE

If the Forest Service succeeds in getting back into its murderous clutches some of the areas it has been forced to disgorge in the past, the people can expect to see . . . woodmen cut down the trees that ought to be a heritage for our children.[2]

HAROLD L. ICKES

AFTER THE 1943 BOUNDARY STUDY had been completed, everyone in Port Angeles knew that the Park Service wanted to get rid of a major part of the park's west-side forests. Its "heart's desire" recommendations for a boundary reduction would accomplish this.

When nothing resulted from the Park Service's forest elimination recommendation throughout 1943 and 1944, a copy of it was given to Harry Henson, probably by Superintendent Macy, in the spring of 1945. Harry Henson was a well-known Port Angeles resident then serving as Senator Hugh Mitchell's secretary. Henson was keenly aware of local pressure to log the park. Instantly, the Park Service's elimination proposals moved to the desk of Congressman Henry Jackson. He called

Drury to his office and demanded "a more logical boundary and which would at the same time make some additional stumpage available for the sawmills and pulp mills of the Olympic peninsula."[3] When Drury reported this meeting to Ickes, he hid from Ickes the Park Service's prior involvement, referring only to "the boundaries suggested by Congressman Jackson," as if they had originated with Jackson and not the Park Service. When Regional Director Tomlinson heard of Jackson's move, he worried about Mrs. Edge's reaction. "We all realize some boundary adjustments should be made," he told Macy, "but . . . in view of the well known attitude of Mrs. Edge and her committee towards Bogachiel and other areas of the western part of the Park,"[4] adjustments would be difficult.

Henry Jackson, however, was not put off by Park Service hesitancy. "I feel that certain features of the Western boundaries cannot be justified either from a park standpoint or from an economic standpoint," Jackson told Drury, "and the sooner we obtain a rectification of this situation, the better. . . ."[5] Jackson sent a copy of his letter to Ickes. Ickes responded, absolutely at variance with every move he had ever made with Drury. He told Jackson, "I am asking Mr. Drury to have a complete study made of the western boundary of Olympic National Park and to submit a report and his recommendations to me for consideration as soon as practicable."[6] The Park Service now had what seemed to be secretarial sanction to move ahead. Drury ordered a review of the 1943 boundary recommendations and charged Regional Director Tomlinson with getting all the Park Service troops lined up behind the forest eliminations. " . . . it is essential," he said, "that we all be in agreement with the stand to be taken."[7]

As Jackson continued his pressures on the Park Service, Drury told him what the elimination would mean to the mills of the Olympic Peninsula. Using the latest figures available, the Park Service calculated that the areas Jackson wanted eliminated "would supply the sawmills for slightly less than one year, and would furnish stumpage for pulp production . . . for three years."[8] Nothing deterred Jackson, not even data about the insignificant impact on the economy of the peninsula against the national interest in preserving them. Jackson viewed himself as the general going into battle. "I believe," he confided to Drury, "that a good general always figures out his strategy and has his ammunition ready for any possible attack prior to the battle."[9] As Drury stalled, Jackson agreed not to rush things.

In January of 1946, *The West Coast Lumberman,* a forest industry publication, had a leading article that headlined, "TIMBER SUPPLY OF WASHINGTON AND OREGON PLACED AT 438.1 BILLION FEET." The article disclosed, "that is a comfortable backlog — it would for example, supply materials to build 73 million five room houses, without any changes in utilization or logging methods. That is two houses apiece for every family in the United States."[10] William Greeley, still ever creative in his attacks on the park, then launched the veterans' housing attack. Greeley claimed that providing housing for returned World War II veterans demanded the park's timber, ignoring the article in his own trade publication.

Senator Warren G. Magnuson asked both Drury and Lyle Watts, chief of the Forest Service, for their views on a possible bill that would eliminate park lands "in order that cutting of timber thereon might be permitted."[11] Before he could get his inquiry answered, the newspapers exploded with Greeley's new campaign to get at the trees in the park to maintain the overbuilt mills of the peninsula.

With Ickes' resignation in February of 1946, the timber industry had renewed hopes. "Emergency legislation by Congress to open up billions of feet of Douglas fir timber locked up in the Olympic National Park . . . was predicted here today . . . ," reported the *Seattle Post-Intelligencer.* "Ickes successor, Julius Krug, . . . is expected not only to take a favorable view towards opening up of the reserve but to lend his active support because of the extreme housing emergency."[12]

Assistant Park Superintendent Fred Overly, now back from the Navy, where he had been since July of 1942, decided to jar the Park Service out of its seeming slowness. Referring to the 1943 special boundary investigation committee he wrote:

> This report recommends the elimination of certain lands in the Bogachiel, Hoh, and Quinault areas. . . . A large portion of this area [the Bogachiel] has . . . little to recommend it for park purposes. . . . I believe the Service would do well to endorse the elimination of these areas from the park. . . . Those who believe the park to be too large could then point with pride to the accomplishment of having the boundary revised to provide materials for home building purposes.[13]

As Overly's memo circulated through the system, no one in the Park Service thought it unusual that the park's assistant superintendent wanted to "point with pride" to the park's destruction for raw materials, materials that only three months before had been declared to be available in abundance by the same industry that coveted them. Again, the Park Service was so confused that it simply did not know what its mission was. It had been that way ever since Mather launched it. The public would pay dearly for this chaos. Superintendent Macy joined wholeheartedly with Overly. "We believe that now would be the opportune time," Macy told Drury, "to adjust the boundary of the park. . . ."[14] Thus, the two most senior local officials entrusted with preserving the park's forests unimpaired for future generations, were again plotting to give those forests to the loggers in their own generation. Their major impediment, Harold Ickes, had resigned as secretary the previous month. There was no reason to believe that his successor, Julius Krug, would not take the guidance from the Park Service that Ickes never had.

Irving Clark found out by chance what was going on and declared war on the Park Service, telling Macy that "he is taking immediate steps to garner all of the forces together" including Rosalie Edge and Irving Brant. Macy was indifferent to Clark's challenge. "Therefore, we know some of our conservation friends will be advised of the matter,"[15] Macy told Drury. In attempting to divest the park's forests, the Park Service might have thought it prudent to discuss such a move with the Emergency Conservation Committee, which had fought the hardest to preserve those forests and could be expected to fight to retain them. For that reason alone, perhaps, it is likely that contact with the ECC was avoided.

The Park Service's boundary study of 1943 moved forward with the regional director affirming that "the lines recommended would have been the same even if the committee had been making the study free from wartime needs and pressures," noting in passing that the timber was not needed at all for housing.[16] Park Service Regional Forester Burnett Sanford, from the San Francisco regional office, supported Overly and the recommendation of the Port Angeles Chamber of Commerce which would eliminate the forests west of the line between Range Nine and Ten.

While all of this was occurring, the Forest Service was answering Congressional inquiries by saying it would willingly be the "alternative to national park management" if "some part of the present park area should be released to permit its industrial utilization."[17] Former Olympic Forest Supervisor, H. L. Plumb, now working for the mill owners as manager of Grays Harbor Industries, announced that the cutting of park timber "can be accomplished without any harm to the recreational or scenic values of the park area" and again pleaded the need for wood to alleviate housing shortage, despite facts to the contrary.[18]

While all this activity was occurring, Secretary of the Interior Krug was uninformed about any of it. Krug told the editor of *The West Coast Lumberman* that it was national policy to maintain inviolate national park forests and cited the industry's own figures on abundance of timber. Drury did the same. His continuing reaffirmation of the preservation purposes of the park, when he knew that the park's forests were headed for the mills in an effort that he was leading, was not seen as unusual within the Park Service.

By May of 1946, Overly turned in yet another timber study that affirmed that 80 percent of the timber in the Hoh Valley could be harvested economically and that in the Bogachiel Valley 75 to 80 percent of it was merchantable. Overly made clear the continuing attraction of the Calawah and Bogachiel areas to the mill operators. In speaking of the high yield per acre, Overly said, "Anyone of the local pulp companies would jump at the chance to tie up this timber and it would make an excellent sustained yield forest area."[19]

The Park Service continued to implement the Forest Service's 1930's cutting plans for these forests, but the public had no knowledge of what was occurring, nor did the secretary's office. Many inquiries from the public kept pouring into the Interior Department asking whether the department had agreed to selective logging of the park. Finally, Under Secretary Oscar Chapman concluded that perhaps the Civilian Production Administration's Housing for Veterans Expediter was behind it. Chapman, in the dark about what was going on inside the Park Service, told Krug, "I strongly urge that every effort be made to oppose opening the Olympic National Park to lumbering. I am convinced that there is no present or foreseeable condition that would justify any change in the present law or policy." The degree to which Drury had succeeded in hiding the Park Service's role from the secretary's office illustrated by Chapman's closing sentence to Krug: "The National Park Service is prepared to present definite proof that no plea of a shortage of stumpage in the Northwest could logically be offered in support of a proposal to open the Olympic National Park to logging."[20] Krug issued a press release strongly affirming the Park Service in its preservationist role.[21] By the end of May, Assistant Superintendent Fred Overly, in a continuation of his timber studies, disclosed that if all the spruce and Douglas fir in the whole park were made available at the existing capacity of the Olympic Peninsula mills, "it would last them only an additional 8 years." On a sustained-yield basis, the volume available would be insignificant, he said. "As long as there are trees left in the park, the Grays Harbor plants will want them."[22]

With the west-side forest eliminations of the 1943 study reexamined and reaffirmed throughout the Park Service, with the timber volume and availability studies complete, Drury issued a personally signed three-page press release attacking Greeley's veterans' housing thrust against the park. The press release ended with a call to protect the very forests he was preparing to send to the mills:

> If any modification of the boundaries of the Olympic is to be made, the national interest, rather than local, commercially motivated pressures must determine it; under no circumstances should any changes be permitted which would rob Americans of this or future generations of the inspiration of the grand sweep of this virgin forest.[23]

By 1946, Olympic National Park had still not been dedicated because of the intervention of World War II, the subsequent death of Roosevelt, and the later resignation of Ickes. Finally in the late spring of 1946, the decision was made to have a dedication ceremony.

No park in the history of the park system had a more bizarre dedication than did Olympic. A few persons gathered at Rosemary Inn on Lake Crescent for the dedication on June 15, 1946. It was a group containing no one who had actually worked for Olympic's creation. Interior Secretary Krug, not knowing that Drury and the staff of the park were working to give the best of Olympic's forests to the loggers, gave a speech in defense of park preservation.[24] Senator Hugh B. Mitchell, who introduced him, did the same. Despite the fact that he was demanding the Calawah, Bogachiel and Hoh valleys for the mill operators, Congressman Henry Jackson told the assembled group, "It is gratifying to share this platform with those who have contributed so much to the preservation of the most majestic, untouched, primitive areas in America." Contrary to the views of those who "mistakenly advocate that national parks are properly for the exclusive pleasure of the hearty and toughened sportsman," Jackson announced that he had gotten the Park Service to request funds for a mountain lodge "with simple and adequate accommodations."[25] The chambers of commerce now had evidence that the wilderness imperative Ickes had imposed on the Park Service could be broken.

At the same time, William Greeley again launched his boundary-commission proposal for the park, this time at a Seattle Chamber of Commerce luncheon in June of 1946. The same commission had been proposed by Greeley when the mill owners had lost in the closing days of the park battle in 1938. Drury saw Greeley's moves for a commission as a challenge to the prerogatives of the Park Service.

Three weeks after the park dedication, Drury decided to involve Krug for the first time in what the Park Service was thinking: " . . . we are prepared to defend revisions," Drury told Krug, of areas of "not such outstanding significance that it is essential for retention in the park."[26] These were the Bogachiel, Calawah, Hoh and Quinault, those considered the most valuable by Ickes and the conservationists.

When Senator Warren G. Magnuson introduced a bill, S 2266, to eliminate from the park the 6,000 acres of private lands in the Quinault Valley, Drury explained to Krug that this bill merited a favorable report and should even be amended to increase the acreage to be eliminated to 15,420 acres. "Substantial stumpage will be made available," he said. At the same time, he reassured Krug that the real reason was "to attain a better boundary."[27]

Drury asked Krug to appoint a committee of three, Tomlinson, Macy, and Lee Muck, a forester, "to make specific recommendations to you for future action." Drury warned that there were dangers: "The intense interest of Mr. Irving Brant, Mrs. Charles N. Edge of the Emergency Conservation Committee and Dr. Van Name of the American Museum of Natural History . . . indicate that we need to exercise great caution . . . with the deletion of any park lands."[28]

Krug turned the committee plan over to Assistant Secretary C. Girard Davidson, who rejected it. Drury was in San Francisco when he heard this. He wired back to Demaray:

> I recommend Secretary approve two boundary changes outlined. . . . I see no advantage in prolonging the agony by reviving the issue locally with probability of public hearings that will be as futile as those held previously on Olympic. . . . Believe concessions we are willing to make will satisfy Governor Wallgren and most of the members of Congress from Washington and will not be opposed by conservation organizations. . . . [29]

Drury was now attempting to bypass the public with fast actions in Congress while openly admitting the "concessions we are willing to make" to the timber industry. His view that public hearings on the park bill had been futile was contrary to the facts. The 1936 hearings were critical to the success of the park bill. All the while that Drury was trying to get rid of the park's rain forests, the letters drafted by the Park Service for Krug and Drury continued to reassure the public in the steadfastness of the department's position:

> The fine support for the preservation of Olympic National Park which has been voiced . . . has been most encouraging to me and to the National Park Service.
>
> The loss of such a irreplaceable and priceless heritage to this and future generations of Americans would be most unfortunate.[30]

Greeley was working hard to get hearings of some kind where a forum would be available to him to orchestrate the timber industry demands. Governor Mon Wallgren, who as a congressman had sponsored the creation of the park, wanted no move to be made. "Better to let sleeping dogs lie" he said.[31] With Assistant Secretary Girard Davidson now directly involved in the Olympic National Park situation, it seemed clear that Krug was not letting Drury proceed without close supervision from the secretary's office. Davidson was now getting guidance from Wallgren, Washington's Congressional delegation, and others, without going through the Park Service.

Drury finally got Krug to approve a proposal to get Congressman Fred Norman of Grays Harbor to support a Park Service boundary bill in place of a Congressional boundary-investigation bill he was threatening to introduce. Drury also wanted approval for Chief of Lands, Conrad Wirth, to begin meetings with the timber industry and the Forest Service.[32]

Both Congressmen Fred Norman and Henry Jackson were fighting to get timber out of the park. So was the Park Service, with the Forest Service enthusiastically supporting all efforts while being officially uninvolved. William Greeley shared his plans, sometimes daily, with Forest Service Regional Forester H. J. Andrews, who was to receive the trees if Greeley succeeded. Greeley's strategy, which he openly spoke about, was to get a boundary adjustment rather than a bill to log the park. A bill to log the park would have too much opposition, he said.

When Conrad Wirth came to Portland to negotiate the boundary changes, it was heady wine for the Forest Service. Here was the Park Service confirming what the Forest Service had argued all during the 1930's, that the territory involved was simply not of park caliber. To the Forest Service, Wirth's arrival, representing Drury and Krug, was an incredible turn of events. Never in their wildest imaginings did the Forest Service ever foresee that they would negotiate Olympic boundaries with the Park Service. And they jumped at the chance. Regional Forester Andrews came up with a boundary that would revert much of the forest and half of the timber in the park back to the Forest Service. Wirth brought Fred Overly and Regional Forester Burnett Sanford with him during the negotiations. "When they left," Andrews told the Forest Service chief, "they were profuse in their thanks for the benefit they had gotten from the thorough discussion. . . ."[33]

Wirth talked at length with Greeley to find out what he wanted. He also talked with the timber committees of the various peninsula chambers of commerce, with local timbermen, with Park Service staff members and with Macy and Overly. Everyone wanted the west-side forests out. Some wanted more. Greeley wanted everything and he clung tenaciously to his commission idea as the route by which he could get it. "It would be very beneficial to the National Park Service," he told Drury, "to support and join in the sort of inquiry which Mr. Norman proposes," ignoring the fact that everyone knew he had written Norman's bill himself.[34]

Wirth's report, submitted to Drury on March 2, 1947, confirmed the underlying forces driving Drury and the whole Park Service:

> In accordance with your instructions, I have analyzed the park boundary problem in an effort to see if any changes could be made *that would aid the economic interest* of the Olympic Peninsula. . . .
>
> It is my opinion that there are some lands now in the park that are not necessary from a park standpoint and, therefore, should be eliminated from the area and put *to a higher economical use.*

The area to be added is high alpine country and *has no timber of commercial value* (italics mine).

Opposed to Olympic National Park in the first place because of its failure, in his opinion, to measure up to "park standards," Wirth was now to be the legislative architect of the long-brewing internal plan to get rid of the park's most valuable forests. In describing his meetings with Greeley on park boundaries, Wirth said to Drury, "I told him (Greeley) of your admiration for him and I thought that perhaps if you and he could get together something might be worked out."[35] For Drury's subordinates to think that Drury had admiration for the arch-enemy of the Olympic National Park says much about the nature of Drury's Park Service.

When in Seattle, Wirth had lunch with Irving Clark and never mentioned the boundary changes underway. Prophetically, though, he told Clark, "I feel we are going to have plenty of trouble on this Olympic problem and your support and understanding of our difficulties is going to be a great source of comfort to us."[36] Wirth was wrong. Support for sending Olympic's forests to the mills was never going to come from Clark.

To deflect Congressman Norman's support for the commission that Greeley wanted, Wirth drafted a letter for the secretary to send to Norman offering to draft a boundary bill, presumably with the eliminations Wirth had gotten everyone to agree to on his trip west. To entice Norman to accept his boundaries, Wirth had the secretary tell him that, with the amendments being recommended for Senator Magnuson's bill S 711, the Park Service "would make available to local lumber industries some 555,699,000 feet of timber." Then to further entice him, Wirth added, "This is only part of the adjustment we feel should be made as a result of our studies."[37]

Two days later, the Park Service bill with Conrad Wirth's eliminations was offered to Congressman Jackson. "These changes are the result of the studies which you asked us to make sometime ago," Jackson was told. Not to be upstaged by Norman on a park-boundary bill, Jackson introduced in his own name the Park Service bill that Wirth had prepared, the same day that Norman introduced his.

To coincide with the introduction of the bills, Drury personally prepared a press release which would later prove to be his undoing. The release, prepared, Drury said, "for the information and guidance of interested conservation organizations," was a jumble of double talk. "The purpose of the Service's recommendation," he said, "is to attain a better boundary from the standpoint of administration and protection. . . ." Two paragraphs, buried on different pages of the four-page release in the middle of preservationist rhetoric told the real story:

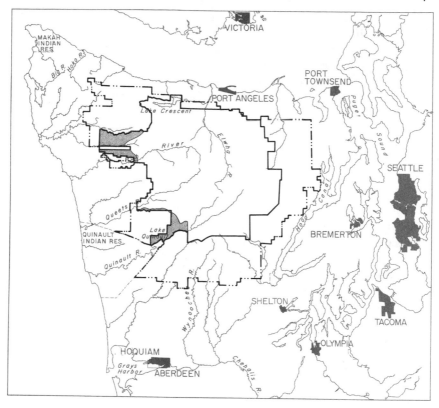

NATIONAL PARK SERVICE FOREST ELIMINATION PROPOSAL S 1240,
HR 4054, HR 2750, HR 2751 1947

The Park Service responded to the demands of the Port Angeles owners by moving to give them nearly all of what they wanted plus an additional 15,000 acres of mostly rain forest in the Quinault. Congressmen Henry M. Jackson and Fred Norman both introduced bills drafted by the Park Service to give it to them.

The integrity of the great natural spectacle in Olympic National Park will be maintained, but the boundary changes, if adopted, will eliminate from the park 56,000 acres containing 2½ billion board feet of merchantable stumpage which will then be available for use by local industry.

Fortunately for local lumbermen, the adjustments proposed effect the exclusion of considerable merchantable timber from the park. In fact, it gives them a considerable part of the forest stand that could be immediately accessible. . . . To eliminate further stands, were this advisable from an administrative or protective standpoint, would involve forests that would be extremely difficult and costly to harvest.[38]

Drury's revelation that the Park Service itself was engaging in an exercise to maximize the profits of the loggers by giving up all of the park forests that could be logged immediately at the least cost shocked the whole of the conservation movement as it had never been shocked before. Drury had not remembered that it was a powerful conservation constituency that had defeated the timber industry to get an Olympic National Park in the first place.

The immediate result of Drury's press release was to reactivate the Emergency Conservation Committee. No group ever moved with such skill, commitment, and dedication as did its members, Willard Van Name, now seventy-five-years old, and Rosalie Edge, now sixty-nine. Harold Ickes, who was seventy-three and now one of the highest paid columnists in the country, became a *de facto* member of the loose confederation of activists that made up the ECC. Irving Brant was, for the moment, in isolation on Vancouver Island, finishing the second volume of his biography of James Madison. But Irving Clark, at sixty-five years of age, stood ready in Seattle to join in bringing the Park Service and Drury down. The new ECC coalition, now augmented by Harold Ickes, was a triumph in geriatric activism.

What they brought to the battlefield was a detailed understanding on how to involve the public and how to emasculate the power of the Park Service. Their experience with the Forest Service in the 1930's immediately led them to work on Secretary of the Interior Krug and President Truman. It was not going to be easy. Rosalie Edge expressed the anguish of the whole conservation community at what the Park Service was attempting: "All the work of many years thrown away," she said, "the property of the people handed officially to the despoilers. The green and living legacy left to us by our great president to be guillotined in the saw mill."[39]

Within two weeks of Drury's press release, Ickes was on the attack in his widely read column. "The tree butchers, axes on shoulders," he told his readers, "are again on the march against some of the few remaining stands of America's glorious virgin timber. . . . And the tree butchers have, as guides for their assault, Secretary of the Interior Julius A. Krug and with Newton B. Drury, Director of the National Park Service in immediate command."[40] In a later column, Ickes brought up Drury's wartime logging efforts, charging that "Director Drury was willing to permit the tree butchers to invade the park under the plea of war necessity." Charging further that the timber-giveaway bill was drafted by the Park Service itself, he told his readers, "the National Park Service does not seem to have thought that since this wonderful timber belonged to the people, they should have been consulted."[41]

Readers were outraged and the avalanche of letters that began pouring into the Park Service reflected that outrage. Ickes felt personally responsible for the Park Service attack on the Olympic forests because it had been he who had put Drury in place. "Unfortunately too," Ickes told Van Name, "I am responsible for the naming of a gutless pigmy as Superintendent [sic] of the National Park Service."[42] Therefore he worked hard to undo the damage he believed his appointment of Drury was inflicting on the nation.

Everyone had accepted at face value Drury's story that the Park Service elimination proposals were the result of Congressman Norman's bill to activate the boundary commission that Greeley wanted. Such a proposal could never have passed Congress, so Drury was in the uncomfortable position of offering to give up park forests because of a bill introduced by an obscure congressman representing a local special interest. In reality, Drury was using Norman's bill to rationalize the elimination move that the Park Service itself had indeed been working for since 1934.

Working as a well-functioning machine, the aging ECC made the same moves that had proved to be winners during the first park battle a decade earlier. Willard Van Name, with the energy of the damned, turned out letter after letter to senators, congressmen, other officials and to every major newspaper in the country. In many cases, Van Name's letters generated other letters from the editors themselves to Secretary Krug asking what was going on. Rosalie Edge produced a pamphlet, *The Raid on the Nation's Olympic Forests,* which turned out to be the most widely distributed of all of the ECC's pamphlets. The New Yorker cartoon that had been so devastating to the timber industry in her pamphlets ten years earlier had even greater effect this time. The Sierra Club sent a sixteen-page pamphlet into national circulation. The Wilderness Society distributed nationally a reprint of an article by Irving Clark. So many letters from the public poured into the Interior Department and Park Service that mail-answering processes ground to a halt and they were reduced to sending out hand-addressed form letters. Congress was also flooded. Finally, by June of 1947, the Park Service warned Congressman Jackson that they were "receiving scores of letters each week protesting the elimination of *any* lands from Olympic National Park. To date we have received just one letter in support of opening a portion of the park to logging."[43] Drury was still plunging ahead, even as Irving Brant desperately tried to save Drury from himself.

Brant wrote to Drury in June, 1947, constructing a step-by-step rationale that would enable Drury to extricate himself. Congressman

Norman, who had gone ahead and introduced Greeley's boundary commission bill, had died not long after introducing it. "With him gone," Brant told Drury, "there is an excellent opening for the Interior Department to take the stand it should for protection of the park." Brant told Drury, "I have talked often enough with President Truman to know that he will never cave in to the commercial despoilers of national parks. . . ."[44] Drury ignored the advice and took no action, even in the face of a threat of presidential veto.

Rosalie Edge had been gently rebuffed twice by Mrs. Roosevelt when she attempted to involve her in the battle. She then asked Harold Ickes to see what he could do. Ickes wrote a long letter to Mrs. Roosevelt on the history of the creation of the park and included details about Drury's wanting to log the park during World War II. "I came to be disturbed at what seemed to me to be Mr. Drury's willingness to yield to this pressure," Ickes told her, "but I never thought that he would go as far as he apparently now has gone, in permitting a raid by the lumber interests upon the magnificent trees which constitute the only rain forest in the whole world."[45] Mrs. Roosevelt reproduced Ickes' letter and sent it to Krug with a cover letter that got his attention. " . . . I can only think that Mr. Drury has been weak enough to be bowled over by the lumber interests," she told him, "and that you have been too busy to find out the history of the whole situation." Calling for Krug to fire Drury, Mrs. Roosevelt ended her letter with: " . . . I think it is essential that if possible Mr. Drury be changed and this be stopped since it can only be a precursor of many similar raids on national territory."[46]

If Ickes could succeed at the barbed letter, Edge thought she would give it a try. With the sarcasm of which she was capable, she wrote to Drury:

28 June, 1947

Dear Mr. Drury,

Let me add this personal word to tell you how sorry I am that you, who have shown me frequent courtesy and kindness, should find yourself in your present embarrassing position.

I find that others, though unalterably opposed, like myself, to the policy which you have embraced, feel little resentment against you personally. You have, indeed warm friends, among whom I hope you will count me. Among them, the feeling expressed is rather one of pity—feeling that you have, somehow, been forced into your present unhappy position without knowing how to extricate yourself.

Older than yourself, and in some ways more experienced, may I say that I believe that the only honorable thing you can do is to resign— resign in such a way as to clear your name from collusion with the present unfortunate deal to give the forests of the Olympic National Park to the lumbermen.

I say this to you because perhaps there is no one else who can say it. The personnel of the Park Service is bound to give you lip service and a show of respect. But what can they think, some of your splendid super-intendents and office associates, of the Department of the Interior plan to give up the forests of the Olympic National Park, without a fight?

Without a fight! That is what hurts your friends. I beg you to clear your name, and sustain your fine reputation.

Believe me with regards,

Sincerely your friend,
Mrs. Charles Noel Edge[47]

Edge had accepted Drury's explanation of the eliminations as being related to Congressman Norman introducing Greeley's commission pro-posal. What no one saw was that Drury was simply representing the Park Service's real philosophy—that there is nothing unique in old-growth forests and therefore the Park Service does not exist to preserve them.

When the Interior Department's favorable report on the elimination, written by the Park Service, was seen by Congressman Richard Welch, chairman of the Public Lands Committee, he was infuriated at the In-terior Department's stance and called the secretary's office to notify them he was opposed to boundary changes and that the Interior Depart-ment should not report favorably on the bill. With the whole depart-ment buried in an avalanche of hostile mail, Under Secretary Oscar Chapman told Welch to withdraw the report.[48] With the withdrawal of departmental support, the Park Service was now in the exact posi-tion that the Forest Service had been in with the Secretary of Agricul-ture ten years earlier.

Drury became desperate to justify the elimination of the Bogachiel Valley as the attacks poured in. He wrote that it was "made as the result of abandonment of the original apparent intent of the Forest Service acquisition of the nine sections, a nine mile long, one mile wide strip in the Bogachiel Valley, owned by Crown Zellerbach that had been or-dered by President Roosevelt to be acquired by the Forest Service for addition to the park." In fact, the Forest Service had already acquired all but 160 acres of the nine sections and they were awaiting addition to the park. When Macy discovered that Drury was using this ploy, he moved to get Tomlinson to stop him: " . . . the abandonment of intent, if any, appears to rest with the National Park Service,"[49] he said. Macy even began to have second thoughts about the elimination. Tomlinson reminded Macy that it was his 1943 committee report that "the Director

Newton B. Drury.
National Park Service.

and I have based our recommendations on."[50] His message to Macy was handwritten, probably to bypass the regional office. Macy moved back into line. It was becoming clear that no one wanted to bear the account-ability for any part of what was unfolding.

By the time hearings were announced on the park elimination bills, the Park Service was going into the hearings on its own bills to eliminate the most important part of Olympic National Park, with the Interior Department having withdrawn support. Deluged with hostile mail, newspaper articles, letters to the editors, and nationwide campaigns against it, the Park Service had now lost control of the situation. Congressman Henry Jackson, who had launched the whole thing, now was sidestepping by pinning his bill on the Park Service, claiming his bill was only introduced at the Park Service's request.

The hearings were held at Rosemary Inn on Lake Crescent on September 16 and 17, 1947. Minutes into the hearing on the first day, Assistant Secretary Davidson destroyed the Park Service's "improving the park" stance for once and for all. "The total area in the national park system containing timber of merchantable value," he pointed out, "probably amounts to less than one half of one percent of the total forested area of this country. Now this is so small a portion that the United States can well afford to maintain its park boundaries and the park without any inroads of commercial logging." His statement was a blow to Drury.

Davidson's testimony ended with an unequivocal statement: ". . . it is the position of the Department of Interior that the forests of the Olympic National Park should be preserved in their natural state for the enjoyment of future generations."[51]

With the Interior Department taking this stance, the support that the timber industry had carefully negotiated with Conrad Wirth earlier was now meaningless. Russell Mack, who had replaced Fred Norman as congressman from Grays Harbor, gave an angry response. He inserted into the record "a letter showing that the Park Service, of its own volition, drafted these bills, and itself specified the areas that went to make up the 56,000 acres suggested for elimination from the park."[52] Witness after witness then confronted the Park Service with its 1934 boundary-proposal report. It was entered intact into the record, with attention drawn to the fact that it had specifically excluded restoring Mount Olympus National Monument to its original boundaries because it "includes much valuable timber on areas that are not of national park caliber . . . for the same reason we do not favor the area as proposed by the Emergency Conservation Committee."

Even though Congressman Henry Jackson and all of the Park Service entourage present knew that the elimination bills under discussion were a direct result of his pressure on Drury, Jackson, facing the same deluge of angry mail that had buried the Park Service, changed his story. "Now, let me say at the outset that it at no time did I ever endorse this proposal. . . . I introduced it by request so that the people at least would have an opportunity of having this matter presented."[53] What was being proposed had become politically untenable. Everyone who could weasel out of it was doing just that, but the Park Service couldn't.

William Greeley had timber industry and chamber of commerce witnesses primed to support his boundary commission plan. Greeley said, "You cannot separate the Olympic National Park from the economic problem of the Olympic Peninsula." In fact, the economic problem to which he referred was the result of the industry's liquidation logging practices that had been underway for seventy years.

Greeley's friend and former Forest Service associate James. W. Girard, now a consulting forester representing the mill owners of both Grays Harbor and Port Angeles, delivered the most damaging testimony. When Girard testified, he laid out the timber industry's plan for Olympic National Park which included the removal of nearly every tree that in the foreseeable future could have any commercial value. This amounted to about 60 percent of the timber volume in the park, comprising ten billion board feet, with no assurances that when that was gone they would not be back for more. Girard, however, reassured his listeners

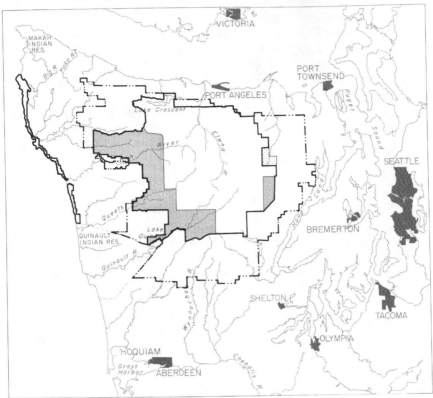

Former Forest Service official James Girard was hired in 1947 by the mill owners of Port Angeles and Grays Harbor to lobby for the timber they wanted out of Olympic National Park—all of what was then merchantable (area shaded on the map). His proposal had the effect of making Director Newton Drury's moves to placate the timber industry look ridiculous. *Girard Report, 1947.*

that his boundary "would, however, retain in the park sufficient areas of fine quality commercial timber to diversify its scenery and retain forever in its virgin condition, splendid examples of the rain forests of the Olympic Peninsula."[54]

The Interior Department, represented by Assistant Secretary Davidson, was forced to take all Olympic National Park decision-making out of the Park Service's and Drury's hands. Davidson's testimony at the hearings had been a repudiation of the Park Service's position. From that moment on, he was the contact point with the conservation community which had brought the Interior Department to its knees. Secretary of the Interior Julius Krug himself had been badly damaged because it now appeared as if popular outrage had forced him to retreat from what he really wanted to do—log the park. The public didn't know he had been led, almost tricked, into the Park Service's position.

Just six weeks after the hearings, in recognition of the power of Rosalie Edge and the Emergency Conservation Committee, Assistant Secretary Davidson went to New York to call on Edge personally. When he explained to her that it was now the Interior Department's policy to oppose all Olympic National Park boundary bills, Edge insisted that he spell out in detail the department's new position in a letter to her. "I asked what I could do with the letters, and he said 'anything you like; give it to the press, if you want to,'" Edge told Brant in recounting the meeting. Edge reproduced Davidson's capitulation letter and sent a thousand copies to newspapers and conservation organizations around the country.[55] The *New York Times* headlined their story, "NEW FIGHT BEGUN TO SAVE FORESTS."[56]

Brant, although busy in Florida on his Madison biography, had been

Congressman Henry M. Jackson and Olympic Park Superintendent Preston P. Macy worked throughout the 1940's to make the park's rain forests available for logging to satisfy the demands of the Port Angeles mill operators. Jackson continued these efforts throughout his political career. *University of Washington.*

busy on Olympic, too. After talking to Krug, he reported to Ickes, " . . . the Interior reversal is genuine. Krug made it plain to me that he felt he had been misled and given bad advice by the NPS."[57] Brant had again succeeded in cutting the Park Service off at the secretarial level, as he had with the Forest Service earlier. What remained was the presidential level. In the outside chance that a park bill were to pass, a presidential veto was the last recourse. Brant then wrote directly to Truman, with a cover letter to Charles G. Ross of the White House staff, who could carry it directly to Truman. "I have taken the matter up with the Secretary of Interior," Truman told Brant after reading his memo, "and I think things will work out all right."[58] Brant confided to Edge: "That was about as near as he could very well come to saying that he would veto any such bill if it passed."[59] The ECC strategy that had created the park had triumphed again, using direct involvement of the public through pamphlets and various other media to pressure the Interior Department and Congress, to separate the secretary from the Park Service, and to gain the commitment of the president to intervene at appropriate junctures. Edge, Brant and Van Name had become so adept at using this strategy that it had taken only eight months from the time that Drury had issued his infamous press release to the capitulation of the Interior Department by the delivery of Davidson's letter to Edge. Actually they had succeeded in a little over two months — Under Secretary Chapman had withdrawn the department's favorable report on the bills at the end of May.

Now painted with the timber industry's brush, Congressman Jackson was forced by the hostile reaction to withdraw his bill and to defend himself. He worked hard to portray himself as the innocent victim of the Interior Department instead of the translator of Drury's 1943 boundary report into action. "The Department of the Interior requested that this bill be introduced . . . " he said in withdrawing it. "In view of the fact that the Department has indicated its opposition to this bill which I introduced by request, I respectfully ask that HR 2751 be withdrawn. . . . "[60]

The timber industry responded with the introduction of more boundary-commission plans through a willing Congressman Mack and Senator Harry Cain. They also published a glossy booklet attacking the existing park boundaries and sent it to every member of Congress. But the avalanche of hostile public opinion left all of these bills dead in the water.

In the few short months that the second battle of Olympic National Park raged, Director Drury was destroyed, both personally and professionally. When the Interior Department reversed itself on the boundary bills, Drury was left as the focal point of everything that was wrong in the Park Service. Chief of Lands, Conrad Wirth, who had conducted the timber industry negotiations and recommended the elimination action, quietly slipped away as did Assistant Superintendent Fred Overly, who helped him draft the bills. Regional Director Tomlinson and Superintendent Macy, both of whom had been working for years for the elimination, also stepped off the stage and into the shadows.

"Of one thing you can be certain," Drury assured Brant when no one any longer cared, "the National Park Service did not in anyway initiate the issue. . . ."[61] Drury actually had initiated it all personally by ordering the 1943 boundary recommendation, which then proved to be so enticing to Congressman Henry Jackson that he demanded action.

In her press release enclosing Assistant Secretary Davidson's capitulation letter, Rosalie Edge went after the Park Service directly, to Drury's horror:

> To the astonishment and dismay of conservationists, they were informed that the bills originated in the National Park Service, which had capitulated to the pressure of a few lumbermen in the State of Washington, and were supported by the Department of Interior.
>
> The forest is a precious possession of every citizen of the United States, and conservationists throughout the land rose in its defense, protesting to government officials and against the proposed shameful lumber grab, endorsed by the National Park Service.[62]

These two sentences forced Drury to react. In his defensive answer to Edge's charges, Drury disclosed for the first time that the boundary chosen was "one which accorded with the recommendations of [the Park Service] field representatives at the time extensions were underway in 1940 . . ." Finally, Drury was admitting that the Park Service's "heart's desire" boundary had fueled its continuing attempts to keep the west-side forests from being added. He told Edge, "while I may deceive myself, I believe that there would be few indeed who would consider that a 'shameful lumber grab' would be endorsed by the National Park Service." Not only had the Park Service endorsed it, it had also originated it. Edge ignored him and never again acknowledged anything he ever wrote to her.

Already alienated from the conservation community, the timber industry now turned on Drury as well. To extricate himself from the untenable position into which the Interior Department's reversal had placed him, Drury stated in much subsequent correspondence that "at the Congressional hearing held in the park in September, representatives of the lumber interests clearly stated that their support of pending boundary adjustment bills was only a first step towards getting the remaining accessible and merchantable virgin forests of the Olympic Peninsula excluded from the park."[63]

William Greeley was furious when Drury's statements kept appearing in Congressional correspondence and everywhere he turned. They got in the way of Greeley's new legislative thrust to get the boundary commission established. Defending the Girard proposals to take out 10 billion board feet of timber, he told Drury "not to misrepresent the position of the Northwestern lumber communities. They want to retain a magnificent park . . . but they feel the *question of size* should be reexamined in relation to the industrial needs and employment of the region." Drury was now isolated and alone in the Interior Department, viewed with contempt by the whole environmental community, and treated as enemy by the timber industry he had attempted to serve.

Drury remained as a lame-duck director until 1951 when Oscar Chapman became Secretary of the Interior. It was Chapman who had signed letters for the Interior Department, drafted by the Park Service, justifying Drury's moves to give the Bogachiel, Calawah, and Quinault areas to the loggers. He was embarrassed by these letters, which were circulated by environmental organizations around the country, illustrating how far the department had sunk since Ickes had left office. To insiders, it was no surprise when one of Chapman's first moves as Secretary of the Interior was to force the resignation of Drury as director. When pressed by the *Washington Post* for a reason, Chapman, however, was gentle in assigning the primary cause: "Mr. Drury has not been sufficiently aggressive in resisting some would-be encroachments on the national parks — for example, the attempt to open Olympic National Park to lumbering during World War II."[64]

When the ECC, augmented by Ickes, heard that Drury had been fired and that he was being considered for appointment as California Director of Beaches and Parks upon leaving the Park Service, they mounted a campaign to do everything possible to prevent it. Brant wrote a lengthy letter to Governor Earl Warren of California citing in great detail Drury's unfitness during his reign as director of the Park Service. Brant said, "It would be a grievous thing if the protective silence which has shrouded his shortcomings in the National Park Service should be allowed to work harm to the country's greatest system of state parks."[65] Two days later, Harold Ickes followed with a four-page letter detailing all the events of Drury's history for Governor Warren. "On balance," Ickes told Warren, "considering the two attempts of Newton Drury to turn the lumbermen loose in Olympic National Park and his leagues' failure to lift so much as a little finger to save any trees but Redwoods in California, I would say that Newton Drury is on the side of lumbermen and no one can make conservationists out of them."[66]

When Rosalie Edge learned that Brant and Ickes had sent letters, she asked Brant to draft a telegram to Governor Warren over her signature:

For sake of California parks and welfare your administration, I beg you probe underlying weakness Newton Drury's record as Director National Parks. He repeatedly jeopardized national park system by craven surrenders to lumbermen and other commercial interests, at same time protecting himself with conservation organizations by concealing policies or falsely blaming them on superiors. He served three conservation-minded Secretaries of Interior, all of whom lost confidence in him. Drury is the only National Park Chief who ever was forced to resign. Please ask Ickes, Krug and Chapman what his record has been.[67]

When Governor Warren hired Drury in 1951 despite this onslaught from the Emergency Conservation Committee, the second battle for Olympic National Park had finally been brought to an end. It turned out to be Ickes' last campaign. He died ten months later in 1952 at age seventy-eight.

After 1947, a permanent legacy of underlying contempt for the Park Service fell on the conservation community of the Pacific Northwest. But the simple fact was that the preservationists had nowhere else to turn but to the Park Service for the protection of resources "that will leave them unimpaired for the enjoyment of future generations." This binds the preservationists to the Park Service but, to the continuing anguish of the preservationists, has never bound the Park Service to them. After it became clear to Irving Clark in 1947 what the Park Service stood for, he formed Olympic Park Associates, using the principles in the 1916 Park Service Act as its charter, to be a watchdog group over the Park Service in Olympic National Park. Olympic Park Associates' ongoing task soon became "to save the park from the Park Service." The Park Service continued its assault on the preservation of the park's forests—next by launching a logging program inside the park itself.

16 LOGGING THE PARK

I am very glad to inform you that there is no authority to permit the cutting of timber on Government owned lands within the Olympic National Park.[1]   FRANKLIN D. ROOSEVELT

The national policy of maintaining inviolate national park forests established by law has been strengthened by general public acceptance of it over the long period since Congress began giving park status to the nationally significant areas of this country.[2]   JULIUS A. KRUG,
SECRETARY OF INTERIOR

O F ALL THE REASONS that led to the creation of the Park Service in 1916, the most important was the continuing insistence of Gifford Pinchot that trees in national parks should be subjected to the practice of forestry. His views were rejected repeatedly by the public between 1895 and 1913 and by Congress. When the long-simmering battle over San Francisco's attempts to flood Yosemite's Hetch Hetchy Valley finally came to a head in 1913, Pinchot's views were an impediment. When he realized that public opinion made logging the parks unattainable, he was forced to declare the inviolability of the national parks' trees at the final Hetch Hetchy hearings. Public opinion was so strong for the absolute preservation of Yosemite's forests that not enough votes could be garnered for the Hetch Hetchy flooding without assurances that trees would be protected everywhere except the actual reservoir site.[3] Pinchot capitulated to public opinion.

In the thirty years between the birth of the Park Service and World War II, the tree-preservation issue that had driven the passage of the 1916 Park Service Act had been forgotten. Nonetheless, the rhetoric of the Park Service paid heed to preservation because the 1916 Park Service Act mandated that the resources be passed "unimpaired for the enjoyment of future generations." So concerned about trees were the drafters of the 1916 Park Service Act that they allowed for the handling of forest disease in much the same way that a surgeon is given license to cut away part of a person's body in order to save the whole. Thus, the secretary was given the power to cut timber "in order to control the attacks of insects or diseases" in the event that a national park forest might be endangered. When the act passed with the insect proviso intact, the American Forestry Association, in a 1917 editorial in *American Forestry,* anticipated the problems that were to come.

> National Parks are created for one definite purpose, to preserve untouched the beauties of natural scenery, with its forests, waterfalls and wildlife. . . . Most unfortunately, the new law already . . . permits timber cutting under the guise of protection from insect ravages. If the public desires to protect the National Parks and preserve them as nature planned them, two things must be demanded—the absolute prohibition of all commercial uses and the establishment of a nonpolitical and efficient park management. . . .[4]

The insect provision receded into the backwaters of memory as preservationists became occupied with issues of road building, predator extermination, and the other crises that Park Service Director Mather's pro-development presence had created. It would take thirty years for the insects to move from the 1916 Park Service Act to the Olympic forests—in fulfillment of *American Forestry*'s 1917 warning.

In the quarter century that unfolded between the Park Service's start-up under Mather and the adding of Olympic's west-side forests, the Park Service had three directors. Each of these directors had measured Park Service success by how many tourists could be attracted to the parks as compared with the year before, and by the numbers of facilities that were constructed to accommodate them. Mather, in his nearly fourteen years on the scene in those crucial years, had produced an organization that could ignore the law or the Park Service's own published guidelines whenever an administrator found it expedient to do so. Mather himself did so often. Because Mather was first and foremost a developer, he understood that to get the freedom to do whatever he wanted, he had to tell the public what they wanted to hear—preservation talk. Thus, a continuing rhetoric of preservation was built into the very fabric of the Park Service's existence, while many problems in the park system were solved with little consideration of preservation issues at all. On top of this were Mather's continuing attempts throughout his tenure to make deals with Chief Forester William Greeley to trade park areas with the largest trees for "scenery," the high alpine country, which the Forest Service was happy to give up. And from the Park Service's earliest days was yet another dynamic. Willard Van Name had continually intervened all through the 1920's on behalf of the preservation agenda defined in the 1916 Park Service Act that Mather's presence as director made impossible. Van Name and all the other preservationists were derisively dubbed "the purists" by Mather and Albright.

Mather's successors, Albright and Cammerer, were also Mather men, and when Olympic National Park's west-side forests were added and Cammerer departed, the Park Service was still Mather's. It was able to tolerate ambiguity and had no organizational commitment to preservation, although it spoke preservation-talk fluently.

This was the Park Service that Newton B. Drury inherited when he took over from Cammerer. Drury became the pawn of the Park Service organization itself. He moved according to the heartbeat that Mather had left behind in the body of the Park Service when he died in 1929. When World War II began twelve years after Mather's death, the Park Service, its duplicitous ethic kept intact by Albright and Cammerer, now reacted to new pressures. Guiding Olympic National Park were a regional director, a superintendent, and an assistant superintendent who not only represented the Mather value system but were also closely linked to the local logging community of Port Angeles, the park's headquarters.

Park Service Chief of Lands, Conrad Wirth, was hired by Horace Albright in 1930, and by the time World War II broke out he had learned in detail how the internal political processes of the Park Service worked. Wirth had become a major player in these processes of power and influence. As Chief of Lands, Wirth would apply his considerable administrative skills to the formidable task of launching a logging program inside the park to placate the continuing demands of both the timber industry and the local Park Service administrators.

Separate and apart from the war-related logging thrust, covered in a previous chapter, was another timber industry thrust—the timber exchange process. This is an *integral* part of all timber operations and absolutely essential to a timber operator's ability to maximize profits. Whenever a timber operator can continue to cut in an area where he already has roads constructed and equipment in place, profits are maximized.

Conrad Wirth.
National Park Service.

In 1937, more than a year before the Olympic Park bill finally passed, Park Ranger Fred Overly, a former logging engineer for Crescent Logging Company, was asked by his former boss at Crescent to arrange for an exchange of government timber in an area about to be added to the park. Overly quickly arranged this exchange on behalf of his friend. Thus the Park Service was placed in the position, even before the creation of the park, of assisting in the maximization of a local logger's profit with trees destined for the park. In the timber-cutting society of Port Angeles, it was good to be known as "cooperative," irrespective of whatever advantage or conflict of interest might accrue to the government from such an exchange.

In February of 1941, Petrus Pearson, general manager of the Crescent Logging Company, again approached his former employee to work out another exchange. (Overly had been cooperative before; he had even gotten the Park Service to eliminate the hillside to the north of Lake Crescent on the second park bill so that Pearson's railroad would not be in the park.) Park Service Chief Counsel Moskey rejected Overly's proposal. "A careful review of the law does not disclose any existing authority to permit the exchange," he said. Overly persisted. "Under the Act of August 25, 1916," he wrote to Drury, "the Secretary is authorized 'to sell or dispose of timber in those cases where in his judgment the cutting of such timber is required in order to control the attacks of insects or diseases or otherwise conserve the scenery or the natural or historic objects in any such park, monument or reservation." He explained that because the park timber would be subject to windthrow after the private timber had been logged, it "will result in a serious fire hazard not to mention possible bark beetle infestations." Overly closed with: "Please advise us of your opinion concerning the Secretary's authority to dispose of the timber under existing law."[5] Overly's headquarters ally, Conrad Wirth, endorsed Overly's request to the chief counsel.[6]

Overly had brilliantly constructed the exact rationale that in the timber-hungry environment of World War II the departmental solicitor could accept. "In my opinion," said Solicitor Nathan Margold, "Section 3 of the act of 1916 authorizes the exchange of timber on park lands for privately owned cut-over lands within national parks. . . ."[7] Overly now had an officially sanctioned license to cut park timber that *might* fall down along with trees that *could* be exposed to insects or *could* be construed to be a fire hazard. The 1916 Park Service Act had now been turned against the very resource it had been designed to protect. This monumental change had occurred in only twenty-five years from the Park Service's creation. The Park Service was now in the same relationship with timber operators that the Forest Service was in. It was this very relationship that Willard Van Name repeatedly had attacked the Forest Service for — acquiring logged-off lands in return for creating more logged-off lands out of publicly owned old-growth forestlands.

With the authorization to proceed with a logging program at hand, the Park Service then produced in 1942 "Timber Disposal Regulations" for Olympic National Park and proclaimed them in the Federal Register, defining which of the park's trees it considered merchantable:

> All Douglas fir, Sitka spruce and western white pine logs are considered merchantable which are not less than 20 feet long and at least 12 inches in diameter. . . .
>   All western red cedar logs, chunks and slabs are considered merchantable which are not less than 20 feet long, at least 12 inches in diameter. . . .[8]

By issuing these regulations, the Park Service confirmed the fears, expressed in 1917 by *American Forestry,* that the insect clause in the 1916 Park Service Act would lead to loss of the forests without "the absolute prohibition of all commercial uses." By defining what was merchantable for disposal purposes, Drury's Park Service had entered the logging business, guaranteeing that the operation would be profitable for the logger. Ironically, the possibility of fire hazard and insects still remained in the material left behind after the merchantable logs were removed, as in any other logging operation.

All this activity occurred concurrently with Drury's other attempts to open Olympic National Park to World War II logging. Secretary of the Interior Ickes had no knowledge of what was happening. Nor did the conservation groups have even the slightest suspicion that the long-standing "no commercialization of resources in the parks" norm had been breached. It all had occurred quietly and routinely within the normal processes of the Interior Department.

Before any action could be taken on the ongoing requests now flowing in from Superintendent Macy to trade park logs for logged-off land, an internal movement began inside the Park Service to head off using the logging in the park authorization. Forester Lee Muck in the secretary's office confronted Drury with reasons why he should not approve Park Superintendent Macy's requests for exchanges. "The proposal to add devastated lands to the park," he said, "is not consistent with the policy which has governed the establishment of these reserves."[9] Regional Director Tomlinson told Macy, " . . . It is a very serious matter to permit salvage logging inside the park proper. Once we permit loggers to enter the park, even though they are restricted to down timber, pressure will increase tremendously for extending cutting operations to the standing timber."[10] Associate Forester Jack Dodd tried to head off the logging through Tomlinson. "All such operations should be discouraged since once they start it it's hard to stop them," he said.[11] Even Regional Chief of Planning Ernest Davidson, from his obscure position in the region, put himself on the line to stop the logging. He called on the Park Service to demand of the loggers that they "convincingly prove there is an existing shortage of vital material, not elsewhere available before logging of any kind, down or standing, is thought of in park lands."[12]

It was all to no avail. Macy and Overly had Wirth on their side and Wirth had Drury. The exchanges proceeded as submitted.

It was inevitable in the fall of 1942, when a blowdown of Douglas fir along Finley Creek in the Quinault area of the park occurred, the newly acquired Timber Disposal Regulations would be put to immediate use. Park Forester Reino Sarlin enthusiastically moved ahead "with the knowledge that we are contributing from this blowdown area critically needed peeler logs. . . ."[13] Macy told Drury before proceeding, "we are being much criticized for not selling this timber under war needs,"[14] whereupon Drury readily approved the sale, and 2,346,000 board feet of mostly old-growth Douglas fir flowed to the Grays Harbor mills from Finley Creek. When the logging operator who had gotten the Finley

Quick, Men, the Paris Green

The 75-year-old Willard Van Name was particularly successful with the *New York Times* and the *New York Herald Tribune* in his 1947 impassioned letter writing spree in defense of the park's forests. The *Herald Tribune* published this Olympic logging cartoon by Ding Darling, an Iowa friend of Irving Brant's, following several of Van Name's letters to the editor. *New York Herald Tribune, November 1, 1947; National Archives.*

Creek timber contract finished his logging, he launched a campaign with Washington's Congressional delegation demanding more. By now, nearly everyone on the Olympic Peninsula knew that the Park Service's preservation rhetoric was for the tourists and that there would be logging contracts for the locals. What Superintendents Macy and Overly had to face from now on was that every new contract would create its own demand for more. Both believed it was good public relations for the Park Service in the local community.

As soon as word spread through Washington's timber operators that the Park Service could cut a timber deal if insects were involved, the ever-alert West Coast Lumberman's Association announced to the press that 100,000 acres of Olympic National Park were infected with the black-headed hemlock budworm "and the infestation may make extensive logging in the park necessary." The newspapers informed their readers that "lumberman said salvage logging should be started immediately. . . ."[15] Thus the first of many insect infestations in Olympic National Park was launched, not by insects but by the word *insect* in the 1916 Park Service Act. Before Overly had succeeded in his timber-exchange program based on the insect clause, the Park Service view had always been as expressed by Regional Planner Davidson:

> The argument of clearing out down stuff to avoid disease etc. is not valid. Down trees, great blowdowns etc. have occurred for countless centuries; they are part of natural forest growth, not hazards to forests.[16]

No change as fundamental as this could go on without some wrenching internal stresses as the organization tried to reconcile the preservation mission stated in the Park Service's rhetoric with the logging program it had launched in Olympic National Park. The whole forestry staff both at headquarters and in the regions opposed the logging program from the start. They maneuvered to undermine its expansion and to stop it at whatever point they could do so. They had tough opposition. Comprising the pro-logging group were Superintendent Macy, Assistant Superintendent Overly (in the Navy from 1942 to 1945), Overly's replacement, Reino Sarlin, and O. A. Tomlinson, the regional director. Tomlinson had misgivings but in the end always actively supported his subordinates. The power of the pro-logging group to prevail was due to the presence of Conrad Wirth, Chief of Lands, in Washington, D.C. With persistence, skill and understanding of how the Park Service worked, he orchestrated what needed to be done to guarantee the expansion of the logging program in the face of considerable opposition.

As the loggers presented proposal after proposal, it was clear that the insect and fire-hazard limitations imposed by the solicitor's opinion were too restrictive to be able to accommodate the demand. Conrad Wirth was at the ready to expand the authority to cut. Under part of the 1916 Park Service Act which read "or otherwise conserve the scenery or the natural or historic objects . . . " he moved to get that authority expanded.[17] When Chief Counsel Jackson Price reasserted the insect and fire hazard restrictions,[18] Wirth responded by rejecting his whole approach. "It seems to me," he told Price, "that whenever we can exchange lands, that by so doing we improve or otherwise conserve the scenery or the natural or historic objects we should do so." He wanted Price to make his case for the solicitor. "Your help in obtaining a liberal interpretation will be appreciated," Wirth told Jackson.[19] Wirth was an aggressive advocate for the logging program. The forestry group that was opposing it was no match for Wirth's skill and persistence and his crucial position next to the director of the Park Service, Drury.

While Ickes was successfully fending off the War Production Board and the Park Service's other efforts to log for war purposes, the logs quietly flowed from the park to the mills without Ickes' knowledge or that of anyone else on the national scene. The 1916 Park Service Act had restricted the power to log the park and to accept title to lands to the Secretary of the Interior. This had given Ickes control in rejecting Drury's moves during World War II. But it also meant that each logging contract had to be approved in the secretary's office. Just six months after Harold Ickes left office, the Park Service tried to change that. In an order of delegation in an obscure corner of the Federal Register for August 21, 1946, they moved control from secretary to director:

> The Director of the National Park Service may provide for the cutting of timber pursuant to Section 3 of the Act of August 25, 1916, and may approve the sale or disposition of such timber.[20]

The agency created by the Park Service Act of 1916, passed thirty years earlier to preserve park forests unimpaired, had now maneuvered itself into position to log the very forests that the act intended to preserve. Using the act itself as the authority for the logging was ironic because the passage of the bill in 1916 followed an intense twenty-year public policy debate over cutting trees in the parks. The Park Service was now implementing Pinchot's rejected park logging program, intact.

By this time, the staff at Olympic Park had also lost control of the logging program in the Queets Corridor to the loggers themselves. The state of Washington was letting logging contracts on areas of the corridor owned by the Park Service which had been set aside to be preserved, and trespasses had become routine. Loggers were not establishing lines as required before they began logging. They simply kept cutting.

Superintendent Macy passively accepted it all. "It appears," he said, "that some legal action might be necessary to protect the interests of the United States."[21] He took no action, however, and with twenty-year cutting rights in force, there would be much more cutting before it ended.

Months before Macy expressed his complaints about the way things were going, Park Service Regional Forester Burnett Sanford had witnessed enough logging inside the park to take on, all alone, bringing it to a halt. He wrote to Tomlinson, his boss, but sent copies directly to Drury and Macy to make certain his message got around. It was a bold move. Writing as a professional forester, he said:

September 18, 1946

On numerous occasions I have opposed timber sales of all classes in the Olympic National Park. I still feel very strongly that the Service should adopt a policy of "no logging within the Park boundary," for the following reasons:

1. It is my firm conviction that the removal of logs *increases* the fire hazard. The tractor or donkey logging cannot help but knock down a large proportion of the small coniferous trees, hardwoods and brush, which are left in windrows in the worst possible condition for controlling fire. The removal of this ground cover permits the rapid drying of the finer fuels greatly increasing the fire hazard. The tops of limbs, which constitute the most inflammable portions of the trees, are exposed to the sun, and left on the ground. Observation of several sales in the western portion of the Park before and after logging has satisfied me that we have increased the fire hazard wherever timber has been sold.

2. The sale of timber from the Park has afforded accessible high quality timber to several "gypo" loggers who have become more or less dependent upon National Park lands for their livelihood, and as long as the sales are continued the pressure is going to be increased for additional sales. These sales and exchanges cannot help but influence the minds of the local people, who are not fully informed as to the principles governing the transactions, and thereby create the impression that under certain circumstances timber products are available within the Park. They do not inquire into the circumstances, and as a result may feel that selective logging over the area could be practiced if the Park officials would just be agreeable.

3. The National Park Service is not organized to administer a timber sale business and lacks the trained personnel to supervise the sales. Several years' experience administering National Forest timber sales with trained men on the ground, a hard and fast sale contract, and a strong forest management branch behind the timber sale man convinces me that any National Park Service sale will result in the operator taking many advan-

tages beyond those granted in his contract. This will result in unnecessarily rough logging, the removal of standing trees, and the leaving of low-grade but merchantable material in the woods. All of these advantages are taken by the operators on Forest Service timber sales, but to a greater degree on our sales with insufficient supervision.

4. Most of the Olympic National Park sales have been made in the form of exchanges whereby the Service acquired cut-over private lands in exchange for stumpage. Recognizing the advantage to the Service through the acquisition of alienated land within the boundaries, I feel that the destructive results of the logging operations more than outweigh the advantage, and increase the total amount of National Park area left in an unnatural condition.

5. Most of the sales have been in areas of forest where a large percentage of the trees have been thrown by wind. In almost every instance these areas are adjacent to logging operations and are a result of the loss of mutual protection which standing trees afford each other. Wherever these areas of windfall occur, they result in an unstabilized condition, since additional trees are exposed to the wind. Experience has demonstrated that stabilization will result in time if the area is left alone, but the removal of dead, broken-topped and otherwise injured trees from among the windfalls cannot help but result in delaying the stabilization of the stand as a whole, and thereby increasing the area of the windfall.

I feel that the sale of timber from the Olympic National Park is not advantageous to the Government, does not decrease the fire hazard, and should be stopped by means of a definite policy statement from the Director.

An adjustment of the Park boundary through exchange with the Forest Service could result in the acquisition of all private lands by the Government without any increase in the cut-over area of the Park.

Burnett Sanford,
Regional Forester[22]

Sanford had confronted the Park Service, but it did not matter. By the time his memo was written, Overly had returned from his wartime service in the Navy and was working closely with Wirth and Drury to eliminate the Bogachiel, the Calawah, and the Quinault areas from the park for the benefit of the lumbermen. Sanford, sitting in the regional office in San Francisco, could be ignored and he was. No one even bothered to acknowledge his memo.

In the meantime, the explosive forest elimination plan of 1947 that Wirth and Overly had engineered had begun Drury's downfall. As Rosalie Edge and her cohorts basked in the triumph of having beaten the Park Service on boundary changes, the Park Service prepared for a real logging program ahead.

In another delegation of power away from the secretary's office engineered by Wirth, the Park Service director was given the power to accept the deeds to the lands given by loggers in return for timber.[23] Bypassing the secretary's office was now complete. The Park Service had internal control over its logging program. Three months later, Wirth gave Drury a logging proposal from the Standard Lumber and Manufacturing Company that virtually gave a blank check to the Olympic National Park superintendent to log at will in the future. Citing the authority of the director first to dispose of timber and second to receive deeds, Wirth recommended that a tract on Lake Crescent be exchanged for park timber adjacent to an existing logging operation. "The Government timber, windthrown *or subject to windthrow* [my italics] is on the fringe of a logged-off area in private ownership," Wirth told Drury, "and constitutes a fire hazard and source of beetle infestation."[24] It was seemingly so innocent and yet such a bold move to broaden the logging program that he got Chief Forester John Coffman and Counsel Jackson Price to co-sign it with him. Coffman could not accept the beetle infestation statements and wrote after his signature, "I concur except as to the threat of beetle infestation."

Because all forests are *subject* to windthrow along the edge of existing logging operations, Wirth had given to the superintendent, with Drury's approval, the power to negotiate a deal with any logger cutting on private land in the park whereby he could keep cutting into park timber as long as he could come up with something of value that the Park Service wanted locally (sometimes lumber, sometimes labor and use of heavy equipment). Wirth and his local Park Service cohorts had constructed a permanent rationale for cutting park trees. After the logger had finished cutting park timber, the trees newly exposed on government land would also be subject to windthrow, so the logging could go on and on.

Only seven years had gone by since Fred Overly had used the insect provision in the 1916 Park Service Act on behalf of his former employer, the Crescent Logging Company. In that period, a group of park administrators had been able with great ease to move the Park Service to a position where it could sell the very trees that conservationists had fought for nearly fifty years to preserve.

By the end of 1948, the Park Service had removed 10,950,700 board feet of timber from the park[25] and the annual rate of removal was accelerating. Fred Overly and Conrad Wirth were now a team. Wirth had transferred Overly to Washington, D.C. in August of 1948 to head the real estate branch, from which he continued to manage Olympic National Park's logging program. Wirth became assistant director of the Park Service in July of 1949.

All through the years that the logging in the park was expanding and accelerating, the Park Service continued its pro-preservation rhetoric with the public and with Congress. When logs were flowing daily from the park to the mills of both Port Angeles and Grays Harbor, the Park Service prepared a statement for Representative Emmanuel Celler, for a Congressional hearing:

> The national policy stated in [1916 Act and the Olympic National Park Act] these acts, to maintain the inviolate character of national park forests, has been strengthened by general public acceptance over a long period of time. Only in these areas of nationally significant forest scenery will Americans of the future be assured of an opportunity to see and enjoy the majesty and beauty of the natural forests.
>
> Logging in any form, even if confined to removal of overmature or dying trees by careful selective means, cannot be accomplished without serious loss of natural values. It is contrary to the whole theory upon which national parks are established.
>
> The Olympic National Park contains one of the last extensive, unmodified remnants of the once vast area of virgin forest which was the glory of the Pacific Northwest. . . . It is my considered opinion that the forests of Olympic National Park, including overmature and dying trees, will serve their most useful purposes to the American people by continuance of these long established and generally accepted policies, and that their importance to the Nation will increase with time.[26]

As Drury's tenure drew to a close in a cloud of conservationist contempt, Conrad Wirth had maneuvered himself into position to ascend to the Park Service throne. No one had any idea that a full-blown logging effort had been laid out during Drury's regime during the distraction of the 1947 boundary-change battle. For the Park Service, the logging program constituted its only success. Every other move it had attempted since 1934, when its first Olympic National Park boundary recommendation had been brushed aside by Ickes, had failed. At last the Park Service administrators who were directly involved with Olympic National Park could finally console themselves that they had a winner — logs were flowing to the mills. That would satisfy the loggers. The conservationists, they thought, would be satisfied that the private land in the park, often in critical locations, was being systematically acquired and without the appropriation process to contend with.

The only flaw in it all was that the American public was deeply committed to inviolate preservation of the park's forests. Director Arno B. Cammerer's absolute commitment, reiterated over and over during the 1930's park battle, that "there would be no timber cutting within the park . . . "[27] had now been long forgotten by the Park Service. Perhaps, by constantly restating their preservation charter, the Park Service could convince everyone of their good intentions.

17 TIMBER FLOWS

I think Fred Overly has done an outstanding job . . . by exchang-
ing timber which is valuable from the lumberman's standpoint
but has very little, if any, value to the National Park.[1]

CONRAD WIRTH, DIRECTOR,
NATIONAL PARK SERVICE

To Fred Overly: "You are destined to be the subject of a biography,
a book, I mean. Maybe to be safe you had better write it yourself."[2]

IRVING CLARK

EARLY IN 1951, when Secretary of the Interior Oscar Chapman forced
Drury out of the directorship of the Park Service, largely over his
handling of Olympic National Park, his choice for successor was
Conrad Wirth. He would become director after a short courtesy appointment of Arthur Demaray. The long internal struggle over the logging
of Olympic National Park was now laid to rest. The pro-logging forces
inside the Park Service had won control at the top and the fight was over.

While Wirth was director designate, he moved Fred Overly from his
Washington, D.C., position as chief of the real estate branch, back to
Olympic as superintendent. At the same time, Macy was moved back
to Mount Rainier, from which he had been transferred to Olympic in
the days of the Mount Olympus National Monument. Overly had been
running Olympic National Park's logging program from Washington,
D.C., since 1948, so everyone close to Olympic National Park knew there
would now be a real logging program but the general public and park
visitors still believed the preservation rhetoric.

Wirth had been in the inner circle of Washington, D.C., Park Service
administrators for over twenty years when he became director. As early

Clear cutting became a part of the Wirth-Overly logging program early on. The M & D Timber Company left this clear-cut on the lower Hoh in 1956. *National Archives.*

as 1932, Wirth was on record saying that the Olympic region did not "come up to the standards set for national parks."[3] Two years later, when Willard Van Name launched the ECC park campaign, Wirth attempted to deflect any Park Service commitment to it by quoting from an earlier memo opposing an Olympic National Park because of the "fact that the mountain and surrounding area, to a large extent, would duplicate Mt. Rainier National Park, in the same state. We have consistently recommended," he said, "against its establishment as a national park."[4] Wirth had then worked continuously within the Park Service to keep the westside forests out of the park during the park battle. During the Drury regime, it was he who had held what Willard Van Name had charged

The hillside above Olympic Hot Spring was given over to clear cut logging in 1956 even though it was adjacent to the visitor parking lot. Overly defended it but Wirth said it was a mistake. *National Archives.*

were secret meetings with the timber industry on forest eliminations. Wirth had also produced the actual boundary recommendations eliminating the Bogachiel, Calawah, Hoh and Quinault forests from the park in 1947. "His general attitude is that national parks are glorified state parks," Fred Packard of the National Parks Association warned Mrs. Edge, "and . . . that inviolate protection of the national parks is a wild eyed dream." Because Packard knew him personally, it was an ominous warning. "I know him and his background too well," he said, "too well to believe he should ever become Director." Prophetically, he told Edge, "we can expect drastic changes of policy if and when Wirth takes over."[5]

None of Wirth's intimate involvement in Olympic's timber affairs was visible to outsiders, including Irving Brant. Brant had a high regard for Wirth's ability but had to confess to Edge, "I never have known whether he was a convinced and thorough conservationist, or one merely capable of carrying out somebody else's conservation policy effectively."[6] Wirth's ascent to the directorship thus was a mixed bag for everyone. Key conservationists viewed him with general distrust from twenty years of watching him in action, but at the same time they admired his skill and political acumen. For the staff at Olympic National Park, the team of Wirth and Overly meant only one thing—logs would flow from the park to the mills. By 1952, so much timber had begun to flow from Olympic National Park that Washington State's timber harvest statistical records could not accurately account for the quantity produced. For the first time, a special category had to be added to the state's timber harvest report—*National Park Timber Harvested—Western Washington 1952.*[7]

All the basic changes necessary to implement a logging program in Olympic National Park had been put into place, piece by piece by Wirth and Overly, throughout the preceding decade. What the 1916 Park Service Act originally required of the Secretary of the Interior regarding tree cutting, had now been delegated to the director. He in turn had delegated the decisions to the park superintendent, who in turn had delegated to the park forester the determination of which trees would be sent to the mills. Ironically, the 1916 Park Service Act, passed to

Major log landings were constructed to handle the volume of timber being removed from the park. The M & D Timber Company constructed this landing on the Hoh in 1956. *National Archives.*

A heel boom track loader at work loading Douglas fir at a log landing in the Quinault Valley in 1955. Note the size of the old-growth Douglas fir being removed. *National Archives.*

prevent logging in the parks for all time, was the cited legal authority for the logging now underway.

When a group of Seattle investors wanted to drill for oil at the mouth of the Hoh River on lands in the park's coastal strip, Wirth obligingly suggested to Representative Henry Jackson that if they "could arrange to do the actual drilling on privately owned lands, this Service would recommend issuance of a lease to provide for slant drilling under Government lands. . . ."[8] The havoc caused by such drilling in the wilderness of the coastal strip was never even considered.

The timber industry, using the Port Angeles Chamber of Commerce again, mounted another attack on the park which ran in the local paper over a period of nine weeks. Its purpose was to rally support to make 300,000 acres of west-side forests available for logging. "The case for Park reduction is clear," one of the articles said, "Many people in all walks of life will benefit."[9] Willard Van Name, now seventy-nine but still with his uncanny, intuitive sense of danger to the park, told the readers of letters to the editor section of the *New York Times* that the lumbermen were still at work attempting to destroy Olympic National Park. "The lumbermen do not want the treeless or poorly forested mountain areas of the park," he said. "They want the rain forest, every tree of it."[10]

By 1952, the coastal strip and the Queets Corridor had been a part of the park for thirteen years, although not legally in it. The timing had never been right for the Park Service to add it to the park. When Macy finally requested that action be taken to place those areas in the park, Overly, still in Washington, D.C., but superintendent-designate of Olympic National Park, drafted a letter for Wirth's signature rejecting the idea.[11]

Irving Brant saw a great threat to the park in the nine-mile-long, mile-wide strip running through the Bogachiel Valley which was not yet in the park. It was now owned by the Forest Service following its acquisition from Crown Zellerbach. When Dwight Eisenhower won the 1952 presidential election, Brant anticipated that Secretary of the Interior-designate, Douglas McKay, would never allow further additions. Brant decided the time to get the former Crown Zellerbach lands in the Bogachiel Valley into the park was now or never. The only way was to get Truman to issue the necessary proclamation before he left office. "The real effort," Brant told Truman about the lumbermen's intentions, "is to prevent the addition of 5,760 acres running like a finger, nine miles long into the present park in the Bogachiel Valley. . . . The Grays Harbor sawmill interests want it left out, to afford an argument for eliminating the entire Bogachiel Valley to a depth of nine miles, by act of Congress."[12] Brant was as highly regarded by Truman, who knew him from his Senate days, as he was by Roosevelt. Truman proclaimed the addition on January 6, 1953, just thirteen days before leaving office. As a final touch, Brant was asked to draft Truman's statement on the proclamation, as he had done for many other official documents relating to Olympic Park in the past.[13]

Brant succeeded in totally disrupting the strategy of the timber industry for making another run at the Bogachiel Valley in the new business-oriented Eisenhower administration. Cries of "foul" could be heard from timber industry and chamber of commerce groups. The Seattle Chamber of Commerce charged, in a fit of illogic, that more than 47,000 acres had been taken away from the people of Washington. "This order," charged the chamber, "not only violates basic rights of citizens of this state but is a serious blow to their economy."[14] As usual, both the *Seattle Times* and *Post-Intelligencer* supported the timber industry. The *New York Times* joined the fray on behalf of the environmental organizations. "In brief," it said at the end of a long pro-park editorial, "if local Washington interests are too short sighted to see the permanent values (commercial as well as spiritual and esthetic) in a 900,000 acre Olympic National Park, then it is up to the rest of us to make sure that the nation is not deprived of this priceless and unique asset."[15]

Gordon Marckworth, dean of the University of Washington College of Forestry, began another campaign on behalf of the timber industry.

The Douglas fir trees along the roads, in campgrounds and wherever they could be reached with logging equipment were generally declared "danger trees" (they might fall down), victims of the 1916 Park Service Act as interpreted by Director Conrad Wirth and Superintendent Fred Overly. This photo was taken in 1956. *National Archives.*

He urged all chambers of commerce on the Olympic Peninsula to launch a campaign to achieve what forester James Girard had recommended in the 1947 hearings—removal of at least 300,000 acres of the west-side forests from the park. To spur them on, he sent them a copy of Girard's report.[16]

When Marckworth's efforts came to Washington Governor Arthur B. Langlie's attention, it seemed he would be the right person to implement the boundary-recommendation commission that Greeley had been working on since he failed in the park battle of the 1930's. Greeley had gotten Seattle's newspaper editors to again call for such a commission, so Langlie could now seem to be responding to local demand. After years of trying, Greeley finally got his commission and Marckworth was appointed chairman. The old industry chief, Greeley himself, would be rewarded by being appointed to it, along with a group representing the classic timber-industry triad: the Forest Service, the University of Washington College of Forestry, and the timber industry trade associations.

To give the commission some semblance of credibility, it had to have some members who would not take the industry position. Here, the conservationists blundered. They should have held that the park boundaries had been fixed by Congress when the park bill authorized additions by proclamation, and that these were not open for further negotiation. The governor's committee would have been finished. Instead, several conservation organization members naively jumped on board, giving it the credibility it needed. In the end, after hearings in three towns during which the usual viewpoints were expressed by the usual assortment of individuals, the committee offered a minority report calling for the preservation of what was already in the park, and a majority report that called for referring the whole matter to "two or more men of national standing" to study it further.[17] Greeley desperately worked behind the scenes to get the committee to adopt the 1934 Park Service boundary recommendation. As Greeley told Marckworth, this "would reduce the Olympic National Park by approximately 275,000 acres or 54 percent of the total area of low land forest."[18]

Greeley didn't succeed, however. The commission deadlocked and took no action. The following year, he would be dead at age seventy-

During the years that the logging program was underway in Olympic National Park, logs waiting to be loaded were a common sight along park roads everywhere in the park. This photo was taken in 1956. *National Archives.*

Built to facilitate the movement of logs across the Quinault River by a Park Service logging contractor, this bridge's size suggests the volume of timber being cut to justify the
cost of its construction. Note the size of the old-growth Douglas fir being removed from
the park in 1955. *National Archives.*

six, having spent a major part of his life working to make Olympic's
trees available for the mill owners who paid his salary.

When Governor Langlie learned that of the hundreds upon hundreds of letters that poured into the committee, not one non-timber-
industry source favored a change in park boundaries, he quietly dropped
the whole thing. Another ominous political factor emerged for him:
The woodworking unions and the CIO warned everyone to keep hands
off the park's forests. Governor Langlie got the message.

The Seattle newspapers did not have to think about votes, however.
When the Lumber and Sawmill Workers Union later urged in their annual convention that "the Olympic Peninsula's forests be preserved ... ,"

the *Seattle Post-Intelligencer* moved its attack to the union. Editorializing, it said, "But the *Post-Intelligencer* feels some astonishment that a group of men who make their living from forest products should so misconstrue a basic issue. . . . We can only conclude that the sawmill workers union knows too little about the Olympic National Park. . . . A much smaller area could produce 60 million dollars of new wealth. . . ."[19] What had happened was that the issues of environmental degradation as a factor in the quality of life had reached the economically better-off blue collar workers by the middle 1950's. This represented a major loss to the timber industry, which could no longer orchestrate its workers to get more timber by political action.

Truman's 1953 additions brought about a hearing in Port Angeles by the House Committee on Interior and Insular Affairs. In these hearings, when Overly was pressed to explain the now-institutionalized logging program in the park, he told the committee that "there will always be some timber to remove."[20] Overly had also by charm, assertiveness, and convincing arguments, managed to immobilize Olympic Park Associates, the watchdog group that Irving Clark had begun after the Park Service's 1947 elimination debacle. In 1953, when Olympic Park Associates' representative, John Osseward, was pressed to take a stand by Congressman D'Ewart on logging in the park, Overly triumphed:

MR. D'EWART: My question was, what about these insect infested trees within the park boundary? Do you give your approval to the removal of this timber?

MR. OSSEWARD: When the Park Service says "Yes."

MR. D'EWART: And also windfalls?

MR. OSSEWARD: Only when the Park Service says "Yes."[21]

Overly had previously witnessed first-hand the power of the Emergency Conservation Committee to bring the Park Service to its knees and could not risk an ECC campaign against the logging program. He therefore took great pains to prevent either Rosalie Edge or Irving Brant from getting involved. After Overly had become superintendent at the start of the intensive logging program in 1952, he called on Edge personally in New York and on Irving Brant in Washington, D.C., to appeal for their cooperation in acquiring desperately needed private property, without which the administration of the park was impeded, he told them. It could be done, he said, by sending some fallen trees to market.[22] They each gave their individual assent to proceed.

Having skillfully moved to identify the possible damaging opposition to his logging program, Overly in one way or another immobilized it. By 1952, he had gotten annual timber production in the park up to 7.3 million board feet. A year later, in 1953, he succeeded in

This 8-foot 7-inch diameter Douglas fir was one of the "danger trees," a victim of the Wirth-Overly logging program in 1955. *National Archives.*

doubling it to 14.6 million board feet.[23] By 1953, Overly had become a power broker for gypo loggers in Port Angeles, Forks, and Grays Harbor. Earlier predictions of the Park Service's own forestry staff had come true: The availability of park timber had created its own, ever-increasing demand for more. Overly responded with the same ingenuity that he was able to apply to every challenge. He sent trail crews miles up the trails to begin logging the back-country. The logs were cut and rolled to the rivers to be floated to waiting logging trucks. One such effort involved logging the area of Camp Baltimore on the Elwha Trail and later giving a contract to take driftwood from Lake Mills at the Crown Zellerbach Dam where the logs collected.

Back-country logging, however, could never produce the volume that Overly was looking for. To assist Overly, Wirth requested on March

25, 1953, "that a reconnaissance survey and report be made of a route over Tshletshy Creek Ridge from the North Fork of the Quinault River to the Queets Corridor."[24] Wirth's request produced a road design by the Bureau of Public Roads that included a twenty-six-foot-wide road through one of the most remote of the park's wilderness areas. This road just happened to pass through the areas of densest forest growth in both the Queets and Quinault valleys. The report concluded, "this route when constructed . . . will make accessible to park visitors a large area in the southwest section of the park that can be reached now only by trails." For the many backpackers who were using the area involved, the report could hardly be a comfort. It read, "The area traversed by the route over several miles in the vicinity of Reflection Lake, Kurtz Lake, and Three Prune Shelter will provide a number of places for picnicking and similar recreational development."[25] Overly also talked of a road up the Hoh Valley over High Divide and out the Soleduck, as he did before the Port Townsend Rotary Club in September of 1953. The Park Service, he said, "needed to convert the vast wilderness into something the people can use."[26] But in fact, all Overly's roads would have generated millions more of board feet for the peninsula mills, and destruction of the wilderness the park was created to protect was the price of his program.

Using the cutting of a swath along the 49th Parallel between Canada and the United States as a precedent, Overly planned the cutting of a similar swath just inside the park boundary all around the park.[27] Such a swath would have produced additional millions of board feet over the years.

Overly's policies for Olympic National Park had the full backing of Director Wirth. Overly was cautious, however, in his relations with Wirth. For every logging contract, Overly sent detailed reports, including photographs showing the damage, back to Washington D.C. headquarters. He did not want to be put in the position of having Washington D.C. say later, "we did not know what was going on." Fred Packard's prophecy to Mrs. Edge, just two years earlier, that "we can expect drastic changes of policy, if and when Wirth takes over," had come true.

Ignoring Overly's doubling of Olympic's annual timber production to 14.6 million board feet, Wirth issued a statement on logging the parks, perhaps to deny even to himself what he had set in motion. His statement serves as a masterpiece of bureaucratic hypocrisy:

> There are those who believe it wasteful to permit large and commercially valuable trees to die, fall down and rot when they could have been used commercially. Such individuals have in numerous instances advocated selective logging for the national parks, so as to utilize the mature and

Park Service logging contractor Frank P. Donahue, friend of Superintendent Fred Overly, proudly stands by a 7½-foot diameter, 20-foot long butt cut Douglas fir taken from the Fairholm area of Lake Crescent in 1955. It scaled at 7,700 board feet. *National Archives.*

overmature trees while they are still merchantable. Such logging, no matter how selective or restrictive it may be or how carefully accomplished, is contrary to the principles upon which our national parks and monuments were established. Once logging is introduced, the ecological conditions are changed and the area no longer exists as a superlative virgin forest.

Olympic National Park has been and will no doubt continue to be the prime target of those interests which seek its timber either through selective logging, boundary retraction, or both. Neither can be permitted under present park concept and law, but laws can be changed. The Department and conservationists nationwide have continued to insist that the integrity of the Park be not encroached upon.

When feasible, we salvage park timber of commercial value resulting from road right-of-way clearings or other construction. At Olympic and Yosemite National Parks we are salvaging valuable timber from road clearings and blowdowns, from feathering the edges of tracts that were clear cut before we acquired them, and at Olympic, from streams. In these cases, however, the basis for the salvage is the preservation of the adjacent forest, the control of insects and diseases, or the protection of the land or stream itself.[28]

The cutting of park trees by now could always be justified by the simple statement that it was only being done to preserve the forest itself. For good measure, Wirth's statement quoted directly from the Park Service administrative manual:

Wood Utilization Policy

In conformity with the letter and spirit of the laws relating to national parks and monuments, there shall be no cutting of trees, either live or dead, within the National Park System for forest products by the Service, by concessioners, or through sales, free use or donations, except as specifically provided by law or regulations, unless such utilization shall be incidental to necessary clearings for rights of way or for building or development sites, vista clearings, fire hazard reduction, cleanup operations in windfalls and burns, insect and tree disease control, removal of trees dangerous to life or property, or for esthetic effect or portrayal of the historic picture.[29]

The Wood Utilization Policy, while reaffirming the preservation intent of the 1916 Park Service Act, allowed for any kind of logging the Park Service chose to engage in, including the back-country logging. In fact, the Olympic National Park logging program conformed precisely with the policy defined in the manual, even though on another page of Wirth's statement the preservation mandate was affirmed: "virgin forests remain unlogged to go through their natural cycles."[30] It was administrative behavior right out of Mather's Park Service and Mather had been gone for a quarter of a century.

As the logs flowed to the mills, enormous stress developed throughout the Park Service as preservation values continued to be reasserted, at the same time that logging continued to increase. The local staff split into opposing camps—those who worked on the logging program, and those who hoped to escape damage to their careers for failure to support it. Overly, however, never asked for support. He just wanted no opposition.

The following year, 1954, the timber industry took a bold new stand. The Olympic National Park, supposedly with locked-up timber, was sitting at the doorstep of mills owned by two of the largest operators in the country—Crown Zellerbach and Rayonier. Instead of locking up the timber in the park, the timber was seen as trickling to the mills by the way of high cost, low-efficiency gypo loggers, when it could be flowing properly through large clear-cuts in Forest Service working circles. In the late fall of 1954, the Rayonier Corporation mounted a nationwide campaign to get a sizeable percentage of the park's trees back into the hands of the Forest Service, which knew how to do business with timber operators. Stepping out from behind the protective facade of the industry front groups, that had normally characterized every timber company's political operations, Rayonier's president, Clyde B. Morgan directly mounted a national media campaign. "The inclusion of this commercial forest land in a national park," he said of Olympic

National Park's west-side forests, "is an error that we propose to rec-
tify . . . the commercial forest lands now included in the park should
be removed."[31] Morgan had launched an international sales thrust a
couple of years earlier to take up the slack in Rayonier's overcapacity.
By 1954 that sales thrust had begun to pay off and he needed timber
to sustain it. "It is a crime to see lands adjacent to ours," he said, "lands
that are prime commercial forest land and not of park caliber, locked
up so that they do no one any good."[32] While Morgan was leading his
personal campaign for more timber, his sales vice president, Michael
A. Brown, told the New York stock analysts another part of the Rayonier story. "Once you build a pulp mill," he said, "the cost of doubling
its size is relatively small, and the temptation to do so is almost irresistible."[33]

In the middle of its media blitz against the park, Rayonier opened
up a picnic ministop on U.S. highway 101 south of Lake Quinault. The
dedication ceremony was turned by Rayonier's public relations department into a major Olympic Peninsula media event, complete with a
keynote address from Washington's Senator Warren G. Magnuson. Magnuson made it plain in his address that he contemplated no boundary
changes in the Olympic National Park but that the Forest Service should
make recommendations for possible use of its over-ripe timber. It was
exactly what the newspaper and timber crowd in attendance wanted
to hear. When Superintendent Fred Overly read Magnuson's speech,
however, he believed he was already doing what Magnuson suggested.
"To my way of thinking," Overly said, "the forest salvage operation we
have been conducting is the answer to this problem."[34]

The end result of the Rayonier campaign turned out to be a reacti-
vation of the national conservation lobby. Even Mrs. Roosevelt joined
in, attacking Rayonier in her nationally syndicated newspaper column,
My Day. There was solid union opposition to cutting timber in the park.
"I can assure you," charged A. F. Hartung of the International Woodworkers, "that our organization will fight to the last ditch before we
will allow them to cut down the timber in the Olympic National Park
for their own profits."[35] All in all, the campaign was a disaster for
Rayonier.

One of Superintendent Fred Overly's real disappointments in life
was that he had not gone into the logging business himself.[36] He kept
working at it though. In 1948, before his transfer from Olympic National

OPPOSITE: Rayonier's President Clyde Morgan launched a nationwide attack on Olympic
National Park and Rosalie Edge with two-page full color advertisements in national maga-
zines, including *Time, US News and World Report* and in daily papers across the country.
Time, December 27, 1954.

Park to Washington, D.C., he went to the Peninsula Plywood Corporation and offered to work for them, assuring them that he really knew how to get timber. The condition he placed was that he receive a full share in the cooperative, worth about $12,000 at the time. He missed the deal by one vote on the board of directors.[37]

By the end of 1953, with millions of board feet of timber from the park now flowing to the mills, Overly took the plunge to become a logger of park timber himself. His scheme was direct and simple.

As superintendent, Overly headed the Olympic Natural History Association. The park naturalist, Gunnar Fagerlund, served as its secretary. This non-profit private association, authorized by special federal legislation, served as a local vehicle by which the park's visitor centers could stock guide books, maps and slides for purchase by park visitors, as such associations do in most parks. Overly's scheme was to assign logging contracts to this association, which he headed. So blatant was the conflict of interest, that in June of 1954, he resigned as chairman of the association and from its board of directors and put on the board along with the park naturalist, Assistant Superintendent Jerry House and Chief Ranger John Aiton. Overly could now issue logging contracts, in effect to his own subordinates, although officially to the Olympic Natural History Association.[38]

Wirth had rejected Overly's approach to using the Olympic Natural History Association in this manner when he first proposed it a year earlier, but Overly persisted. Overly, as superintendent, could now finance projects that caught his attention by selling off park resources through the Olympic Natural History Association, which he controlled. The revenue generated could then be directed wherever he pleased. The Port Angeles Visitor Center was financed largely in this manner.

In May of 1955, the Interior Department Solicitor determined that the 1942 decision allowing park timber to be exchanged for private land was illegal. Wirth notified everyone immediately that there would be no more timber exchanged for land. Even though this exchange process was now declared illegal, logging went right on, with the proceeds now going to the U.S. Treasury instead of toward land acquisition.

With the appearance of "drift" logs in Lake Mills, a result of back-country logging, the Olympic Natural History Association seemed to Overly to be a natural to receive the contract to pick them up. Overly decided that the shores of Lake Mills could just as well be logged at the same time. The Olympic Natural History Association continued on as logging contractor, now actively engaged in the destruction of the primeval back-country of the park.[39] Periodically, the park naturalist would be handed a check for proceeds of the operation, which he dutifully deposited in the association's account.

When the backcountry logging up the Elwha and on the hillsides above Lake Mills was completed, the logs gathered behind Glines Canyon Dam. A contract was then let for the gathering of "driftwood in Lake Mills." The photo was taken in 1956. *National Archives.*

As the logging continued year after year, the stress rose in the local Park Service staff. The greatest stress was on the park's seasonal naturalist staff, all of whom were housed together in a small enclave on Lake Crescent. This was the staff that had to face angry inquiries about logging when park visitors saw it. Hardly was an evening campfire program completed without a hostile comment about logging in the park from one or more of the visitors. In fact, it was from visitor contacts that the naturalist staff became aware of the extent of the logging. Often by chance, while photographing the park, one of the naturalists would stumble across an area with all of the large, old-growth Douglas fir removed, as one saw when taking pictures across the Hoh River from Hoh Ranger Station.

Every public organization which relies on seasonal employees is vulnerable to internal problems when the stated values of the organization differ from what its operational values actually are. Permanent employees soon become immune to these differences, often for the sake of keeping their jobs.

Seasonal employees, on the other hand, are only present during the busiest time of the year, with minimum contact with the permanent staff. Seasonal naturalists in most parks come with a highly developed preservationist viewpoint. In fact, a major function of their jobs is to articulate the Park Service's role in preservation.

Because of the disparity between the Park Service's articulated values and the park logging in which some of the permanent staff was vigorously engaged, the seasonal naturalist staff was chronically outraged. To have the Olympic Natural History Association and Gunnar Fagerlund, the park naturalist whom they all idolized as a role model, involved in logging the park, was taken as almost a personal insult.

The seasonal naturalist staff, therefore, became the focal point of opposition inside the Olympic National Park organization itself. Because of this, even many permanent employees were ventilating their outrage along with the seasonal naturalists by the summer of 1956.

The naturalist staff had long sessions over cheap jug wine in the Morganroth log cabin on Lake Crescent, which was occupied by lead seasonal naturalist, Grant Sharpe. These sessions became known as "logging the park" sessions because that was almost the only subject discussed. Sharpe was then working on a dissertation on the rain forest for a Ph.D. in forestry. These sessions went on through the summers of 1954 and 1955. Sharpe did not appear in the summer of 1956, having left to finish his dissertation. He was replaced by Paul Shepard, an ecology graduate from Paul Sears' well-known program at Yale University. At that time, Shepard had an academic appointment at Knox College in Illinois and was serving as conservation chairman of the National Council of State Garden Clubs, with a total membership at the time of 250,000.

Shepard, from the moment of his arrival, was stunned by the ever-present logging occurring everywhere in the park. His reaction proved to be enormously validating for the rest of the seasonal staff. As Overly used the term "birdwatchers" as a term of derision for them, the naturalist staff wore it with increasing pride as their new lead naturalist reacted with the same abhorrence they felt towards what was going on.

In the middle of the summer of 1956, Overly unwittingly issued the order that was the beginning of the end for him and for the logging program. He ordered the naturalist staff to photograph all back-country areas where tree damage had resulted from winter avalanches, a part of the natural processes of nature in the park. To the staff, this meant back-country everywhere in the park now was going to be systematically logged, with the trees going down the rivers and tearing up fish-spawning beds in the process. It also involved the naturalists directly in the logging process although this had probably never entered Overly's mind. The rest of that summer, the "logging the park" group therapy sessions gave way to serious planning around Paul Shepard's table.

The naturalists believed, from the reactions of the tourists in the park, that the logging program could not stand public scrutiny. Silence

Major logging operations were found to be underway throughout the park by the joint environmentalist committee as the allegations of the seasonal naturalists were corroborated. The committee photographed the Park Service contractor's loading yard next to the Quinault River deep inside the park in 1956. *Carsten Lien.*

was what had enabled it to go on. Earlier in that summer of 1956, one of the naturalists found in the park's headquarters a statement personally signed by Wirth in 1954 that lent credence to what appeared to be a systematic cover-up. In his two-page statement, Wirth said:

> . . . the American people, through its Congress, long ago determined that there shall be both national parks and national forests. That is why the relatively small acreages set aside by the people as national parks cannot be tampered with if any unaltered exhibits of nature's handiwork are to be kept in trust by the Nation for the benefit of this and future generations. That is why from the viewpoint of the National Park Service, the rain forests of Olympic National Park cannot be selectively logged or eliminated from the park for timber production. To do so would defeat the very purposes of the park and the expressed will of the Nation to which it belongs.[40]

From this flagrant misstatement of what was occurring, they deduced that if a national campaign with enough publicity could be mounted,

All of the enormous Douglas fir trees the park was created to preserve were cut by the Park Service wherever they could be reached by logging equipment in the Wirth-Overly logging program. This nine-foot diameter giant was felled at LaPoel on Lake Crescent (1956) where such trees were once common. *Carsten Lien.*

Wirth would run rather than try to defend logging. Shepard, as conservation chairman of the National Council of State Garden Clubs, had ties throughout the East. They also discovered they had direct ties to all the environmental groups in the Pacific Northwest.

There were two problems, however. One was that they believed the local conservation organizations had been gutless in dealing with the Park Service on the logging in all the previous years. Because of this local penchant for passivity and inaction, the naturalists developed a plan that every environmental organization outside of the Pacific Northwest would ask Wirth for logging to cease pending an investigation. Local groups would then be forced into only having to decide whether to join the action or not. Even if they chose not to, the efforts would go right on without them. The second problem was that if the naturalist staff were visibly involved, the whole effort would be laid right on Park Naturalist Gunnar Fagerlund's doorstep by Overly. To avoid this problem for their revered boss, who was not a willing party to the logging scheme, the naturalists decided that Paul Shepard would be the front man. The plan would unfold without Fagerlund's knowledge.

After the naturalist group had split up at the end of the season of 1956, a working group dubbed the *Joint Committee on SLONP* (Salvage Logging Olympic National Park) formed in Seattle representing the Sierra Club, the Mountaineers, Seattle Audubon Society, Olympic Park Associates, and the Federation of Western Outdoor Clubs. Their judgment that local inaction would again prevail was wrong. The local groups jumped into action. Congressman Jack Westland's administrative assistant, Jim Dolliver, in whose district the park lay, had been a seasonal ranger in the park and a personal friend of one of the naturalists. He was asked to request from Wirth on behalf of Westland a detailed accounting of every logging contract Overly had granted. Congressional involvement could seem ominous to Wirth, they believed. They were right.

By the end of the following week, letters and telegrams were pouring in to Wirth from conservation organizations, national and local, demanding a cessation of all logging in the park. In the meantime, the Joint Committee had undertaken a field trip to logging sites in the park to corroborate the accuracy of what the naturalists were telling them. Any lingering doubts vanished when they found a logging crew in the Bogachiel Valley, four miles into the back-country from the trail head. Supposedly salvaging a log jam, the crew was actually dropping large Douglas fir trees in the adjacent forest. The whole operation was photographed.

Shepard, from his role with the National Council of State Garden Clubs, had not only pieced together a coalition of eastern and national groups to respond to the logging but also stepped in to confront Wirth directly. Shepard wrote Wirth:

> We are familiar with the ring of logged land that now practically surrounds Lake Crescent, with the logging on park lands in the Sol Duc area, the intensive cutting going on near Kalaloch, the so-called salvage operations in the Bogachiel and Hoh Channels, the removal of down trees at the Hoh Ranger Station, the logging at the forks of the Quinault, far up the Elwha and at Olympic Hot Springs. We know that plans are afoot to salvage avalanche timber from deep within the park and that a right-of-way widening program will remove a large amount of timber from each side of roads, if it is carried out.[41]

Overly had recognized from the start the power that Irving Brant could wield in bringing an Olympic Park logging program to a halt. He chose not to start logging unless Brant would approve in advance and now it was paying off.

When the joint committee of environmental organizations arrived at the backcountry site of what was supposed to be a logjam logging operation on the Bogachiel, four miles from the trailhead, they found the Park Service logging contractor busy logging, not the logjam, but the adjacent forest of the largest Douglas fir trees that could be located. The committee photographed the loading of some of these newly cut green Douglas fir logs in 1956. *Carsten Lien.*

Overly, however, had so completely taken in Irving Brant and Rosalie Edge on his logging program that Brant instantly dismissed the whole thing. Overly had, in effect, made Brant a part of it. Brant explained to Edge how Overly had involved him in the logging program:

> Overly talked to me . . . before he started, saying that by salvaging the down trees in the Sol Duc windthrow he could raise enough money to buy all the private timber lands around Crescent Lake, preventing the destruction of the beautiful forest at the west end of the lake and stopping lumbering operations on the north side. He would not do it, he said, unless I approved it. . . . I told him he ought to go ahead. . . .[42]

Brant's support of Overly was a relief for Rosalie Edge. Then seventy-eight years old, she had been intensely involved with Olympic National Park for nearly thirty years and was just not up to more. "When I came home and found all the correspondence about the Olympic Park on my desk," she told Brant, "I simply couldn't face it." Thanking Brant for his explanation, she told him, "I know Paul Shepard quite well. He is intelligent and well meaning but not too experienced in conservation."[43] With that declaration she withdrew, relieved that Brant was satisfied that everything was proper.

Shepard had sent forty-eight long telegrams to each of the state presidents of the garden clubs. As a result, Wirth was deluged by letters and telegrams from all over the country and with similar responses from all of the conservation organizations in the country. Wirth started to make moves to contain the attack on the Park Service and, inferentially, on him. Congressman Westland's request for a complete accounting of every logging contract represented a real danger and the fact that objections to the logging were coming in from every state also meant real danger for him.

The Park Service was again in the middle of a crisis. On September 25, 1956, just three weeks after the Lake Crescent seasonal naturalists had launched their plan, Regional Director Lawrence Merriam called Overly from San Francisco and later summarized his message in writing to make absolutely certain Overly got it:

1. That there will be no contract involving salvage logging at the Staircase area awarded tomorrow, September 26.

The joint committee photographed a logging contractor's truck as it departed from the Bogachiel backcountry in 1956. Note the size of the old-growth Douglas fir being taken and the riverbank that had to be bulldozed to get the logs out. Upset by the picture taking, the crew shut down the job for the day after this truck departed. *Carsten Lien.*

2. That there will be no extension granted to Abel [a logger] beyond October 15 in connection with the removal of blowdown in the Hoh area.
3. That there will be no further contracts entered into involving salvage logging between now and October 15.
4. That after October 15 no salvage logging contracts will be entered into without taking the matter up first with this office.[44]

The naturalists' working premise that logging the park could not stand up to public scrutiny was proving to be correct. Overly had lost control of the logging processes in the first bureaucratic reaction to that public response. Without knowing they were doing so, the naturalists were acting out Willard Van Name's first rule of conservation activism — change only happens when the public is involved.

Given the task of investigating the logging, Merriam proceeded to the park with Regional Forester Maurice Thede to meet members of the Joint Committee at some of the more notorious logging sites in the park. The Joint Committee refused to have Overly present, so Park Forester Floyd Dickinson attended as an acceptable local park official. "Have you ever seen anything like this in a national park?" Phil Zalesky of Olympic Park Associates asked Merriam of the destruction in front of them. "No," said Merriam, with chagrin, "I have never seen anything like this in a national park before."[45]

By this time, whole delegations of executives from various conservation organizations had called at Park Service headquarters in Washington, D.C., to discuss logging. Contingents from the National Parks Association, the National Wildlife Federation, American Civic and Planning Association, and others, had all emphasized to the beleaguered Park Service that the crisis was real.

Paul Shepard's role as conservation chairman of the National Council of State Garden Clubs had put him on the Natural Resources Council, a league of conservation groups. In that autumn's meeting in Chicago, he met with the directors of all the major conservation organizations in the country. "I was disappointed," Shepard said later, "in the relatively modest response of all those organizations." Just before Merriam began his Olympic National Park investigation, he attended a meeting of the Sierra Club board of directors in Yosemite and faced a hostile resolution demanding a stop to the logging. He was not even allowed to see the photographs of the logging and the reports that had circulated to everyone else, so high was the distrust of the Park Service within the conservation community.[46]

On October 3, 1956, not yet a month into the naturalists' project to stop the logging, Wirth met in his office with Dave Brower of the Sierra

Club, Fred Packard of the National Parks Association, and Joe Penfold of the Izaak Walton League. Wirth told them that the Park Service would no longer cut "potential bug trees." He assured them the Park Service would not go into the interior of the park to remove avalanche-damaged timber and that there would be no more sales of timber in the interior of the park away from presently constructed roads. As the public dialogue over logging the park continued, Wirth was yielding, but always insisting that "nothing illegal was being done or had been done."[47]

Director Wirth decided that he had better start protecting himself. When the Joint Committee requested a meeting with him in Seattle, he accepted. The naturalists were delighted. The fact that Wirth would meet with them had to mean that he was concerned.

The leadership of the conservation organizations of the Pacific Northwest was present for the meeting with Wirth and Merriam, held at the SeaTac Airport. Even Dave Brower, executive director of the Sierra Club at the time, had flown in from San Francisco to be present. The park naturalists stayed away from this meeting out of concern that it would lead to retaliation against the park naturalist, Gunnar Fagerlund, an innocent party. Everyone knew, including Wirth, that this meeting would determine whether the logging crisis could be mopped up or not. Without Wirth's knowledge (although no effort was made to hide it), a verbatim transcript of everything that was being said at the meeting was recorded in shorthand by Polly Dyer, a member of the group. Because the distrust level was running high and because commitments were going to be made, a transcript seemed important.

Wirth took control of the meeting immediately, making it clear that a change in policy on logging was in progress. " . . . Ever since the beginning of the program—I don't know, maybe ten years ago," he told the group, "we were taking a calculated risk in doing this . . . we took that risk. . . ." And that risk had gotten him into the uncomfortable situation in which he now found himself. To get the logging situation defused, he assured the group directly that, outside of a few situations like road building and campground development, nothing would be removed at all, whether alive, dead, or windfall, without a specific review passed through regular channels to the regional office and the Washington, D.C., office. Then to further allay fears that the program might continue as before, Wirth went on to say that he couldn't anticipate "any of those cases."

Wirth continued to tightly control the course of the meeting. When he finally got around to dealing with "irregularities" referred to in telegrams from conservation organizations, it became clear that "irregularity" was in fact, a real concern and that it meant to him what it had meant to the seasonal naturalists—"That it might be interpreted," he said, "as a violation of a particular law or a matter of honesty." When one of the group pressed for the stump cruises that the naturalists wanted, a key member of the group jumped in and said with great finality, "That won't be necessary." Stump cruises would have reconciled the volumes stated in the contracts with what was actually removed. Wirth had masterfully given the group the guarantees of change they wanted without any argument in return. Having gotten all the changes and reassurances they had been seeking, some members of the group then lost their drive to pursue the matter further.

Wirth told the group, "I'm awfully sorry that this thing got the wide distribution it did. . . . We are in the position to have to explain to a lot of friends that have lost confidence in the National Park Service." Everyone there, including Wirth, knew that without "the wide distribution" Wirth was talking about, he would not have so magnanimously announced changes.

By attending the meeting and quickly yielding, the threat to his directorship had been greatly reduced. Conservation groups and the naturalists got what they wanted—a stop to the logging. The naturalists had lost the logging audit they wanted, but that was of little consequence compared to the stopping of the logging.

As the meeting wound down and Wirth began to justifiably bask in the warm glow of a successful meeting and the personal skill on his part that had gotten things to where they now were, he decided to share with the group his personal philosophy regarding preservation in the national parks:

> One more word and I hope what I say is understood. You people, and I would like to include ourselves in "you people" are of a mind that believes in strong conservation protection of these things that we're talking about. The Olympic is in the neighborhood of a group of people that are, for lack of a better term, and not a disrespectful one, a community of loggers, and they are very sensitive to logs on the ground. . . . Where a log can be picked up that doesn't affect the parks—No I'm not saying it right—if we can keep them quiet by giving them a log or two in a developed area so they don't see it lying there or burned up by us, but put in the mill this will do our public relations much good. On the other hand, if we have a snag in a developed area, road area or administration area and can give it to them and let them make a peeler out of it or whatever you call it, it improves our public relations. . . .

After saying that he did not believe in any of the most commonly understood principles of preservation in national parks, Wirth added a final note to the amazement of everyone:

I am a firm believer that there is no such thing as compromising a principle. As soon as you compromise a principle, you have lost everything.
One can't do that, and I wouldn't sacrifice a principle for anything.[48]

In an unguarded moment, Wirth had disclosed the underpinnings of
the logging program that had been underway for the last fifteen years —
it existed to placate the local loggers. Everyone present already knew
that the program was economically driven. This had even been
confirmed two weeks earlier by Park Forester Floyd Dickinson on the
inspection trip with Merriam. The Bogachiel Valley log jam, he said,
was being logged because "people outside the park exerted a lot of pressure to log the jam rather than let it go to waste." This refuted his earlier
reason — that it was to keep the river from being diverted into the adjacent forest.[49]

Wirth was sent a copy of the transcript of the SeaTac Airport meeting and asked to confirm its accuracy and, if not accurate, to revise it.
Dumbfounded that a transcript of the meeting existed, he could only
say, "It is a little startling sometimes to have an exact transcript of an
informal discussion. . . ." No one else thought that the discussion was
informal and the presence of an exact transcript affirmed dramatically
that fact. Wirth knew it too, so he told the group, "You have done a
fine job of getting down the sense and meaning of my remarks."[50] Two
days after the meeting, Wirth announced to the conservation organization executives in Washington, D.C., that a new tree-cutting policy
was being written that severely restricted the role of the superintendent. While Wirth officially moved to mop up the logging program on
one front, he was actively fighting on other fronts.

Paul Shepard had put a three-page series of questions and answers
about Olympic National Park's logging into national circulation through
the garden club network. When he returned from the SeaTac Airport
meeting, Wirth decided to answer each of Shepard's questions himself,
contradicting the answers Shepard provided. The first question was
"What kind of logging practices are being carried on in Olympic National Park?" Wirth's answer set the tone for how the Park Service would
respond from then on: denial. Wirth said, "We do not believe any 'logging' as such is being carried on."[51] The Washington, D.C., office's statement was that "the principal basis for the concern of conservationists
was based largely on cutting operations on privately owned lands over
which we have no control or lands that were logged before title passed
to the government." This was an ingenious device by which the logging
issues could be side-stepped completely. In the fall of 1956, *Living Wilderness* magazine printed pictures of logging in the park taken by the Joint

Committee, the impact was so devastating that the Park Service's "private land" ploy was very useful. Overly was asked by the Park Service to "comment" on each of the pictures, a request he took to mean "give us something with which we can defend ourselves." He fabricated what he believed was a plausible story for each picture to account for the devastation shown in each of them. Overly's "comments" became the Park Service's position, even though in many instances they were at total variance with the facts.[52]

At this point it did not matter. It was untenable for the Park Service and for Wirth to defend the logging. The only remaining question was how long Overly would remain as superintendent at Olympic Park.

To the loggers and other locals, Overly accounted for the abrupt stopping of the logging by explaining that the Park Service forced him to stop because the support of conservation groups in the on-going boundary fight was needed. The Park Service couldn't afford to alienate them, he said. He never admitted that the logging might have been wrong or that he approved of the decision to stop. As close as he ever would come was, "I admit some errors in judgment,"[53] a statement made to Fred Packard of the National Parks Association.

In his continuing defense of everything that had gone on, even his clear-cutting of trees at Olympic Hot Springs, Overly got encouragement from Wirth. Wirth even told Dave Brower of the Sierra Club in March of 1957 that the logging pictures that had run in *Living Wilderness* were of scenes outside the park.[54]

A constant stream of logging requests had continued to come in to Overly during 1957. Most were denied. In August of 1957, when a Boy Scout troop reached North Fork Ranger Station at the end of a trek through the park, they found a logging operation underway at North Fork Campground. Outraged, they wrote directly to Wirth, sending pictures of it all. "The Douglas fir were sound trees and beautiful four-, five-, and six-foot specimens," they said. "One eight-foot Sitka spruce was also sound as a dollar, as the pictures show."[55] Wirth's letter of response talked about windthrow and insects. This was not what they saw, the Boy Scouts told Wirth in their reply. The Boy Scout troop confronted Wirth with sarcasm: "We wonder how the magnificent forests we once had ever come into being with the black bear, porcupine, woodpeckers and insects killing so many trees."[56]

Because there was a legitimate blowdown being cleared down the road and the equipment was present, it was an irresistible attraction to take the trees from the campground under the terms of the new regulations "to provide under approved development programs, for safe use and full enjoyment of the areas by the people."[57] This logging seemingly was an open challenge to the shut-down that Wirth had ordered.

In fact Overly had confronted Regional Director Merriam in his quest to continue logging: "Timber salvage for the protection of the remaining forest," he said, "has developed into quite a controversial thing, but I can see no other way out in discharging our forest policy than to conduct forest salvage operations of one nature or another."[58]

By continuing the logging program in the face of all that had transpired, Overly now became a threat to Wirth's survival at the Park Service. Every conservation organization in the country was watching how the new tree-cutting policy was implemented. However much Wirth might have wanted to keep Overly as superintendent in Olympic Park, Overly had to go.

On February 12, 1958, Overly was transferred to Great Smoky Mountain National Park. Before he left, the Port Angeles Chamber of Commerce gave a banquet in Overly's honor. Conrad Wirth and Regional Director Lawrence Merriam were there. Senator Henry Jackson and a whole coterie of state elected officials were there. Crown Zellerbach's retired public relations officer was master of ceremonies.

Senator Jackson praised the fine relationship Overly had created between the Park Service and the people of the state. Wirth told the crowd that Overly was "going on to bigger things." Overly was made a life member of the Port Angeles Chamber of Commerce, the park's number one enemy since 1934. He received a pair of silver candelabra as a memento of his tenure as superintendent.[59]

Overly's banishment from Olympic Park was openly discussed by everyone, including Overly himself. He told Irving Brant that he was being "exiled." Even the Port Angeles newspaper played with the subject. "Scribe is tempted to remind Fred of the school book poem, Woodman, Spare That Tree, for who knows that even in the thickets and bracken of the Big Smokies, Bird Watchers may be lurking, twittering among themselves and listening not only for bird songs but for the sounds of a woodman's ax."[60]

Fred Overly himself was in no humorous mood about his transfer. Within the confines of an Olympic National Park party for him later, he summed it up for everyone: "I cut too goddamn many trees."[61]

In spite of the careful precautions of the seasonal naturalists to avoid involving the park naturalist, Gunnar Fagerlund, Overly went after him. Fagerlund explained, "Overly must have strongly suspected me—that I was collaborating with Paul Shepard, for he called me on the carpet one day in the Spring of 1957. He was angry. . . . In late summer '57, [Assistant Superintendent] Jerry House told me that 'everyone knew that either you or Fred Overly would have to leave.' Soon after that I moved to Washington [D.C.]."[62]

Just as the naturalists had anticipated, the Park Service then turned on Paul Shepard for disloyalty. He was officially forever banned from employment in the national parks by Regional Director Merriam himself.[63] Shepard then became a folk hero, but that was no consolation to him since he had enjoyed being a seasonal naturalist. In stopping the logging, Olympic's seasonal naturalists could stand beside the seasonal rangers who stopped the pelican killing in Yellowstone by stealing the files and sending them to Rosalie Edge when Director Albright denied the killing in 1932. They can also stand beside the seasonal fire guards in Olympic National Forest who wrote to President Roosevelt about the sign moving during the presidential visit in 1937.

From 1941, when the logging began, until it completely ended at the end of 1958, approximately 100 million board feet were recorded as sent from Olympic National Park to the mills of the Olympic Peninsula (probably much more was sent, if there is any validity to the widespread "sweetening the load" deals that were once rampant).

Future generations now will never be able to see the up to nine-foot diameter Douglas fir trees that were once easily accessible to motorists everywhere in the park. They all went to the mills as "danger trees" or as *potential* bug trees if they happened to have taken root a thousand years ago in a place where logging equipment could get at them. Even though the illusion of virgin forest is present for the visitor today, the Park Service achieved the destruction of the largest and most magnificent of Olympic Park's trees in the face of an absolutely clear mandate from society to preserve them.

18 THE COASTAL STRIP PRESERVATION DENIED

I am disturbed . . . by three matters which I realize we cannot accomplish under the recent Olympic National Park Bill. The first of these relates to the preservation of the Pacific Shore line. . . . *Second, my authority does not extend to the acquisition of a strip . . . down the Queets River Valley from the National Park to the ocean. I think it is of the utmost importance that such strips be made a part of the Olympic National Park. Third, I think we should have legislation for the* preservation of all the remaining timber *in the Quinault River Valley . . .*[1] *[emphasis added].*   FRANKLIN D. ROOSEVELT

The Coast Strip was acquired as a Public Works Project for the express purpose of constructing a highway along the coast.[2]
FRED J. OVERLY

IN THE FINAL FLURRY of effort to get an Olympic National Park bill passed in the spring of 1938, the preservation of a strip along the ocean and forested corridor to the sea that Roosevelt had personally insisted on got lost in the shuffle. Governor Clarence Martin rejected the ocean park because it involved the acquisition of lands owned by large timber operators. "A park along the ocean beach . . . is impractical for park purposes,"[3] he told Roosevelt, dismissing the whole idea out of hand.

When Roosevelt read Irving Brant's recommendations for additions to the park later that year, he wrote to Ickes asking for legislation to create an Ocean Strip and a forested corridor (the Queets Corridor) and to purchase the remaining old-growth timber on the Quinault Indian Reservation. "I have personally seen what amounts to criminal devastation without replanting on the Reservation,"[4] he told Ickes. Brant revised his boundary recommendations to allow for a 57,000-acre Ocean Strip and Queets Corridor, eliminating the upper Dungeness, Dosewallips, and Hamma Hamma areas in order not to exceed the Congressionally mandated size limitations.

The Port Angeles Chamber of Commerce reacted with fury. "Lake Ozette should not be included . . . ," Chamber President Thomas Aldwell said. "The lake shore is needed for docks and booming grounds."[5] The Park Service gave the chamber what it wanted.

Rather than go through the legislative processes which would provide a forum for more timber-industry acrimony, Ickes came up with $1,750,000 of Public Works Administration money for the Ocean Strip and Queets Corridor. The PWA was a depression-era agency devoted to creating jobs by building public improvements of all kinds. The project was officially "for the construction of roads, trails, firebreaks, lookout towers, ranger cabins, public beach facilities and utilities. . . ." The project was also officially described as being for the "preservation" and "the protection and conservation" of the ocean.[6] To Fred Overly, however, the purpose of the project was to construct a road the length of the Ocean Strip. As a timber technician, Overly had been present at the meeting in 1939 with Irving Brant, Ickes, and Roosevelt at which the PWA route to funding was agreed to. Because the PWA authorization included roads amongst other developments, and because he had been the only Park Service person present at the meeting, Overly insisted there was presidential intent for a road the length of the Ocean Strip.

No specific mention of the road Overly was proposing appeared in the project authorization, only the generic "roads, trails . . . etc." Nevertheless, he stridently insisted that the building of the road was now national policy emanating from the president's office. Former Assistant Director Harold C. Bryant, who was acting as a PWA consultant to the Park Service, immediately agreed with construction of a road, which Tomlinson also did. "To me, the best use of this strip will be as the basis for a highway or parkway all the way along the coast to Neah Bay," Bryant told Regional Director Kittredge.

Kittredge, however, had never accepted Overly's story and moved to block any further thought of a road. The Park Service was thus split internally into two camps — pro-preservationist and pro-development. Kittredge told Bryant:

> I have disclaimed all knowledge or interest in this [road]. I still feel that
> the road if we have anything to do with it, should be a long way back
> from the coast in many places and that it should leave great areas of coast-
> line entirely free from road.

Kittredge further declared himself unequivocally for preservation and
gave Bryant what amounted to a policy directive:

> It seems to me that we must do this if we are to follow our policy of
> preserving the natural vegetation and coast undisturbed.[7]

Bryant responded:

> As I reported to you the matter of a road up the coast has been settled
> in Washington so we do not have to make the decision. Mr. Overly reports
> that at a conference at the White House in Washington, both the Presi-
> dent and Irving Brant concurred in a plan for a road.[8]

Bryant's recommendations included not only the road as Overly wanted
it, but also lateral access roads to the beaches along the length of the
strip so park visitors could drive their cars on the beach at low tide.
"This," he said, "would afford a trip by auto along the beach and afford
access to specified beach picnic grounds."[9]

Kittredge decided to fight on. He sent to Director Drury a line by
line analysis of Bryant's recommendations. When he got to Bryant's road
recommendations, Kittredge said he wanted only the two existing roads
to the strip improved—one to the mouth of the Hoh River and the other
to the mouth of the Quillayute River. "This plan of road development,"
he said, "would not open any country not now opened to roads. . . ."[10]
However, he found that Overly had captured the thinking in the director's office and that Overly, in the Park Service barely five years, was
going to prevail over an old pro like himself. Arthur Demaray, as acting director, wrote back to him supporting Overly's plans, including
that the language of the "PWA allocation was so worded that construction of the parkway road is authorized." To end the discussion, Demaray gave a direct order to Kittredge: "You are instructed, therefore, to
include this item in the development program."

Even in the face of this direct order from Washington, D.C., Kittredge
continued to fight to keep Overly's road from destroying the wilderness.
Quoting Demaray's memo expounding Overly's story as fact, Kittredge
sarcastically replied, "We are glad to have these statements for we had
no idea that the purpose of the acquisition was for 'providing a scenic
parkway road along the ocean!' " He went on to say that he had searched
the files and found no such wording, and that the only printed reference to such a road had appeared in the *Port Angeles Evening News*.[11]

But after two months of hard internal fighting, Kittredge gave up. To contain the damage, he recommended that the road be built from Ruby Beach to La Push, which would have kept it away from Lake Ozette and Cape Alava. It was approved immediately.

Overly now had a partial road committed for the Ocean Strip. By the end of the year, however, the full road as Overly wanted it would again emerge. A speech, probably written in large part by Overly, was delivered in December 1940, by Preston Macy to the major timber-industry gathering of the year in Portland. The speech laid out a new rationale for the construction of the coastal highway — "unquestionably a practical defense measure," "bring the benefits of . . . new economic enterprise," "opening additional scenic benefits," "confidently expect the Olympic park and the new Olympic ocean parkway to bring to it a fuller measure of productive security."[12]

Just six weeks after Kittredge thought he had partly contained the road, a road the whole length of the Ocean Strip was being touted as a national defense project. World War II eventually intervened to put the road on the back burner of the Park Service's priorities.

When Overly later became park superintendent, in 1951, the Ocean Strip road appeared on the park's master plan again. It was not until a ten year project to upgrade National Park facilities, called Mission 66, began that the road could become a reality. With funds now available, Overly expected that finally his long-fought-for road project would begin, but it was rejected in Washington, D.C., upon review. Fighting like fury, Overly wrote and called Director Wirth, still arguing that "the Coastal Strip was acquired . . . for the express purpose of constructing a highway along the coast."[13] In September of 1956, Overly was given $2,806,500 plus $414,000 for utilities and buildings for the road.

But, just as the money was finally in hand, Overly's logging program in the park became a public controversy and threatened to bring down the administration of Conrad Wirth. Thus, Wirth was forced in his SeaTac Airport meeting about park logging to agree to conservationists' demands that the road be eliminated from the master plan. "In view of the numerous conflicting factors," Wirth wrote to the regional office to fulfill his private commitments to the environmentalists in the logging imbroglio, "it appears that the Service has not yet found the best solution to the Coastal Strip. I believe little good would be accomplished by continuing your route studies. . . ."[14] Overly never learned that the road he had been fighting for for nearly two decades vanished from his grasp as a result of his logging activities in the park. The following year, 1958, Wirth was bolstered by a Pacific Coast Seashore Survey staff report that stated, "no coastal road should be constructed within the Olympic Coastal Strip . . . its present wilderness qualities should be

In July of 1958, Supreme Court Justice William Douglas (on the left) entered the campaign to stop the Park Service from destroying the wilderness of the coastal strip with a road. He led a group of 70 on an overnight protest hike and faced the harassment campaign organized by the Port Angeles Chamber of Commerce at its conclusion. *Bob and Ira Spring.*

retained."[15] In July, 1959, when Justice William O. Douglas led a march of some seventy hikers down twenty-two miles of the coast to protest the possibility of the road, the road seemed doomed. However, everyone underestimated the determination of Fred Overly, who would present his road again eight years later from his position as regional director of the Bureau of Outdoor Recreation.

The most important dynamic of the Ocean Strip and Queets Corridor project was that it was being forced onto the Park Service from the outside by a presidential decision in which the Park Service had not been involved. Not only did the Park Service see very little use for the Ocean Strip, except to provide picnic sites for car users, but it had open hostility to being involved in the taking of more old-growth forest *by condemnation.*

Nonetheless the Park Service proceeded with the acquisition as ordered by Ickes in fulfillment of Roosevelt's wishes.

The Ocean Strip and Queets Corridor project tangled with the timber companies, the most uncooperative of which was the Polson Logging Company which had gotten 10,040 acres of its west-side holdings in the Timber and Stone Act fraud in the notorious Olympic Forest Reserve eliminations at the turn of the century, forty years earlier.[16] No sooner had acquisition negotiations with Polson begun in 1940 than the Park Service's acquisition agent warned that "they intend to make a fight, utilizing every possible point, including oil, in an effort to save their spruce timber or build up excessive damages."[17]

With no commitment to preservation, the Park Service's acquisition focused on the path of least resistance, which was of course, to give Polson and the other operators the timber on the lands being acquired. The Park Service then acquired the land on that basis, in direct contradiction to Roosevelt's intent toward tree preservation. Later on, when funds started running low, the Park Service did not suggest that more money was imperative. Having discovered that the timber companies would cooperate if they could retain cutting rights on the timber on the lands being acquired, there was now a basis for acquiring land without asking for more money, even if it defeated the preservation intent of creating the corridor and strip in the first place.[18]

By 1942, having gotten everything it wanted from the Park Service, Polson began upping its demands. Arnold Polson now wanted cutting rights extended into the far future. "I would suggest," he said, "that either a very substantial term of years should be given in which to log timber, or a flexible arrangement be made so as to fully protect our interests. . . ."[19] Eventually, Polson was given fifteen years to log the timber off the lands being acquired for the park. The University of Washington, which owned school lands in the strip was given twenty-year cutting rights, an incredible giveaway considering that the project was a preservation project.

Polson still pressed for more. Up until early 1942, the cutting rights had involved spruce. With the Park Service now only focused on how inexpensively it could acquire stump land, Polson went to the next logical step: swapping old-growth trees for clear-cut land. In expectation of saving $75,000 the Park Service proposed, at Arnold Polson's instigation, the clear-cutting by Polson of 1,200 acres between Kalaloch and Ruby Beach. "Timber is 80 percent or more cedar, nearly all of which is over mature," wired the acquisition coordinator asking Drury's approval.[20] Fred Overly had proposed it and negotiated the deal with Polson. What Polson got was cutting rights for fifteen years on 1,291 acres of former Polson land in the Ocean Strip, plus similar cutting rights on 991 acres of old-growth forest acquired by the Park Service from other owners.

The Park Service's program of acquiring old-growth forest for a presidentially ordered preservation project, only to clear-cut it so that what was acquired was stump land, continued unabated. Drury kept Ickes informed and pointed with pride to the fact that the land was being acquired "without incurring a deficiency."[21] Ickes was so busy with World War II that he paid little heed to this aspect of the park acquisition program. With constant reassurance that everything was going well, Ickes may never have read the reports from Drury.

By 1953, when Truman added the Queets Corridor and Ocean Strip to the park by proclamation, the total acreage of the park would have exceeded the size limitation imposed by Congress by more than 6,000 acres. To handle this problem, the Park Service simply eliminated 6,000 acres from amongst the thousands of acres of stump land it had created out of the virgin forest it began with. This in turn gave Superintendent Fred Overly near six square miles of timberland with which he could wheel and deal with the peninsula loggers.

With more than six thousand acres available for trade, environmental groups saw the opportunity to extend the park up the coast to include the dramatic Shi Shi Beach and the east shore of Lake Ozette. Superintendent Fred Overly was not interested and even moved to dispose of the islands in Lake Ozette already acquired by the Park Service.

When the Queets Corridor and Ocean Strip were acquired in 1940, the state faced condemnation proceedings against some of its own timberlands and its tidelands. The beach itself was considered to be such an integral part of the Ocean Strip that the Interior Department moved to acquire not only the beach but the submerged tidelands out a half-mile from extreme low tide. Washington State authorities quickly moved to head off the taking of the tidelands: oil was seeping out of the ground at the mouth of the Hoh River. Two different geological reports showed there was a possible oil dome present. State Land Commissioner Albert Martin, speaking of the oil domes, told the Park Service in 1940 "that if this was found to be true, development of such dome would be advantageous to the state and it would not be advisable to have a reservation on the statutes preventing it."[22] Having disclosed that the state of Washington fully intended to put oil-drilling rigs on the tidelands whenever the opportunity presented itself, he asked that the tidelands be dropped from the condemnation proceedings. Martin had openly made the Park Service privy to the state's plans for the tidelands, which if ever acted upon would make the Ocean Strip irrelevant for park purposes. Oil rigs and wilderness beaches were hardly compatible.

Arno Cammerer, in his final days as Park Service director, wrote back:

We appreciate your statements that the state would be willing to administer such lands in a manner consistent with our use of the adjacent
uplands after their acquisition by the Federal Government. Should it sub-
sequently develop that the tide and submerged lands were put to uses
which conflict with, or did irreparable damage to . . . the immediate adjacent uplands . . . we would be in an embarrassing position.[23]

A week and a half later, the U.S. attorney general requested that the
tidelands be dropped from the condemnation suit for the moment because title to them might already reside with the United States government and not Washington State. Washington State did not want to drop
the matter, however. Even with the tidelands temporarily dropped from
the suit, both the state's Attorney General and the Land Commissioner
pushed on when they discovered there was no resolve within the Park
Service to pursue the tidelands. Washington's attorney general then organized a formal proposal from the State Land Board, a group including the governor, state land commissioner, attorney general, and the
state superintendent of Public Instruction. He proposed that in turn
for the state abandoning the tidelands, the board would give to the Park
Service a policy statement "expressing it to be the policy of the State
of Washington that the ocean tidelands abutting upon the Olympic Public Works Project will be maintained for the benefit of the public and
will be administered in such a fashion as not to affect adversely the
adjacent recreational area. . . ."[24] In the face of the state's earlier declaration that it intended to put oil rigs on the beach, the Park Service
moved to accept the state's offer. Joseph E. Taylor, the Park Service Land
Acquisition Coordinator, made every aspect of the state's campaign his
own, telling Drury in enthusiastic endorsement of the state's offer:

I was informed that the elimination of the tidelands would be a big step
toward settlement of the entire litigation since we have widely divergent
views of the value of these lands and, since the state is willing to give
all assurance possible and the tidelands are to be administered for the
public anyway, they feel that elimination of these tracts from the litigation by dismissal is the best possible solution.[25]

When Superintendent Macy learned of the proposal to drop the tidelands, he told Drury, " . . . such action is highly undesirable. The tidelands are perhaps the most desirable part of our acquisition area and
without proper protection our purposes will be defeated." Macy virtually demanded the tidelands be acquired "in order to afford complete
protection to wildlife, marine life, and natural features."[26]

Macy, having lived through the park battle, knew the state of Washington well. Prophetically he told Drury, "While a statement of policy by the state authorities will be of great benefit, we feel that changing administrations will find these policies also changing, and we will be unable to have the proper protection along our beaches."[27] Macy had good reason to have personal anguish about eliminating the beaches. Two years earlier, he had moved to include the offshore islands and rocks in the park because the State Fisheries Department was making trips to the islands, breeding grounds for sea lions, and "shooting the sea lions wholesale," he said. Speaking of Ozette Island, he said, "This island would be extremely valuable for the preservation of sea lions, which suffer great damage from those who feel that they may be inter-fering with some of the fish population."[28]

The director's office gave no credence to Macy's urgent plea to ac-quire the tidelands. Saving money was reaffirmed as the driving force in the acquisition when Demaray ordered the Declaration of Policy from the state of Washington to be executed. Macy had pushed so hard that in his directive to Taylor ordering the dropping of the tidelands, Demaray felt compelled to acknowledge the fight that Macy had fought. "We dislike very much to take action which is counter to Mr. Macy's recommendation," Demaray wrote to Taylor for Macy's benefit, "but he will no doubt recognize the compelling reasons for our position."[29] The decision to drop the tidelands was a political disaster. From the mo-ment of its signing, Washington State ignored its own Declaration of Policy, as if it had never existed. And Macy, as superintendent, along with all his successors, would have to live with the disaster.

After legally binding the state with two documents to the satisfac-tion of the federal government's attorneys, the state succeeded immedi-ately in defeating the intent of the documents which declared:

1. that no part of the tidelands along the shore of the Pacific Ocean from the northern boundary of the Quinault Indian Reservation shall ever be sold or otherwise disposed of
2. the state shall not use or allow any part of said tidelands to be used for any purpose detrimental to the public parkway and recreational area now being established by the United States of America[30]

A week later, the commissioner of Public Lands notified Washington's attorney general and the Park Service, "I have entered an order setting forth the Declaration of Policy . . . ," a stipulation of the federal govern-ment so that the Declaration of Policy would bind the department to the order. Having notified everyone that he had entered the order, the Commissioner then failed to do so, leaving the State Land Office blind to the fact that such an order even existed. In addition, no word was ever sent to the Department of Game or the State Fisheries Department. They continued killing wildlife on the beach and on the offshore rocks and islands as usual.

State ownership of the beach meant "people taking guns out on the beach for target practice." As Fred Overly pointed out to the Department of Game, they "have also indiscriminately shot coons, bear, and deer on the beach." The Department of Game insisted, when confronted, "that flights of brant and geese and some shore birds pass this area in their migrations and that residents of Forks have no other place to shoot birds."[31] For people who complained about hunting on the beach, the Department of Game reminded them, " . . . bears have been declared predatory animals in Jefferson County and may be shot at any time of year." For those who objected to the killing of seals along the beach, they received a reminder that the Washington State Legislature had put a bounty on seals and that they were under the jurisdiction of the State Fisheries Department.[32] Never once in all the years that these moves by the state took place did the Park Service even attempt to invoke the Declaration of Policy to restrain the state. The Declaration of Policy remained silently in the files.

By 1959, the whole concept of an Ocean Strip with state tidelands had reached the point that superintendent Dan Beard questioned its continuation. "It is very obvious to me that state ownership of the tidelands is a real threat to the park." Beard had replaced Overly as Olympic superintendent. "I cannot help being concerned," he lamented, "about spending federal money for developments on the lands which are dependent entirely on the beach and intertidal area that we do not have anything to say about." He reported that "bulldozers work up and down the beaches salvaging logs. Elk, deer and raccoon are killed along the beaches on state land and sometimes ours. Seals are shot for bounty in the breaker line and on offshore rocks."[33] Beard responded to the beach problems by recommending that the park boundary be extended seaward to include them all. Because the seals preyed on the same fish as the commercial fishermen, Washington State had long been involved in killing seals on behalf of the fishermen. The U.S. Fish and Wildlife Service, which administered the offshore islands and rocks, ignored the fact that the area was a designated wildlife refuge.

In 1959, at the moment that Superintendent Beard was attempting to include the tidelands and offshore rocks and islands, State Land Commissioner Bert Cole got the Washington State Legislature to amend the Tidelands Protection Act with the addition of two words: "*or minerals.*" With this addition, the tidelands could be "disposed of or leased" by the State Land Commissioner now for minerals as well as "petroleum and gas." By this new law, he had legislative authority to lease the park's beach for minerals, in direct contradiction to the Declaration of Policy that declared "that no part of the tidelands . . . shall ever be sold or otherwise disposed of."[34] The Declaration of Policy remained invisible.

Within a day of the amendment going into effect in June, 1959, every acre of beach on the park's Ocean Strip had been leased by Washington State at $5 a year for forty acres. The state reassured environmentalists, who were outraged, that "granting of mineral leases would not close the beach areas to recreational use,"[35] a bizarre assertion in view of the fact that there were no restrictions on how the mining of the beach for minerals would take place. The state only demanded that in the event anything of commercial value was found, a mining contract be issued doubling the fee to $10 per year for forty acres, plus one percent of the value of the minerals extracted per year. With 2,000 acres of beach under lease for mining purposes, all of Macy's predictions seventeen years earlier, had dramatically come to pass. Olympic National Park's beach was now entirely in the hands of private lease holders.

Environmental activist groups in the Pacific Northwest took action. A copy of the Declaration of Policy was hand-carried by a member of Olympic Park Associates to the State Land Commissioner's office in the state capitol, and it was confirmed that the Declaration of Policy had never been entered in the records of the department. After its authenticity was established, Volume 82 of Commissioner's Orders, where it should have been entered, vanished. Since only its own staff had access to these files, chicanery was strongly suspected.[36]

Conservation organizations expected that when a copy of the Declaration of Policy was given to Park Superintendent Dan Beard, the Park Service would assert its position on the beach, but it took no action of any kind.

The Park Service accepted the leasing of the beach with the same passivity that it accepted state-authorized killing of wildlife and salvage logging. "It is not believed," said Acting Superintendent Oscar Sedergren later, "there is any way which we could reach agreement with the state to hold up authority to commence operations along the stretch adjacent to the Olympic National Park."[37] The beach was saved only by the fact that no commercially valuable minerals were found.

By 1970, the Park Service had administered the Ocean Strip for thirty years, during which time two superintendents had vigorously recommended including the offshore islands and rocks in the park. When no move to do this had occurred, the environmental groups in the Pacific Northwest succeeded in getting Congress to create the Washington Island Wilderness out of them all. They would now at least have the protection of the Wilderness Act of 1964.

Then, in 1976, Olympic Park Associates let an environmentally oriented governor, Dan Evans, know that the stretch of beach north to the Makah Indian Reservation had never been added to the park. It contained Shi Shi Beach, the longest single stretch of wild sand beach in the country which was not in public ownership. Evans and his staff took it on as a project. Using all of the power of persuasion of the governor's office, Evans managed to bring a resistive group of large timber companies to agreement on a minimal area for inclusion in the park. The advantage of his approach was that, even though small in area, the addition could appear as a non-controversial housekeeping measure in the Omnibus Park Bill of 1976.

Evans also succeeded in getting a tiny strip on the east shore of Lake Ozette included, surrounding the lake for the first time with park land even though the lake itself remained under the control of Washington State. His success represented a start at correcting the Park Service's original error in judgment in leaving the lake out of the park at the insistence of the Port Angeles Chamber of Commerce.

As early as 1941, the local Olympic National Park staff had attempted to sell the Navy on the idea of turning Lake Ozette into a seaplane base and having the Navy acquire a minimum of a half a mile of timber around the lake. When World War II ended, they expected that the land in public ownership could be turned over to the Park Service.

Owen Tomlinson wrote to the commandment of the 13th Naval District promoting the seaplane base:

> The entire east shoreline of the lake is in private ownership and contains a stand of fir and hemlock timber which . . . is prepared for logging in the near future. It is this timber to which your attention is directed as of possible value for camouflage and sea plane operation purposes. Perhaps the trees along the east shore of the lake are more valuable to the government than if cut into lumber.[38]

The admiral was interested. Three days later, Tomlinson was informed that the admiral had forwarded a request to the Navy Department that the Ozette timber be acquired by the Navy.

When Irving Brant learned of the seaplane base efforts then underway, he went straight to Lake Ozette, took a number of pictures, and sent them directly to President Roosevelt with a letter. Brant urged Roosevelt to take action. "It will be nothing less than criminal," he told Roosevelt, "to allow the protective cover to be cut off, but it will be done, and done soon, unless the government acquired it."[39] Brant also sent a copy to Ickes, adding, "As the President was personally responsible for the seashore project," he said, "he ought to be sympathetic to this move."[40]

Roosevelt was interested and checked with the Navy personally. With tongue in cheek, Roosevelt responded back to Brant:

> The active interest in national defense which prompted this recommendation is deeply appreciated. Frankly, however, I must say that the Navy Department has recommended against using Lake Ozette at the present time for a naval air base. The Department insists that such use would necessitate the construction of a costly highway and railroad. Besides this those who have studied the terrain are of the opinion that the surrounding mountains present a hazard to flight operations under poor visibility conditions, and a further argument against the site is that it is not capable of sufficient expansion.[41]

The acquisition of Lake Ozette and the surrounding lands emerged in formal boundary recommendations again in 1943 and then continuously until 1966. Citizen-activist intervention was the critical ingredient that finally got it added to the park in the end.

By 1986, time for the Ocean Strip had run out. Rising population, ever-increasing interest, and easy accessibility had turned the Ocean Strip into one of the most heavily used areas in the park. In 1984, 389,471 park visitors used the beaches; in 1985 there were 621,265 visitors, a 60 percent increase in one year. The Park Service was reeling from the impact of humans on every square foot of the beach environment. While the Park Service kept attempting, mostly by bluff, to prevent damage to the tidal pools and the displays of shellfish and crustaceans on the rocks, the State Fisheries Department threatened to commercially harvest several tons of mussels from those same rocks annually. Still the Declaration of Policy remained silently unused in the Park Service's files.

Former Governor Dan Evans, now a United States Senator and still oriented toward finding solutions for Olympic National Park's problems, was approached again by Olympic Park Associates. Evans sponsored a bill to put the tidelands and Lake Ozette into the park, but he refused to proceed without concurrence of the governor, Booth Gardner. With the State Parks Director Jan Tveten taking the lead, the governor was told that every single department of state government was opposed to adding the beach to the park. The governor, therefore, felt compelled to say no. The bill proceeded without the beaches. The Department of Natural Resources had been one of those departments characterized by the state parks director as opposed to adding the beaches to the park, which precipitated a response from it to the contrary. In a strongly supportive memo circulated throughout the state and even to Senator Evans' office, Cleve Pinnix of the Department of Natural Resources called for state support for Evans' bill. "The boundary adjustments proposed in Senator Evans' current legislation," he said, "may afford the state an improved opportunity to work with the National Park Service to better protect this magnificent area." With the bipartisan help of Representative Al Swift in the House, whose district contains the park, Evans' bill sailed through Congress in 1986 with not only the beaches and Lake Ozette, but also the offshore islands and rocks.

After nearly a half century, the Park was basically complete. What remains a mystery is why the Park Service never used the legal tool at its fingertips — the Declaration of Policy — to protect the tidelands in federal court. Was it the general administrative passivity of the Park Service or did successive administrators lose track of its existence? In any event, the notorious 1942 Declaration of Policy was made moot by Evans' park bill of 1986, forty-four years later.

When Senator Evans' park bill was wending its way through the legislative processes in the fall of 1986, the Fish and Wildlife Service approved of putting the offshore rocks and islands into the park. Later it denied this after its various constituent groups objected. One year later, the Fish and Wildlife Service got the House of Representatives to pass an amendment to HR 2583 which would return the park's offshore rocks and islands to the Fish and Wildlife Service, while leaving the area inside the park. Even Senator Evans supported this, and the measure sailed through the Senate as it had the House, as a simple housekeeping measure.

By leaving the area inside the park boundaries and at the same time removing the national park laws and restoring the much less protective wildlife refuge laws, a number of potentially damaging factors for the future of Olympic National Park were created:

1. For the first time, an enclave inside a national park where national park laws do not apply has been created, providing a precedent for the whole park system by which resource exploiters can attempt to get relief from the restrictive park laws.
2. The preservation shifts from the law itself under the national park laws to the discretion of the Secretary of the Interior under wildlife refuge laws. For instance, Olympic National Park is bound by the provisions of 56 Stat 151: "all hunting or the killing, wounding, capturing at any time of any wild bird or animal . . . is prohibited." This law also requires "the preservation from injury or spoilation of all timber, mineral deposits, natural curiosities or wonderful objects within the park, and for the protection of the animals and birds in the park from capture or destruction. . . ." HR 2583 removed those laws from the offshore areas of the park and substitutes instead, that "the Secretary . . . may . . . permit the use of this area for any purpose

but not limited to hunting, fishing, public recreation and accommodations and access whenever he determines such areas are compatible. . . ." The Fish and Wildlife Service is authorized "to occupy any such area for any purpose" and specifically restores the mining and mineral leasing laws to the area.

3. With the Secretary of the Interior agitating to begin oil drilling immediately adjacent to this area of the park, the importance of this area to the wilderness coast is magnified considerably. The thin veneer of the Wilderness Act of 1964, easily modified, will be the only barrier to oil drilling closer in if oil is discovered. And that will hardly be a barrier because the Wilderness Act applies only to the islands themselves, not the submerged lands between them. The chairman of the House Merchant Marine and Fisheries Committee, who would have jurisdiction over this area of the park, has already declared that he is in favor of oil drilling in the Arctic National Wildlife Refuge, also under his jurisdiction. The combination of a key House committee chairman favoring oil drilling in wildlife refuges, an Interior Secretary with discretionary power over the area, and a state government unable to resist the lure of oil, has the power to destroy the last wilderness coast in the contiguous forty-eight states.

In a move consistent with its past in Olympic National Park, the Park Service supported taking the critical offshore rocks and islands from its control. Thus, the Park Service was yet again a party to reducing the level of preservation in the park. The Park Service also saw no concern for the precedent being established. The groups fighting for preservation were once again having to fight to keep the Park Service administering an area critical to the future of wilderness on the coastal strip. This time, the Park Service was able to defeat the preservationists by openly supporting the bill. Now the Park Service has added to Olympic National Park's many firsts the precedent of an enclave inside its boundaries in which national park laws do not apply but the less protective laws of another agency do. With oil-drilling rigs about to emerge adjacent to this area of the park, many will be watching to see if a Secretary of the Interior can resist the new power he has been given in Olympic National Park by the Wildlife Refuge Act. This authorized the secretary to use the offshore rocks and islands "for any purpose" and gave the Fish and Wildlife Service the power to "occupy any such area for any purpose." Only the Wilderness Act stands as a legal deterrent to the full exercising of this power.

Dominating the land acquisition process of the Ocean Strip from the very beginning has been the presence of the Ozette Indian Reservation, which the strip enclosed. It sits astride Cape Alava, in what is

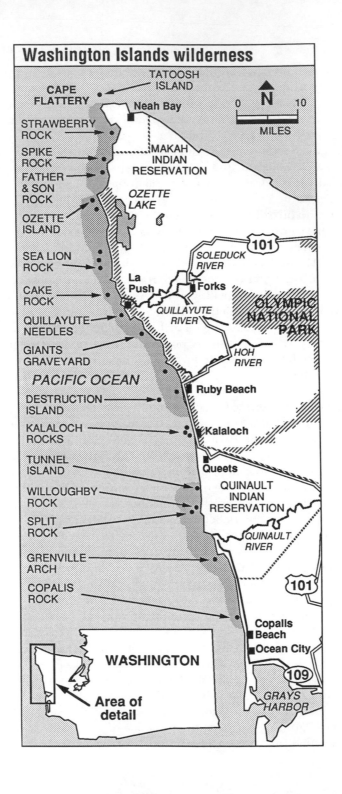

Washington Islands wilderness

TATOOSH
ISLAND

CAPE
FLATTERY

Neah Bay

0   N   10

MILES

STRAWBERRY
ROCK

SPIKE
ROCK

FATHER
& SON
ROCK

MAKAH
INDIAN
RESERVATION

*OZETTE
LAKE*

OZETTE
ISLAND

101

SEA LION
ROCK

*SOLEDUCK
RIVER*

La
Push

Forks

CAKE
ROCK

OLYMPIC
NATIONAL
PARK

*QUILLAYUTE
RIVER*

QUILLAYUTE
NEEDLES

GIANTS
GRAVEYARD

*HOH
RIVER*

PACIFIC OCEAN

Ruby Beach

DESTRUCTION
ISLAND

KALALOCH
ROCKS

Kalaloch

TUNNEL
ISLAND

Queets

WILLOUGHBY
ROCK

QUINAULT
INDIAN
RESERVATION

SPLIT
ROCK

*QUINAULT
RIVER*

GRENVILLE
ARCH

COPALIS
ROCK

101

Copalis
Beach

Ocean City

WASHINGTON

109

Area of
detail

*GRAYS
HARBOR*

perhaps the most spectacular wilderness of the whole coast. So spectacular was this area that Mount Olympus National Monument's custodian, Preston Macy, recommended more than a year before the 1938 park bill passed that Cape Alava be made into a national monument. He wanted the Interior Department to transfer the Ozette Reservation to the Park Service because no Indians were then living there.[42]

In fact, all the Indian families who had lived there left in 1903, when, owing to a lack of school facilities, the government insisted that the young children go to school in Neah Bay. The reservation itself was viewed as public land by the Interior Department.[43]

There had been a major oversight in drafting the 1938 Olympic National Park bill. It only authorized the addition of lands by proclamation from within the boundaries of Olympic National Forest and lands which could be acquired by gift or purchase. Lands already in United States ownership, such as the Ozette Reservation, were excluded by omission from the proclamation. This oversight set in motion a struggle that lasted for more than thirty years.

Life for Elliott Anderson, the last surviving Ozette Indian, became more and more uneasy at Neah Bay among the Makah tribe, with which he had never identified. He asked his friend Charles Keller, who lived at Lake Ozette, to see "about National Park if will buy My Reservation . . . If buy my Res. I will get homestead at 3 miles North of Ozette River Near late Frank Mair's homestead. That's best place I like [sic]."[44] When Macy got Anderson's request, he instantly wrote to Drury, ". . . everything possible should be done to acquire Mr. Anderson's interest in the Ozette Reservation."[45] When nothing happened, Anderson wrote to Macy directly asserting his claim as "sole owner of Ozette" and complained of his lack of status as an Ozette on the Makah Reservation, " . . . no one formers Ozette get money," he said. "Makahs hate me just as if I was a itchy dog what ever I have they want to take away from me [sic]."[46]

Believing that as the last surviving Ozette he owned the reservation, Anderson thought he could sell it to the Park Service. Preston Macy made a recommendation that it be purchased or somehow acquired forthwith. He wrote directly to Ickes and a month later, he got a copy of a letter to Drury from the chief counsel's office which killed the effort. Assuming that funds would have to come from the Public Works project, Chief Counsel D. E. Lee told Drury that no part of the acquisition money should be "diverted to the acquisition of the Ozette Reservation."[47]

OPPOSITE: In 1988 after years of effort, environmentalists succeeded in getting the offshore rocks and islands added to the park. The Park Service supported legislation to remove them from the protection of the park the following year. *Ed Walker, © 1988, Seattle Times.*

Even the daily press has begun to reflect the public's belief that offshore oil drilling se-verely threatens the wilderness of the Olympic Coastal Strip. *Copyright 1987, Brian Bassett, Seattle Times.*

Elliott Anderson struggled on in his attempts to get the Park Ser-vice to buy the reservation even while he was incapacitated in the Ta-coma Indian Hospital. "I have a useless Indian reservation . . . ," he said. "If national park can buy my land I can sell it."[48] The following spring Macy again recommended action and this time he got it but it was killed on the spot by the Park Service's 1947 attempt to eliminate the Bogachiel, Calawah, and Quinault areas to placate the timber industry. "The trend of these bills," Acting Director Tolson said, "is toward a reduction of the Park and adjacent areas. Any proposal to add lands to the Olympic area by legislation in the face of this trend would likely have little chance of success and might easily incite the interests advocating a reduction of the park to renewed efforts in that direction with a possible adverse effect upon the overall interests of the Service."[49]

By aborting the move to acquire the Ozette Reservation, not only could a possible conflict with the timber industry be avoided but avoided also would be the internal Interior Department conflict with the Bu-reau of Indian Affairs. The BIA could be expected to attempt to retain the reservation so when legislation to move control to the Park Ser-vice emerged "it would impose upon the Department the necessity of resolving the apparent conflicting interests of the two Services by de-termining the paramount use to which the land should be devoted."[50] The avoidance of conflict would again rule the day in the Park Service.

The Park Service, however, had underestimated the Bureau of In-dian Affairs. By 1952, it was ready to liquidate the Hoh Reservation be-cause there were no legal heirs and no timber, as well as the Quillayute

Reservation, because all the timber had been cut and it was not worth protecting for the small amount of timber it might produce in seventy or more years. The same was true for the Ozette Reservation. The Park Service was asked by the Bureau of Indian Affairs to signify its interest in the reservation and it did so,[51] but in the following five years, it took no action, probably as a result of pressure from the Makah tribe.

Ever since 1941, the Makahs had asserted their interest in the Ozette Reservation by requesting its transfer to them. When the Makah Tribal Council attempted to construct a hunting lodge on the Ozette Reservation in 1955, permission "was denied on the ground that no tribal funds should be used to make improvements on land until the tribe was found to have an interest in the land." When the Interior Department's Solicitor responded to the Makah's formal petition claiming the Ozette Reservation in 1957, he found that "the mere fact the Ozettes were historically a branch or part of the Makah tribe does not give the Makah tribe any rights to the Ozette reservation." He determined that descendents of Ozettes " . . . relinquished all rights thereon when they did not return to cast their votes to determine the future of reservation lands when the election was held in 1935."[52] Sensitive to the fact that the reservation was an island inside Olympic National Park and that it dominated the future of preservation in the Ocean Strip, the Makahs now knew that getting the reservation was going to be political. The Makah Tribal Council wrote directly to President Eisenhower:

> We vigorously protest adding this land to the Olympic National Park . . . their claim has no merit when compared with the claims of the Makah Indian Tribe.
>
> The reason the Tribe is so desirous of obtaining this land is because of its tie in with past history and culture. It is the intention of the Tribe, once the land is obtained in their name, to make a park out of the area and eventually turn it over to the State of Washington as a Makah Memorial Park.[53]

In spite of these disclaimers from the tribe to use it as park land, when Congressman Jack Westland introduced HR 10800 to transfer the Ozette Reservation to the Makahs, the Pacific Northwest environmental community rose up in arms against it, fearing that the Makahs would allow the same logging devastation the timber companies had wrought on both the Quinault and the Makah reservations. "We hope you will go on record," the president of the Mountaineers wrote to Westland, " . . . as favorable to the interests of all of the citizens of the United States including the Indians, instead of appearing favorable to a proposition which would convey to a tiny special interest group what amounts to a part of our National Park system." "HR 10800 would," he said, "open to logging and roads the most heavily used trail area of the Olympic Coastal Strip."[54]

The environmental groups were adamant that the Ozette Reservation was not going to become yet another sea of devastation. The Makahs were equally as adamant that the reservation properly belonged to them to do with as they pleased. Congressman Westland, in whose district both the park and the Makah Reservation lay, was caught in the crossfire. When he reintroduced his bill to transfer Ozette to the Makahs, it failed again. Westland then moved to resolve the matter with HR 12131, which would give the reservation to the Park Service, designate it the Makah Memorial Park Area and create a location for a Makah Indian Fishing Camp. That failed. He tried again with HR 2329, the same bill reintroduced, again with no luck. Lloyd Meeds replaced Congressman Jack Westland. Conservationists discovered that Meeds' part-Indian heritage proved stronger than his ties to preservation. He supported the Makahs in their quest for the Ozette Reservation. With his position on the House Interior Committee, he could move the bill fast in the House.

Finally, in 1970, Senator Henry Jackson took on the task of transferring the Ozette Reservation to the Makahs in HR 9311. Immediately, the bill was confronted with an Interior Department report:

> The bill gives the Makah Tribe the beneficial use of the land and under the provisions of the bill they will be able to develop it and use it for the benefit of tribal members. However, because the reservation is adjoined by the Olympic National Park ocean strip and possesses some outstanding natural values . . . we recommend that the bill be amended to provide that the development of the reservation be in conformance with regulations to be prescribed by the Secretary of Interior. . . . This amendment would, while allowing the tribe to develop the land for their benefit, give this Department sufficient control over any development to insure that it would be in keeping with the surrounding area. . . .[55]

The Makahs reacted to the threat of Interior Department controls on their development plans by producing a policy statement in which they said, "the tribe is willing that this declaration of policy regarding the use of Ozette be incorporated in any act or resolution of Congress placing the land in trust for the Makahs."[56] So concerned were they that the issue of preservation might derail the transfer, they were even willing to have their policy written into the law itself. They came forth with an attempt to placate the environmentalists with an on-the-record statement of their preservation intent.

Resolved, that the policy of the Makah Tribe regarding Ozette is as follows:

FIRST: The Makah Indian Tribes desire to preserve the Ozette Reservation as a modern monument to its ancient past.

SECOND: Consistent with this, the Makah Indian Tribe declares that Ozette shall be dedicated to the use of the Makah who wish to reside there, either permanently or in temporary camps, and for use by Makahs in fishing, hunting, berry picking, and related uses.

THIRD: The Tribe will maintain its traditional hospitality toward non-Indian visitors to the area but will permit no acts or conduct by such visitors which would damage or desecrate the natural beauty of Ozette.

FOURTH: The Tribe will not lease or otherwise permit any commercial development of the area or use inconsistent with its primary use by Makahs, as here stated, or inconsistent with the natural beauty of the area and its surroundings.[57]

So persuasive was the Makah's Declaration of Policy that Jackson chose not to include the language in the bill itself, even with the offer by the Makahs to do so. With the Declaration of Policy, the Interior Department's objections vanished as well. But lingering ominously over the Makahs' Declaration of Policy was the State of Washington's Declaration of Policy nearly thirty years earlier, which the Park Service repeatedly ignored.

Three years later, Joseph Laurence Jr., the chairman of the Makah Tribal Council, wrote to Park Superintendent Roger Allin, that he "would like to emphasize the fact that the Ozette Indian Reservation was set aside by an Act of Congress for the Makah Indian Tribe to use and develop as we please."[58] The Declaration of Policy did not any longer exist in Makah memory in the short span of three years. In spite of this seeming lapse, the Makahs have lived up to the letter and spirit of their Declaration of Policy so far.

Ominously, however, in the 1988 bill to put Olympic's coastal strip under the protection of the Wilderness Act, the Makahs demanded a non-wilderness corridor through the park for access to the Ozette Reservation. It was understood that the move was to facilitate development. To the dismay of the Pacific Northwest environmental community, the Park Service recommended that the park wilderness bill accommodate the Indians' request. With the Park Service's history of never enforcing the preservation commitments made in the past, the future of the Ocean Strip remains perilously in doubt.

Indians and backpackers have so far functioned happily together at Cape Alava. The site of the village at Ozette turned out to be one of the richest archaeological finds ever. Artifacts of a culture dating back four hundred years are displayed with pride by the Makahs in a newly constructed museum at Neah Bay. The Makahs have succeeded to the present time in the first tenet of their stated policy "to preserve the Ozette Reservation as a modern monument to its ancient past." Any move to change that preservation, however, is likely to set in motion a nationwide conservation battle.

Another threat to the park has emerged against a backdrop of the increasing activism of Indians throughout North America in 1990. The Quileute Indians, whose 797-acre reservation is surrounded by Olympic National Park lands, want to expand their reservation for the benefit of the 430 enrolled members who live there and others who may come. Rialto Beach, a popular park tourist attraction, the Quillayute River shore now open to the public and 1,300 acres of park forestland have been put into dispute by the Indians' claims against the park.[59] All of the lands involved were acquired by the United States by condemnation from private owners for public use a half century ago when Olympic National Park was created. Title to the tidelands was acquired by the Park Service from the state of Washington by a purchase/trade. What makes this threat ominous for the future of the Ocean Strip is that the Park Service, in its fifty-year history on the Olympic Peninsula, has never failed so far to at least recommend the yielding of territory in every case in which park territory was demanded. Whether this "lower the conflict" position, normal for the Park Service, will prevail here remains to be seen.

19 SENATOR JACKSON AND FRED OVERLY TEAM UP

> *The proposal to open the Bogachiel-Calawah rain forest to timber cutting is simply outrageous. It is intolerable that the Nation should have to defend Olympic National Park every few years against some new proposal like this for the benefit of the timber industry.*[1]   ANTHONY WAYNE SMITH,
> NATIONAL PARKS ASSOCIATION

> *The return of this area [the Bogachiel and Calawah] to National Forest status would make a significant contribution to the economy of the Peninsula.*[2]   FRED J. OVERLY,
> BUREAU OF OUTDOOR RECREATION

WITH FRED OVERLY GONE from Olympic National Park, exiled to Appalachia, a growing sense that the park might survive after all permeated the environmental community of the Pacific Northwest. Almost as if a signal had been sent to Willard Van Name that his beloved Olympic National Park trees were now safe, he died at eighty-seven in the spring of 1959. Three years later, at age eighty-five, Rosalie Edge, active in conservation to the end, also died. Of the original group who had fought Olympic National Park into reality, only Irving Brant now remained to watch over it.

Overly was embittered at having been banished for carrying out a park logging policy that in fact was the Park Service's and certainly Director Wirth's. "His feeling was that people were entirely too emotional

321

about a few trees," said an Overly acquaintance, "and that he was un-justly treated for using his judgment in selling trees he thought were mature and too valuable to keep standing. He also felt that a standing tree was not a creditable monument when it could do somebody some good. He didn't say so but I got the feeling he also believed that the stump would do just as well to show people how big it used to be."[3]

As the four-year mark of Overly's banishment to Great Smoky Mountain National Park approached, the Bureau of Outdoor Recreation emerged out of the work of an Outdoor Recreation Resources Review Commission, proposed by the Sierra Club's Dave Brower and launched by Act of Congress in 1958. A number of the functions of the Park Service were transferred to the new bureau with its creation in 1962.

The timber industry recognized the threat that an agency focusing on outdoor recreation could pose for logging. The National Lumber Manufacturers' Association retaliated against this threat with the FACTS program, an acronym for *Federal and Community Timber Supply*. The program set out to lobby Congress to remove the Forest Service's management prerogatives and place them into a Congressionally mandated forest policy with four thrusts:

1. To manage the national forests solely as commercial tree farms with little or no consideration for other uses. This abandonment of the multiple-use concept was called "full timber-growth potential from commercial forest areas" and was listed as the prime objective of the program.
2. Eliminate competitive bidding for timber in the national forests, going instead to a system of appraised prices based on average costs of production and selling prices. "The industry which boasts it asks for 'no dole nor subsidy,'" charged *Conservation News*, "instead would seek a guaranteed profit from public resources."
3. Take the appeals process away from the Forest Service. The industry charged that "purchasers are subject to arbitrary decisions by the administrators without the right of appeal outside of the agency." The industry wanted an outside board to which Forest Service decisions could be appealed and which they could control.
4. A complete revision of the timber sale contract form.[4]

With the timber industry trying to stop allocation to recreation of even a quarter section of federal land that could grow trees, the new Bureau of Outdoor Recreation began the process of organizing itself. Overly's career in the Park Service had made him too controversial for most assignments, and his open expression of an anti-preservation, pro-logging point of view did not set well inside the Park Service, which demanded at least preservation rhetoric from its staff.

Even though Overly had never shown even the tiniest spark of in-terest in recreation, he recognized that the new BOR was an escape route from the Park Service. With his usual political acumen, he went to his friend Senator Henry Jackson, chairman of the Senate Interior and Insular Affairs Committee. Overly had maintained close ties with Jackson for more than twenty years. Jackson had legitimized Overly's logging program by openly supporting it after his forest elimination bill had had to be withdrawn in 1947. One of Overly's daughters had even worked as Jackson's secretary in Washington, D.C.

After failing in a try to become director of the BOR itself, he now tried for regional director of the Bureau of Outdoor Recreation in Seat-tle. Senator Jackson went to work for him and he was appointed in May of 1963. This discredited Interior Secretary Stewart Udall and the con-servation movement for being unable to resist Senator Jackson. In ad-dition, it undermined the credibility of Edward C. Crafts, the new BOR director in Washington, D.C., who had come to BOR from the Forest Service and therefore was viewed as pro-logging. Overly's presence as BOR's regional director launched the new agency in a cloud of distrust. These two anti-preservation men were now in a position to greatly affect the volatile old-growth forest, wilderness preservation and other issues that dominated the environmental agenda of the Pacific Northwest.

Overly soon dropped his first bombshell: "A new government agency has recommended construction of a controversial highway along the wilderness beach area of Olympic National Park," the *Seattle Times* in-formed its readers in April of 1964.[5] The road along the wilderness beach of the Ocean Strip was widely viewed as a timber-to-market road to assist Rayonier, Crown Zellerbach, and other large timber operators cutting on the west side of the Olympic Peninsula. If built, it would destroy the only roadless coastline area remaining in the contiguous forty-eight states. At this time, the conservation organizations of the Pacific Northwest were working actively to create a North Cascades Na-tional Park. Now they also had to resist Overly's coastal road.

During this same period, Overly had sat next to Secretary of the In-terior Stewart Udall on a flight from Juneau to Seattle and had steered the conversation toward his views on possible Olympic National Park deletions, development, and roads. Overly gave his views to Udall on the plane and followed up in writing, bypassing any review by the Park Service or the Bureau of Outdoor Recreation. In an attack on the con-cept of wilderness and forest preservation, Overly laid out all of his Olympic National Park plans for Udall:

1. *The elimination of wilderness from the Ocean Strip.* "Construction of a road to Cape Alava and a connecting road from Cape Alava across the

Ozette River to the park boundary to join with a road coming down from the north; building a large campground in the vicinity of Cape Alava; establishment of a concession for overnight accommodations and creation of an archaeological exhibit."

2. *Clear-cutting the Bogachiel and Calawah rain forests.* "Managed on a sustained-yield basis by the U.S. Forest Service, this exclusion could add significantly to the economy of the peninsula. Harvesting of the timber by clear-cutting in blocks would produce browse . . . " for game.

3. *Elimination of 16,440 acres from the Quinault* "containing an estimated 586 million board feet of timber."

4. *Elimination of Alckee Creek plus some very minor ridge-top additions.*

Overly ended his nine-page memo to Udall on the hopeful note that "2.6 billion board feet of timber would be removed," but that "it would not be unrealistic to assume that the volume of timber to be excluded from the park would exceed the estimated 2.6 billion board feet by one half again as much."[6]

Overly followed his forest-deletion memo with a second memo on roads and development. Emerging with new life was Overly's Tshletshy Creek Road. Planned over a decade earlier to increase the timber volume being cut from the park during his logging program, the road was routed through the densest forests in the park and into some of the most pristine wilderness. The road that vanished with Overly's departure was now alive again as a result of Senator Jackson's power to put him in the BOR. The road was to run on the route of the Queets-Quinault Skyline Trail, down Tshletshy Creek and the Queets Valley. Overly told Udall the road would give visitors "opportunity to see the big game — deer, bear and elk in the high country and some unspoiled virgin timber stands along the Quinault and Queets Rivers. . . . In my opinion," Overly said, "it would develop into one of the most popular drives in the country." What he chose not to disclose was the millions of board feet of timber that would be made available for logging by the building of the road.

Overly also wanted a road to connect Deer Park with Hurricane Ridge and a road on the Lake Crescent railroad grade (putting highways at water's edge on both sides of the lake). He wanted the old road to Hurricane Hill from Whiskey Bend on the Elwha River opened and paved and the East Fork of the Quinault Road extended farther up the river. To conservationists, it was as if Overly had designated himself to be the agent to destroy what had by then been a seventy-six year struggle to preserve some of the wilderness resources of the Olympic Peninsula in a park.[7]

Edward Crafts had also brought his timber-cutting views from his role as assistant chief of the Forest Service to his new role as director of BOR. The head of the BOR and his seniormost official in the Pacific Northwest were now working together on behalf of the timber industry to increase the federal land available for logging in an area long ago set aside to be preserved. This perversion of the intent of the executive order creating the BOR had occurred within three years of its establishment. This was comparable to the perversion of the 1916 Park Service Act through the logging policies Overly had carried out in the 1940's and 1950's.

Finding himself in complete accord with Overly on the need to get the old-growth rain forests of the Bogachiel and Calawah rivers out of the park, Crafts wrote to Udall:

> . . . my recommendation is legislation that would transfer about 59,000 acres of National Park land and 3 billion board feet of timber to the Olympic National Forest. This is also Overly's recommendation and it is very similar to a bill that Jackson sponsored when a Congressman in 1947.[8]

In a repetition of Newton Drury's 1947 Olympic National Park boundary-change fiasco, Crafts told Udall this "will establish boundaries better suited to practical administration of both the National Park and the adjacent National Forest lands." Crafts picked up Overly's exact language in his earlier memo to Udall. "Harvesting of the timber by clear cutting in blocks would produce browse and contribute substantially to the elk range, increasing the harvest for sportsmen."[9]

Crafts wanted the Olympic National Park boundary-change issue "brought out in the open" at the press conference scheduled in Seattle the following week on the results of the North Cascade National Park study. Even though Crafts did not want it "to look like a *quid pro quo* for a North Cascades Park," he was willing to run the risk.

At the press conference in January of 1966, Jackson arranged for Overly to have equal billing with Stewart Udall, Secretary of the Interior and Orville Freeman, Secretary of Agriculture, and with Overly's own boss, Edward Crafts. Jackson's strategy was to tie Overly's Olympic National Park proposals so tightly to the North Cascades Park proposal that it could not move forward without the Olympic reduction. Jackson planned hearings to consider both at the same time.

When Overly got up at the press conference and began his statement, the carnival atmosphere at the Washington Athletic Club, with klieg lights, television cameras and flash bulbs, was well suited for the explosion that Overly's Olympic proposal turned out to be. The newspaper reporters present instantly saw the reality of what was unfolding and reported: " . . . it was unusual for Overly to be introduced by Jackson from the same platform occupied by two cabinet members," said the *Seattle Times.* "Obviously what Overly had to say was considered important by his political peers. Its importance was magnified a few minutes later when, in answer to a question, Senator Jackson made it clear that his Interior Committee hearings would consider both the study team report and the Overly recommendation together. The senator refused to separate or segregate them."[10]

Irving Brant was outraged. Now eighty-one years old, he moved into action again to defend his beloved Bogachiel Valley by writing directly to Secretary Udall:

> Never in my life have I been so astonished and dismayed as on this day, when I received a report of the conference held in Seattle. . . .
>
> I cannot believe that you are entering into this plan with knowledge of the wreckage it would make of the decisions of Congress, President Roosevelt, and President Truman, to preserve an adequate portion of the disappearing rain forest of the Pacific Slope, for the present and future generations.
>
> If you had asked me . . . who would be the worst possible choice among persons with a governmental background outside the Forest Service to make recommendations on Olympic Park deletions, I would have said without hesitation, Mr. Overly . . . for the task currently assigned to him he had two insurmountable disqualifications.
>
> 1. Throughout the years he spent in the National Park Service he remained in fundamental thought the expert logging engineer.
> 2. The bitter personal experience resulting from that trait — his "exile" (as he called it to me) from the Olympic Park superintendent to the Great Smokies — set up a mental torment that was a barrier to important judgment in the matter assigned to him — the Olympic appendage to the North Cascades study. . . .
>
> I visited him [in Great Smoky] several times and could not help observing how bitterly he resented the criticisms of conservation organizations and the actions of the National Park Service in transferring him. I do not say that this was the governing influence in his present recommendations, but in combination with his logging engineer outlook, it virtually eliminated the possibility of a firm stand for the preservation of the Bogachiel Valley from destruction.

Brant went on to refute Overly's report against his own past experience. "I write this letter without knowing to what extent," he told Udall, "you are committed to this destructive invasion of the Olympic National Park. . . . Will you please let me know what your position is?"[11]

Udall responded back that neither he "nor Director Hartzog are committed to any part of it at this point." Brant responded to a friend that the explanation that the Overly proposal is one man's "does not explain how that one man happened to make this proposal. . . ."[12] Referring to Jackson's widely commented-upon identity as "the senator from Boeing," Brant said, "Who then except Senator Jackson? I suspect that the Rayonier Corporation is the Boeing of this affair."[13]

Brant now believed that Jackson had to be the power behind Overly's moves. He wrote back to Udall to drive the wedge he hoped would separate Udall from Jackson. " . . . I have come to believe you have been put into an unfortunate position by Senator Jackson, and have no intention of serving his ends . . . ," he said,[14] hoping that Udall would step away from support of Jackson and Overly.

By the time of the Olympic-North Cascades hearings in February of 1966, the "one-man report" ploy enabled Jackson, Crafts, and Udall to have Overly out front to take the flak. If the Olympic deletions proved to be politically untenable, none of the three needed to take any responsibility at all. Overly was set up to be the patsy, but he embraced the attention as if it were his proper due.

Every politician, public administrator and civic activist showed up to testify at the hearings. Governor Dan Evans opposed the Olympic eliminations and the linking of the North Cascades issue to Olympic National Park. Irving Brant, in a statement given at the hearings by his daughter, Robin Lodewick, following her own testimony, went after both Fred Overly and Senator Jackson: "Mr. Overly's 'one man study' is an obvious assist to the persistent efforts of timbermen to open the Bogachiel and Calawah Valley rain forests to lumbering." After identifying in some detail Jackson's attempts in 1947 to give the west-side forests to the lumbermen, Brant continued:

> I have before me two maps. One shows the Quinault, Bogachiel and Calawah boundaries proposed in the Norman and Jackson bills of 1947. The other shows the boundaries in those areas recommended by Fred Overly in this report last month. The two maps are identical except for a minor contour variation in the Quinault. In other words, the 'one man study' made by Mr. Overly for the benefit of the Secretary of the Interior . . . is a mere pick up of the eliminations sought by Representatives Norman and Jackson in 1947 and rejected by an aroused public and by Congress.[15]

Preston Macy, in retirement since 1961 after thirty-seven years in the Park Service, produced the most curious of all the testimony. He virtually recanted his whole Park Service career and was clearly attempting to distance himself from Overly, with whom his career had been intermeshed for years. " . . . I was the first Superintendent of Olympic National Park," he told the Committee. "Mr. Fred J. Overly served as my assistant. During those years I disagreed sharply with him on many recommendations regarding the release of segments of fine virgin forest from the park. . . . It is a tragedy when one man can, at any time for selfish reasons, cause a threat to the welfare of an area which has been given careful and thorough study by many . . . and . . . have caused our legislators to declare the necessity of preserving it as an outstanding example of our American heritage."[16] As he continued on about the misrepresentation of the need for Sitka spruce in World War II and the importance of the decay-and-rot process in a virgin forest, Macy conveniently overlooked that it was he who had worked vigorously to keep that very forest out of the park in the 1934 and 1943 boundary studies. In 1947, he had actively supported Jackson's elimination bill, nearly identical with Overly's one-man study which he was now attacking. He was park superintendent during a period when the first 11 million board feet of timber were logged out of Olympic National Park. He believed in park logging enough that he brought Overly's logging program to Mount Rainier National Park when he returned there as superintendent. Mount Rainier was logged regularly by Macy until the Olympic logging crisis stopped it.[17] Macy's statement from the introspection of his retirement years could be viewed either as a maturing of vision or as a denial of reality.

Senator Jackson's moves to give the timber industry Olympic National Park's west-side forests now backfired for the second time. There was such overwhelming and universal condemnation of it and of Overly that it became untenable for Jackson to pursue it. By the end of the hearings, Jackson felt the need to publicly defend both Overly and himself.

After the last witness had been heard from, Jackson turned to Overly and said that because of the response to Overly's report, "made at the request of the Secretary of the Interior and myself, I think it is appropriate that he make whatever comments he desires to make at this time."

Overly got up and commented on the barbs he had received. "I am an unnumbered witness," he said, "but not unmarked." He then went on to detail a conversation with Associate Director Arthur Demaray, supposedly held during the final days preceding the passage of the park bill, that contradicted both the record and Irving Brant's testimony of his role at the time:

> One of my first jobs in the Department of Interior was to appraise all of the timber in the then proposed park. . . . I was to appear the next day as a witness [in the hearings]. I went to the Associate Director of the National Park Service and I said: "Mr. Demaray, I have observed that every

witness has asked one question: 'Do you think this is a good bill' and I said: 'If I am asked that question, I will say "No" because I believe that it encompasses too much timber.' " Mr. Demaray said: "Fred, I am surprised, he says, "You have worked very closely with us for several years on this, and I thought you were a believer in the park," and I said: "I am," but I said: "No one asked me what my opinion was as to the volume of timber that is being included, and if I am asked that question, that is the answer I will give." I did not appear as a witness.[18]

Overly finished his testimony with a rambling statement about the Bogachiel Valley timber not being worthy of preservation because of "better examples of the timber types elsewhere in the park." This was the same argument William Greeley of the West Coast Lumberman's Association had used about those same forests, over and over again. For the regional director of the Bureau of Outdoor Recreation to say such a thing was tantamount to saying that the timber industry controlled the BOR. Environmentalists in the Pacific Northwest believed that BOR was the enemy from that point on, akin to the timber industry itself.

The hearings had brought into focus Senator Jackson's attempts twenty years earlier to give the park's west-side forests up for logging, and Jackson moved to defend himself as best he could:

> Mr. Overly, I want to say while you are still here, that in 1947 I introduced a bill which I believe covered about 56,000 acres which was worked out with Newton B. Drury, who was a great conservationist and then Director of the Park Service. The feeling was, and it was from the very beginning of the establishment of the park, that there were areas which certainly were questionable as to whether or not they met the proper requisites for a national park, and I want the record to show that there was general agreement in 1947 that those changes should be made. I have been a good conservationist all these years. . . .
>
> . . . the bill was drafted in the Park Service and it was the general position of the Park Service that it was a proper bill and I want the record to show that. What Mr. Overly has suggested here, I think, is about 3,000 acres more. . . . [19]

Senator Jackson simply put the blame again on the Park Service, sidestepping the fact that it was he who had requested the draft of the 1947 bill. Jackson was protective of Overly to the end. He closed with a final salvo on Overly's behalf. "Mr. Overly's participation in 1947 was with the full support of the Director of the Park Service at that time," he said, " . . . and he acted for and in behalf of the National Park Service." Jackson even went so far as to warn those in attendance "not to impute or impugn the motives of Overly."[20]

Just days before the Olympic-North Cascades hearings, the Forest Service became aware that Fred Overly was going to call for eliminations from Olympic National Park as a trade-off for a North Cascades Park. Jackson had thrown a real curve ball to the Forest Service which was desperately trying to hang on to the North Cascades area it controlled. With the Forest Service's commercial focus under attack among those promoting a North Cascades Park, it tried desperately to distance itself from Overly. "I know of no commitment by the Forest Service," explained Olympic National Forest Supervisor R. E. Worthington, of the Bogachiel elimination, "to sell this timber should the land be returned to National Forest administration. . . . Certainly, some of the area discussed . . . must be of high recreational value or it would not have been included in the National Park in the first place." Even though no one believed him, Worthington went on, "Such recreational land would continue to be managed by the Forest Service for its recreational values, and little if any timber would be cut from it." Expressing surprise that a report such as Overly's could be "released at this time," the supervisor claimed the Forest Service "was not even aware that a study was being made by the Bureau of Outdoor Recreation." He said, " . . . the Olympic proposal only clouds the basic issue originally put before the public, that is, should National Forest lands in the North Cascades be made into a national park."[21]

The Park Service refused to defend the Bogachiel Valley, an area that had been under its administration now for over a quarter of a century. Olympic National Park Superintendent Bennett Gale went on the chamber of commerce luncheon circuit to broadcast the agency's position. He informed everyone that the Park Service's attitude towards Overly's recommended reduction was, "We'll be glad to study it."[22] It was a bad position for the Park Service to put itself into, at the same time the forest supervisor of Olympic National Forest was on the same circuit emphasizing the Bogachiel Valley's recreational and esthetic values, and that "little if any timber would be cut" because of this, even if the Forest Service got it back. Superintendent Gale presented both the timber-industry position in wanting the Bogachiel-Calawah area out of the park and the environmentalist's position in wanting it preserved. That the Olympic National Park superintendent was unwilling to make a case for continued preservation of the Bogachiel Valley in the park without also presenting the timber industry's case produced contempt within the whole of the conservation community.

Overly went on the chamber of commerce luncheon circuit promoting his proposal for an Olympic National Park reduction. As his boss, Edward Crafts was attempting not to have the Olympic National Park elimination look like a *quid pro quo* for North Cascades National Park,

Overly boldly said, "The presently proposed boundaries [North Cascades] includes little marketable timber, but if it is enlarged and takes valuable timber, then it gives all the more reason for a reduction in Olympic National Park."[23]

Shortly after the Olympic-North Cascades hearings were over, Senator Jackson again moved to get an Olympic National Park boundary reduction bill underway. Jackson told Udall that he wanted the Park Service, the Bureau of Outdoor Recreation, and the Forest Service to conduct an Olympic National Park boundary study leading to a recommendation from the administration by the following January, 1967. This way, he would seem to be acting on behalf of administration recommendations even though he was generating them himself from behind the scenes. It was to be an exact replay of Jackson's 1947 attack on the park. If it blew up again he could always say he was acting on request.[24] Jackson ignored completely the outrage that the proposed Olympic National Park eliminations had aroused at the hearings.

Senator Jackson worked hard to get the Forest Service involved again in the dismemberment of Olympic National Park, but the agency wanted no part of it. Secretary of Agriculture Orville Freeman side-stepped Jackson's insistence that the Forest Service take part in a joint boundary study, telling Udall, " . . . we believe that any determination that substantial areas are no longer essential to fulfill the objectives and programs of Olympic National Park should be made by the Department of the Interior."[25] He told Jackson the same thing, but Jackson would not take no for an answer and Freeman finally allowed the Forest Service to provide technical assistance. The Forest Service wanted no part of any decision to eliminate trees from Olympic National Park at the same time it was calling on the American public to believe it should be entrusted with management of a North Cascades Recreational Complex, its alternative proposal to head off the creation of a North Cascades National Park.

Meanwhile, Director Crafts of the Bureau of Outdoor Recreation moved to give every possible assist to Jackson's efforts by appointing Overly to represent the BOR on the committee to develop "recommendations . . . concerning revisions in boundaries of Olympic National Park."[26] Secretary Udall's press release stated "the Department is making a study of boundaries of the park in order that it can recommend to Congress early next year boundary adjustments required to facilitate park administration,"[27] was a stunning blow to environmentalists. They now had to drop the North Cascades fight to fight yet again the Olympic battle of 1947, a battle that had been fought and won over and over. It seemed ludicrous that again twenty years after the Park Service had attempted to "improve administration" by eliminating Olympic's forests, the same issue had to be refought.

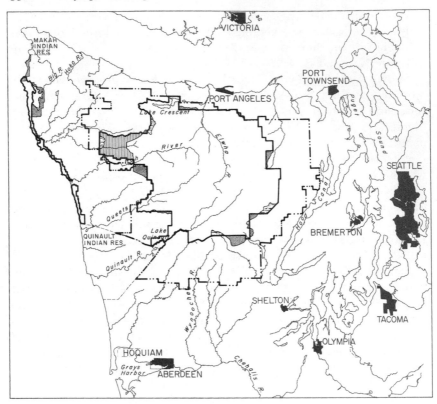

NATIONAL PARK SERVICE BOUNDARY PROPOSALS 1966

The Park Service again in 1966 recommended giving up part of the Bogachiel as a compromise with Fred Overly, Senator Henry M. Jackson, and the timber industry. All wanted the Bogachiel available for logging.

In the eyes of the environmental community the fact that the study was underway at all was stark testimony that the Park Service stood for nothing. If a discredited logger/ex-superintendent could move the Interior Department to attack again the integrity of Olympic National Park from within with such ease, there seemed to be no hope. It was a political triumph, however, for Fred Overly. It had taken him barely three years since he returned from exile in Great Smoky to put the most valuable of Olympic National Park's trees at risk again. The *Seattle Times,* having editorially supported Overly's park reductions with great enthusiasm from the start, led their news article on the study with an open disclosure of the reality of the situation. "A seven man team was named today to study possible changes in the boundary of Olympic

National Park *to release quantities of timber for harvest.*" [italics added][28] This newspaper account was a call to arms for every environmental organization in the country.

Olympic Park Associates, the watchdog group founded by Irving Clark in the aftermath of the Park Service's 1947 boundary debacle, now moved to involve every conservation organization in the country in what was unfolding. Under the leadership of Phil Zalesky, Olympic Park Associates dropped the passivity that had nearly destroyed its credibility in the past. "The worst part of having Fred Overly on this committee," Zalesky wrote to Stewart Brandborg of the Wilderness Society, "is that he has a strong and dominating personality, bullish, and stubborn. This is almost certain to result in forcing the members of the committee to reach a compromise with him. . . . The NPS may feel they can handle Fred Overly or this committee. I do not believe it! Overly will force them into concessions that will tamper with the integrity of the park. If the NPS now compromises with the Overly Report, how can they expect us to support its administering of the lands of the North Cascades?"[29] Zalesky detailed for Brandborg what Olympic Park Associates considered to be the sorry history of Park Service administration of Olympic National Park, including Overly's logging program.

Zalesky continued the environmentalists' attack with letters to both Director Hartzog and Secretary Udall. Referring back to Jackson's recently completed hearings, he summed up the nearly universal anger at the Park Service that had spread throughout the conservation organizations at the prospect of another boundary study in Olympic National Park. "For every person who favored the Overly Report," Zalesky said, "there were 20 who opposed it. That, I would think, is conclusive evidence as to what the people think should be done to Olympic National Park. And if we must suffer through another study, it is simply unthinkable that such an outspoken critic of Olympic National Park, Fred J. Overly, should be appointed to the study committee. Must we deliberately send the fox to guard the chickens again?"[30] Zalesky continued, "By placing Fred Overly on this committee, you are asking us to suspect the motives and results of the committee before it has ever commenced. He is simply persona non grata as far as we are concerned."[31]

The boundary committee that emerged consisted of Park Service personnel augmented by a member of the National Park Advisory Board, along with Overly, and his BOR subordinate, Sid Malbon, who also had worked under Overly in Olympic National Park. Chaired by Olympic National Park Superintendent Bennett Gale, the committee acted as had been predicted by the environmental organizations.

The Park Service stood firm against what Overly really wanted, but the Park Service majority recommended giving up the western end of the

Bogachiel Valley arm, all of the Alckee Creek drainage, the headwaters of the Wynoochee River and all of the Hamma Hamma River drainage. The predicted compromise was a reality. Done under the guise of hydrographic divide adjustments, the timber volume in the Bogachiel Valley elimination far exceeded the minor additions recommended.[32]

Overly produced a minority report that explained his boundary recommendation in one area as being drawn "to exclude commercially valuable timber." He challenged the Park Service's continuing presence on Lake Quinault and even its use of "Federal zoning regulations and other Federal manifestations of the police power to control the use of private land. "If adopted," he said, "such regulations would put the National Park Service in the position of governing a small community. . . ."[33]

Overly said he would agree to an adjustment on the South Fork of the Hoh River and the adjacent state lands "only if an equivalent value of Federal land and timber can be exchanged" for it. Although this was a boundary study, he also threw in his demand for the coastal road he wanted. "This road should be constructed within the confines of the present Pacific Coast Area from the vicinity of Mora north to the west side of Ozette Lake to connect with the existing road." Overly's minority report closed with an attempt to assist the local loggers. He proposed that another mile-wide corridor be created the length of the Bogachiel Valley, this time to straddle the township line between T27 and T28 north, and that this corridor revert to the Forest Service. "We recommend," he said, "that any land north or south of this corridor . . . not needed for land exchange purpose revert to Olympic National Forest . . . north of the corridor in the Bogachiel drainage we recommend that *preference first be given to private land owners* [italics mine].[34] The private land owners were the large timber companies.

This time, the Park Service recommendation did not give Senator Jackson enough timber to justify proceeding ahead with a bill, so his efforts quietly receded into the background. As this was occurring, the North Cascades Park bill wended its way through the legislature. Jackson took the boundary decisions for the new park away from the park's promoters and gave them to the Forest Service. Thus the boundary of the North Cascades National Park was established to accommodate the commercial exploitation plans of local economic development groups, as defined in each Forest Service Ranger District. The North Cascades National Park Bill passed. A year later, in 1969, Jackson's re-election fund drive was led by timberman William Reed, owner of the huge Simpson Timber Complex and much of the redwood forests of northern California that would soon be in conflict with national park proposals there. So much money flowed to Jackson from Reed's efforts that *Argus Weekly* reported that "Republicans nearly have given up trying to find a candidate to oppose Jackson . . . with their principal money-sources dried up be-fore the campaign even starts they have good reason."[35]

Overly's career in BOR was finished even before he was assigned to the Olympic boundary study committee. This may have given him the freedom to blatantly demonstate his loyalties to the peninsula logging community. Director Crafts of the BOR told Overly in a letter of repri-mand in April of 1966:

> . . . the character, tone and content of your letter are provocative and destructive of the close working relation and mutual respect that must exist between an agency head and his regional directors if an agency is to function effectively. To put it mildly, your statement is extraordinary, defiant, indicates a personal grievance toward me and dissatisfaction with my conduct of Bureau affairs.
>
> As long as I am director of this Bureau I am responsible for its opera-tions, shall execute the duties of my office to the best of my ability, and expect good will, responsiveness and conformance to policy from mem-bers of my staff.
>
> Although as you point out, your time until retirement is relatively short, your letter leads me to feel that you might be happier in another agency. If you wish to initiate action toward a transfer, I shall not object.[36]

Overly still had Senator Jackson, chairman of the Senate Interior and Insular Affairs Committee as an ally. That proved to be enough to en-able him to remain in office at the BOR until he retired in March of 1972.

Upon retirement, Overly organized a timber industry front group, the Olympic Peninsula Heritage Council. All the big timber operators were financial supporters in equal share: Merrill and Ring, Simpson Timber Company, Rayonier, Mayr Brothers, Weyerhaeuser, Boise Cas-cade and Crown Zellerbach. Payments to Overly totalling $2,577.32 com-prised 97 percent of total expenses of the group for the month of November, 1972. This was the only month for which a financial report is available.[37]

The first task the Olympic Peninsula Heritage Council undertook was to remove the forest areas in the park from "wilderness" designa-tion under the Wilderness Act. Deleting wilderness status would have removed another layer of protection from the park's forests and it would have retained the possibility of reinstating the park's logging program. Crown Zellerbach's spokesman explained precisely why the timber in-dustry was directing so much energy towards keeping wilderness desig-nation out of the park:

> By stressing wilderness use and de-emphasizing the development of a va-riety of opportunities and facilities for the outdoor recreative public, the

park plans [for wilderness] in effect divert public recreation pressure to the National Forests, state and private lands. These latter lands are being called upon to provide a raw material base for the economy of the peninsula, and we do not believe that they should be asked to meet an inordinate demand for recreation from people attracted to the peninsula by the National Park.[38]

As Fred Overly worked with the Olympic Peninsula Heritage Council to prepare for the forthcoming park wilderness hearings to begin five weeks hence, he died suddenly, at age sixty-six. Enormous relief spread throughout the community of environmental organizations nationwide. However, the Park Service was still very close at hand and ready to strike again.

The whole concept of wilderness status for Olympic National Park came under attack by the Park Service in the first wilderness plan it produced. They proposed twenty-acre enclaves situated in the depths of the wilderness where a hostel, a meal, or a shower in a permanent building might be available to the weary back-country traveller. The Park Service said the hostels were for "those who desire and would appreciate an overnight or short experience in backcountry, but who do not have the necessary equipment or know how to encounter the backcountry alone."[39] The proposal would eliminate the Mount Angeles-Morse Creek area from wilderness consideration to allow for a tramway.

Conservation groups attacked the enclave proposal so hard it became untenable for the Park Service to proceed with the concept, even while the timber industry was supporting it wholeheartedly.

Two months after Overly's death, the Olympic Peninsula Heritage Council's recommendations were presented. They included nearly every one of Overly's development proposals for the park, as presented to Udall seven years earlier. Among them were:

1. No wilderness status for areas containing commercially valuable forest.
2. Permit salvage logging.
3. Open Whiskey Bend-Hurricane Hill Road.
4. Expand enclave idea in the wilderness.
5. Build a road up Little River to Mount Angeles with tramway connecting to Hurricane Hill.
6. Build a road connecting Deer Park and Obstruction Point, and a road connecting Sol Duc Hot Springs and Olympic Hot Springs.
7. Build the Tshletshy Ridge-Nork Fork Road.
8. Extend East Fork Quinault Road.
9. Build a tramway near Mount Steel.[40]

The Park Service's proposal for the park vanished as Senator Jackson removed Olympic National Park wilderness considerations from his legislative agenda.

Irving Brant died in 1976 at the age of ninety-one. He spent the last few years of his life writing a memoir, finished in 1976, of his experiences in conservation. Brant's passing marked the end of nearly a half century of personal environmental activism. Willard Van Name's vision that the public had to be involved in environmental issues was embodied in every move that Brant made. They both believed that control over public land decision-making had to be wrested from those who profited from its exploitation. Irving Brant, along with Rosalie Edge and Willard Van Name, not only succeeded in leaving a heritage of preservation in forests and wildlife, but also succeeded in changing the national environmental agenda and the methods by which the public can have access to that agenda.

20 SUMMARIZING THE PAST

It would be a great mistake to include in parks great bodies of commerical timber. . . . This would result either in preventing the use of the timber or having a national forest under the name of a park.[1] HENRY S. GRAVES,

U.S. FOREST SERVICE

The Forest Service has always been and is the bitter and most dangerous enemy of the national park system, which it seems to regard as a silly concession to weak sentimentality.[2]

WILLARD VAN NAME

THE LONGEST RUNNING and most intense of the nation's conservation battles has been the Olympic National Park tree-preservation battle, during which a powerful industry and two government bureaus under its influence vied with environmental activists at the game of capturing Congressional votes.

Preserving the environment through direct citizen activism, as we know it today, had its beginnings in the Olympic National Park battle. The Emergency Conservation Committee's triumph in adding the rain forests of the Quinault, Bogachiel, Calawah, Hoh and Queets valleys to the park was the triumph of democracy in action: the public was led to demand a say in how publicly owned resources would be allocated. Three persons began and led the campaign: Willard Van Name, Irving Brant, and Rosalie Edge. In the end, hundreds of thousands of people in forty-eight states were fighting the fight as their own. In 1925, fifteen years before Roosevelt's Olympic National Park proclamations of 1940, H.H. Chapman of the Yale Forestry School asked the crucial question:

> Shall trees be cut down and used and the forest perpetuated by reproducing it through forestry methods, or shall the trees be preserved to be enjoyed as they are now? We cannot do both. . . . If a tree or stand is worth more to civilization by leaving it as it is than by cutting and reproducing it, then it should be preserved from the ax. Who is to determine this? In the final analysis, the public.[3]

The problem was there had been no vehicle by which the public could speak. Those who were profiting from the economic utilization of the trees, and the Forest Service which administered these resources, were both happy to keep it that way. In the 1920's environmentalist Willard Van Name crowded his way into this comfortable relationship between the timber industry and the Forest Service with a demand that the public be heard. He added an optimistic corollary to Chapman's statement:

> Most of our Senators and Congressmen . . . are only too glad to do the will of the people if it is clear to them. In too many cases the public fails to make its views and desires known or even to give evidence of having any. This is the first condition we have to remedy.[4]

Van Name was struggling alone by the time he wrote *Vanishing Forest Reserves* in 1929. When he linked up with Rosalie Edge and Irving Brant in forming the Emergency Conservation Committee in 1930, he found complementary personalities to breathe life into his concept of public involvement.

Willard Van Name defined the "will of the people" in his pamphlet *The Proposed Olympic National Park* in 1934, which launched the park battle, and which he paid for out of his own pocket. It was Van Name who induced environmentalist Irving Clark to join in the fight in 1934. It was Van Name who recognized that Congress needed to understand the "will of the people" and who personally paid the salary of William G. Schulz as the ECC's lobbyist in the state of Washington. Without Van Name's enormous financial commitment, the park bill might well have failed. He would have felt honored by what Secretary of the Interior Krug said of him later, in 1947, "Dr. Van Name is . . . the hairshirt that the National Park Service has worn, perhaps for the Nations' sins against conservation generally, since the days of Stephen T. Mather."[5]

Rosalie Edge brought not only a sharp mind, acid tongue and quick wit to the fight, but also organizational skills without which the whole effort would have failed. An excellent writer, Edge knew instinctively what would capture the public: sometimes a cartoon, sometimes a map, sometimes a picture. One after the other, they found their way into

ECC pamphlets. With pamphlets, letters, and phone calls she contacted anyone and everyone who could help. Edge's position in the New York social register gave her access to nearly everyone she chose to have access to. She worked tirelessly for those conservation goals in which she believed. The Olympic National Park campaign was only one of Rosalie Edge's many conservation activities, yet the saving of its rain forests in the sixty-third year of her life became one of the high points in her career.

Irving Brant was the master strategist who had understood every nuance of power in the domain of politics and public administration. He knew the power of proximity to power, the power of access to power, and he used it so effectively that before the park battle was over, he was a power in his own right. Probably no citizen-activist before or since ever ended up so deeply involved in the processes of government. Brant attended all the top-level meetings between the president, the cabinet secretaries involved and the governor of Washington, not as a resource person but as a key participant. He was as deeply involved inside the Congress as he was inside the executive branch. Key committee chairmen looked to him for strategy and allowed him to participate in the selection of committee members involved in the passing of the 1938 park bill. Without Brant's presence there would have been no Olympic National Park.

Two other citizen-activists completed the team: Irving Clark, a wealthy, liberal Seattle lawyer, had long been involved in environmental activities as the secretary of the Mountaineers. He was on a first-name basis with nearly every politician and environmentalist in the Pacific Northwest. He was the critical link to the infrastructure of Pacific Northwest politics and conservation that enabled ECC lobbyist William Schulz to drive a wedge between the timber industry and Washington State's Congressional delegation.

William Schulz, a young, true-believer in the saving of trees, was an excellent writer. He produced pro-conservation articles that appeared in national publications and the daily press throughout the Pacific Northwest. A community organizer, he filled Washington State with letters to the editor and press releases. His direct memos to Secretary of the Interior Harold Ickes induced Ickes to hire him as a personal representative.

These were the five people who were most responsible for creating Olympic National Park, although thousands participated. Never in American history had any conservation battle lasted so long or had such politically significant consequences. The triumph in it all was that a group of citizens, beginning with nothing, could achieve what they set out to achieve in the face of the massive resources committed to defeating them. They did it by involving the public.

Natural resources on public lands belong to the public. This was the Emergency Conservation Committee's presumption and the driving force which defined its relationship to both the Park Service and the Forest Service. Neither the Park Service nor the Forest Service has ever accepted the validity of the ECC's simple and direct operating presumption and both were in constant conflict with it and the public as a result.

The ECC followed a strategic plan to pass a national park bill that becomes apparent on analysis but was probably not followed consciously:

1. Define a specific minimum area that must be in the park and explain why it must be included.
2. Continually work to capture the cabinet-level secretaries to the cause by any means available to provide a counterforce to the Park Service and the Forest Service in their support of local economic interests.
3. Build trusting personal relationships with the Congressional leadership and members of appropriate Congressional committees.
4. Capture the support of Washington's State Congressional delegation through public involvement.
5. Capture the support of Congress through a nationwide publicity campaign aimed at the public.
6. Use conflict with opponents and communication with the public as weapons to build support and keep opponents on the defensive and to keep the issue active in the media.

In addition to the clarity of their strategy for the passage of an Olympic National Park bill, the ECC followed intuitively "the law of effective reform," a basic principle for getting change in government. In using this principle with institutions such as Congress, courts or agencies, one must assert:

1. The factual basis for the grievance and the specific parties involved.
    The ECC's grievance: The Forest Service and the timber industry are planning together to send the last remnants of America's old-growth heritage to the mills without saving even a sample for future generations to experience.
2. The legal principle that indicates that relief is due (Constitutional provision, statute, regulation, court or agency decision).
    The ECC's legal challenge: The Forest Service's planned cutting circles have allocated every tree in Olympic National Forest ultimately for logging, contrary to law and its own statements.

3. The precise remedy sought (new legislation or regulations, license revocation, fines or an order changing practices).

The ECC's solution: The bill to create an Olympic National Park will preserve a minimum sample of Pacific Northwest forest for future generations.

Nicholas Johnson, who served a seven-year term on the Federal Communications Commission from 1966 to 1973, observed these principles in action many times. "When this principle is not understood, which is most of the time," Johnson said, "the most legitimate public protests from thousands of citizens fall like drops of rain upon lonely and uncharted seas. But by understanding and using the right strategy the meekest amongst us can roll back the ocean."[6] And roll back the ocean the ECC managed to do.

The ECC wanted change in national assumptions about how natural resources are allocated, along with a reallocation. When such fundamental change is attempted, groups who are profiting from the status quo can be expected to fight to retain their favored positions in the existing situation. The ECC understood this well.

From the beginning, the ECC set out to use the conflict generated as a weapon to achieve their goals. Dave Brower's laws of conservation action had not been promulgated when the ECC began but they were embraced by Van Name, Edge and Brant as if they had written them themselves:

1. Conflict gets attention and educates the public.
2. Mediation does neither and lets the industrial Godzilla stomp Bambi in private.
3. Sell the alternative good over the proposed bad.

Rejecting mediation and preferring open conflict to arouse the public, Van Name, Edge, and Brant knew that any move towards being "reasonable" would result in failure. Political scientist Grant McConnell described this dynamic of environmental mediation which the ECC successfully resisted:

> The implicit argument is a comparison with a market bargain: you offer me something at a price. I offer in return a lesser amount; we dicker, and then agree on something in between the two; both of us are better off than we were before. And it's all *reasonable*.
>
> By contrast, you ask me for agreement to the building of two dams in the Grand Canyon or for a number of 2000 year old redwoods. I refuse; you say let's be reasonable: agree to building just one dam or somewhat fewer redwoods. I again refuse. You tell me I am stubborn and irrational. But any way I agree with you, I lose. The fact is that the only way

you could provide an analogous bargain with the market situation is if you offered me a brand new Grand Canyon in place of the one you want to destroy or some brand new 2000 year old redwoods.[7]

The potential for conflict could not have been greater when Willard Van Name produced his ECC pamphlet, *The Proposed Olympic National Park*, in 1934, as the "alternative good" to what the Forest Service was planning for the trees of the Olympic Peninsula. The criteria for the use of conflict strategy was present in the Olympic National Park situation and the ECC used it well, however unconsciously:

1. *Where power disparities exist so that one group dominates another.*

The ECC had a keen understanding of the power disparity that existed between it and those aligned against it. Aligned with the timber industry to commit all of the Olympic Peninsula's resources to economic utilization were the Forest Service, colleges of forestry, chambers of commerce, newspapers, and state, county and municipal governments. Held together by a commonly shared value in the primacy of utilization over every other value, the timber industry coalition seemed unbeatable to everyone but the ECC. The ECC counted on the public.

2. *Where conditions are win-lose.*

Hardly a more dramatic example of win-lose has ever existed. With the practice of clear-cutting in the Pacific Northwest and no part of the Olympic Peninsula assigned to be preserved by the Forest Service, every acre of the remaining forest would be devastated by logging if the park bill failed.

3. *Where sharp cleavages of interests exist.*

The ECC asserted that the public's interest lay in preservation of the last remnants of the vast forest domain. They continually confronted the public with dramatic illustrations of what maintaining the status quo meant for the future — future profits for mill owners and loss of a great natural heritage.

The ECC, in following conflict strategy, continually sought out *those things which divide people*. The conflict strategist will try to divide people along the cleavages that already exist in American society. The conflict strategist also attempts to bring people together in these same interests. Rosalie Edge got the New York Zoological Society, the Philadelphia Academy of Sciences and similar scientific and educational groups to pay for and distribute copies of her pamphlets to their own memberships, convincing these organizations that the preservation of eco-systems was in their interest and that the enemy, the timber industry-Forest Service coalition, wanted them destroyed by logging. Thus her role as organizer was to rub raw the latent sores of resentment that lay dormant. In this manner, component parts of the public, targeted by Edge, saw that their real interests were in the creation of an Olympic National Park.

In the use of conflict strategy, *communication is a weapon.* And Rosalie Edge was a master in its use. First, a conflict tactician makes strategic use of information. Needs, goals or conditions will be disguised so as to manipulate the situation to advantage. For example, Rosalie Edge consistently refused to reveal the size of the ECC's membership, which for the most part consisted of three persons. It was not to its strategic advantage to do so.

Second, to establish advantage for negotiation, the conflict strategist overstates objectives. He will ask for more than he knows he will get, so that hopefully when the negotiation comes, he will get more than he would have otherwise. When the ECC issued Willard Van Name's 1934 pamphlet, *The Proposed Olympic National Park,* they demanded much of the remaining west-side forest as a *minimum* addition to the existing Mount Olympus National Monument. Van Name's "minimum" boundaries became the baseline by which the ECC could attack all other park proposals as inadequate. In 1938, the ECC began listing the forest and wildlife resources it was "actively campaigning for the protection of." First on the list was "Virgin Forests," by which Rosalie Edge meant *all* publicly owned old-growth forests. Calling for the protection of all virgin forests labeled Edge a fanatic extremist in her day. "No virgin forest of outstanding beauty," she said, "should be touched until the extreme limit of necessity has been reached. Such forest cannot be replaced. . . ."[8] But as a result of this grandiose goal, thousands of acres of forest land were preserved. Thus, demanding the preservation of *all* old-growth forest was a useful overstatement of objectives for the ECC, right out of the conflict strategy textbook.

Third, the conflict strategist will use (or withhold) communication to keep the situation ambiguous and uncertain for opponents. By using the element of surprise and behaving in unpredictable ways, the opponent can be kept off balance. Thus, when Rosalie Edge produced and distributed her pamphlet, *Double Crossing Mount Olympus National Park,* attacking the Park Service for trying to keep the rain forests out of the park, she blamed the rewritten bill on the Forest Service, even with the full knowledge that the Park Service was really to blame and not the Forest Service.

In conflict strategies, *the opponent is the enemy,* and is treated as such. One of the first tasks of a conflict strategist is to discover the enemy and give it a name. The ECC made the Forest Service their targeted enemy. Irving Brant succeeded year after year in undermining the

Forest Service's relationship with President Roosevelt, Secretary Wallace and with their assistants in the White House and in the Department of Agriculture. Finally, at the close of the park battle, when the ECC issued Brant's pamphlet, *The Olympic Forests for a National Park,* he openly ridiculed the Forest Service by using its own statistics on economic necessity to support his position. The pamphlet was even reprinted in the *Congressional Record,* to the dismay of the Forest Service, which as a result ended up being unable to defend itself to the Secretary of Agriculture.

As easily as conflict strategy came to the three individuals in the Emergency Conservation Committee, there is nothing to suggest that any one of them consciously operated within any formal framework. It was probably all instinctive, based on empirical knowledge gained through years of working for change in other contexts. Brant, Edge and Van Name were middle-aged when they launched the Olympic National Park battle. They brought with them personal storehouses of data on how to succeed in political action and put these storehouses to use continually.

The conflict strategies employed by the ECC left William Greeley and his West Coast Lumberman's Association continually off balance. Greeley, however, was a master of consensus strategy. In this strategy, power must be shared; there must be a balance of power so that equals are dealing with equals. For Greeley this worked well between his group and other timber organizations, the Forest Service, the colleges of forestry, the chambers of commerce and the newspapers. Each shared a common belief in the primacy of the economic utilization of trees over every other use.

A consensus strategy is more useful when goals are distributable, i.e., when both sides can get something they need, and when it is not a win-lose situation where one side must give up what it wants to the other. Greeley insisted that the timber industry wanted an Olympic National Park and, therefore, his goals were the same as the environmentalists. It was, he said, just a matter of size. Since his goals were the same as the environmentalists, surely a reasonably sized park could be negotiated, one that met everyone's needs, the timber industry's needs for timber and others' needs for recreation. Owen Tomlinson of the Park Service, likewise, believed that the whole park issue could be resolved by consensus between the Park Service and Forest Service. Greeley was so successful in his consensus strategy that the Park Service moved continually to give the timber industry at least some of the forest areas that the environmentalists had succeeded in getting preserved. Over and over, the timber industry attempted to gain consensus by promulgating a "we can have our cake and eat it too" viewpoint. The industry said, "Let us have magnificent areas of primeval forest; let us maintain the herds of lordly elk in their native habitat; let us provide recreation and inspiration for all America. But let us also have the ordered use of our waters and minerals. Let us have the controlled use of our timber resources. . . . " To achieve these conflicting goals, the industry proposed returning Mount Olympus National Monument to the Forest Service and the implementation of its Cleator Recreation Plan,[9] which called for the eventual logging of every merchantable tree on the Olympic Peninsula whenever it was needed. After the Park Service's 1947 failure to give the industry the west-side forests it wanted, the industry began a new campaign in Congress. In a large color pamphlet, the industry declared in very large print: "On Any Lands Added to the Olympic National Forest All Recreational Values Would be Preserved."[10] As hard as the industry worked to convince the public that its goals were compatible with preservation, it failed. The public rejected the compatibility viewpoint as completely as it rejected Gifford Pinchot's turn-of-the-century views about logging the national parks.

Finally, consensus strategy is most effective in situations where people share values, interests and goals. For the powerful triad of timber-industry trade associations, colleges of forestry, and the Forest Service, consensus strategy was the glue that held them together functioning as one, giving them much greater strength than they might otherwise have had. William Greeley of the West Coast Lumberman's Association was able, by the use of consensus strategy, to almost (but not quite) keep the rain forests out of the park. Later, he almost (but not quite) got them out of the park even after they were put in by legislative consensus.

The ECC succeeded because it had proximity to power, gained through Irving Brant, the capacity to communicate with the public and to Congress, provided by Rosalie Edge, and a vision of how the world ought to be, which came from Willard Van Name. The timber industry, the Forest Service and the Park Service believed that the Emergency Conservation Committee was unreasonable in what it wanted. George Bernard Shaw's view of reasonableness might well be applied to the ECC in the Olympic battle. "Reasonableness," he said, "never yet achieved anything great."

Stephen Mather's development program for national parks amounted to a massive attack on the concept of preservation that the 1916 Park Service Act mandated. On top of it all, he permanently disrupted the balance in the park's wildlife populations with his wildlife extermination program. In Director Cammerer's regime, every move was made to prevent the preservation of the commercially valuable forests in the park. Director Drury tried to give the most valuable of the park's forests back to the Forest Service to be logged. When that failed, he actually began his own massive logging program in the park. Conrad Wirth carried the park's logging program so far that he succeeded in getting over 66 million board feet to the mills during his regime (and another 37 million before becoming director). The Park Service today daily demonstrates that it does not have an organizational culture that will support the preservation that the law requires and that the public believes is happening. In the fifty-four-year history of Park Service administration on the Olympic Peninsula, the Park Service merits an *F* on courage and must join the Forest Service in receiving an *F* on management, at least as measured against their statutory mandates.

Ironically, the Park Service and the Forest Service both have failed in large part because of the management behavior of their first leaders. Gifford Pinchot imprinted the Forest Service so deeply with his economic-utilization values that it has been unable to extricate itself in order to serve the modern society in which it now exists. Stephen Mather, on the other hand, had no particular plan for the Park Service except to have the parks make money. Instead of imprinting the Park Service with a value system that could support the great mandate of preservation inherent in the 1916 Park Service Act, he imprinted the Park Service with his own confusion and ended up with an organization incapable of meeting the needs of a modern, increasingly urbanized society, exactly where the Forest Service is.

Mather left the Park Service with the management philosophy that drives it to this day: *the avoidance of conflict.* Just as the timber industry moves to *maximize profits,* and the Forest Service moves to seek *economic utilization,* the Park Service imperative is *rock no boat.*

What distinguishes the Park Service from the normal bureaucratic tendency for conflict avoidance is that it is driven by lack of values at its organizational core. This characteristic is present to such a degree that it will not even defend its own turf, as defined by law, and as the public expects it to. Any administrator who must manage in an environment which is ungrounded in a value system cannot commit himself or herself on anything that might be controversial. At the same time, the no-conflict option generally imperils the resources that both the law and public expectation require be protected.

When the New Deal struck in 1933, the Park Service attempted to avoid taking over Mount Olympus National Monument despite a presidential order to do so. The Park Service tried repeatedly between 1934 and 1938 to keep the rain forests out of Olympic National Park to avoid conflict with the Forest Service and local chambers of commerce. Later,

348   *Olympic Battleground*

it connived to eliminate the Bogachiel, Calawah, Quinault and Queets valleys in the misguided belief that if it yielded to the timber industry, the conflict would go away.

The Emergency Conservation Committee's success in preserving the Olympic rain forests in a national park represented such organizational failure within the Park Service that as soon as the forests were added, it moved to undo the preservation with which it was charged. Here are some of the moves the Park Service has made to lower the conflict and increase its comfort level in the local scene:

1. Attempted to keep commercially valuable forests out of the various bills to create Olympic National Park.
2. Managed the acquisition of the Queets Corridor and Ocean Strip so that the timber companies could retain cutting rights to the old-growth timber as the Park Service acquired the land for park purposes.
3. Attempted repeatedly during World War II to open the Bogachiel and the Hoh for logging, areas that it did not want in the park.
4. Set up a logging program in the park which ran from 1942 until 1958, removing on the record over 100 million board feet but probably closer to 150 million board feet.
5. Attempted to placate the timber industry by legislation in 1947 to remove 63,000 acres of the most heavily timbered and most valuable old-growth areas of the park, in the Calawah, Bogachiel, Hoh and Quinault valleys.
6. Refused to enforce the provisions of the contract with the state of Washington to protect the tidelands of the coastal strip.
7. Attempted to divest the western end of the heavily timbered Bogachiel Valley in 1966 along with the headwaters of some other drainages.

In 1988, there were two excellent illustrations of the *avoidance of conflict* dynamic at work. For more than ten years the Crown Zellerbach Corporation has operated a power dam on the Elwha River inside Olympic National Park with only an annual license. It was the assumption of environmental groups that with the glut of power in the Pacific Northwest, the license would not be renewed. If this dam and a lower one were removed, restoration of a legendary salmon run into a natural, free-flowing Elwha River would be possible. In fact, Fish and Wildlife Service studies indicate that the economic value of a restored Elwha salmon run would far exceed the value of the power generated by the dams. Despite agitation by many environmental groups for the removal of the dam, and even with a local United States Senator in agreement, the Park Service opted to support retention of the dam in the park and to experiment with transporting fish over the dam. The no-conflict option avoided a confrontation with a major industry and allowed the park superintendent to live more comfortably in the local community with the mill manager, chamber of commerce, and other pro-timber-industry groups. Even with the economics of the situation on the side of removal and clear interest in a restored river valley, the Park Service was unable to make a decision for preservation that might have generated conflict. The Park Service, however, suddenly reversed its dam retention position in 1990. Conflict was being heightened by then with its retention stance. With leading newspapers calling for the dam's removal, with Indian tribes, every environmental organization, the U.S. Fish and Wildlife Service and several state agencies joining them, the Park Service for the first time enthusiastically embraced removal. By doing so, it returned to the low-conflict position in which it is most comfortable.

Another current park issue is non-native mountain goats placed in the area by the Clallam County Game Commission before the park was created. The goats have multiplied to the point where the native plants and ground cover the park was created to preserve are being destroyed. Erosion is permanently damaging and even denuding many areas. For years the Park Service has avoided the issue, experimenting with heli-copter removal of goats without really affecting the numbers or the problem. An internal Park Service committee has now recommended, in the face of the damage being caused, that shooting the goats is the only way that numbers can be decreased fast enough. Shooting, how-ever, opens up the specter of animal rights groups on the one hand demanding that the goats be left alone to multiply at will, even if this means the destruction of the park, and hunters on the other hand, demanding that if any shooting is to be done, they will do it. Whether the Park Service will triumph over preservation and perhaps even com-mon sense in dealing with the goats remains to be seen.

What the Forest Service was supposed to deliver, upon its founding by Gifford Pinchot, was:

1. Break even within five years and make a profit after that.
2. Stop destructive logging practices through education and control over cutting on private land.
3. Provide a role model for what is good forestry practice to demon-strate that, in the end, this is the best economics.
4. Eventual public ownership of all forestland.
5. Honest and corruption-free administration.

None of these has come to pass. In fact, the tree-cutting on Forest Ser-vice lands is now undistinguishable from that on private lands. Its focus is the maximization of profit for the logger, just as it is on private land. The view that the Forest Service is essentially the governmental arm of the timber industry seems to be borne out by the subsidization of the private ownership of forestland and the now-routine subsidized-cutting contracts. The Forest Service has been a massive management failure. Even Pinchot's concept of a corruption-free Forest Service has been lost in Olympic National Forest. A felony indictment of an Olympic National Forest employee in 1988 for conflict of interest with loggers resulted in a guilty plea. He was given a jail sentence and fined $1,000. Others have left under a cloud.

It was Gifford Pinchot who had the great vision that created the Forest Service, and ironically, it was he who, by excluding the public, destroyed the potential it had to fulfill that vision. The public was excluded by his insistence on the economic-utilization imperative and by the absolute primacy of the judgment of the Forest Service technician, a deadly combination. Pinchot, for all his arrogance, may have had some doubts, however. "Unless the Forest Service has served the people," he said, "and is able to contribute to their welfare, it has failed in its work and should be abolished."[11] Irving Brant probably spoke the public viewpoint as precisely as anyone, as he did so many times. "Never, from the day of its organization," Brant said, "has the Forest Service genuinely accepted the doctrine that preservation of a great distinctive forest growth which lies within reach of a lumber mill is part of national policy."[12]

Ben Twight's 1983 study of the Forest Service's behavior in the Olympic National Park situation offers an insight that perhaps comes closest of all to explaining the dynamics involved in its clinging to a losing ideology:

The structure of the Forest Service caused rigidity because it was patterned after the eighteenth-century European, bureaucratic "machine" model, which emphasized reliability of behavior to maintain central control. Use of this model tends to result in increased impersonality and increased internalization of rules and values, to the point where means become substituted for ends. Such structural characteristics can be expected to prevent anticipation of change and responsiveness to new sources of power in the organization's environment. Thus, an innovative response to a new stimulus would not be predicted. On the contrary, the opposite would tend to occur. That is, a consolidative response—an attempt to satisfy external forces for change by reordering or revising programs within the organization's existing framework of values and norms—would be expected. A problem with consolidation behavior, however, is that by the time an adequate response is made, the organization

tends to be on the defensive and its options are limited. Thus, the organization has less control over its future and its domain than has an
organization which anticipates institutional trends and adapts innova-
tively to change.[13]

In its first open confrontation with the public in the Olympic National
Park battle, the Forest Service lost everything it wanted to retain. The
public, acting through Congress, simply took the trees away from the
Forest Service and gave them to the Park Service to be preserved. Since
then, the Forest Service has lost over and over again, continuing to assert its economic-utilization imperative. The North Cascades were lost
to it for the same reason.

The Forest Service's management imperative, since its earliest beginnings with Pinchot, can be stated: *Economic utilization is the only value.*
William Greeley dramatically reinforced that management imperative
when he moved to make the interests of the Forest Service synonymous
with the interests of the timber industry in the 1920's. At the onset of
the New Deal, the Forest Service and the timber industry stood as one,
supported by an ideology that mandated the economic utilization of
every forest resource. "Their fundamental belief is that the only use
for a mature tree is to cut it,"[14] Irving Brant complained about the Forest Service, as he began to prepare for attack against it and its timber-
industry allies.

Having lost control of the Mount Olympus National Monument to
the Park Service by executive order in 1933, the Forest Service fought
on, trying to prevent its enlargement into a park by reasserting Pinchot's dogma, handed down as law in 1905. Oblivious to the societal
changes that demanded wilderness designations from 1925 onward, the
Forest Service yielded not an inch. Bolstered by its timber industry and
chamber of commerce constituency and legitimized by the colleges of
forestry, the Forest Service clung to Pinchot's rules as if they were
natural law.

The Forest Service thought it was the "irrational sentimentalism" of
the public, worked up by the Emergency Conservation Committee, that
had caused the Olympic National Park bill to pass. The Olympic National Park loss did force the Forest Service, however, to totally revise
its Primitive Area definitions, which had allowed for economic utilization of all resources and road building. Having done this, it abolished
the remnants of the Olympic Primitive Areas not included in the park
over the objections of its own recreation division.

Congress, in the end, intervened. After the Wilderness Act of 1964
took away the Forest Service's discretionary decision-making over its
own lands, Congress took more of Olympic National Forest. Several

Corruption of Olympic National Forest officials was front page news in 1987 and 1988 with the disclosure of massive stealing of timber with the connivance of forest officials. Ironically, this was the very corruption that Gifford Pinchot created a Forest Service to overcome. *Copyright 1987, Steve Greenberg, Seattle Post Intelligencer.*

significant wilderness areas were created on the park's boundaries, many in areas of the former Primitive Areas which had been abolished. But in other areas the Forest Service fought on, sometimes even when it lost in Congress, as it did in 1976, when it asked President Ford to veto the Alpine Lakes Wilderness bill for Washington State. Today, Alpine Lakes is the third most used wilderness area in the United States and is in a crisis of over-use for which the Forest Service has no solution.[15]

When a goal is approached with absolute clarity of purpose, its achievement is much more likely. In order to be able to continue in its quest for maximized profits, the timber industry has been creative, has hired exceptionally skillful men, has intervened in politics, and has done whatever it needed to do to achieve that end. Against numerous countervailing pressures in American society, it triumphed over and over again. If judged solely on its goal of maximization of profit, the timber industry would win management accolades.

William Greeley, upon leaving the role as chief of the Forest Service in 1928, went straight to the West Coast Lumberman's Association, where he succeeded for the next quarter of a century in piecing together a powerful coalition of interests to watch after the timber industry's well-being. He brought together the colleges of forestry, the Forest Service, and various timber companies and trade associations to make up the "timber-industry triad." This powerful group not only promoted its single commonly held ideology but also provided employment opportunities, as Forest Service employees flowed to the colleges of forestry and industry employees flowed to the other two points of the triad. A maverick in any part of the triad was instantly labeled and isolated, diminishing his career potential. Identifying the industry position as the public-interest position, and therefore their own, the colleges of forestry were reinforced by state governments.

The colleges of forestry ended up emasculated by this simple development. By 1916 in Washington State, the sawing capacity of the mills exceeded by one half the greatest cut of lumber they had ever made.[16] This overcapacity in the mills was exacerbated by the fact that the industry did not restock the mile upon mile of clear-cut lands left behind. E. G. Griggs, who headed the National Lumber Manufacturing Association while also heading the St. Paul and Tacoma Lumber Company, said it all in 1911: "Reforestation will come when it is profitable,"[17] dismissing all concern for the fact that literally millions of acres were being left unstocked for future generations.

Although it occurred decades late, natural restocking eventually did occur on some of the private lands. Twenty years later, in 1932, the Olympic National Park battle began, largely because the overcapacity of the mills demanded the consumption of all the old-growth forests within reach. At that same time, Dean Hugo Winkenwerder of the University of Washington College of Forestry defended the practices of the timber industry, even to the point of irrationality. "At present we are cutting our timber three and one half times faster than we are replacing it by reforestation," he told a radio audience in 1937. "It is evident that only a disastrous result can be the outcome of this practice," he concluded. Having called attention to the forthcoming disaster, Winkenwerder reassured his listeners, "There is no need to force the lumber and timber industries to curtail operations." He assured everyone that the annual cut need not be reduced. "Under the proper forest management," he maintained, "this figure [5 billion board feet] can be maintained and even increased."[18] Greeley had been so successful in forging his industry triad that Washington's College of Forestry, along with those of the other timber states, became little more than arms of the industry itself.

Greeley's program, which drove his every move in politics, in public relations, and in his relationships with the colleges of forestry and the Forest Service, advocated three essentials:

1. Free enterprise (the maximization of profits).
2. Education at the grass roots (to insure continuing public and political support for the other components).
3. Cooperation without dictation from national agencies (cooperation is the industry euphemism for subsidy—subsidies without conditions being imposed by the Forest Service) [parentheses are mine].[19]

It did not matter to Greeley that lumbermen "were almost in the class of Public Enemy No. 1," as Greeley's own poll indicated.[20] What mattered was that the three essentials of his program functioned well, and they did.

When the timber industry had to meet the public head on, as it did in the Olympic National Park battle, the confrontation precipitated by the Emergency Conservation Committee caused Greeley and the industry to lose big. The public was sensitized by the ECC to the fragile nature of the Olympic Peninsula's forests. Nonetheless, Greeley kept the battle going, resurrecting out of nothing, time and time again, new opportunities for a diminished park boundary.

When such a small organization as the Emergency Conservation Committee could lead the public to assign industrial forestlands to be "locked up," it became clear to the timber industry that more trouble might be coming. With demands for more dedicated wilderness areas also looming on the horizon, the timber industry turned toward state legislatures, traditionally the industry's home turf. The industry's three-point program to foreclose the possibility of another national park was simple and direct:

1. "All further extension of parks and monuments should be made only with the consent of the legislatures of the states concerned."
2. " . . . their boundaries should be restricted to the smallest area . . . "
3. "The establishment of monuments, like the establishment of parks, should be exclusively in the hands of Congress."[21]

Had this program existed in the past, there would have been no Mount Olympus National Monument and certainly no Olympic National Park, a fact that the drafter of the program (probably Greeley) had in mind.

The timber industry's singular focus on profit was justified as being in the general welfare. The protection of private timber with tax money would prevent forest fires, thus preserving the country's resources. Lower taxation of timberlands would eliminate the necessity of a hurried conversion of timber into logs. If taxes did not endanger future profits, the timber owners would preserve his trees. Lower taxes on logged-off lands would make it possible to reforest denuded lands, guaranteeing an adequate future timber supply. Forest fires, heavy taxes, high railroad rates and low prices for lumber caused waste of timber.[22]

In the 1980's, when the Japanese were willing to pay much more than independent Olympic Peninsula mills could afford for unprocessed logs, George Weyerhaeuser justified shipping the logs to Japan on the basis of reducing our international trade deficit. Further, he wanted to make increased government assistance to export firms a national goal.[23] As early as 1972, when Congress placed a ceiling on log exports from federal lands, timber-industry demands for increasingly larger cuts from the national forest became more strident. Direct conflict with environmental organizations increased dramatically as the industry's quest for profits conflicted with concerns for preserving old-growth trees that would provide those profits.

Since the 1940's the industry has promoted its "Tree Farm" program to allay fears that over-cutting can lead to shortages. To qualify for "Tree Farm" status, owners simply have to sign a statement agreeing to follow three basic rules:

1. Keep "Tree Farm" land in good condition to produce timber crops.
2. Protect trees from fire, disease, insects and other damage.
3. Harvest "Tree Farm" timber in such a way that the land will continue to produce timber for future use.

In reality, the owner makes no pledge to match cut with growth, leaving the tree farm land to be cut as before, to maximize the profits.[24]

As the industry turned to the Forest Service as a major supplier of raw material to make up for shortages on its own lands, the Forest Service increased its timber cutting from 5.6 billion feet in 1950 to 13 billion feet in 1969. As this political push by the industry for more and more raw material from the national forests continued, conservationists turned to Congress. Congress responded with more wilderness designations. The battle today is continuing. The Forest Service responded to timber-industry pressure by removing in fiscal 1987 alone, 5.6 billion board feet from the national forests of Oregon and Washington, the second highest yield since 1946, in open defiance of public concern.

The timber industry's success with the Forest Service was documented by former Assistant Chief Edward Crafts before the House Agriculture Committee. The Forest Service had made a grave error by permitting the term "allowable cut" to be substituted for "sustained yield," he said. "Allowable cut used to be the ceiling above which the cut would not be allowed to go. Then it became the floor below the cut would not be allowed to fall."[25]

Nowhere in the national forest system has any company been as successful in dealing with the Forest Service as has the family-owned Simpson Timber Company on the Olympic Peninsula. By 1947, most forestlands owned by Simpson had been completely cut over. At the same time, the adjacent Olympic National Forest lands had experienced very little timber cutting. With the economic stability of the local communities of Shelton and McCleary in question, where Simpson had mills at stake, the Forest Service entered into an agreement with Simpson in 1947. The largely old-growth timber on an entire ranger district of 113,000 acres would be combined with the company's 159,000 acres of cut-over lands for the purpose of calculating the allowable cut. In the deal, Simpson would get the exclusive right to buy the Forest Service timber without competitive bidding.

The Forest Service was surprised to find that when the private and public lands were combined, their calculations yielded a 50 percent greater increase in cut than if the lands were calculated separately. Combining the two resulted in increased cutting rates because the old-growth surplus federal forest could rely on the cut-over lands to provide additional sustained-yield capacity after the old growth was gone. With the discovery of this 50 percent increase in cutting rates from combining lands, the Forest Service began in 1960 to combine ranger districts to achieve that end. Then in the 1970's, it began combining forests themselves to justify further increasing the cut. Thus, such combinations as Mount Baker Snoqualmie National Forest came into existence.[26]

Besides enabling the Forest Service to increase the cut, the Simpson agreement had other effects as well. Randal O'Toole, in *Reforming the Forest Service,* stated it simply. "The lack of competition cost taxpayers tens of millions of dollars per year in potential revenues in the late 1970s, yet no jobs were created by the unit that would not have existed somewhere in the vicinity.[27] Instead, the millions of dollars of revenue losses simply represented a transfer of wealth from U.S. taxpayers to Simpson Timber Company stockholders."[28] Made possible by "the fruit of industrial support in Congress,"[29] the law that made such agreements possible, was supported by Senator Henry Jackson throughout his career. It enabled Simpson during the 1960's and 1970's to clear-cut an average of almost 2,000 acres of old-growth forest per year, all without competitive bidding.[30]

Preservation considerations, as mandated by the National Environmental Protection Act (NEPA) in 1969 and the Roadless Area Review and Evaluation (RARE) in the decade which followed, got short shrift at the hands of the Olympic National Forest as it interacted with the

Simpson Timber Company in the Shelton Ranger District. Here is how Randal O'Toole describes what happened:

> One example of the Forest Service's attitude toward wilderness and road-less areas can be found in a series of memos between the Region 6 office and the Olympic National Forest at about this period of time. The Shelton Ranger District of the Olympic Forest was part of the Shelton Cooperative Sustained Yield Unit, and Simpson Timber Company considered all the timber in the district to be part of its private reserve. When the time came to prepare a plan for the Shelton Unit, the Olympic Forest asked the region if the roadless areas could be ignored.
>
> The region replied that the court cases were clear: All roadless areas had to be considered for wilderness. But the Olympic National Forest wrote another memo warning that the Simpson Timber Company would probably sue if Shelton roadless areas were even considered for wilderness. Although the region again responded that roadless areas must be evaluated for wilderness suitability, the Shelton Plan never mentioned the existence of the roadless areas. New road construction soon eliminated the roadless areas, and environmentalists did not learn about the roadless areas until after the roads were built.[31]

By administrative manipulation both the law and the Forest Service's own procedures were flagrantly violated and the public was cut out of the process. Because the violation reinforced the timber production imperative of the Forest Service, there were no consequences for the violation, which was tacitly understood by everyone involved as being proper.

The kind of public involvement that the Emergency Conservation Committee used in confronting the Park Service, the Forest Service, and the timber industry, they all found hard to accept. The Park Service reacted by committing its internal decision-making to benefit the timber industry, even to the point of logging the park, contrary to law and public expectation. It did this while reiterating the rhetoric of preservation that it knew the public wanted to hear.

The Forest Service ignored the law just as flagrantly. To forestall public demand for preservation in national forests, the Forest Service tried to head off public involvement with agreements with the Park Service for creating small park areas to thwart large park efforts from the public later. The timber industry attempted to impede public involvement by forcing the public to fight the national park battles in state legislatures as well as Congress. The timber industry expected to dominate the legislative processes at the state level if they could not at the national level. Removal of the president's proclamation power became a timber-industry focus as well.

The success of the Emergency Conservation Committee opened up a new vision of what was possible with public involvement. Because nearly everything the ECC succeeded in preserving had very high economic as well as esthetic value, it still remains at risk today and will be at even higher risk in the future.

21 THE PRESENT

The Secretary's office has consistently squelched plans prepared by Park Service professionals. Watt and Hodel have attempted to weed out and isolate park professionals who see things differently. Assistant Secretary William P. Horn changed the Park Service director's performance rating of one regional director from "excellent" to "marginal" after the director refused to sign a statement saying Yosemite would never need to acquire any of the privately held lands inside the park.[1]

PETER STEINHART, IN *the seattle times*

THROUGHOUT THE 1990's, the Forest Service was accused of systematically violating the law in administering the national forests. In an attack on the Forest Service backed by nearly every environmental group, the Wilderness Society charged that:

1. The law prohibits timber sales on national forest land that is not physically suitable for logging. The Forest Service is breaking the law by planning to log hundreds of thousands of acres where erosion will destroy watersheds and fisheries and where logged hillsides cannot be reforested.
2. The law prohibits the Forest Service from logging land that is economically unsuitable. The Forest Service is breaking the law by planning to log so much unsuitable land that taxpayer subsidies of timber sales could rise to $270 million per year or more.
3. The law prohibits clear-cutting except where it is the "optimum" method of logging. The Forest Service is breaking the law by making clear-cutting its top choice nationwide.
4. The law requires the Forest Service to provide for "the diversity of plant and animal communities" in the national forests. The Forest Service is breaking the law by planning to destroy old growth forests and the habitat of threatened species that depend on them.[2]

Ironically, more than sixty years ago, the Emergency Conservation Committee presented the American public with virtually these same concerns about the Forest Service. Each time the ECC involved the public, the Forest Service lost as Congress opted for preservation. As the Forest Service in the 1990's asserted again and again the primacy of the economic utilization imperative laid out for it by Gifford Pinchot in 1905, Congress and the courts intervened to stop it. The battle over the saving of trees had clearly caught the fancy of the public nationwide, resulting in the Forest Service losing control over its own territory as the courts and Congress, sometimes with very negative results, intervened on behalf of the law.

Today the Forest Service finds itself at odds with the American public as it plans how it will operate for the next fifty years. Finally, however, with old growth nearly gone and with the public clamoring for change, those years ahead will see the very last of the old growth forests either go to the mills or be saved. Some of this past clamor resulted in open rebellion over logging contracts in recreation-oriented areas in the 1980's and the "spiking" of trees by the radical environmental activists. (Such metal spikes in the trees made the trees dangerous to cut by chainsaw and valueless at the mills because of the damage the spikes do to machinery.)

The continued use of logging contracts subsidized by the Forest Service had become so routine that some activists saw sabotage as the only alternative. Even the General Accounting Office attacked the Forest Service for the economic disaster it promoted by way of its subsidies to the timber industry. Another GAO report found that the federal treasury took in less than 10 percent of the nearly $2 billion sold by the agency to private loggers during the last three years. *The Seattle Times* pointed out the following to its readers:

> Out of $1.85 billion in timber sale revenues, a mere $124.5 million was returned to the treasury. The remaining $1.7 billion was siphoned off into off-budget slush funds beyond Congress' reach. The booty is used to pay for salvage logging, and for credits to private timber purchasers who build logging roads on national forests. . . . Every year, the feds lose hundreds of millions of dollars by charging timber companies far below what it costs the agency to prepare and administer timber sales.[3]

With the Forest Service controlling 8.5 percent of the country's public land; more than half of the Wild and Scenic River System; 100,000 miles of trail (compared with the Park Service's 7000 miles); and 80 percent of the wilderness in the contiguous forty-eight states, it is facing a very strong challenge from a now organized and rapidly growing urban public. That public has managed over the years to put into place a series of environmental laws, such as the National Environmental Policy Act, the Endangered Species Act, and the National Forest Management Act, all of which are supposed to govern federal public land management. However, because employee performance in the Forest Service is based on timber production, the requirements of fish and wildlife, recreation, water quality, and forest protection for future generations often conflict grossly with the agency's reward system. With the current Forest Service chief (as of January 2000) coming from a fisheries biology background and the current Olympic National Forest supervisor coming from a forest recreation background, fundamental changes seem to be underway within the Forest Service, even if those changes are occurring after most of the old growth has been logged.

Since its beginning, the Forest Service has maintained a system of administrative appeals by which the public could object to agency decisions in recognition of the internal conflicts between timber production and all the other values needing consideration. The process has not worked well, however. One Forest Service employee articulated the appeal process as he saw it operating in the real world:

> What have we learned from appeals? The biggest lesson is that we don't always follow our own rules. We have been inconsistent in how we apply them, seemingly doing what is right and proper when it is convenient and doing something else when it is not. We haven't always given people notice of proposed actions so they view some actions as end runs to avoid involving them in planning. Our documentation is often incomplete. Our written decisions are often unclear and our writing too often fuzzy and obtuse. We've relied on after-the-fact explanations to satisfy NEPA obligations instead of doing NEPA correctly in the first place. Often, Deciding Officers make decisions that are reserved to Reviewing Officers. Lastly, as GAO [General Accounting Office] reported, we seldom meet required timelines. In summary, our record hasn't been good.[4]

The reality of the Forest Service's public involvement has served more to make it seem real rather than to make it real, a fact well known and understood by armies of environmental activists.

The timber industry and its allies could be expected to attempt to maintain the status quo as the winds of change in forest administration reached hurricane force. The timber industry wanted a Forest Service focused on timber production above all other values, as in the past. Indeed, that is exactly what the industry achieved with the Logging Rider tacked onto the Fiscal Year 1995 Emergency Supplemental

Appropriations for Disaster Relief and Rescissions Act. When the forests simply could not sustain the accelerated cutting during the 1980's and provide essential habitat for endangered and threatened species, clean water, and viable fish runs, federal land managers began to stop many harmful timber sales. Although spurred by lawsuits and citizen appeals of forest plans, they began to revise various forest management plans to reflect the needs of all users of the forest, not just maximum timber production for the benefit of the timber industry. The industry responded with a vengeance. The timber industry's lobbyists managed to attach a rider to a popular bill providing relief for victims of the Oklahoma City bombing and the California floods, a measure that could not have withstood the light of day in the regular legislative process.

> "The Logging Rider took environmental laws and citizens out of federal forest management in two ways. First, for whole categories of new timber sales, the rider truncated the required environmental analysis, eliminated administrative appeals, and rendered federal environmental and natural resource laws unenforceable. Through these devices, the rider left forest management entirely to the discretion of the agencies with little input from or oversight by the public. Second, the rider micromanaged forest decision making by resurrecting and mandating logging of over one hundred old-growth timber sales that had previously been stopped because they violated environmental laws."[5]

The rider passing into law was a disaster for the environment and a bonanza for the timber industry.

Now faced with disturbingly hostile public demonstrations requiring the summoning of police as a result of the Forest Service's cutting practices and plans, it faces an uncomfortable dilemma: a rapidly growing urban population at the forests' doorstep stridently calling for preservation and, at the same time, groups adversely affected by reduction of timber cutting who cry "unemployment" and "economic stagnation." It is thus caught, in part a victim of its own past, in part a victim of external societal circumstances in which it now finds itself.[6]

This peculiar Forest Service drama is causing the break up of the hitherto tight relationships within the timber-industry triad: the colleges of forestry, industry trade associations, and the Forest Service. Professor Barney Dowdle, a forest economist at the University of Washington, has been labeled a "crank, crackpot, and a troublemaker" in the *UW Daily* for his continued insistence that "much of the problems of the troubled timber industry goes back to the creation of the national forests" and that "creating these forests had been a mistake." Ninety years after the timber industry succeeded in privatizing and liquidating three-fourths of the timber in the Olympic Forest Reserve at the turn of the twentieth century by the Timber and Stone Act fraud, Dowdle insists that the industry was only acting within the economics of the situation at that time. The Simpson Timber Company, which successfully privatized 12,360 acres[7] of the Olympic Forest Reserve for itself at the turn of the twentieth century, sided with Professor Dowdle and may try for even more national forest privatization. John Walker, vice president of the Simpson Timber Company, claims that "the basic approach to national forests in this country was wrong from the start," agreeing with Dowdle. Walker said the only way to correct the matter is to "stand on the courthouse steps and auction off the National Forest Service's property." Professor Steve H. Hanke, of Johns Hopkins University and a collaborator of Dowdle's, took up Dowdle's attack on continued public ownership of forestlands in an August 1988 article in the *Wall Street Journal.* "The National Forest mess," he told his readers, "is a consequence of the neglect that accompanies public ownership and management." Privatizing the national forests would result not only in more timber but also in more "environmental outputs!" In conclusion, Hanke said, "Private ownership generates asset care and public ownership produces asset neglect," a haunting deja vu of the privatization of the best of the Olympic Forest Reserve at the turn of the century.[8]

In the same week that the *Wall Street Journal* article supported the idea of turning the national forests over to the timber companies, *Time* magazine reported that, in effect, this may already have occurred. In Olympic National Forest, less than half of the old-growth trees claimed to be present by the Forest Service still remain, only 106,000 acres of the 217,000 claimed. Researchers found that this pattern existed elsewhere as well. In six national forests examined in Washington and Oregon, they found that only 33 to 50 percent of the sample tracts listed as old-growth forest by the Forest Service were still forested. Most of them had been clear-cut and trucked off. "Overestimating the amount of old growth still standing by underreporting clear-cuts or by counting mature second growth as primal forest," said the *Time* article's author, John Skow, "is convenient because it reduces the urgency of squawks from environmentalists."[9] Environmentalists concluded that the Forest Service is still attempting to deceive the public.

According to the Forest Service's own statistics, expenditures exceeded revenues in 76 of 120 national forests as of November 28,

1988. To accommodate the loggers' demands for timber, Congress provided $167 million in 1987 for building roads in national forests. To justify continued cutting in areas like the northern Rocky Mountains, the Forest Service has spread road costs over periods from 122 to 331 years, so only a fraction of the road costs are charged against timber receipts in any year. The Forest Service has at the same time closed campgrounds in many national forests. The Wilderness Society, which employs three forest economists, charged the Forest Service with losing $223 million on timber sales in 1987 and losing an average of $406 million a year between 1982 and 1987.[10]

In reaction to public interest in saving old growth forests, Forest Service Chief Dale Robertson announced on December 12, 1988, that logging would be barred in certain parts of Oregon and Washington national forests to expand protection for the spotted owl. In Olympic National Forest, Robertson said, these areas may be as large as 3000 acres but generally would be 1000 to 2000 acres in extent.[11] "It's a farce," said Andy Stahl, a forester with the Sierra Club Legal Defense Fund. "This decision means about 9 percent of the owl habitat will not be logged." Timber industry trade associations recommended that no areas be set aside for the spotted owl. What everyone in the battle tacitly understands, however, is that the owl is a surrogate stand-in for the trees themselves.[12]

The Northern Spotted Owl's only habitat is old-growth forest, and its survival is dependent on the presence of that forest. In June 1990, the U.S. Fish and Wildlife Service, after much delay, declared the owl to be a threatened species under the Endangered Species Act and thus entitled to protection. One month later, Olympic National Forest adopted a management plan that reduced annual timber sales from 225 million board feet to 111 million board feet per year. The average for the decade was 248 million board feet. The plan would prevent building roads on 57,500 roadless acres of the 632,000-acre national forest and even called for 141 miles of new trail.

When Forest Service officials announced that the new plan would leave intact 141,500 of the forests with 266,000 acres of remaining old growth, the Wilderness Society charged that "wildly inaccurate" figures for the amount of virgin forest were being used by the Forest Service. Wilderness Society attorney Melanie Rowland pointed out to the press that only two months earlier the Wilderness Society's audit of the Olympic National Forest showed that there were only 94,000 acres of true old growth left, not 266,000, and that 185,000 acres of what was labeled old growth was actually just older forest.

Even more upsetting to the environmental organizations was

The harsh reality for the loggers of the Olympic Peninsula is encapsulated in this 1992 cartoon. It has been hard for loggers to accept that when the last available trees finally have been cut, as they now are, their jobs are gone, probably forever. Copyright Joel Pett, *Lexington Herald-Leader.*

the admission by the Forest Service that if the recommendations of the interagency scientific committee to protect the spotted owl were followed, Olympic National Forest would have had to reduce the annual cut to 43 million board feet, instead of the 111 million planned.[13] The 111 million board feet timber cut in Olympic National Forest in 1990, however, had dropped to 4 million board feet per year by 1997— a virtual collapse of the old-growth logging program. When compared against the 380 million board feet annual cut of the 1980's, the 4 million board feet cut represents approximately one percent of the cut that occurred then.

Charlie Miller, in the logging business for forty years and a part of Olympic National Forest's logging constituency, summed up what he thought of the plan and the concept of preserving old growth trees for the Forest Service and the environmental organizations. "They're over-ripe," he said, "those trees should have been logged years ago. Our forest is just like a cornfield in Nebraska. When the cornfield is ripe, you've got to cut it."[14] He probably spoke for the whole industry. Faced on the one hand with the demands of loggers for more trees and the

ever louder voice of the public for preservation on the other, Forest
Service Supervisor Ted Stubblefield explained the reduced cut in
Olympic National Forest with the simple statement, "The values have
shifted in our society."[15] Stubblefield's ironic comment was soon reinforced by further cut reductions under a logging ban by Federal
Judge William Dwyer in an environmentalist lawsuit under the Endangered Species Act of 1991. Settled two years later by the introduction of the Northwest Forest Plan, the ban was lifted, but the cut was
reduced even more.

While the Forest Service is in conflict with both the timber industry
and the nation's environmental groups, the Park Service lies in
shambles. Now politicized by White House appointments, it has little
power or influence. Robert and Patricia Cahn, in a recent article in
National Parks magazine, said:

> With the advent of James Watt and the Reagan administration in 1981
> came the attempt to make drastic changes. The Watt train brought an
> antigovernment "sagebrush rebellion" philosophy and a tilt toward
> development and privatization, which they aggressively sought to im-
> pose on the Park Service. Watt's idea of preserving the parks meant a
> $1 billion program to restore sewage systems, roads, buildings, and other
> facilities while ignoring programs to protect natural resources. He tried
> to stop all funding for new parkland. . . . [16]

The Reagan Administration gave key Park Service positions to people
fundamentally opposed to the intent of the 1916 law establishing the
Park Service. Included in this group of senior Park Service administrators are former lobbyists for the National Rifle Association and
National Inholders Association (a group opposed to purchasing the
private lands in the parks) and a former oil company geologist who is
an advocate of sport hunting, commercial fishing, and off-road vehicle
use in park areas. Recently, Regional Director Howard H. Chapman
has become the target of what he calls "a vendetta" after he resisted
Assistant Secretary William Horn's order to sign a document stating
that the Park Service would not acquire any more privately held land
in Yosemite. (Chapman claimed it would have been illegal.)[17]

The Park Service entered the Reagan era weak and plagued with
the legacy of Directors Mather, Albright, Drury, Wirth, and several
others, all of whom savagely attacked the concept of preservation. It
exited the Reagan era further ravaged by the ideology of the su-
premacy of the private interest. In most environmental conflict situations, the public assumes the public's interests are being guarded by

the Park Service. The reality is quite different from what the public assumes. Contempt for the legal mandate to leave parks "unimpaired for the enjoyment of future generations" is the pattern established by the Park Service's historic administrative behavior. As the 1900s came to a close, the Park Service continued its antipreservation moves to the ongoing anguish of interested activists. In 1985, for instance, the Park Service attempted to rebuild the 12-mile long Sol Duc road in Olympic National Park with a design that would have removed 3800 old-growth trees. Citizen intervention stopped the road as designed in its tracks when they established that the road plan had completely ignored the agency's own published road design guidelines. Although wilderness status for Lake Ozette was called for by every environmental organization in the country, the Park Service opposed it. In addition, the Park Service's support of the successful efforts to remove the park's offshore rocks and islands from the protection of national park laws has left a lingering aftertaste of distrust.

Environmentalists are yet again organizing for a battle with the Park Service over its attack on the integrity of the park regarding "the Quilcute matter." Activated by the Service's response to the Quileute Indians' demands for land in order to expand the boundaries of their reservation, accusations of "give away" and "management failure" abound.

The Quileute reservation is bounded by the park on three sides and by the Pacific Ocean on the fourth. All the parkland surrounding the reservation is land that was condemned from its private owners for park purposes in the acquisition of the park's coastal strip. Ownership of the land when in private ownership was never in dispute, and its owners vigorously fought condemnation for national park purposes in court in 1940.

The problem for the continuing integrity of the park began in 1976 when the Park Service agreed to transfer to the Quileutes more than 200 acres of parkland outside of the then boundaries of the reservation in LaPush, the small village on the reservation. But for the creation of the park and the turning of private land by condemnation into public land, such a move would not have been possible. This transfer to the tribe occurred in a large multipark omnibus park bill, buried in its fine print without public knowledge or involvement. Also buried in the bill was the transfer of $13 million dollars to the tribe, originally for an easement that was never given.

The fact that the reservation was now surrounded by public land owned by the U.S. Department of the Interior presented an enticing opportunity to the tribe. Armed with the knowledge that the Park

Service was willing to give up its parklands with little resistance, the Quileutes began their campaign for more. By 1990 the tribe's demands for more land from the park became louder. Tribal Chairman James Jaime laid the Quileutes' demands on the line. "We are bounded by the ocean on one side and on three sides by the national park," he said. "We have no alternative but to push against our land borders." In a letter to the Park Service, the tribe asked that parkland to the east, north, and south of the reservation be transferred to them. In laying out their demands, the Quileutes laid legal claim to 400 acres and made clear that they wanted 1200 acres more, in all, more than 2-square miles of critical national park land at the mouth of the Quillayute River[18]—critical because of its location, great beauty, and heavy use by the visiting public.

Upping the ante, the Quileutes decided unilaterally that Rialto Beach, a narrow 8-acre jetty of accreted rock and sand at the mouth of the river, was really a part of their reservation and not a part of the park at all as a result of the meandering of the river in the distant past. Although it has no inherent value, Rialto Beach has been the focus of the Park Service's development efforts for sixty years. It was here that the parking lot, picnic tables, restrooms, and other visitor facilities had been constructed to serve those who wanted to wander on one of the park's major beaches. Rialto Beach is a major park tourist destination and the Quileutes' claim was a vexing intrusion to the Park Service.

With a dubious claim to parklands on its hands and with demands for up to 2-square miles of parkland lurking on the horizon, there was only one possible move for the Park Service to make to protect the public's interest in maintaining the integrity of the park—*do absolutely nothing*. That would have forced the Quileutes tribe, if it thought it had a defensible case, to present it in court where it could be adjudicated on its merits.

Instead, the Park Service reverted to its short-term avoidance of conflict strategy, a strategy that had failed both it and the public again and again ever since the agency's first arrival on the Olympic Peninsula in 1934. It was forced against its wishes by executive order to take over Mount Olympus National Monument because it wanted to avoid conflict with the Forest Service and its timber industry allies. The "no conflict" approach failed repeatedly with the timber industry—no matter what they got, they only wanted more. It failed with the Elwha Dam removal proposal—their lack of support for removing the dams quickly turned to support when support became the low-conflict option. A trial over the merits of the Quileute claims, if it ever were to occur, would have placed the Park

Service into direct conflict with the tribe, a situation in which in the end there would be a winner and a loser. The public's interest, however, would have been protected by forcing the tribe to make its case where it can be challenged.

Instead, the Park Service decided to negotiate an agreement with the Quileutes to avoid, they said, "a long and costly trial." To negotiate an agreement with a group that had nothing to negotiate except the assertion of ownership of 8 acres of rock and sand, the park and the public could only lose and lose big. The Quileutes' *unsubstantiated claim* to Rialto Beach, considered by most to be dubious at best, caused the Park Service to enter negotiations as if the Quileutes in fact owned Rialto Beach and the park was illegally occupying tribal land by its very presence there.

The park's superintendent, Maureen Finnerty, in office since January 1990, took on the task of getting an agreement with the Quileutes apparently at any cost. She entered that task with great vigor and even greater irresponsibility, if looking after the public interest is judged to be important in the work of a public administrator. She responded to tribal Chairman Jaime's demand for parkland as if the land involved were her personal property. "The Service," she pronounced, "will recognize tribal claims to parcels 1 and 2 and transfer these lands to the tribe." Without a thought for what she was giving away, or what her responsibilities to the public might be, Finnerty added for good measure that, "the Service will recognize tribal claims to the riverbed adjacent to parcels 1 and 2."[19]

By the end of 1993, Finnerty had an agreement in hand that had the effect of privatizing again the whole of the area at the mouth of the Quillayute River, the very condition that the original condemnation suit sought to correct in the creation of the Olympic Coastal Strip. What the Park Service completely ignored was that the Federal Courts sixty years ago determined that in relation to the very land that the Park Service was now so casually about to give away that:

1. "The land to be acquired *will be used to conserve the natural resources* of the United States."
2. "The conservation of natural resources promotes the general welfare of the United States and *is clearly a public use.*"
3. *"The condemnation of land for park and recreational purposes is for public use* of the United States."[20]

The Interior Department was called upon to justify to the court the taking of this land from its private owners and it did:

The [Ocean Strip] will make possible the preservation and development of one of the most scenic portions of the seashore, with its characteristic vegetation, for the benefit of the public. This is becoming
increasingly important because less than 1 percent of the ocean beaches
in the United States is now in public ownership.[21]

Ignoring that there had been a long and bitter fight to acquire and
put into public ownership this coastal parkland in the first place,
Finnerty came up with an agreement with the Quileutes that gives
away 315 acres of some of the finest and most important parkland in
the park in return for the Quileutes giving up their *unsubstantiated
claim* to the 8 acres of accreted sand and rock that is Rialto Beach.
For good measure, she threw in a half mile of the river itself. In an
unprecedented move, the Park Service agreed to have the boundary
at the high-water level instead of the customary low-water mark in
such situations, which moves the Quileute reservation boundary on
the north side of the river right to the edge of the Rialto Beach road.
Right away Finnerty saw the problems ahead. Writing to the regional
director about the agreement and the problems ahead, she said:

> Our greatest concern is the redescribed boundary between Olympic
> National Park and the Quileute Indian Reservation along the north-
> ern high-water mark on the north shore of the Quillayute River. The
> definition of "high-water mark" would include some lands on the north
> shore of the river adjacent to, and possibly including, parts of the Park
> Service road to Rialto Beach. Hunting, wood cutting, permanent camps,
> and off-road vehicle travel by tribal members could occur immediately
> adjacent to a heavily traveled visitor road noted for its scenic and wild-
> life attractions. Roadway jurisdiction might be questionable. The NPS
> would have no jurisdiction on these tribal lands below the high-water
> mark. . . . A second concern is that under the redescribed boundary,
> the Quileute tribe would gain complete control of about one-half mile
> of the Quillayute River that is currently considered by us to be part of
> Olympic National Park. . . . The tribe would have the legal power to
> close this section of river to sport fishing . . . even a possibility of
> closure could create strong controversy when this agreement is ex-
> posed to public scrutiny.[22]

Having laid out the reality that the Park Service was creating administrative chaos for itself and both chaos and loss of critical land for
the park visitors to come, Finnerty proceeded to move the "give away"
effort forward without the public being involved. "At this point in

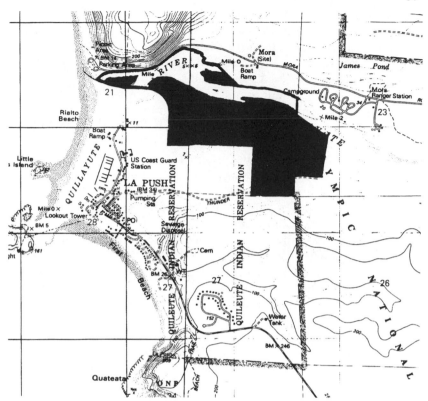

The Park Service is proposing to give away more than 315 acres of parkland at the mouth of the Quillayute River, condemned for park purposes sixty years ago from its private owners. The give away includes the river itself and would greatly diminish the public's use of the area and completely destroy the environment of Mora Campground.

time," she said, "there has been no significant public, state, or local participation in these negotiations . . .we thought it best to limit formal negotiations to NPS and the tribe."

In any event, Finnerty was transferred to Washington, D.C., in November 1994 and replaced as superintendent by David Morris, who had a chance to review with a fresh eye the whole sequence of events that Maureen Finnerty, his immediate predecessor, had set in motion. Although these events were in the process of leading to the divestiture of some very important lands in the park, for reasons unexplained, Morris embraced what was going on as if it had been his project from the beginning. In less than a year after arriving, he had finished negotiations and submitted the draft legislation to achieve what the

Quileutes wanted. In his transmittal letter to the Park Service, he asked that the various offices of the National Park Service "be made cognizant and prepared to move ahead quickly in support of this legislation." "We support fully," he said, "the tribe's proposal for the needed legislation."[23] "I am pleased," he said further, "that after years of negotiation, agreement about how to resolve this boundary conflict has been reached." The problem for Morris, at this point, was that none of the requirements of the National Environmental Policy Act had been met and the public had never been involved. In fact, the public deliberately had been kept in the dark about the whole affair on the grounds that it was a "government-to-government" negotiation. So far it had been as if the land involved was the Park Service's, to be disposed of at will by its employees if they chose to do so. The $13 million dollars the Quileutes wanted thrown in for good measure seemed to follow the logic that if $13 million was achievable in 1976, it was achievable today. Reportedly, this gave Washington State Congressman Norm Dicks pause when the Park Service could not support that transfer of funds. He was on record as being willing to introduce any legislation to which the Park Service and the tribe agreed.

What Morris now had on his hands was an agreement that gave the Quileutes everything they wanted without the park getting anything, not even an environmental impact statement that would have defined the damage to the park. Even the issues of hunting, wood cutting, permanent camps, fishing, and off-road vehicle travel, which Superintendent Finnerty had raised earlier, were handled in the final agreement as *guidelines,* which are not legally binding on the Quileutes at all. Even at that, the guidelines applied only to the small area of land north of the river. Completely left out were any provisions to protect the interests of the public, which meant that the pristine area immediately across the river from Mora Campground faced immediate development into trailer parks, motels, housing, casinos, or any other development that might turn a profit. What *was* binding on all parties, however, was that all of the parkland involved in the agreement, including the Quillayute River itself, henceforth was to be under the sole control of the tribe: On all lands made a part of the Quileute Indian Reservation as a result of this agreement, the tribe shall have the same jurisdiction and authority as it does on other tribal land that is part of the Quileute Indian Reservation.

This simple provision, most believe, guarantees that the lands that would be acquired by the tribe will soon reflect the appearance of the rest of the reservation, just as the lands received in 1976 now do.

Mora Campground will be devastated by implementation of the agreement. Park visitors will find themselves camping immediately adjacent to the urbanized extension of the town of LaPush. Whenever the tribe wants to again turn up the heat for more land and another agreement, the public will have to face the possibility of exclusion from the river or the lands involved. In a bizarre reaction to these realities of the agreement's impact on the park, Superintendent Morris assures those who write expressing concern about the agreement: "We continue to feel that the proposed management agreement with the Quileute tribe will promote the long-term stewardship of the natural resources of Olympic National Park, and best serve visitors to the Mora area."[24]

Both Finnerty and Morris completely ignored their statutory mandate from the 1916 Organic Act creating the National Park Service—to leave the park "unimpaired for the enjoyment of future generations."

The seeming incapacity of the Park Service to protect the public's interests in maintaining the integrity of the lands within the park against the skills of the high powered law firms and lobbyists engaged by the tribe is illustrated by comparing what happened in the 1976 divestiture of lands with what is being proposed today. In order to get those 200 plus acres in 1976, the Quileutes agreed to three provisions, which appeared in the draft of the bill submitted to Congress:

This transfer of lands and the payment to the tribe as authorized pursuant to this Act shall constitute just and final settlement of all claims of the tribe for lands and waters which are located within the National Park.

The National Park Service is authorized to accept and manage as part of the National Park an easement for parking and foot access along a trail across the reservation to Second Beach within Olympic National Park.

The Secretary is authorized to make a payment to the Quileute tribe in the amount of \$_____ as settlement of any and all claims of said tribe to lands within the National Park. This payment includes just compensation for the United States to hold and manage the easement described in section 5(b) of this Act.

The intent of these provisions was absolutely clear. In return for a huge payment—\$13 million—the park would be free of the Quileute pressure against its lands and it would have in return an easement for the Second Beach trail as well, a part of which crosses tribal lands.

The Park Service was no match for the skill of the tribal-hired lobbyists, however. When the bill began to wend its way through the legislative processes of Washington, D.C., it emerged in an omnibus park bill involving several parks. The clause providing for the settlement of all claims had vanished from the bill along with the easement for the Second Beach trail. Left intact, however, was the provision for a $13 million payment to the tribe now with an entirely new focus unrelated to the transfer of lands from Olympic National Park to the tribe.

> There is hereby authorized to be appropriated not to exceed $13,000,000 for the acquisition of lands, privately owned aquatic lands, or interests therein in accordance with the provisions of this title.

It was with this money from the U.S. Treasury that the tribe purchased the so-called Jones property adjacent to the park boundary directly to the east of the reservation. As written into the bill that passed, it was free money for the tribe. The Quileutes had to give nothing in return, and the Park Service and the public were left with nothing.

In the pending agreement as of January 2000 and the draft bill to implement it, another $13 million is there for the Quileutes, but this time instead of them giving up further claims against the park, the bill confines those claims to the northern boundary of the reservation, thus setting up the park for another raid on its lands later on:

> This transfer of lands and the payment to the tribe as authorized pursuant to this Act shall constitute just and final settlement of all claims of the tribe to Rialto Beach and of the Reservation's northern boundary with the National Park.[25]

In addition, what was an unconditional easement for the access to Second Beach in the 1976 bill has now become, in effect, no easement at all because the current bill as drafted conveys to the Quileutes the power to unilaterally terminate the easement at any time. The Park Service, by agreeing to such a provision, gave the Quileutes another bargaining chip to be pulled out and used against the park any time in the future. The tribe can simply close the trail to Second Beach by withdrawing the easement to use the trail:

> The tribe will grant the NPS a conditional nonexclusive easement to maintain and assure use of the existing Second Beach parking lot,

together with that portion of the Second Beach trail that is on tribal land for public pedestrian visitation. Not withstanding this agreed to public access, the *tribe will retain the unilateral right to transfer or terminate this easement* upon prior written notice to the NPS, six months in advance, by the tribe . . .[26]

The details of this noneasement are hidden in the draft of the bill itself except by reference to the agreement, which is directly quoted earlier.

Nowhere in the long history of the National Park Service has there ever been an agreement that so flagrantly gives away park resources to a special interest group, comprising in this case only 386 persons.[27] At the same time, the agreement just as flagrantly flaunts the legitimate public interest in lands condemned from private owners for park purposes. As knowledge of this pending agreement becomes known to the public, the public can be expected to demand a place at the table before the agreement is ever passed into law.

The public began to become involved in the Quileute agreement for the first time in 1997. A local newspaper disclosed that the tribe was about to receive 315 acres at the mouth of the Quillayute River as well as the river itself because they had laid claim to the 8 acres of Rialto Beach. From the kinds of questions asked and the tone of the comments that came in to Superintendent Morris about the agreement, it must have become clear to him that the public had a lot to say about this issue and, if given a chance, would have a lot more to say. To buy some time with which to deal with the lack of public involvement so far and the lack of an environmental impact statement, Park Superintendent David Morris moved further consideration of the issue to within the context of the revision of the park's general management plan in Fiscal Year 2001. Morris has indicated that the present agreement will not now be the Park Service's preferred option for dealing with the Quileutes' demands, but as of January 2000, he had no other options developed. If the agreement appears in the general management plan at all, even as an option, Morris is going to be called upon to explain how an 8-acre, unsubstantiated claim for some rock and sand can result in a Park Service "give away" of 315 acres and a half mile of river. It will not be easy, especially when the fact that all of the area was acquired by condemnation for park purposes from its private owners is factored.

The simple notion that one of a park administrator's roles, perhaps the primary role, is to protect the public interest against all those who claim park resources for private gain, seems far fetched in the current Park Service. Serving the public interest would mean accepting and managing conflict, not a part of the Park Service's organizational culture or something that it rewards when conflict occurs.

The Park Service has been and remains today, the most unreliable and erratic advocate of preservation, in spite of all of the laws and public expectation mandating it to be otherwise. The Park Service continues to keep its preservation rhetoric in the forefront and at the same time its support for local resource exploiting organizations in the background. In its opposition to removing the Elwha dams in Olympic Park (see Chapter 20), the Park Service proposed at first to share half of the annual costs of transporting fish over the dam with the timber company that benefits from the dam. In support of the Park Service proposal to underwrite out of the federal treasury half of the costs of getting fish over the dam, Park Service Director William Penn Mott spoke enthusiastically. "It would be a good example of . . . a good teamwork relationship between private enterprise and government," Mott said. He failed to mention that it also would allow the timber company to maximize its profit, with a Park Service subsidy, to the detriment of the park. Mott opposed a study, which might have demonstrated the folly of the Park Service's position. "Just commencing or suggesting a study," he said, "will create much discussion and controversy in the local community.[28] This was reason enough for him to oppose it. Belatedly in 1990, the Park Service finally joined those calling for removal of the dams. Shortly after, the Elwha River Ecosystem and Fisheries Restoration Act (the Elwha Act) of 1992 authorized the Secretary of the Interior to acquire the Elwha and Glines Canyon dams and to fully restore the river's ecosystem. Although Washington State Senator Slade Gorton succeeded in bringing to a halt all progress toward achieving what the legislation authorized, finally in the spring of 2000 the Park Service expects the acquisition of the dams to have been completed. Gorton relented in the face of great support from the public for restoring the legendary Elwha salmon runs in a free-flowing river. The dams' owners were always eager to sell, given that power was available cheaper from other sources than would be the power from the Elwha dams when the salmon mitigation requirements associated with relicensing were factored. However long it takes, the Elwha River can again look forward to being a free-flowing stream, restored to its former ecological grandeur by the removal of its dams.

Many minor attempts at protection are rebuffed by the local administrators of Olympic National Park. For instance, environmentalists tried in 1988 to protect the tidal rocks from the destructive law that Congressman Al Swift managed to insert in the 1986 park bill when the tidelands were finally added to the park: "Such lands . . . shall continue to be open to fishing and to the taking of shellfish in conformity with the laws and regulations of the State of Washington." The environmental community wanted the wording changed to read, "the taking of clams and fishing in conformity with regulations promulgated by the Secretary of Interior." The then Superintendent Robert Chandler dismissed the effort. He said, "We have a good relationship with the state," as if the park's immediate relationship with the then state director of fisheries was relevant to the long-term preservation of the park. As a result, the State Fisheries Department has the legal right to allow the taking of living creatures from the park's tidelands, acquired to preserve intact ecosystems.

Thus, the environmentalists of today have the same relationship to the Park Service that their predecessors had more than fifty years ago. To the Park Service, they are still "the purists,"—not a complementary term.

22 THE FUTURE

What is past is prologue. The heritage of the past is the seed that springs forth the harvest of the future.

NATIONAL ARCHIVES
WASHINGTON D.C.

But one thing that can't be changed is once a tree is cut down it's cut down.[1]

SAMUEL CONTI,
U.S DISTRICT COURT JUDGE

HE GREATEST CONIFEROUS FOREST ON EARTH, extending from Alaska to California, reached its climax growth on Washington State's Olympic Peninsula. The preservation of a tiny remnant of that vast domain, and the wildness within it, we placed in the hands of the Park Service, believing that our grandchildren and theirs would be able to experience it as we have. There is, however, nothing in the hundred-year history of attempts to preserve trees on the Olympic Peninsula to suggest that this will happen. Massive intervention will be required to keep the trees in Olympic National Park from ending up in the mills, as have those on the millions of square miles of forest from Alaska to California. Without this intervention, it is probable that the old-growth forests as we know them will disappear, perhaps even within our own lifetimes.

First and foremost, the vehicle for any intervention has to be the Park Service itself. Defined today by the *National Geographic Magazine* as the "keeper of America's playgrounds," the Park Service desperately needs to shift to another focus.

The Park Service's lack of strategic planning invites disaster. In Olympic National Park today, there is a trail abandonment process under-way that has confined increasing numbers of trail users on fewer and fewer miles of trail, exacerbating the impact of people. But far more serious than that, trails are being abandoned in the areas of the park with high commercial timber value. For instance, the Park Service has never placed a bridge at the start of the Queets Trail to eliminate the dangerous ford of the Queets River now required of every backpacker

378

who attempts to use the Queets Valley. This virtually eliminates use of the Queets Valley by most backpackers. Having created this low use, the Park Service easily abandoned the Kloochman Rock Trail and the Tshletshy Creek Trail, thereby making the Queets Trail itself a dead end. According to *Signpost* magazine, the upper ten miles of the Queets Trail are now abandoned—"unmaintained and poorly marked."[2] Clearly, it is in the timber industry's best interests to keep use of rain forest areas such as the Queets Valley at an absolute minimum for the day in the future when it will again argue "economic necessity" for logging. The Park Service continues to manage the park, however unwittingly, on behalf of the timber industry.

Other illustrations abound of the Park Service's lack of strategic planning. In 1951, the Forks fire, just outside the park, destroyed the Snider-Jackson Trail which ran into the park through the Bogachiel Valley to the Hoh Valley, originally from Snider Ranger Station in the Soleduck Valley to Jackson Ranger Station, now called Hoh Ranger Station. All the trail signs along the length of the Bogachiel trail which referred to the Snider-Jackson Trail were left in place until 1982, a span of thirty years during which the Snider-Jackson Trail no longer existed. When the road to the Bogachiel Valley washed out, three miles from the park boundary in 1953, it was never repaired, making access to the Bogachiel Valley much more difficult. Today, there is no more evidence of the Park Service's presence in the Bogachiel Valley than there was in 1934 when Willard Van Name proposed its addition to the Mount Olympus National Monument in the first park bill. Even though the rain forests of the Bogachiel Valley are the closest to U.S. Highway 101 of all the park's west-side valleys, there is no sign of any kind to mark the Bogachiel Road. In the event that a park visitor is able to find the road, he would not be able to find the trailhead. It is completely unmarked. The Park Service's lack of visible administration of the Bogachiel area invites the attacks by the timber industry that will come to "use" the area.

In many ways, the Park Service has turned its back on the forests of the park, ignoring the fact that, along with Hetch Hetchy, the most protracted and bitter national conservation battle of the century was fought over them. Ignoring the sensitivities that have grown from this bitter battle, the Park Service's original plan to rebuild the Soleduck Road in 1985 involved the logging of 3,800 old-growth trees to provide the swath into which the new road would run. The design of the road could have come from Mather's Park Service of the 1920's. Luckily, because Director Mott, then brand new on the job, happened to side with the environmental groups which vigorously attacked the road, the road was re-positioned to avoid the loss of so many trees. 1990 brought new attacks on the Park Service from environmentalists because of plans to cut 1,100 old-growth trees to widen Highway 410 in Mount Rainier National Park.

Those who fought for the forests of the park through the decades would like to see an Olympic National Park natural history museum to display the scientific information about the complex interrelationships between all the living things in a primeval forest. Yet, the main exhibit confronting the visitor to the park's Visitor Center in Port Angeles is an exhibit on life in a logging camp. This is an ironic holdover from the days when the Park Service itself was logging the park. It built the museum with wood logged from the park. Its inappropriateness is seemingly unquestioned by a long line of park administrators.

Present-park administrators are no exception to the Park Service's on-going fascination with logging. When the May, 1988, plan for the development of the Quinault Valley was released, logging appeared yet again. This time, at a projected construction cost of $393,000, the Park Service's preferred alternative of those presented in the plan was to interpret logging and homesteading by reconstructing a sawmill and providing interpretive services. At the same time, the single most important factor in providing visitors with a chance to enjoy a visit to the rain forest was ignored — paving the road to remove the clouds of car-generated dust which plague the area in the dry season.

As is often true, a logical and cost-saving operational decision can be a bad strategic decision. Examples of this conflict abound in Olympic. For instance, the Park Service chose to occupy the Forest Service ranger stations at Forks and Hoodsport jointly with the Forest Service. As logical as the move may seem as a cost saver, it represents the giving away of power to the anti-preservation forces by the Park Service because most, if not all, of the visitors who stop are part of the Park Service's recreational constituency. At the Forks ranger station, for instance, visitors are treated by the Forest Service to an educational display on the benefits of logging. No contrasting material on preservation is provided by the Park Service, unless a relief map can be so designated. The Forest Service material informs visitors to their exhibit in this joint facility that:

> A mature stand of timber is largely stagnant. Some liken it to a desert.
> Decay and death of individual trees diminish what's there. Nothing much
> happens until management begins.

This exhibit is a dramatic reassertion of the economic-utilization imperative of the Forest Service. More multi-agency visitor centers are in the Park Service's proposed plans for the Quinault Valley.

It is not that cooperation with a fellow governmental bureau is necessarily bad. It is that this joint operation is occurring between agencies

Confusing an already confused public, the joint NPS/USFS ranger stations serve well to illustrate the internal chaos at the Park Service's value core left by the Mather-Albright regime. *Carsten Lien.*

with charters diametrically opposed and historically hostile to each other. Joint operating agreements will make the preservation task more difficult as the Park Service's avoidance of conflict interacts in its self-constructed trap of cooperation.

The existence of Olympic National Park today represents only the temporary triumph of the preservationists over the economic-utilization value system that generally drives the actions of government and the private sector in our society. Even when all the dedicated, oft-times outstanding employees in the Park Service are taken into account, the organization in which they work is so fundamentally flawed that individual commitments to the preservation task at hand is not organizationally supported.

Because the presence of Olympic's magnificent old-growth forests is a temporary phenomenon (they are always available for cutting at the whim of Congress) and probably always will be, the kind of Park Service which administers them will always be of desperate concern to those who harbor preservationist values and are ready to fight for them. The relationship between the Park Service and the preservationists responsible for its creation has, unfortunately, most often contained a strong undercurrent of mutual contempt and distrust going all the way back to Mather himself. Willard Van Name expressed the dilemma of the preservationists:

> If there were any safer, better protected and more permanent kind of reservations than the national parks, *or any prospect of getting them,* the ECC would be for them. But the National Parks are the best that can be had and if we fail to work for them and fight for their protection we shall save nothing at all[3] [italics Van Name's].

Preservationists also remember Regional Director Frank Kittredge's caveat, "a bureaucrat is held upright by pressure from all directions," which implies that all viewpoints have equal standing with the Park Service. This uncomfortable denial of the Park Service's preservation mandate remains a jarring reality to everyone who is involved.

Can the national park system itself survive as the United States moves from being a resource-surplus society to being a resource-scarce society? That is a critical issue for the nation, and one which the Park Service is now incapable of dealing with. All of our society's laboriously worked-out preservation contracts will now be under attack because the basic premise underpinning them was that we had a surplus of resources. The national parks, National Forest wilderness areas, wildlife refuges, wild rivers, and all the rest will face difficult times as the impact of resource scarcity changes our lives, and as the population is increasingly made up of those who were not part of the original agreements to preserve.

The economic value of the resources inside Olympic National Park far exceeds the sum total of all the resources contained in all the rest of the park system put together. Olympic National Park is already a stress point in the future renegotiation process because of this. When that process begins, it will again be argued, even more stridently this time, that providing a brief period of jobs, critically short raw materials, and economic health for nearby communities and the national security will be the Olympic forest's best use. As this occurs, the Park Service's pattern of discouraging visitor use of the park's forest areas will provide statistical information for the economic-utilization forces to attack again on a cost-benefit basis. In any event, the enormous dollar value of Olympic forests will bring massive political and economic efforts at making them available, just as the possible presence of oil in Alaska's wildlife refuges drives events there. In the end, the Park Service's inability to plan strategically for this future event will make it easier for those forces counting on utilizing the park's trees. Creating the strongest possible Park Service now is the keystone to the survival of the Olympic forests.

Being a resource-scarce society in the future, we are likely to attempt to sacrifice all accessible resources to cling to a standard of living that is doomed in the long run. Our societal refusal to conserve the use of oil, a finite resource, is indicative of this possibility. When that same dynamic hits Olympic National Park, the Park Service may well, as it did in World War II, step patriotically forward to contribute resources under its control for the nation's crisis at hand, or be ordered to do so by an Interior Secretary, as has happened in the past.

A massive White House-directed redevelopment program must now rejuvenate the Park Service or the Olympic Peninsula's past will prove to be the prologue to its future. This effort, in order to succeed, will take at least eight years (two presidential terms), perhaps longer. Even in the best corporations, such programs take a minimum of five years. With the much more limited flexibility of government, it will take much longer for the Park Service. Because such an effort endures powerful opposition, both internally and externally, as a new power equilibrium evolves, it can only succeed if the president remains solidly behind it.

Because the Park Service is confused in its core values, its goals are confused and its structure reflects this chaos.

With the present Park Service structure, it would be impossible to deliver in the field any predetermined goals because there is no discernable accountability anywhere for what occurs. For instance, it is impossible by looking at the reporting relationships to discern who is responsible in direct line to the director for what happens in Olympic National Park. The structure as depicted here reflects the confused inner value and goal core of the organization and total lack of concern for preservation as an organizational value. This has become even more complex as the Park Service has focused on equal employment and law enforcement, both of which began guiding personnel selection and training.

The rebuilding of the Park Service needs to contain the following elements:

1. The Park Service must acquire preservation values and institutionalize them in the organization's core. This is a slow, agonizing process, requiring constant reinforcement throughout the system.

2. The present mission of the Park Service as "keeper of America's playgrounds" must be dropped immediately. If it isn't, we will be told that the sacrifice of our vacation lands is a small sacrifice compared with the survival of our country and the jobs and output that have made us great. There should be a separate mission statement for each of the three major units of the park system, the natural areas, historical areas, and recreation areas, as indeed there was during the administration of Director George Hartzog and long since abandoned. An appropriate statement for the natural areas might be: *To protect remnant samples of the nation's native ground covers and the intact ecosystems and the natural wonders associated with them.* Such a statement would emphasize that the national parks may well hold the native gene pools from which seeds and animal stock for dealing with now-undefined problems, especially in forestry, may have to be extracted.

3. Clarity in the organizational structure of the Park Service will emerge from a clarification of values and appropriate missions for each of its different units.

4. It is imperative to professionalize and de-politicize the Park Service and move it toward becoming a career service. Two steps could immediately assist this process:

   (a) Pass legislation requiring that all employees, including the director, be civil servants selected from within government service and that, generally, employees come up through the ranks.

   (b) All panels selecting key personnel for promotion must have half of their members be citizens representing environmental and scientific societies.[4]

5. Constituency-building needs to be a major thrust of the Park Service. The scientific community should be brought in, together with preservationist organizations, to express to Congress a consistent viewpoint representing the Park Service, the scientific community and the environmental lobby together.

6. All of the existing statutes that authorize logging and other anti-preservation activities in the park system need to be identified and eliminated as a housekeeping update in an omnibus park bill as soon as possible.

In February of 1988, Congressman Bruce F. Vento of Minnesota introduced HR 3964, which if enacted would fundamentally change the Park Service's relationship to Congress and to the Interior Department. This legislation creates a three-member review board to oversee the activities of the national park system and to *independently* submit an annual report to Congress, along with recommendations for the annual budget. The bill requires that the director of the Park Service be appointed

NATIONAL PARK SERVICE

Any recent National Park Service organization chart visibly demonstrates the chaos and confusion in the service's value core and therefore in the organization itself. *The Exchange, March 1987.*

by the president and confirmed by the Senate. In addition, this legislation restores the authority of the director to administer the Park Service, an authority effectively removed by the Reagan administration. If nothing else, this bill may signal the beginning of an era of on-going Congressional concern for the Park Service, and may serve the long-term preservation of the park system. By 1990 the bill had passed the House without the review board and is expected to pass the Senate.

In the local administration of Olympic National Park, the Park Service needs to think of the park's continued presence as a temporary holding mechanism for preserving old-growth trees. Local administrators must understand that because no society has ever before set aside resources of such enormous economic value as Olympic's forests, it is an absolute certainty that their value alone will precipitate continuing attacks. If local Olympic National Park administrators understand this, they may be able to think strategically and ask, what moves do we need to make to assist those who are fighting to preserve Olympic National Park? An immediate response to this question may entail a reversal of the Park Service's present operating focus, among which might be:

1. An immediate restoration of the trail system inherited from the Forest Service in 1938 and 1940, especially the forest trails, the Kloochman Rock Trail, the Tshletshy Creek Trail, the Rustler River Trail, Promise Creek Way, and all the others, along with installing a Queets trailhead bridge to open the Queets Valley to the many backpackers who are not willing to undertake a dangerous ford. At a minimum, a review of the trails master plan in the context of strategic planning is called for.

2. Build a forest museum to interpret to the public the vast and complex ecosystem of which the trees in an old-growth forest are a part. Emphasize the presence of the west-side forests as the reason for Olympic National Park's creation. Acquaint the public with the statistical reality that what is being preserved represents only a fraction of one percent of the original range of the Pacific Northwest's forest heritage.

3. Establish a Park Service presence in the Bogachiel Valley immediately. Whether this means a first-class visitor facility, a ranger station or a museum, there must be recognition that this most vulnerable of all the areas of the park has been, and will be again, under attack from timber interests, and that the Park Service intends to protect it.

4. Educate the public on how tenuous the preservation of Olympic National Park's forests is.

5. Physically separate Park Service public-contact facilities from those of the Forest Service. Confusion of the Park Service's preservation role within its own ranks and with the public will be the price paid for failure to do this.

Even if the Park Service were to do all these things immediately, Olympic National Park will continue to be at high risk.

There are numbers of possible scenarios for projecting the future of the park forests of the Olympic Peninsula. Here are three of them:

Scenario #1: *The Resource-Scarce Future*

YEAR: 2040.

ASSUMPTION: The National Park Service remains as it is today as the United States moves towards becoming a resource-scarce society.

CHANCE OF SCENARIO HAPPENING: 80 percent.

OUTCOME: Trees in the park logged and sent to the mills.

Attendance at Olympic National Park and all other parks drops dramatically as the result of a prolonged shortage of gasoline. Many scientists now believe that the long-projected end of the world's oil reserves may be at hand. In addition, it is clear that Gifford Pinchot's assumption that "timber is a crop" is false; the third-growth forest is sparse and in many areas a fourth growth fails to materialize in spite of great effort. When confronted with this reality, timber-industry representatives still deflect responsibility with their oft-repeated position: "We can't focus on the past. Of course errors were made, but no one had any way of knowing. We now must look to the future security of the country and make the best use of the resources at hand." While the environmentalists continue to focus on the fact that the preserved timber in Olympic National Park only represents a fraction of one percent of the original stand of that type of forest, the industry keeps focusing on the timber volume available in the park for cutting if it could be released. When the timber industry confronts the nation with the lack of actual recreational use of the Queets, Bogachiel and Hoh valleys, the explanation that the cause was the lack of an accessible trail network did little to help.

Another major national conservation battle is underway. The Forest Service remains silent. Finally, as the industry begins to perceive that it may be winning the battle, it becomes bolder and bolder. To those on both sides of the issue who read about the great battle that created the park nearly ninety years ago, it seems as if the same things were being said all over again.

Still driven by the avoidance-of-conflict management style that is now more deeply imbedded in its organization than ever, the Park Service keeps trying to find a compromise that will lower the conflict level. Because park-boundary changes seem to be unacceptable to the public, the industry begins to yield on having the west-side forests transferred to the Forest Service. The Park Service proposes, to the horror of environmental organizations, that its prior experience in logging indicates that park values could be preserved without changing the boundaries while careful logging occurs. It can protect park values better than any other agency, the Park Service argues. The *Seattle Times*' headline announces the solution to the long-fought debate: "PARK SERVICE WINS ON PARK VALUES: TO CONTROL LOGGING IN PARK." Because Olympic National Park is the major stress point in the whole park system, it is clear to the environmentalists that Gifford Pinchot has triumphed in the end: All of the national parks will now provide timber on some basis for their local economies. The timber industry and local chambers of commerce are delighted. Logs will flow to the mills, providing the jobs and the purchases in the stores so sought after by the local merchants. The environmentalists vow to fight on to stop the logging, but in the environment of scarcity, the process is irreversible. A short while after the timber is all cut and gone, the country reverts to exactly the same economic position it was in when park logging began, except now there is nothing of the old-growth forest for future generations to experience.

Scenario #2: *The Organization-Change Future*

YEAR: 2025
ASSUMPTION: That the Park Service undergoes change through a systematic organization development that successfully alters its whole being.
CHANCE OF SCENARIO HAPPENING: 10 percent.
OUTCOME: Trees temporarily preserved.

A strongly pro-environment president comes to power on a "quality of life" campaign in which preservation of the national parks plays a strong part. When given a chance to express their views, the public seems to be solidly behind preservation, as it was in the past every time it was given an opportunity to express itself. The new president counts on that fact to give him the security he needs to proceed.

He finds a Park Service director who not only understands the issues, but also understands management and organization development. The president charges him with producing a Park Service that will be able to deliver on the intent of the 1916 Park Service Act. Immediately, the Park concessionaires organize to defeat the new director. The president, having anticipated this, uses a television address to deal with park issues and asks citizens at the local level to let their senators and congressmen know how they feel. During eight years of this president's administration, serious conflict with the concessionaires and local chambers of commerce goes on. However, the preservation values of the 1916 Park Service Act are reinforced from within by appointments to the key positions in the system at all levels, by training for all employees, and by the continuing speeches and public appearances of the new director and the public dialogue he precipitates. Because the revamped Park Service has become an important part of the president's program, numbers of key senators and congressmen support it. This is easy for them because of its popularity back home. By the end of the president's second term, a powerful network of scientific societies and environmental organizations has joined with the Park Service to insure continuing preservation of natural ground covers and related ecosystems.

As the decades pass, this working coalition grows stronger. Research becomes an important component of the Park Service's program. Because of its political strength, various Secretaries of the Interior and presidents generally leave the Park Service alone. It is accepted that, in the big picture, the park's mineral and timber resources can play nothing but a temporary role and an insignificant one in the long run.

As American society begins to face the crisis of shortage of resources that has been talked about for decades, the environmental coalition forged originally by the new president is able to fend off the destruction of the parks in the rush to maintain a standard of living that is irreversibly disappearing anyway. They believe that if they can hang on until the new standard of living is accepted, the presence of the parks will offer the same amenities to an urbanized population as before.

In spite of continuing attacks from the timber industry, mining interests, water power developers and others, the pro-environment coalition of political power and the Park Service as redeveloped by the new president is able to hold the line against the economic utilization of park resources. As time goes on, the lowered standard of living becomes the accepted norm. The presence of national parks under these circumstances is viewed with awe by nearly everyone, surprised that past generations had the foresight and self-discipline to leave them intact. They become, more than ever, a source of great national pride.

Scenario #3: The New Agency Future

YEAR: 2025

ASSUMPTION: That organizations cannot change. Therefore, dysfunctional organizations must be replaced by new ones which do not bear the impedimentia of the past.

CHANCE OF SCENARIO HAPPENING: 10 percent.

OUTCOME: Trees temporarily preserved.

A strongly pro-environment president has come to power on a "quality of life" campaign in which preservation of the national parks from economic exploitation is an issue. It is natural that the parks become one of the first items for discussion for the new White House group.

The political professionals surrounding the new president are in agreement that bureaus which had evolved dysfunctionally in relation to their assigned tasks should have the most critical of their tasks reassigned to new agencies created for the purpose, or reassigned to existing agencies which demonstrate the capacity to deliver. Nearly all the president's close political advisors come to this view from long years of experience at all levels of government. Their experience has led them to believe that bureaucracies do not change. When this bureaucratically experienced group begins the discussion, there is agreement, almost at once, that the level of effort that needs to be expended on the existing Park Service is not worth it.

As the conversations proceed, the group of presidential advisors agree among themselves that the remaining remnant areas of the continent's natural flora and fauna are far too important to leave to the existing Park Service. Part of the problem is that some of these natural remnants are located in the national park system, some are in the national forests, and some are in the wildlife refuge system. Neither the existing laws under which they are being administered nor any of the agencies involved support preservation. The new president's administration deals with this by presenting the Congress with a bill which combines the wilderness parks and other Park Service areas requiring preservation with the wilderness areas in the national forests and the wilderness wildlife refuges. The bill proposes to create the U.S. Wilderness Service to manage these areas as a unified system focused on maintaining inviolate the natural conditions within them. Under this bill, the Park Service will continue its administration of recreation areas, historic sites, the national capital parks and all developed areas, a task consistent with the Park Service's evolved values. The Forest Service, freed of the burden of conflict with the public over preservation, will then be able to concentrate on increased production of timber, a task consistent with its own embedded values.

Wisely, the bill gives the president the power to transfer each area by Executive Order when the U.S. Wilderness Service is ready to receive it. By taking in each area one by one, the newly created agency avoids being inundated by the existing attitudes of the agencies it is replacing. The new director has the lead time required for him to act as the entrepreneur in developing the new agency's organizational culture to support the preservation mandate in the new law. Under the provision of the bill, the U.S. Wilderness Service is not mandated to employ any existing employee, but is authorized to recruit from amongst them. It has control over its own staff, a critical factor in organizational development.

Because the focus of the new law is to maintain, so far as possible, intact ecosystems, the new law mandates the phasing out of the hunting allowed in some of the wildlife refuges it inherited. It also phases out hunting and livestock-grazing allowed in the former Forest Service wilderness areas. Opposition by those who are profiting from the economic exploitation of these areas is overcome by the demonstration of vast public support.

The new president's administration then places the new U.S. Wilderness Service under the auspices of the Smithsonian Institution to link it to the nation's scientific infrastructure for research purposes. The intent is to make these remnant areas great living museums of nature to educate those who enter them. Because of the Smithsonian's experience in developing conventional museums, a greatly expanded formal museum program to present the natural history drama of each area is envisioned.

After the bill passes, the president's administration finds a charismatic, entrepreneurial director who breathes life into the new agency. With the help of an intensive training program, and the clear transmission of organizational goals, the U.S. Wilderness Service is able to recruit most of its new employees from the old agencies. The U.S. Wilderness Service is mandated to be a career service with promotion from within. A formal system is set up requiring participation in employee promotion panels from the scientific societies and environmental organizations. By this device, the public can participate in the direction and future of the agency. The expectation is that the internal consolidation of the Forest Service around economic utilization and the anti-preservationism displayed by the Park Service can be avoided.

Within four years, the new U.S. Wilderness Service absorbs all the areas it is to receive. With the presidential power to make minor boundary adjustments conveyed by the bill, the Forest Service wilderness areas adjacent to national parks are joined into logical and easily administered combined areas. The greatly increased research focus results in a number of discoveries, some of which assist tremendously in the restocking of denuded forest land. The close working relationships with the U.S. Wilderness Service's natural constituencies result in increased use of the areas but much less visible impact from that use.[5]

Unfortunately there is nothing in the history of American conservation that suggests that anything other than Scenario #1 is likely to occur, or at least some variation of it. Given the right set of circumstances, however, Scenarios #2 and #3 are possible. Only time will tell. Whatever happens in the future, part of the story will be told by what happens in the Park Service itself. In 1972, in *National Parks for the Future,* the Conservation Foundation said it better than anyone else:

> The National Park System can best meet the future needs of all Americans by reasserting its original mission—the preservation and interpretation of natural landscapes and ecosystems. This function, which must involve truly representative citizen participation, can enable the park system to make its most meaningful and lasting contribution to an urban people and can exemplify and inspire an enduring environmental ethic.[6]

The Conservation Foundation's vision for the park system is brought to life by Paul Shepard's challenge to the Park Service to become what its internal culture may now prevent:

The National Park Service should be the instigator, host and collaborator in the development of a wilderness philosophy; this should involve
real philosophers and real theologians, not just backpackers writing for
wilderness publications. I think the service should depart completely from
its military motif, its overview of itself as primarily policeman, and de-
mote statistics on recreation, appreciation and even education to their
appropriate places somewhere below creative studies of the value of
wilderness and the necessity of preserving climax ecosystems regardless
of their public use. The NPS has utterly failed to keep up, much less sponsor inquiry into the meaning of such a radical land use. Much has changed
since the tradition of landscape esthetics produced the parks in the 1860's
and 70's but you would not know it from the picture-postcard mentality
of the NPS or the concessionaires which it franchises. . . . There is room
for a government to recognize and defend the most unusual idea in the
human mode of relating to the natural environment in the history of
the Western world.[7]

In the meantime, readers should schedule a trip to Olympic National
Park's rain forest wilderness while it still exists.

Abbreviations Of Sources

AC	Asahel Curtis papers, University of Washington, Seattle, Washington.
AMNH	American Museum of Natural History files, New York.
BGN	Board on Geographic Names files, Reston, Virginia.
BT	Ben Twight papers, University of Washington, Seattle, Washington.
CFR	University of Washington College of Forest Resources files, University of Washington Archives, Seattle, Washington.
CL	Carsten Lien papers, Seattle, Washington.
ECC	Emergency Conservation Committee files, New York, now located in Western History Department, Denver Public Library.
ESM	Edmond S. Meany papers, University of Washington Archives, Seattle, Washington.
FJO	Fred J. Overly papers, University of Washington, Seattle, Washington.
GP	Gifford Pinchot papers, Library of Congress, Washington, D.C.
HMJ	Henry M. Jackson papers, University of Washington, Seattle, Washington.
HW	Hugo Winkenwerder papers, University of Washington Archives, Seattle, Washington.
IB	Irving Brant papers, Library of Congress, Washington, D.C.
IC	Irving Clark papers, University of Washington, Seattle, Washington.
NA	National Archives, Washington, D.C. and Seattle, Washington, at Sand Point.
NCOR	National Commission on Outdoor Recreation, National Archives, Washington, D.C.
NPSHF	Library and Archival Services National Park Service, Harpers' Ferry, West Virginia.
ONF	Olympic National Forest, Olympia, Washington.
ONP	Olympic National Park, Port Angeles, Washington.
OAT	Owen A. Tomlinson papers in author's possession.
PHZ	Philip H. Zalesky papers, University of Washington, Seattle, Washington.
PPM	Preston P. Macy papers, University of Washington, Seattle, Washington.
PS	Paul Shepard Olympic papers in author's possession.
TTA	Thomas T. Aldwell papers, University of Washington, Seattle, Washington.
WGM	Warren G. Magnuson papers, University of Washington, Seattle, Washington.
WLJ	Wesley L. Jones papers, University of Washington, Seattle, Washington.
WSPC	Washington State Planning Council files, Washington State Archives, Olympia, Washington.

CHAPTER NOTES

CHAPTER 1

1. Badé, William F., *Life and Letters*, vol. 2, p. 403.
2. *Congressional Record*, February 26, 1909, p. 3226, 60th Cong 2 Sess.
3. Olmstead, Frederic Law, "The Yosemite Valley and the Mariposa Big Trees, A Preliminary Report 1865," *Landscape Architecture*, October, 1952, 43(1): 22. See also Shepard, *Man in the Landscape*, for the historic antecedents to preservation.
4. Muir, John, *Our National Parks*, pp. 347–348.
5. Coman, Edwin T. and Helen M. Gibbs, *Time, Tide and Timber*.
6. 26 stat 1103 Act of March 3, 1891, to repeal the timber culture laws.
7. Johnson, Robert U., *Remembered Yesterdays*, pp. 293–294.
8. Ibid., p. 294.
9. Muir, "The Yellowstone National Park," *Atlantic*, April, 1898, 81:509.
10. Wickersham, James, "A National Park in the Olympics . . . 1890," *The Living Wilderness*, Summer-Fall 1961, p. 5.
11. *Report of Lieut. Joseph O'Neil, Fourteenth Infantry, of his Exploration of the Olympic Mountains, from June to October 1890*, Senate Document 59, 54 Cong, 1 Sess.
12. *Forest and Stream*, April 21, 1900, 54:303.
13. Johnson, op. cit., p. 297.
14. Johnson, op. cit., p. 298.
15. Trefethen, James B., *Crusade for Wildlife*, p. 52.
16. Pinchot, Gifford, *Breaking New Ground*, p. 94.
17. Muir, "A Plan to Save the Forests," *Century*, February, 1895, 49:631.
18. Wolfe, Linnie M., *The Life of John Muir*, p. 275.
19. For a detailed account of the situation leading up to this exchange, see Rakestraw, "Sheep Grazing in the Cascade Range: John Minto vs. John Muir," *Pacific Historical Review, 1958* 27(4): 371–382.
20. *Report of the Committee Appointed by the National Academy of Sciences upon a Forest Policy for the Forested Lands of the United States*, pp. 34–35.
21. Muir, "The American Forests," *The Atlantic Monthly*, August, 1897, 80:155.
22. Smith, Herbert A., "Saving the Forest," *National Geographic*, August, 1907, 18:524.
23. *The Lumber Industry*, part 1, p. 100, Dept. of Commerce Bureau of Corporations, 1914.
24. "Weyerhaeuser gets set up for the 21st century," *Fortune*, April, 1977, p. 78.
25. Ibid.
26. *Congressional Record*, vol. 30, part 1, p. 917, 55 Cong, 1 Sess.
27. Ibid., p. 987.
28. Johnson, op. cit., pp. 299–300.

29. *Congressional Record,* vol. 30, part 1, p. 919, 55 Cong, 1 Sess.

30. Pinchot, *Breaking New Ground,* p. 113.

31. Ibid., p. 116.

32. *Congressional Record,* vol. 30, part 1, p. 899–900, 55 Cong, 1 Sess.

33. Ibid., p. 913.

34. Muir, "A Plan to Save the Forests," *Century,* February, 1895, 49:631.

35. Muir, "The National Parks and Forest Reservations," *Harper's Weekly,* June 5, 1897, p. 563.

36. Muir, "The American Forests," *Atlantic Monthly,* August, 1897, 80:145.

37. Muir, "The Wild Parks and Forest Reservations of the West," *Atlantic Monthly,* January, 1898, 81:15.

38. Pinchot, op. cit., p. 116.

39. *Congressional Record,* vol. 31, p. 5633.

40. House Report 2300, 55 Cong, 3 Sess, February 24, 1899.

41. *The Lumber Industry,* op. cit., p. 102 + p. 18.

42. This is almost verbatim as Assistant Attorney General Normal Littel explained it to Irving Clark, Littel to Clark, August 8, 1944, IC.

43. *Congressional Record,* vol. 322, p. 2147, 63 Cong, 3 Sess.

CHAPTER 2

1. Seattle Chamber of Commerce Resolution of November 16, 1899. See *Congressional Record,* June 17, 1913, p. 2063, 63 Cong, 1 Sess.

2. Walcott to Hermann, September 26, 1899, NA. See also *Congressional Record,* June 17, 1913, p. 2063, 63 Cong, 1 Sess.

3. *Report of the Committee Appointed by the National Academy of Sciences upon a Forest Policy for the Forested Lands of the United States,* p. 40.

4. Muir to Sargent, April 30, 1899, quoted in Badé, *Life and Letters of John Muir,* p. 319.

5. Pinchot, *Breaking New Ground,* pp. 126–128.

6. *Report on the Survey and Examination of Forest Reserves (March) 1898,* Senate Document 189, 55 Cong, 2 Sess, pp. 87–91.

7. Rakestraw, Lawrence. *A History of Forest Conservation in the Northwest 1891–1913,* pp. 125–126.

8. Morgan, Murray, *The Mill on the Boot,* p. 155.

9. *Tacoma News,* August 11, 1898, quoted in Morgan *The Mill on the Boot,* p. 155.

10. Foster to Hitchcock and Foster to Hermann, both October 19, 1899, NA.

11. General Land Office *Memorandum on Olympic Forest Reserve,* undated 1899, NA.

12. Walcott to Hermann, March 31, 1899, NA.

13. Pinchot to Walcott, March 13, 1899, NA.

14. Rakestraw, op. cit., p. 130.

15. Ibid., p. 131. See also *Congressional Record,* vol. 298, pp. 2061–2064.

16. Ibid., p. 133–134. See also *Congressional Record,* pp. 2061–2064.

17. *Congressional Record,* vol. 298, p. 2060.

18. Ibid.

19. Annual Report of the Commissioner of the General Land Office, 1901.

20. *The Westerner,* August, 1910, pp. 10–11, also quoted in Robbins *Our Landed Heritage,* p. 373.

CHAPTER 3

1. Muir, "The National Parks and Forest Reservation," *Harper's Weekly,* June 5, 1897, 41:566.

2. Pinchot, *The Fight for Conservation,* p. 42.

3. Pinchot, *Breaking New Ground,* p. 321.

4. Ibid., p. 167.

5. Hays, Samuel P., *Conservation and the Gospel . . . ,* pp. 40–41.

6. Cox, John, *Organization of the Lumber Industry,* p. 174.

7. Ibid., pp. 174–175.

8. Pinchot, *The Fight for Conservation*, p. 43.

9. Pinchot to Madson, May 28, 1906, in Johnson *Remembered Yesterdays*, pp. 307–308.

10. Annual report of Secretary of Interior, 1909.

11. See Nash Roderick, *Wilderness and the American Mind*, p. 154.

12. *Forest and Stream*, May 19, 1900, 54:331.

13. *The Seattle Mail and Herald*, Dec. 17, 1904, 8:37.

CHAPTER 4

1. Stanard to Ballinger, April 30, 1909, NA.

2. Graves to Secretary of Agriculture, December 10, 1914, NA.

3. *Port Angeles Evening News*, February 15, 1940.

4. Report 1874 to accompany HR 10443, March 23, 1904, page 4.

5. Ibid., p. 2.

6. Port Angeles Newspaper article identified, March 11, 1904, PPM.

7. *The Seattle Mail and Herald*, Dec. 17, 1904, 8:33.

8. Chapter 172 Section 7 Laws of 1905, p.351, Chapter 151 Section 15 laws of 1915, p. 437.

9. *1917 National Parks Conference Proceedings*, pp. 215–216.

10. Robbins, Roy M., *Our Landed Heritage*, p. 349.

11. Ibid., p. 350.

12. *The Mountaineer*, vol. 4, 1911, p. 56.

13. *The Mountaineer*, vol. 2, 1909, p. 42.

14. 35 Stat 2247.

15. *Colliers*, April 10, 1909, p. 12.

16. *Congressional Record*, vol. 43 part 4, page 3821 and p. 3819.

17. W. E. Humphrey to Secretary of Interior, June 11, 1911, NA.

18. See Ickes "Not Guilty . . . ," *Saturday Evening Post*, May 25, 1940 for the case for Ballinger. See Richardson, *The Politics of Conservation*, pp. 84–85 for a review of the incident.

19. Harris and Johnson pamphlet, *The Neglected West*, pp. 9–11, no date.

20. Pamphlet *Attitude of Seattle Chamber of Commerce on Conservation*, March 22, 1910, CL.

21. HR 12532 July 15, 1911, S5257, February 13, 1912.

22. Curtis to E. T. Parsons, May 21, 1912, AC.

23. *Concerning legislation with a view of changing the character of the Mt. Olympus National Monument and the Creation of Olympus National Park*, Jan. 12, 1912, The Seattle Chamber of Commerce Monument Reduction Report, BT.

24. Ibid.

25. *Seattle Post-Intelligencer*, January 14, 1912.

26. P. S. Lovejoy to District Forester, Dec. 22, 1911, NA.

27. Wright to Sweeney, October 8, 1914, NA.

28. Curtis to W. E. Colby, March 16, 1912, AC.

29. Ibid.

30. Twight *Organizational Values and Political Power*, pp. 34–35.

31. *Congressional Record*, vol. 297, p. 1891.

32. Greeley, *Shall the National Forests Be Turned Over to the States* Manuscript, July 20, 1912, NA 95.

33. *Congressional Record*, vol. 297, pp. 1862–1863.

34. Ibid., p. 1867.

35. Ibid., vol. 50, part 6, 63 Cong, 1 Sess, p. 5979.

36. Ibid., p. 5979.

37. Ibid., vol. 297, p. 1890.

38. Ibid., vol. 50, part 6, p. 5971.

39. Ibid., vol. 50, part 6, p. 5972.
40. Ibid.
41. Ibid.
42. *Congressional Record,* vol. 297, p. 1890.
43. Wright to Sweeney, October 8, 1914, NA.
44. Solicitor to Graves, November 30, 1914, NA.
45. Ibid.
46. Twight, *Organizational Values and Political Power,* p. 37.
47. Grave's Monument Report in Fringer, *Olympic National Park Administrative History,* p. 58.
48. Lane to West, April 8, 1915, NA.

CHAPTER 5
1. Teal, E. W., *The Wilderness World of John Muir,* pp. 312, 314, 320.
2. Pinchot, *The Fight for Conservation,* 1910, pp. 51–52.
3. Ibid., p. 42.
4. Annual Report of the Secretary of Interior, 1908.
5. From Samual P. Hays' excellent summary in *Conservation and the Gospel of Efficiency,* pp. 195–196.
6. Proceedings of National Park Conference 1911, pp. 63–64.
7. Ibid., p. 68.
8. Report of Secretary of Interior, 1913.
9. Hearing on S3463 on Bill to Establish a Bureau of National Parks, April 17, 1912, p. 8.
10. HR 22995 S3463, 62 Cong, 2 Sess, 1912.
11. Hearing before the Committee on the Public Lands on H.R. 6281, June 25, 1913, p. 25.
12. Ibid., pp. 26–27.
13. Wolfe, Linnie Marsh, *Son of the Wilderness,* p. 341.
14. HR 15522, May 10, 1916, 64 Cong, 1 Sess.
15. Report No. 700 to accompany HR 15522, p. 4.

CHAPTER 6
1. Albright, Horace M., "Our National Parks as Wildlife Sanctuaries," *American Forests,* August, 1929, 35:356.
2. Grinnell and Storer, "Animal Life as an Asset of National Parks," *Science,* September 15, 1916, 44:378.
3. Pinchot, *The Fight for Conservation,* p. 42.
4. Graves to J. Horace McFarland, NPS Hearings, April 5, 1916, p. 58.
5. Houston, David, "The National Forest Enterprises," *American Forestry,* December, 1916, 22:750–752.
6. Ibid.
7. Ise, John, *Our National Park Policy,* p. 287; Rakestraw, Lawrence, *History of Forest Conservation,* p. 263.
8. Shankland, *Steve Mather of the National Parks,* p. 7.
9. *Progress in the Development of the National Parks,* U.S. Gov't. Printing Office, 1916, page 10, quoted in Ise, *Our National Park Policy,* p. 198.
10. Mather, Stephen, "The National Parks on a Business Basis," *American Review of Reviews,* April 1915, 51:429.
11. S778, 64 Cong, 1 and 2 Sess, Stat 39 1122.
12. Senate Report No. 452, Serial 6899, House Report 1354, Serial 7110, 64 Cong, 1 and 2 Sess.
13. Ibid.
14. Shankland, Robert, *Steve Mather of the National Parks,* pp. 40, 62.
15. Ibid., p. 265.

16. Ibid., pp. 266–267.
17. Ise, John, *Our National Park Policy*, pp. 244–245; Shankland, p. 82.
18. Swain, Donald C., *Wilderness Defender*, p. 69.
19. Ibid., pp. 89–90.
20. Cameron, Jenks, *The National Park Service*, pp. 15–19.
21. Ibid.
22. Mather "The National Parks on a Business Basis," *American Review of Reviews*, April, 1915, 51:429.
23. Ibid.
24. Shankland, Robert, *Steve Mather of the National Parks*, p. 159.
25. Report, Director National Park Service 1924, p. 14, quoted in Ise, *Our National Park Policy*, p. 646.
26. *Harper's Magazine*, April, 1930, quoted in Ise, op. cit., p. 652.
27. Swain, Donald C., *Wilderness Defender*, p. 96.
28. Robert S. Yard to G. B. Grinnell, September 18, 1926, quoted in Fox, *John Muir and His Legacy*, p. 204.
29. Hawthorne and Mills, *Enos Mills of the Rockies*, p. 226.
30. Swain, *Wilderness Defender*, p. 96.
31. Hawthorne and Mills, op. cit., p. 228.
32. *Reedy's Mirror*, St. Louis, March 4, 1920.
33. Shankland, op. cit., pp. 77–78.
34. National Lumberman's Association Ninth Annual Convention 1911 *Official Report* p. 130, quoted in Cox *Organization of the Lumber Industry*, p. 177.
35. Memo to Mt. Rainier Advisory Board, April 7, 1922 by Ashael Curtis, AC.
36. *The Administration of the National Parks*, The Mountaineers, 1922, WLJ.
37. Ibid., p. 10.
38. Cahalane, Victor, "The Evolution of Predator Control Policy in the National Parks," *Journal of Wildlife Management*, July, 1939, 3:232.
39. Ibid., p. 233.
40. Ibid., pp. 233–34.
41. Report of Director 1919, p. 35.
42. Report of Director 1920, pp. 279, 312.
43. Ibid., p. 273.
44. Cahalane, op. cit., p. 234.
45. Mather, op. cit., p. 429.
46. Mather, "The National Parks on a Business Basis," *American Review of Reviews*, April, 1915, 51:429.
47. Cameron, Jenks, *The National Parks Service: Its History, Activities and Organization*.
48. Cahalane, op. cit., p. 234.
49. Adams, Dr. Chas. C., "Ecological Conditions in National Forests and in National Parks," *Scientific Monthly*, June, 1925, p. 570.
50. Moore, Barrington, "Importance of Natural Conditions in National Parks," *Hunting and Conservation: The Book of the Boone and Crockett Club*, p. 353.
51. Ibid., p. 347.
52. Cahalane, op.cit., p. 235.
53. Albright, "The National Park Service's Policy on Predatory Mammals," *Journal of Mammology*, May, 1931, 12:185.
54. Chase, Alston, "Sometimes What Threatens Our Parks Is the Park Service," *Wall Street Journal*, April 8, 1986.
55. Wright, George M., and Ben H. Thompson, *Fauna of the National Parks of the United States*, p. 22.

56. Albright, "Our National Parks as Wild Life Sanctuaries," *American Forests,* August, 1929, 35:506.
57. 39 Stat 243–246.

CHAPTER 7
1. Pinchot, Foreword to Ahearn, *Deforested America,* p. vi.
2. Greeley to Winkenwerder, Jan. 11, 1923, CFR Box 12.
3. Secretary Wilson to Gifford Pinchot, drafted by Pinchot, *Breaking New Ground,* pp. 261–262.
4. Munger, Thornton, "My Thirty-eight Years in the Forest Service 1908–1946," *Timberlines,* Dec. 1962.
5. Pinchot, *The Use Book* (1907–08), p. 76.
6. See McConnell, "The Multiple Use Concept . . . " *Sierra Club Bulletin,* October, 1959, p. 24.
7. For a discussion of Pinchot's role in the context of the times, see McConnell, "The Conservation Movement . . . ," *Western Political Quarterly,* September, 1954, pp. 463–478.
8. Chapman, H. H., "A Program for Private Forestry," *American Forestry,* Oct. 1919.
9. Griggs, E. G., address to 3rd National Conservation Congress 1911, p. 246.
10. Greeley, *Forests and Men,* p. 102.
11. Greeley, *Some Public and Economic Aspects of the Lumber Industry,* U.S. Department of Agriculture Report 114, Washington 1917.
12. Morgan, George T., *William B. Greenley, a Practical Forester,* p. 37.
13. Ibid., p. 49.
14. Senate Document No. 12, 73 Cong, 1 Sess, known as Copeland Report, quoted in Frome, *The Forest Service,* p. 19; Robert Marshall, *The People's Forests,* p. 126.
15. "Forest Statistics for Grays Harbor County, Washington" U.S. Forest Service, July 25, 1938, quoted in *Seattle Post-Intelligencer,* October 23, 1938.
16. *Port Angeles Evening News,* February 7, 1945.
17. *Master Plan for Forestry in Washington,* Washington State Planning Council, 1936, pp. 41–42.
18. Greeley, *Forests and Men,* p. 45.
19. Marshall, Robert, *The People's Forests,* pp. 90–91.
20. C. B. Sanderson to Hugo Winkenwerder, July 10, 1929.
21. Morgan, op. cit., pp. 63–64.
22. Curtis to Underwood, February 26, 1926, AC.
23. Tomlinson to Cammerer, January 23, 1937, NA.
24. Van Syckle, Edwin. *They Tried to Cut it All,* pp. 256–257.
25. *A Brief Asking the Federal Forest Service for the Allocation of Timber in the Olympic National Forest,* March 1, 1929, Chambers of Commerce of Grays Harbor County.
26. Report of the Forester, 1930.
27. Pinchot to Robert Y. Stuart, November 15, 1928, Pinchot papers, Box 294, quoted in Morgan, George T., *William B. Greeley, a Practical Forester.*
28. Greeley testimony before the House Public Lands Committee, December 13, 1921, quoted in *National Parks Association Bulletin* 25, January 30, 1922.
29. Fox, Stephen, *John Muir and His Legacy,* pp. 204–205.
30. Greeley, testimony December 13, 1921, op. cit.
31. Van Name, "A Menace to the National Parks," *Science,* December 22, 1922, p. 706.
32. Van Name, ibid., p. 706.
33. Mather, letter published in *Fresno Republican,* October 1, 1927, quoted in Van Name *A New Raid on the Yosemite National Park,* p. 3.
34. Cammerer to H. S. Watson, May 19, 1922, quoted in Van Name, ibid., pp. 706–707.

35. Van Name, *A Grab for Half the Sequoia Park,* broadside ESM Box 25.
36. Van Name, *Vanishing Forest Reserves,* p. 82.
37. Moore, Barrington, "The Proposed Roosevelt-Sequoia National Park and the Barbour Bill," *Science,* January 19, 1923, p. 83.
38. Leopold, Aldo, "The Last Stand of the Wilderness," *American Forests and Forest Life,* October, 1925, 31:601.
39. National Conference on Outdoor Recreation proceedings, page 42, NA.
40. Greeley to Van Name, April 19, 1922, quoted in Van Name *Hands Off the National Parks,* p. 2.
41. Van Name, *Hands Off the National Parks,* p. 6.
42. Ibid., pp. 6–7.
43. Ibid., p. 7.
44. Ibid.
45. Ibid.
46. Charles Sheldon to Arthur Ringland NCOR Box 10.
47. Arthur Ringland to Barrington Moore, March 3, 1926, Barrington Moore to Arthur Ringland, March 2, 1926 NCOR Box 10.
48. Chapman, H. H., "Recreation as a Federal Land Use," *American Forests and Forest Life,* June, 1925.
49. Timber Management Plan ONF quoted in Twight, Ben *Organizational Values and Political Power,* p. 42.
50. Leon Kneipp memorandum, Sept. 8, 1928, NA, p. 7.
51. Ibid.
52. Beezley, B. F., *Report of Investigation to Determine Eligibility of Dosewallips — East Fork Route and North Fork — Elwha Route for Classification as Forest Highway,* ONF 1926.
53. N. F. Staley to District Forester, September 8, 1926.
54. Twight, *Organizational Values,* p. 12, quoting Gilligan *The Development of Policy,* pp. 97–124.
55. Twight, op. cit., p. 12.
56. Olympic Forest Recreation Plan, p. 5, NA.
57. See Kneipp, "Recreational Use of the National Forests," *Journal of Forestry,* May, 1930 for an exposition of Forest Service views and for an example of its attempts to deceive the public about Primitive Areas.

CHAPTER 8

1. Brant to Senator C. C. Dill, February 15, 1933, IB.
2. Van Name to Irving Brant, July 24, 1930, IB.
3. Report of the Chalet Committee to the Hoquiam Chamber of Commerce, September 25, 1925, p. 1, AC.
4. Ibid.
5. Cammerer to Johnson, June 29, 1926, NA.
6. HR 13069, 69 Cong, 1 Sess, June 26, 1926.
7. Grant to Mather, October 26, 1928, NA.
8. Mather to Grant, October 26, 1928, NA.
9. Van Name, *Vanishing Forest Reserves,* p. 173.
10. Report of Director of National Parks for 1923 p. 15, quoted in Van Name *Vanishing Forest Reserves,* p. 172.
11. Van Name, *Vanishing Forest Reserves,* p. 172.
12. Van Name, ibid., p. 181.
13. Van Name, ibid., p. 159.
14. Van Name, "Maintaining the Standard and the Scientific Usefulness of the National Parks," *Science,* August 7, 1928.

15. Edge, Rosalie, *An Implacable Widow*, autobiographical manuscript, unnumbered pages.
16. Miner, Roy W., memorandum on Van Name's pamphlets, January 31, 1929.
17. Ibid.
18. Edge, op. cit.
19. Van Name, *Vanishing Forest Reserves*, p. 190.
20. Peter Edge to Lien, undated, February, 1988, CL.
21. Edge, op. cit.
22. Edge, op. cit.
23. Peter Edge to Lien, February 19, 1988.
24. Edge, *In Memoriam Willard Gibbs Van Name*, April, 1959, CL.
25. Van Name, *The U.S. Biological Survey*, p. 1.
26. Edge, *The Slaughter of the Yellowstone Park Pelicans*, p. 4.
27. Interview with Mrs. Edge, July 1959. See also Taylor "Oh Hawk of Mercy," *New Yorker*, April 17, 1948, for a short summary of this event.
28. Edge, *An Implacable Widow*.
29. Mrs. Edge interview July, 1929.
30. Ibid.
31. Van Name, *Report on Forest and Wild Life Protection in the Olympic Peninsula Washington*, December 1, 1932, pp. 10–11, AMNH.
32. Ibid., p. 11.
33. Ibid., p. 12.
34. Ibid., p. 25.
35. Brant to Albright, May 5, 1932, IB.
36. Albright to Brant, February 19, 1932, IB.
37. Irving Brant to J. F. Allen, February 2, 1932, IB.
38. Brant to FDR, March 31, 1933, IB.
39. *A National Plan for American Forestry*, Senate Document 12, 73 Cong, 1 Sess.
40. Van Name, *Vanishing Forest Reserves*, p. 40.
41. *A National Plan for American Forestry*, op. cit., quoted in Marshall *The People's Forests*, pp. 92–93.
42. See wilderness writings in Grinnell, *Book of Boone and Crockett Club*, 1925; Aldo Leopold wilderness article, 1925; and Robert Marshall writings and The Mountaineers campaign against Mt. Rainier road building and other development.
43. See Robbins, *Lumberjacks and Legislators*, for a detailed account of the evolving industry-Forest Service relationship.
44. The Pinchot quotes are from the Secretary Wilson letter to himself which he drafted, *Breaking New Ground*, p. 261.
45. Swain, Donald C., *Wilderness Defender: Horace M. Albright and Conservation*, p. 182.
46. Shankland, Robert, *Steve Mather of the National Parks*, pp. 295–296 quoting Albright to Robert Sterling Yard.
47. R. Y. Stuart to Albright, March 3, 1932, NA.
48. Van Name, *Hands off the National Parks*, February, 1926.
49. Robinson, *The Forest Service*, p. 257.

CHAPTER 9

1. Ickes column 540, "Save Our Trees," *New York Post*, January 26, 1949; appears to have been written by Irving Brant for Ickes. This statement reflects exactly how Ickes viewed the Forest Service during the whole of his tenure as secretary.
2. Madsen speech to Port Angeles Chamber of Commerce, July 13, 1934; given also on several other occasions as Park Service policy, NA.
3. Executive order 6166, June 10, 1933, NA.

4. C. J. Buck to *The Forester,* Sept. 20, 1933, NA.

5. L. F. Kneipp to F. V. Horton, Nov. 6, 1933, NA.

6. To Secretary of Agriculture from Harold L. Ickes, November 11, 1933, NA.

7. See Alston Chase's *Playing God in Yellowstone* for an excellent review of the role of the wildlife division.

8. Ben H. Thompson to director, May 22, 1934, NA.

9. Conrad L. Wirth to director, May 26, 1934, NA.

10. Policy statement, Olympic Forest, Washington, March 15, 1934, NA.

11. Administrative Statistics, Mt. Olympus National Monument in Olympic National Forest, undated 1934, NA.

12. Irving Brant to FDR, March 31, 1933, IB.

13. Brant to Ickes, May 26, 1933, IB.

14. Ibid.

15. Martin F. Smith to Edge, May 15, 1934, ECC.

16. Cammerer to Brant, February 24, 1934, NA.

17. C. J. Buck to Irving Clark, May 29, 1934, IC.

18. Van Name to Clark, June 5, 1934, IC.

19. Madsen, chamber of commerce speech transmitted to director, July 17, 1934

20. Ibid.

21. Kneipp to Buck, June 4, 1934, NA.

22. Kneipp to F. V. Horton, July 9, 1934, NA.

23. Paper on park delivered to Special Committee on Mt. Olympus National Monument, State Planning Council, August 24, 1934, NA.

24. Clark to Ovid Butler, June 12, 1934, IC.

25. Silcox to Ovid Butler, June 25, 1934, NA.

26. E. A. Sherman to regional forester, July 8, 1932, NA.

27. Macy to Tomlinson, August 20, 1934, NA.

28. Preliminary Report, Mt. Olympus National Monument, October 5, 1934, NA.

29. Tomlinson to Tiffany, October 10, 1934, HW.

30. Interview with Mrs. Edge, July, 1959, HR 7086.

31. Tomlinson to director, February 10, 1935; Madsen to director, March 26, 1935, NA.

32. Wallgren to Asahel Curtis, April 16, 1935, AC.

33. Drake to Cammerer, June 13, 1935, NA.

34. Cowan, "The Proposed Mount Olympus National Park," *Journal of Forestry,* August, 1936, 34:747–749. First sentence is from Cowan's manuscript, edited out of the published article, OAT.

35. Curtis to Cammerer, April 27, 1935, AC.

36. *Seattle Municipal News,* April 27, 1935, HW.

37. Demaray to Mathias, May 21, 1935, NA.

38. Van Name to Brant, February 4, 1936, IB.

39. Van Name to Yeon, February 4, 1936, NA.

40. Buck to Silcox, April 12, 1935, NA.

41. Curtis to Cammerer, April 27, 1935, AC.

42. Earl Clapp to Yard, March 24, 1936, NA.

43. Kizer to Martin, January 24, 1936, WSPC.

44. Yard to Clark, April 23, 1936, OAT.

45. Ibid., and Mount Olympus National Park Hearing before the Committee on Public Lands, House of Representatives, 74 Cong, 2 Sess, on HR 7086, p. 10.

46. Yard to Clark, April 24, 1936, OAT.

47. Hearings, p. 57.

48. Yard to Clark, April 25, 1936, OAT.

49. Yard's handwriting was illegible. Quote completed from hearings, p. 79.
50. Yard to Clark, April 27, 1936, OAT.
51. Yard to Clark, April 28, 1936, OAT.
52. Yard to Clark, April 30, 1936, OAT.
53. Hearings, p. 225.
54. Hearings, p. 275.
55. Hearings, pp. 251–261.
56. Ibid.
57. House Report 2658, 74 Cong, 2 Sess, Hearings.
58. Van Name to Ickes, May 6, 1936, NA.
59. Edge to Brant, June 5, 1936, IB.
60. Edge, *An Implacable Widow*, p. 109.

CHAPTER 10

1. Van Name to Ickes, May 17, 1937, NA.
2. Curtis to Messingale, May 18, 1936, AC.
3. Port Angeles Evening News, May 7, 1936.
4. Brant to Ickes, February 13, 1936, IB. Also in *FDR and Conservation,* pp. 483–485.
5. *Seattle Times,* July 30, 1936.
6. *National Parks Bulletin,* February, 1937.
7. Bulletin of Wilderness Society, November, 1936.
8. Ibid.
9. Report on Olympic Primitive Area, July 7, 1936, NA.
10. Ibid.
11. Watts to Secretary of Agriculture, March 23, 1943, and Modifications of Plan, April 8, 1943, NA.
12. Curtis to Cammerer, June 2, 1936, AC.
13. Curtis to Mathias, May 21, 1936, AC.
14. Cammerer to Mr. E. B. Ackerman, undated copy, OAT.
15. Horning, W. H., *The Proposed Mount Olympus National Park and Its Probable Effect on the Olympic National Forest and Economic Interests of the Olympic Peninsula,* hereafter referred to as the Horning Report, p. 9, OAT.
16. Ibid., pp. 213–214.
17. Macy to Tomlinson, August 18, 1936, NA.
18. Van Name to Brant, November 13, 1936, IB.
19. Schulz to Brant, January 10, 1937, IB.
20. Demaray to Poole, January 28, 1937, NA.
21. Kneipp to C. J. Buck, October 8, 1936, NA.
22. Graves to Herbert A. Smith, December 29, 1936, BT.
23. Silcox to Wallace, February 12, 1937, NA.
24. Outgoing letters from March 1937 onward re HR 4724.
25. Brant to Wallace, March 7, 1937, IB.
26. Brant to Wallace, April 24, 1937, IB.
27. Edge to Ickes, February 19, 1937, NA.
28. Edge to West, April 2, 1937, NA.
29. Wallgren to Edge, April 2, 1937, NA.
30. Interview with Mrs. Edge, July, 1959.
31. Wallgren to Edge, April 2, 1937, NA.
32. Edge to Ickes, April 12, 1937, NA.
33. Cammerer to Ickes, May 6, 1937, OAT.
34. Cammerer to Coward, June 4, 1937, NA.

35. Slattery to Demaray, June 11, 1937, NA.
36. Peninsula Profile #76 *Port Angeles Evening News,* undated.
37. October 1960 interview with Overly transcript National Park Service, Harper's Ferry, West Virginia.
38. Overly to Macy, September 5, 1936, p. 10, OAT.
39. Overly to Macy, February 20, 1937, NA.
40. Interior Report on HR 4724 to Chairman Committee on Public Lands, undated 1937, NA.
41. Marshall Memo, "Reasons Why," May, 1937, NA.
42. F. H. Brundage Memorandum for Files, June 4, 1937, NA.

CHAPTER 11
1. Van Name to O'Hare, May, 1937, undated, ECC.
2. Cammerer to Myers, June 4, 1937, NA. Letters with this same wording were sent by the hundreds to justify the Park Service's position.
3. Rejected Draft Report HR 4724, undated spring 1937, NA.
4. Agriculture Report HR 4724, August 13, 1937, NA.
5. Carter to Kneipp, June 7, 1937, NA.
6. Ibid.
7. Edge to Carney, June 1, 1937, ECC.
8. Brant to Roosevelt, September 22, 1937, IB. Both quotes from this letter.
9. Ibid.
10. Quote and preceding material from *Port Angeles Evening News,* October 1, 1937.
11. Macy, Tomlinson, Bruckhart and Buck all wrote detailed memoranda to the files following the meeting in Roosevelt's cottage. All agree exactly on what happened and what was said. The quotes are from these memos. NA.
12. *Port Angeles Evening News,* October 1, 1937.
13. Tomlinson to files, October 4, 1937, OAT.
14. Fromme, Rudo, *Olympic Memoirs,* p. 65, Fromme, RLF.
15. Anonymous to Roosevelt, undated October, 1937, NA.
16. Silcox to Buck, November 22, 1937, NA.
17. Morgan, Murray, *The Last Wilderness,* p. 185.
18. Brant to Herman Kahn, May 3, 1954, IB.
19. *Ickes Diary,* vol 2, page 320, February 16, 1938.
20. Brant to Ickes, October 4, 1937, IB.
21. Ickes to Brant, October 29, 1937, NA.
22. Horning to Demaray, October 21, 1937, NA.
23. Ickes to Demaray, October 26, 1937, NA.
24. Clark to Ickes, December 29, 1937, NA.
25. Brundage to Chief, October 29, 1937.
26. *The National Parks Bulletin,* December, 1937, p. 12.
27. For a discussion of the NPA ties to the timber industry, see Fox, *John Muir . . . ,* pp. 204-205.
28. Van Name to Brant, November 18, 1936, Brant to Van Name, November 19, 1936, IB.
29. Van Name to Brant, August 20, 1937, IB.
30. Brant to Edge, September 14, 1937, IB.
31. Brant to Edge, September 20, 1937, IB.
32. Edge to Brant, September 23, 1937, IB.
33. Brant to Schulz, September 25, 1937, IB.
34. Edge to Brant, October 20, 1937, IB.

CHAPTER 12
1. Van Name to Roosevelt, April 23, 1938, IB.
2. Van Name to Brant, May 27, 1938, IB.
3. Edge to Brant, November 11, 1937, IB.
4. Tomlinson, Macy, Overly to director, November 24, 1937, NA.
5. Brant to Ickes, January 16, 1938, IB.
6. Schulz to Brant, January 25, 1938, IB.
7. Ickes to Brant, Janaury 24, 1938, IB.
8. Tomlinson memo to files, March 9, 1938, OAT.
9. Appleby to Silcox, January 14, 1938, NA.
10. Granger memorandum, January 21, 1938, NA.
11. Appleby to Silcox, January 14, 1938, NA.
12. TWN to Granger, January 25, 1938, NA.
13. Carter to Silcox, January 28, 1938, NA.
14. Brundage to Buck, February 1, 1938, NA.
15. Silcox to Appleby, February 15, 1938, NA.
16. Silcox to Tiffany, February 23, 1938, WSPC.
17. Ickes to Brant, January 24, 1938, NA.
18. Cammerer to Demaray and Wirth, February 8, 1938, NA.
19. Brant to Schulz, February 12, 1938, IB.
20. Buck to Brundage, February 15, 1938, NA.
21. Tomlinson to James, March 1, 1938, OAT.
22. Woods to Tiffany, March 1, 1938 telegram, WSPC.
23. Woods to Greeley, March 3, 1938, WSPC.
24. *Ickes Diary*, vol. 2, April 21, 1938, p. 374.
25. Smith to Tiffany, April 19, 1938, WSPC.
26. Edge to Brant, May 4, 1938, IB.
27. Brant to Roosevelt, May 28, 1938, IB.
28. Ibid.
29. Brant to FDR, June 6, 1938, IB.
30. Edge to Brant, June 10, 1938, IB.
31. Brant to FDR, June 14, 1938, IB.
32. Brant to Van Name, June 17, 1938, IB.
33. Ibid.
34. Ibid.
35. Edge, *Conservation—Come and Get It*, ECC Report for 1938, pp. 3–4, CL.
36. Edge to Brant, June 20, 1938, IB.

CHAPTER 13
1. *Ickes Diary*, vol. 2, August 6, 1938, p. 438.
2. Cammerer, "Maintenance of the Primeval in National Parks," 1938, pp. 210–211, quoted in Runte, *National Parks*, p. 175.
3. S1188, 76 Cong, 1 Sess, February 6, 1939, IB.
4. Ickes's speech to Commonwealth Club of San Francisco, February 15, 1939, written by Irving Brant, IB.
5. Schulz to Brant, August 28, 1938, IB.
6. Roosevelt to Ickes, December 10, 1938, NA.
7. Brant, *Adventures in Conservation*, p. 316.
8. Burlew to Roosevelt, December 11, 1939, NA.
9. Burlew to Roosevelt, December 12, 1939, NA. Written by Brant.

10. Wallace to Roosevelt, December 18, 1938, NA.
11. Brant to Van Name, December 20, 1938, IB.
12. *Ickes Diary,* vol. 3, December 24, 1939, p. 94.
13. Ibid.
14. Aldwell to Zellerbach, November 30, 1939, TTA.
15. Brant, *Adventures in Conservation,* p. 333.
16. *Ickes Diary,* vol. 2, March 5, 1939, pp. 584–585.
17. Ibid., vol. 3, September 16, 1939, p. 9.
18. Ibid., vol. 3, December 3, 1939, p. 72.
19. Ibid., vol. 3, December 30, 1939, p. 103.
20. *The National Parks Bulletin,* July, 1940, p. 22.
21. Greeley, *Forests and Men,* p. 217.
22. Chapman, "A Program for Private Forestry," *American Forestry,* October, 1919, p. 1405.
23. *Forest Statistics for Grays Harbor County Washington,* Pacific Northwest Forest and Range Experiment Station, Portland, Oregon, 1938, NA.
24. Clark to Buller, June 12, 1934, IC.
25. Senator Pittman, December 20, 1938.
26. Clark to Marshall, December 22, 1935, IC.
27. Ferris to Magnuson, March 7, 1938, WGM.
28. Pinchot, *The Fight for Conservation,* p. 43, address, Forest National Conservation Congress Proceedings, p. 72. See also pp. 51–52, *Fight.*
29. *Ickes Diary,* vol. 2, February 16, 1938, p. 320.
30. Brant to Schulz, August 4, 1940, IB.
31. Wallace to Roosevelt, January 18, 1939, NA.

CHAPTER 14
1. *Seattle Post-Intelligencer,* June 9, 1943, NA.
2. Norman quote from *Tacoma Tribune,* quoted in NPS memo, July 9, 1943, NA.
3. Andrea S. Lanning, Potlatch, to Secretary of Interior, June 24, 1943, NA.
4. Brant to Edge, August 4, 1940, Brant annotation on file copy, IB.
5. Brant to Edge, June 26, 1940, IB.
6. Schulz to Brant, July 24, 1940, IB.
7. Resolution of February 26, 1940, in Mathias to Curtis, March 2, 1940, AC.
8. Kittredge to director, July 16, 1940, NA.
9. Overly and Dodd, *Sitka Spruce in the Olympic Acquisition Area,* February 14, 1941, NA.
10. Ibid., p. 4.
11. Overly, *Sitka Spruce in the Olympic National Park,* April 25, 1941, p. 59, NA.
12. Burlew to Roosevelt, December 12, 1939. Drafted by Brant, NA.
13. Drury to Coffman, May 7, 1941. Hand-written note on archives copy of Overly report.
14. Overly, op. cit., p. 4.
15. Greeley to Nelson, January 28, 1942, OAT.
16. Greeley to Macy, May 25, 1942, NA.
17. Tomlinson memo, May 28, 1942, NA.
18. Graves to Drury, November 23, 1941, NA.
19. Sarlin, *The Availability of Vital Woods . . . ,* p. 23, NA
20. Ibid., p. 20.
21. Ibid., p. 23.
22. *Conservation for Victory,* ECC annual report for 1942, p. 8, CL.
23. Brundage to Ickes, January 20, 1943, OAT.
24. Drury to Ickes, January 21, 1943 (never sent), NA.
25. Condon to Muck, December 7, 1942, OAT.

26. Ickes to Roosevelt, March 29, 1943, NA.
27. Demaray to Drury, January 13, 1943, NA.
28. Ickes to Roosevelt, March 29, 1943, NA.
29. Greeley to Mathias, April 11, 1942, NA.
30. Henson to Jackson, May 26, 1943, HMJ.
31. *Seattle Times,* June 2, 1943, NA.
32. *Seattle Post-Intelligencer,* June 6, 1943, IB.
33. Drury to Ickes, June 21, 1943. Summary of memo in *Olympic Spruce*—correspondence and events of significance in relation to the 1940 attempt of lumbermen and WPB to open Olympic National park to logging, October 1, 1943, p. 4, NA.
34. Drury to secretary, July 3, 1943, Ickes to Chapman, July 6, 1943, Ibid., p. 4.
35. Ickes to Nelson, July 12, 1943, NA, OAT.
36. Preston to Drury, July 20, 1943, detailed coverage of hearings, NA.
37. Lawrence to Jackson, June 9, 1943, HMJ.
38. Nelson to Ickes, July 27, 1945, HMJ.
39. *Washington Post,* September 3, 1943, NA.
40. Bloedel to Ickes, September 6, 1943, NA.
41. Ickes to Nelson, September 14, 1934, NA.
42. Nelson to Ickes, September 23, 1943, NA.
43. Maier to Macy, September 2, 1943, NA.
44. Macy to Drury, September 23, 1946, NA.
45. Drury to Brant, October 29, 1943, IB.

CHAPTER 15
1. Aldwell, Thomas T., *Conquering the Last Frontier,* p. 157.
2. Ickes column 16, No. 540, January 26, 1949, *New York Post,* et. al., IB.
3. Drury to Ickes, April 9, 1945, NA.
4. Tomlinson to Macy, April 11, 1945, PPM.
5. Jackson to Drury, April 12, 1945, NA.
6. Ickes to Jackson, May 12, 1945, NA.
7. Drury to Tomlinson, May 21, 1945, NA.
8. Drury to Jackson, June 25, 1945, NA.
9. Jackson to Drury, July 9, 1945, NA.
10. MacDaniels, E. H., "Timber Supply of Washington and Oregon Placed at 438.1 Billion Feet," *West Coast Lumberman,* January, 1946.
11. Magnuson to Drury, March 15, 1946, NA.
12. *Seattle Post-Intelligencer,* March 17, 1946,
13. Overly to Macy, March 22, 1946, NA.
14. Macy to Drury, March 22, 1946, NA.
15. Ibid.
16. Maier to Drury, April 2, 1946, NA.
17. Watts to Magnuson, March 15, 1946, WGM.
18. Plumb press release, April 11, 1946, NA.
19. Overly to Macy, May 8, 1946, NA.
20. Chapman to Krug, May 20, 1946, NA.
21. Press release, June 1, 1946, NA.
22. Overly *Statistics Relative to Adjustments of West Boundary,* May 27, 1946, NA.
23. Undated NPS press release by Drury, June 13, 1946, OAT.
24. *Congressional Record,* Vol. 92, part 12, page A3781.
25. Dedication speeches, June 15, 1946, OAT.
26. Drury to Krug, July 8, 1946, NA.

27. Ibid.

28. Drury to Krug, July 8, 1946, NA.

29. Drury to Demaray, August 2, 1946, NA.

30. Krug to Downey, August 9, 1946, NA. Typical of all letters.

31. Davidson to Krug, October 8, 1946, NA; Davidson is quoting Wallgren.

32. Drury to Krug, December 13, 1946, NA.

33. Andrews to McArdle, January 16, 1947, NA.

34. Greeley to Drury, February 28, 1947, NA.

35. Wirth to Drury, March 3, 1947, NA.

36. Wirth to Clark, March 5, 1947, NA.

37. Chapman to Norman, March 12, 1947, NA.

38. Drury, *National Park Service Reports on Results of its Study of Olympic National Park Boundaries,* March 18, 1947, NA.

39. Edge, *An Implacable Widow,* p. 120.

40. Ickes column, April 8, 1947, *New York Post,* IB.

41. Ickes column, April 10, 1947, *New York Post,* IB.

42. Ickes to Van Name, June 11, 1947, AMNH.

43. Tolson to Jackson, June 25, 1947, NA.

44. Brant to Drury, June 17, 1947, IB.

45. Ickes to Mrs. Roosevelt, June 7, 1947, NA.

46. Mrs. Roosevelt to Krug, June 12, 1947, NA.

47. Edge to Drury, June 28, 1947, IB.

48. Wirth to Drury, May 29, 1947, NA.

49. Macy to Tomlinson, June 19, 1947, NA.

50. Tomlinson to Macy, July 30, 1947, PPM.

51. *Hearings before the Committee on Public Lands Pursuant to HR93 September 16–17, 1947,* Washington, D.C., Government Printing Office, 1948, page 14.

52. Ibid., p. 24.

53. Ibid., pp. 27–28.

54. Hearings, op. cit., p. 70.

55. Edge to Brant, November 17, 1947, IB.

56. *New York Times,* November 27, 1947, IB.

57. Brant to Ickes, December 1, 1947, IB.

58. Truman to Brant, January 5, 1948, IB.

59. Brant to Edge, February 9, 1948, IB.

60. Jackson to Welch, January 27, 1948, NA.

61. Drury to Brant, September 5, 1947, IB.

62. ECC press release, November 20, 1947, NA.

63. Drury signed statement, *The Olympic Boundary Question,* November 14, 1947, NA.

64. *Washington Post,* February 17, 1951, "Parks for People."

65. Brant to Earl Warren, March 31, 1951, IB.

66. Ickes to Warren, April 2, 1951, IB.

67. Edge to Warren (telegram), April 4, 1951, IB.

CHAPTER 16

1. Roosevelt to Fairfield Osborne, December 26, 1940, in *FDR and Conservation,* p. 486.

2. Krug to Crosby, May 1, 1946, NA.

3. See pp. 26–27, *Hearings before Committee on Public Lands on HR6281,* 1913.

4. *American Forestry,* January, 1917, editorial, 23:48–49.

5. Overly to Drury, September 16, 1941, NA.

6. Wirth to Moskey, October 3, 1941, NA.

7. Interior Department Solicitors Opinion M 31545, January 21, 1942, NA.
8. USC Title 36, Chapter I, part 26, Olympic National Park; Timber Disposal regulations, approved April 13, 1942.
9. Muck to Drury, May 12, 1942, NA.
10. Tomlinson to Macy, May 15, 1942, NA.
11. Dodd to Tomlinson, May 15, 1942, NA.
12. Davidson to Tomlinson, May 16, 1942, NA.
13. Sarlin to Macy, March 16, 1943, NA.
14. Macy to Drury, March 17, 1943, NA.
15. September 9, 1944, newspaper clipping "Worms attack 400,000 acres of Pacific Northwest Timber," NA.
16. Davidson to Tomlinson, May 16, 1942, NA.
17. Wirth to Price, January 11, 1945, NA.
18. Price to Wirth, January 26, 1945, NA.
19. Wirth to Price, February 2, 1945, NA.
20. 11 FR 9083, August 21, 1946.
21. Superintendent's Monthly Report, May, 1947, NA.
22. Sanford to regional director, September 18, 1946, NA.
23. 13 FR 361, January 27, 1948.
24. Price, Wirth, Coffman to Drury, May 7, 1948, NA.
25. Drury to Mylrea, March 17, 1949. Drafted by Overly, NA.
26. Drafted for Secretary of Interior L. F. Cook of the Forestry Division, September 12, 1950, NA. Hearings before the Subcommittee of the Study of Monopoly Power of the Committee of the Judiciary, House of Representatives, 81 Cong, 2 Sess, July 18, 1950.
27. For one of these, see Cammerer to Yard, January 7, 1936, NA.

CHAPTER 17
1. Wirth to Webster, March 26, 1952, NA. Webster was editor and publisher of the *Port Angeles Evening News*.
2. Clark to Overly, September 9, 1952, IC.
3. Wirth to Bryant, May 17, 1932, NA.
4. Wirth to Cammerer, May 26, 1934, NA.
5. Packard to Edge, January 25, 1951, IB.
6. Brant to Edge, February 12, 1951, IB.
7. *1952 Timber Harvest Report,* Washington State Division of Forestry.
8. Wirth to Jackson, August 6, 1951, HMJ.
9. *The Peninsula Herald,* June 14, 1951, CFR.
10. *New York Times,* December 9, 1951, NA.
11. Wirth to regional director, March 13, 1951, NA.
12. Brant to Truman, December 24, 1952, IB.
13. Statement by the President Relating to the Enlarging of Olympic National Park, Washington, January 6, 1953, NA.
14. Strack to Wirth, January 8, 1953, NA.
15. *New York Times,* February 15, 1953.
16. Marckworth to several chamber of commerce secretaries, March 13, 1953, HMJ.
17. Report of Olympic National Park Review Committee, April, 1954, NA.
18. Greeley to Marckworth: A Recommendation, November 23, 1953, CFR.
19. *Seattle Post-Intelligencer,* August 23, 1955.
20. *Transcript, Hearings Committee Interior and Insular Affairs,* Port Angeles, September 26, 1953, p. 14.
21. Hearings, op. cit., p. 29.

22. Interview with Rosalie Edge, July, 1959.
23. Washington State *Timber Harvest Reports*, 1952, 1953.
24. Carpenter to Chief Western Office, Division of D. & C., July 30, 1954, NA.
25. *Reconnaissance Report for a Road over Tshletshy Creek Ridge*, Olympic National Park, July 30, 1954, NA.
26. *Port Townsend Leader*, September 17, 1953, reported by Irving Clark to Samuelson, October 9, 1953, IC.
27. Interview with Fred Packard, October, 1956.
28. *Encroachments on and Resource Utilization in Areas of the National Park System*, August 28, 1953, pp. 8-9.
29. Ibid., p. 8.
30. Ibid., p. 1.
31. Morgan to Packard, August 29, 1955, NA.
32. *Port Angeles Evening News*, September 27, 1955.
33. *Time*, August 24, 1962.
34. Overly to regional director, May 9, 1955, NA.
35. Hartung to Overly, January 4, 1955, NA.
36. Interview with Frances Fagerlund, May 1, 1986, reporting on conversation with Overly's wife.
37. Interview with Glenn Gallison, April 15, 1986, reporting on conversation with Fred Overly.
38. Olympic Natural History Association Narrative Report, 1954, NA; interview with Gunnar Fagerlund, May 1, 1986.
39. Contract No. 14-10-447-295, February 14, 1956.
40. Two-page Wirth statement, *What are National Parks?*, November 29, 1954, ONP.
41. Shepard to Wirth, September 18, 1956, PS.
42. Brant to Edge, November 9, 1956, IB.
43. Edge to Brant, November 19, 1956, IB.
44. Merriam to files, September 25, 1956, NA.
45. Interview with Phil Zalesky, May 7, 1986.
46. *A Log of Action on the Olympic National Park Situation*, October, 1956, NA.
47. Ibid.
48. Transcript, Special Meeting with National Park Service Director and Regional Director re Olympic National Park, October 15, 1956, and from interview with Phil Zalesky, May 7, 1986, who was present, CL.
49. Notes on Joint Field Trip to Study Salvage Logging in ONP, September 30, 1956, CL.
50. Wirth to Goldsworthy, October 30, 1956, CL.
51. Questions and Answers about Logging in Olympic National Park by Paul Shepard, comments by Director Conrad L. Wirth on Questions and Answers about Logging in Olympic National Park, NA.
52. Overly to Wirth, May 14, 1957, NA.
53. Overly to Packard, January 7, 1957, NA.
54. Goldsworthy to Brower, March 24, 1957, PHZ.
55. Alverts, *et al.* to Wirth, August 19, 1957, NA.
56. Alverts to Wirth, September 26, 1957, NA.
57. Policy on cutting and use of forest material, November 20, 1956, NA.
58. Overly to Merriam, May 6, 1957, NA.
59. *Port Angeles Evening News, April* 21, 1958.
60. Ibid.
61. Interview with Glenn Gallison, April 30, 1986.

62. Fagerlund to Lien, March, 1988 (no date), CL.
63. Merriam to Shepard, February 19, 1957.

CHAPTER 18
 1. Roosevelt to Ickes, December 10, 1938, NA.
 2. Overly to Wirth, March 1, 1950, quoted in *History of Coastal Road 1957*, NA.
 3. Martin to Roosevelt, March 31, 1938, NA.
 4. Roosevelt to Ickes, December 10, 1938, IB.
 5. Aldwell to Wallgren, March 14, 1938, OAT.
 6. PWA Project 723, April 19, 1939, NA.
 7. Kittredge to Bryant, February 21, 1940, OAT.
 8. Bryant to Kittredge, February 27, 1940, OAT.
 9. Bryant, *Development Plan for the Queets and Ocean Strips, Olympic Peninsula*, April 2, 1940, pp. 6, 18, OAT.
10. Kittredge to director, June 1, 1940, OAT.
11. Demaray to Kittredge, October 30, 1940, OAT.
12. "The Olympic Parkway and National Defense." Speech delivered by Preston P. Macy before the Western Forestry and Conservation Association, December 12, 1940, Portland, Oregon, NA.
13. Overly to Wirth, March 1, 1956, in *History of Coastal Road 1957*, NA.
14. Wirth to regional director, May 14, 1957, in *History of Coastal Road 1957*, NA.
15. Collins to Wirth, July 14, 1958, in *History of Coastal Road 1957*, NA.
16. Congressional Record, House, June 17, 1913, p. 2060.
17. Myers to chief counsel, May 4, 1949, NA.
18. Taylor to Drury, November 7, 1941, NA.
19. Polson to Taylor, February 4, 1942, NA.
20. Taylor and Lee to Drury, March 9, 1942, NA.
21. Drury to Ickes, June 17, 1942, NA.
22. Martin to Lee, March 1, 1940, NA.
23. Cammerer to Martin, March 19, 1940, NA.
24. Taylor to director, May 14, 1942, NA.
25. Ibid.
26. Macy to Drury, May 18, 1942, NA.
27. Ibid.
28. Macy to Cammerer, February 13, 1940, NA.
29. Demaray to Taylor, June 2, 1942, NA.
30. Declaration of Policy signed by Governor Arthur B. Langlie and Jack Taylor, Commissioner of Public Lands, September 16, 1942, NA.
31. Overly to regional director, March 5, 1953, NA.
32. Crouse to Goldsworthy, November 8, 1955, CL.
33. Beard to regional director, March 12, 1959, NA.
34. House Bill 216, January 26, 1959.
35. *Port Angeles Evening News*, June 13, 1959.
36. Hastings to Toni, September 19, 1986, CL.
37. Sodergren to regional director, November 23, 1959, NA.
38. Tomlinson to Freeman, April 8, 1941, OAT.
39. Brant to Roosevelt, July 27, 1941, OAT.
40. Brant to Ickes, July 28, 1941, IB.
41. Roosevelt to Brant, August 18, 1941, IB.
42. Macy to Tomlinson, April 27, 1939, PPM.

43. Interior Solicitor's Opinion M–36456, November 21, 1957, NA.
44. Anderson to Keller, February 24, 1941, OAT.
45. Macy to Drury, April 13, 1941, OAT.
46. Anderson to Macy, September 14, 1941, OAT.
47. Lee to Drury, November 17, 1941, OAT.
48. Anderson to postmaster, September 8 or 9, 1946, OAT.
49. Tolson to regional director, August 18, 1947, NA.
50. Ibid.
51. Overly to regional director, March 17, 1952, OAT.
52. Interior Solicitor's Opinion M36456, November 21, 1957, NA.
53. Makah Tribal Council to Eisenhower, December 19, 1957, NA.
54. Wiseman to Westland, April 11, 1958, CL.
55. Interior Report to accompany HR 9311, Report 91–1222, 91 Cong, 2 Sess.
56. Ibid.
57. Ibid.
58. Laurence to Allin, November 16, 1973, NA.
59. *Seattle Times*, June 26, 1990.

CHAPTER 19
1. Smith to Udall, January 19, 1966, FJO.
2. North Cascades-Olympic National Park Hearings, February 11–12, 1966, p. 56.
3. Hallia to Jackson, January 12, 1966, HMJ.
4. *Conservation News*, October 15, 1962.
5. *Seattle Times*, April 19, 1964.
6. Overly to Udall, August 27, 1965, FJO.
7. Overly to Udall, August 30, 1965, FJO.
8. Crafts to Udall, December 31, 1965, FJO.
9. Statement on Olympic National Park-National Forest Boundary, October 29, 1965, transmitted with Crafts to Udall, December 31, 1965, NA.
10. *Seattle Times*, January 9, 1966.
11. Brant to Udall, January 22, 1966, IB.
12. Udall to Brant, January 24, 1966, IB.
13. Brant to Osseward, January 26, 1966, IB.
14. Brant to Udall, February 7, 1966, IB.
15. North Cascades-Olympic Hearings, February 11–12, 1966, p. 302.
16. Ibid., p. 591.
17. For timber volume removed from Mt. Rainier, see *Timber Harvest Report* of State Division of Forestry from 1954 onward.
18. North Cascades-Olympic Hearings, February 11–12, 1966, pp. 516–517.
19. Ibid., p. 517.
20. Ibid., p. 518.
21. *Port Angeles Evening News*, April 3, 1966.
22. *Port Townsend Leader*, February 24, 1966.
23. *Port Angeles Evening News*, March 3, 1966.
24. Jackson to Udall, March 3, 1966, NA.
25. Freeman to Udall, April 26, 1966, NA.
26. Crafts to Overly, June 16, 1966, FJO.
27. Office of the Secretary, press release, July 3, 1966, NA.
28. *Seattle Times*, July 12, 1966.
29. Zalesky to Brandborg, July 14, 1966, PHZ.
30. Zalesky to Hartzog, July 16, 1966, PHZ.

31. Ibid.
32. Olympic National Park Boundary Study Committee Report, September 2, 1966, NA.
33. Ibid.
34. Ibid.
35. *Argus,* July 25, 1969. For Director Hartzog's views of Senator Jackson's involvements in the North Cascades and the Redwoods fights, see Hartzog, *Battling for the National Parks,* pp. 159–175.
36. Crafts to Overly, April 5, 1966, FJO.
37. Minutes, Olympic Peninsula Heritage Council, November, 1972, FJO.
38. ONP Master Plan Hearings, November 3, 1973, p. 10.
39. *Port Angeles Daily News,* 1973 (undated clippings quoting the Master Plan).
40. Olympic Peninsula Heritage Council Master Plan Hearings, November 2, 1973.

CHAPTER 20

1. Graves, Proceedings of the 1915 National Park Conference, p. 145.
2. Van Name, *Vanishing Forest Reserves,* pp. 163–164.
3. Chapman, *American Forests and Forest Life Magazine,* June, 1925 (reprint—no page number).
4. Van Name, *Vanishing Forest Reserves,* p. 184.
5. Krug to Waldrop, July 22, 1947, NA.
6. Johnson, Nicholas, "The Easy Chair," *Harper's,* February, 1969, p. 14.
7. McConnell to Lien, October 31, 1988, CL.
8. *Conservation for Victory,* ECC Report for 1942, p. 9, CL.
9. *An Olympic Peninsula Answer to the Wallgren Bill,* 1936 timber industry pamphlet, pp. 2–3.
10. *Investigate Please,* 1948 timber-industry pamphlet, p. 17.
11. Pinchot, *The Fight for Conservation,* p. 51.
12. Brant to Wallace, April 24, 1937, IB.
13. Twight, *Organizational Values and Political Power: The Forest Service versus the Olympic National Park,* p. 109.
14. Brant to Maury, February 2, 1932, IB. For a modern update of this essential aspect of the Forest Service, see O'Toole, *Reforming the Forest Service.*
15. Johnston, Greg, "Urban Forests Fighting Overuse," *Seattle Post-Intelligencer,* August 22, 1990.
16. Greeley, *Forests and Men,* p. 46.
17. Address by E. G. Griggs to Third National Conservation Congress, Kansas City, 1911.
18. Winkenwerder interview on station KJR, Seattle, July 2, 1937, CFR.
19. Greeley, *Forests and Men,* p. 236.
20. Ibid., p. 217.
21. Chamber of Commerce of the United States, *What to Do With 500,000,000 Acres of Government Land,* 1945.
22. Cox, *Organization of the Lumber Industry in the Pacific Northwest,* pp. 179–180.
23. Brown, *Mountain in the Clouds,* p. 184.
24. House Agricultural Committee Hearings on HR 10344, May 23, 1969, p. 220.
25. Testimony of Edward C. Crafts, former Assistant Chief of the Forest Service, before the House Agriculture Committee, May 23, 1969, quoted in Michael Frome, *The Forest Service,* pp. 84–85.
26. See O'Toole, *Reforming the Forest Service,* pp. 147–148.
27. Surveys and Investigations Staff, Committee on Appropriation, U.S. House of Representatives, *Timber Sales Process of U.S. Forest Service,* Washington, D.C.: House of Representatives 1982, p. 41, quoted in O'Toole, op. cit., p. 202.
28. O'Toole, op. cit., p. 202.

29. Clary, David A., *Timber and the Forest Service,* 1986, p. 126, quoted in O'Toole, op. cit., p.202.
30. "Fish, Trees, and the Law," *The Seattle Times,* July 6, 1980.
31. O'Toole, op. cit., pp. 161–162.

CHAPTER 21
1. Steinhart, Peter, "Reagan Administration Steps Up War on Park Service," *The Seattle Times,* August 29, 1988.
2. Frampton to Wilderness Society members, May 10, 1987.
3. "More Timber Folly," *The Seattle Times,* November 27, 1998.
4. Hill, Larry, *A Glimpse of the USDA Forest Service Administrative Appeals Process,* Address at Congressional Research Service Symposium on Appeals 6-7, November 17, 1989, quoted in Goldman, Patti A., and Boyles, Kristen L., "Forsaking the Rule of Law" 27:1039.
5. Goldman, Patti A., and Boyles, Kristen L., *op. cit.* 27:1048.
6. *Seattle Post-Intelligencer,* April 22, 1988.
7. *Congressional Record,* June 17, 1913, 63rd Congress.
8. Hanke, Steve H., "Privatize the National Forests," *Wall Street Journal,* August 23, 1988.
9. Skow, John, In "Washington Lighthawk Counts the Clearcuts," *Time,* August 29, 1988, p.12.
10. *Seattle Post-Intelligencer,* December 15, 1988.
11. *New York Times,* December 13, 1988.
12. *The Seattle Times,* December 13, 1988; *Seattle Post Intelligencer,* December 13, 1988.
13. *The Seattle Times,* July 30, 1990.
14. *Aberdeen Daily World,* June 25, 1990.
15. *Seattle Post-Intelligencer,* July 31, 1990.
16. Cahn, Robert, and Patricia, "Disputed Territory," *National Parks,* May/June, 1987, p. 30.
17. *San Francisco Chronicle,* April 21, 1987.
18. *Seattle Post-Intelligencer,* June 26, 1990.
19. Finnerty to Jaime, September 28, 1990.
20. *United States of America v. John B. Aaker et. al.*
21. From the justification submitted to President Roosevelt by the Administrator of Public Works for the private land acquisition in the Olympic Coastal Strip. Ok'd personally by Franklin D. Roosevelt, April 19, 1939. In case file, United States vs. John B. Aaker, et al.
22. Finnerty to Regional Director, November 19, 1993.
23. Morris to Bill Walters, Deputy Field Director, September 18, 1995.
24. Morris to Phil Pearl, August 29, 1997.
25. Draft of the implementing bill as negotiated with the Quileute Tribe.
26. Draft agreement (with the Quileute Tribe).
27. The 386-membership figure for the Quileute tribe is for 1985 and comes from *A Guide to the Indian Tribes of the Pacific Northwest,* revised edition, by Robert H. Ruby and John A. Brown, Norman and London: University of Oklahoma Press, 1992.
28. Mott to Hodell, August 28, 1988.

CHAPTER 22
1. Court transcript, Sierra Club vs. Forest Service, p. 5.
2. *Signpost,* September 1987, trail report from an NPS ranger.
3. Van Name to Clark, June 5, 1934, IB.
4. I am indebted to Ben Twight for this thought.
5. See Twight and Lyden, "Multiple Use vs. Organizational Commitment," *Forest Science,* June, 1988, vol. 34, no. 2. I am indebted to Ben Twight for suggesting the elements of this scenario to me.
6. *National Parks for the Future,* The Conservation Foundation, March 1972.
7. Shepard to Lien, February 17, 1988.

BIBLIOGRAPHY

BOOKS

Abbey, Edward. *Desert Solitaire: A Season in the Wilderness.* New York: Ballantine Books, 1968.

Albright, Horace M. (as told to Robert Cahn). *The Birth of the National Park Service: The Founding Years 1913–1933.* Salt Lake City: Howe Brothers, 1985.

————. *Origins of the National Park Service Administration of Historic Sites.* Philadelphia: Eastern National Park and Monument Association, 1971.

Aldwell, Thomas T. *Conquering the Last Frontier.* Seattle: Superior Publishing Company, 1950.

Badé, William F. *The Life and Letters of John Muir.* Boston and New York: Houghton Mifflin Co., 1924, 2 vols.

Barney, Daniel R. *The Last Stand: Ralph Nader's Study Group Report on the National Forests.* New York: Grossman Publishers, 1974.

Brant, Irving. *Adventures in Conservation with Franklin D. Roosevelt.* Flagstaff: Northland Publishing, 1988.

Brockman, C. Frank, and Lawrence C. Merriam, Jr. *Recreational Use of Wildlands.* New York: McGraw Hill, 1973.

Brown, Bruce. *Mountain in the Clouds: A Search for the Wild Salmon.* New York: Simon and Schuster, 1982.

Cameron, Jenks. *The National Park Service: Its History, Activities and Organization.* New York: D. Appleton and Company, 1922.

Chase, Alston. *Playing God in Yellowstone: The Destruction of America's First National Park.* Boston & New York: Atlantic Monthly Press, 1986.

Coman, Edwin T., and Helen M. Gibbs. *Time, Tide and Timber.* Stanford: Stanford University Press, 1949.

Conservation Foundation. *National Parks for the Future.* Washington, D.C.: The Conservation Foundation, 1972.

Crawford, Kenneth G. *The Pressure Boys: The Inside Story of Lobbying in America.* New York: Julian Messner, Inc., 1939.

Darling, F. Fraser, and Noel D. Eichorn. *Men and Nature in the National Parks — Reflections on Policy.* Washington, D.C.: The Conservation Foundation, 1967.

Dietrich, William. *The Final Forest: The Battle for the Lost Great Trees of the Pacific Northwest.* New York: Simon and Schuster, 1992.

Duerr, William A., editor. *Timber: Problems, Prospects, Policies.* Ames: Iowa State University Press, 1973.

Everhart, William C. *The National Park Service.* Boulder, CO: Westview Press, 1972.

Fausold, Martin L. *Gifford Pinchot: Bull Moose Progressive.* Syracuse: Syracuse University Press, 1961.

Fox, Stephen. *John Muir and His Legacy: The American Conservation Movement.* Boston: Little, Brown and Company, 1981.

Frome, Michael. *The Forest Service.* New York: Praeger Publishers, 1971.

————. *Whose Woods These Are: The Story of the National Forests.* New York: Doubleday and Co., 1962.

Glover, James M. *A Wilderness Original: The Life of Bob Marshall.* Seattle: The Mountaineers, 1986.

Greeley, William B. *Forest Policy.* New York: McGraw Hill, 1953.

————. *Forests and Men.* Garden City, New York: Doubleday and Co., 1951.

Grinnell, George Bird, editor. *Hunting at High Altitudes: The Book of the Boone and Crockett Club.* New York: Harper and Brothers, 1913.

Grinnell, George B., and Charles Sheldon, editors. *Hunting and Conservation: The Book of the Boone and Crockett Club.* New Haven: Yale University Press, 1925.

Gulick, Luther Halsey. *American Forest Policy: A Study of Government Administration and Economic Control.* New York: Duell, Sloan and Pearch, 1951.

Hartzog, George B., Jr. *Battling for the National Parks.* Mt. Kisco, NY: Moyer Bell Limited, 1988.

Hawthorne, Hildegarde, and Esther Burnell Mills. *Enos Mills of the Rockies.* New York: Houghton Mifflin, 1935.

Hays, Samuel P. *Conservation and the Gospel of Efficiency: The Progressive Conservation Movement 1890–1920.* Cambridge: Harvard University Press, 1959.

Ickes, Harold. *The Secret Diary of Harold L. Ickes.* New York: Simon and Schuster, 1953.

Ise, John. *Our National Park Policy: A Critical History.* Baltimore: Johns Hopkins Press, 1961.

————. *The United States Forest Policy.* New Haven: Yale University Press, 1920.

Johnson, Robert Underwood. *Remembered Yesterdays.* Boston: Little, Brown and Company, 1923.

Kaufman, Herbert. *The Forest Ranger: A Study in Administrative Behavior.* Baltimore: Johns Hopkins Press (published for Resources for the Future), 1960.

Kinney, Jay P. *The Development of Forest Laws in America.* New York: John Wiley and Sons, 1917.

McGeary, M. Nelson. *Gifford Pinchot Forester Politician.* Princeton: Princeton University Press, 1960.

Marshall, Robert. *The People's Forests.* New York: Harrison Smith and Robert Haas, 1933.

Mason, Alpheus Thomas. *Bureaucracy Convicts Itself: The Ballinger Pinchot Controversy of 1910.* New York: Viking Press, 1941.

Morgan, George T. *William B. Greeley, A Practical Forester 1879–1955.* St. Paul: Forest History Society, 1961.

Morgan, Murray. *The Last Wilderness.* New York: Viking Press, 1955.

————. *The Mill on the Boot: The Story of the St. Paul and Tacoma Lumber Company.* Seattle and London: University of Washington Press, 1982.

Muir, John. *John of the Mountains, The Unpublished Journals of John Muir,* edited by Linnie Marsh Wolfe. Boston: Houghton Mifflin Company, 1938.

————. *Our National Parks.* Boston: Houghton Mifflin Company, 1901.

————. "Washington and Puget Sound," *The Rocky Mountains and the Pacific Slope.* New York, San Francisco: J. Dewing Publishing Co., 1890(?).

————. *The Wilderness World of John Muir.* Boston: Houghton Mifflin Company, 1954.

Nash, Roderic. *Wilderness and the American Mind.* New Haven: Yale University Press, 1967.

National Conservation Congress. *Addresses and Proceedings of the First National Conservation Congress Held at Seattle, Washington August 26–28, 1909.* Washington, D.C.: National Conservation Congress, 1909.

————. *Addresses and Proceedings of the Second National Conservation Congress Held at St. Paul, Minnesota September 8, 1910.* Washington, D.C.: National Conservation Congress, 1911.

————. *Addresses and Proceedings of the Third National Conservation Congress Held at Kansas City, Missouri September 25–27, 1911.* Washington, D.C.: National Conservation Congress, 1912.

National Parks for the Future. Washington, D.C.: Conservation Foundation, 1972.

Nixon, Edgar B., editor and compiler. *Franklin D. Roosevelt and Conservation 1911–1945.* Hyde Park: National Archives and Record Service, Franklin D. Roosevelt Library, 1957.

Norman, Charles. *John Muir, Father of Our National Parks.* New York: Juilian Messner, 1957.

O'Toole, Randal. *Reforming the Forest Service.* Washington, D.C. and Covelo, CA: Island Press, 1988.

Peffer, E. Louise. *The Closing of the Public Domain, Disposal and Reservation Policies 1900–1950.* Stanford: Stanford University Press, 1951.

Penick, James. *Progressive Politics and Conservation — The Ballinger-Pinchot Affair.* Chicago: University of Chicago Press, 1968.

Pinchot, Gifford. *Breaking New Ground.* New York: Harcourt, Brace and Company, 1947.

———. *The Fight for Conservation.* New York: Doubleday, Page and Company, 1910.

———. *The Use Book: Regulations and Instructions for the Use of the National Forest Reserves.* Washington, D.C.: Government Printing Office, 1907–1908.

Progress in the Development of the National Parks. Washington, D.C.: Government Printing Office, 1916.

Reich, Charles A. *Bureaucracy and the Forests.* Santa Barbara: Center for the Study of Demographic Institutions, 1962.

Richardson, Elmo R. *The Politics of Conservation: Crusades and Controversies 1897–1913.* Berkeley, Los Angeles: University of California Press, 1962.

Robbins, Roy M. *Our Landed Heritage: The Public Domain 1776–1970.* Lincoln: University of Nebraska Press, 1976.

Robbins, William G. *Lumberjacks and Legislators: Political Economy of the U.S. Lumber Industry 1890–1941.* College Station: Texas A&M University Press, 1982.

Robinson, Glen O. *The Forest Service: A Study in Public Land Management.* Baltimore: Johns Hopkins University Press, 1975.

Roth, Dennis M. *The Wilderness Movement and the National Forests 1964–1980.* Forest Service History Series. Washington, D.C.: USDA Forest Service, 1984.

Runte, Alfred. *National Parks: The American Experience.* Lincoln and London: University of Nebraska Press, 1984.

Sax, Joseph L. *Mountains Without Handrails: Reflections on the National Parks.* Ann Arbor: University of Michigan Press, 1980.

Shankland, Robert. *Steve Mather of the National Parks.* New York: Alfred A. Knopf, 1954.

Shepard, Paul. *Man in the Landscape: A Historic View of the Esthetics of Nature.* New York: Alfred A. Knopf, 1967.

Steen, Harold K. *The U.S. Forest Service: A History.* Seattle and London: University of Washington Press, 1976.

Swain, Donald C. *Federal Conservation Policy from 1921–1933.* Berkeley and Los Angeles: University of California Press, 1963.

———. *Wilderness Defender: Horace M. Albright and Conservation.* Chicago: University of Chicago Press, 1970.

Trefethen, James B. *Crusade for Wildlife: Highlights in Conservation Progress.* Harrisburg: The Stackpole Company, 1961.

Twight, Ben W. *Organizational Values and Political Power: The Forest Service Versus The Olympic National Park.* University Park and London: Pennsylvania State University Press, 1983.

Van Name, Willard G. *Vanishing Forest Reserves: Problems of the National Forests and National Parks.* Boston: Richard G. Badger Publisher, The Gorham Press, 1929.

Van Syckle, Edwin. *They Tried to Cut it All: Grays Harbor — Turbulent Years of Greed and Greatness.* Aberdeen: Friends of the Aberdeen Public Library, 1980.

Vinnedge, Robert W. *The Pacific Northwest Lumber Industry and Its Development.* New Haven: Yale University Press, 1923.

White, Graham, and John Maze. *Harold Ickes of the New Deal: His Private Life and Public Career.* Cambridge and London: Harvard University Press, 1985.
Wild, Peter. *Enos Mills.* Boise State University Western Writers Series No. 36, 1979.
Wirth, Conrad L. *Parks, Politics and People.* Norman: University of Oklahoma Press, 1980.
Wolfe, Linnie Marsh. *Son of the Wilderness: The Life of John Muir.* New York: Alfred A. Knopf, 1947.

PERIODICALS
Adams, Dr. Charles C. "Ecological Conditions in National Forests and National Parks." *Scientific Monthly,* June 1925.
Albright, Horace M. "The National Park Service's Policy on Predatory Mammals." *Journal of Mammology,* May 1931, 12:185–186.
———. "Our National Parks as Wildlife Sanctuaries." *American Forests,* August 1929, 35:505.
Appleman, Roy E. "Timber Empire from the Public Domain." *Mississippi Valley Historical Review,* September 1939, 26:193.
Bates, J. Leonard. "Fulfilling American Democracy: The Conservation Movement 1907 to 1921." *Mississippi Valley Historical Review,* June 1957, 44:29–57.
Buck, C. J. "The Proposed Mount Olympus National Park." *Journal of Forestry.* September 1936, 34:836–839.
Cahalane, Victor H. "The Evolution of Predator Control Policy in the National Parks." *The Journal of Wildlife Management,* July 1939, 3:229–237.
Chapman, H. H. "Against the Park." *The Puget Sounder,* May/June 1936.
———. "A Program for Private Forestry." *American Forestry,* October 1919, pp. 1405–1406.
Chase, Alston. "Sometimes What Threatens Our Parks Is the Park Service." *Wall Street Journal,* April 8, 1986.
Clark, E. T. "Is Olympic National Park Too Big? — Yes." *American Forests,* September 1954, p. 30.
Clark, Irving. "Mount Olympus National Park — Shall It Be Ravished by Greed and Ruined by Ignorance?" *Town Crier,* July 1935, 30:13.
———. "Protect Olympic Park: Here Are the Facts and the Background." *The Living Wilderness,* June 1947.
Clark, Irving, Jr. "Is Olympic National Park Too Big? — No." *American Forestry,* September 1954, p. 31.
Cowan, C. S. "The Proposed Mount Olympus National Park." *Journal of Forestry,* August 1936, 34:747–749.
Crisler, Lois. "Loggers Loot in the Olympics." *The Christian Century,* July 27, 1955, pp. 867–868.
Curtis, Asahel. "The Proposed Mount Olympus National Park." *American Forests,* April 1936, 42:166–169.
Daniels, Mark. "Mount Rainier National Park." *American Forestry,* September 1916, 22:529–536.
"The Dawn of Conservation." *American Forests,* September 1935, 41:446–451.
Drury, Newton B. "The Olympic National Park — Is It Too Large? No." *University of Washington Forest Club Quarterly 1947–48,* vol. 28, no. 3.
Dusha, Julius. "The Undercover Fight over the Wilderness." *Harper's,* April 1962, 224:55.
"The Economic Necessity for Public Forest Ownership." Editorial, *American Forestry,* February 1917, pp. 110–111.
Edge, Mrs. C. N. "Prosperity and Mount Olympus Park." *The Puget Sounder,* April 1936.
Edge, Mrs. Charles N. "We Were Taken to Task." *Nature,* March 1936, 27:177.
El Comancho. "A Dormant Resource." *Seattle Mail and Herald,* December 17, 1904, 8:33.
Elfring, Chris. "U.S. Parks at a Crossroads." *Bioscience,* May 1986, 36:301–304.
"Extensions of Olympic National Park." *National Parks Bulletin,* July 1940, pp. 20–21.

Foote, James A. "Commercialization and the National Primeval Parks." Editorial, *National Parks Bulletin,* December 1938, pp. 14–15.

———. "Youth on Mount Olympus." *National Parks Bulletin,* December 1937, pp. 10–12.

"The Forest Service Reveals Lumber Industry Conditions." *American Forestry,* February 1917, pp. 105–106.

Freidel, Frank. "Franklin D. Roosevelt in the Northwest." *Pacific Northwest Quarterly,* October 1985.

Fromme, R. L. "The Olympic National Forest — What It Means." *The Mountaineer,* vol. 6, 1913, pp. 9–18.

"For a National Outdoor Recreation Policy." *National Parks Bulletin,* April 30, 1924.

Gill, Tom. "But Who Pays." *Nature,* October 1935, vol. 25–26, pp. 241–242.

Girard, James W. "The Olympic National Park — Is It Too Large? Yes." *University of Washington Forest Club Quarterly,* 1947–48, vol. 28, no. 3.

Graves, Henry S. "Bonding National Forests." *American Forestry,* March 1917, 23:133–138.

———. "A Crisis in National Recreation." *American Forestry,* July 1920.

———. "A Policy of Forestry for the Nation." *American Forestry,* October 1919.

Greeley, William B. "Guarding Our Scenic Heritage." *The Mountaineer,* December 15, 1925, vol. 17, no. 1.

———. "What Shall We Do with Our Mountains." *Sunset,* December 1927, p. 14.

Grinnell, Joseph, and Tracey I. Storer. "Animal Life as an Asset of National Parks." *Science,* September 15, 1916, 44:375–380.

Hanks, Steve H. "Privatize the National Forests." *Wall Street Journal,* August 23, 1988.

Heald, Weldon F. "Shall We Auction Olympic Park." *Natural History,* September 1954, 63:312–320.

"Hold the Olympic Park Intact." Editorial, *National Park Magazine,* July–September 1947, 21:3–4.

Horning, W. H. "The Other Side of Olympus." *Journal of Forestry,* August 1936, 34:750–754.

Houston, David. "The National Forest Enterprises." *American Forestry,* December 1916, 22:750–752.

Humphrey, William E. "Olympic National Monument." *The Mountaineer,* vol. 2, 1909, pp. 41–42.

Ickes, Harold. "Not Guilty: Richard A. Ballinger — An American Dreyfus." *Saturday Evening Post,* May 25, 1940, 212:9–128.

Jones, John. "The Organizational Universe." *The 1981 Annual Handbook for Group Facilitators.* San Diego: University Associates, 1981.

Kneipp, L. F. "Recreational Use of the National Forests." *Journal of Forestry,* May 1930, 28:618–625.

Lane, Franklin K. "National Parks as an Asset." *American Forestry,* January 1916.

Leopold, Aldo. "The Last Stand of the Wilderness." *American Forests and Forest Life,* October 1925, 31:599–604.

Lotszgesell, Mrs. James. "For the Park." *The Puget Sounder,* May–June 1936, vol. 2, no. 5, p. 1.

MacDaniels, E. H. "Timber Supply of Washington and Oregon Placed at 438.1 Billion Feet." *West Coast Lumberman,* January 1946.

McClosky, Michael. "Wilderness Movement at the Crossroads 1945–1970." *Pacific Historical Review,* vol. 41, August 1972, p. 346.

McConnell, Grant. "The Conservation Movement — Past and Present." *Western Political Quarterly,* September 1954, 7:463–478.

———. "The Multiple-Use Concept in Forest Service Policy." *Sierra Club Bulletin,* October 1959, pp. 14–28.

Macy, Preston, and Will Muller. "The Land that Slept Late." *American Forests,* December 1946, 52:568.

Marshall, Robert. "The Problem of the Wilderness." *Scientific Monthly*, February 1930, 30:141–148.

Mather, Stephen Tyng. "The National Parks on a Business Basis." *The American Review of Reviews*, April 1915, 51:429–431.

Mather, Stephen T. "A Glance Backward at National Park Development." *Nature*, August 27, 1927, pp. 112–115.

Meany, Edmond S. "The Olympic National Monument." *The Mountaineer*, 1911, 4:54–59.

———. "Olympics in History and Legend." *The Mountaineer*, 1913, 6:51–55.

Merriam, John C. "The Meaning of the National Parks." *American Forests*, August 1929, 35:471.

Merritt, Dixon. "Exit Greeley: Enter Stuart." *The Outlook*, March 7, 1928, 148:373.

Millard, Bailey. "The West Coast Land Grafters." *Everybody's Magazine*, May 1905, 12:581.

Mills, Enos A. "Exploiting Our National Parks." *The New Republic*, November 10, 1920, p. 272.

———. "Warden of the Nation's Mountain Scenery." *The American Review of Reviews*, April 1915, 51:428.

"Misinformation — A Menace to Conservation." Editorial, *American Forests and Forest Life*, March 1930, 36:161.

Moore, Barrington. "The Proposed Roosevelt Sequoia National Park and the Barbour Bill." *Science*, January 19, 1923, 57:82–84.

"Mount Olympus — Forest or Park?" Editorial, *American Forests*, April 1936, 42:177.

Muir, John. "The American Forests." *Atlantic Monthly*, August 1897, 80:145.

———. "The National Parks and Forest Reservations." *Harper's Weekly*, June 5, 1897, 41:563.

———. "A Plan to Save the Forests." *Century*, February 1895, 49:630–631.

———. "The Wild Parks and Forest Reservations of the West." *Atlantic Monthly*, January 1898, 81:15.

———. "The Yellowstone National Park." *Atlantic Monthly*, April 1898, 81:509.

Murie, Olaus J. "The Olympic Attack." *National Parks Magazine*, July–September 1947, 21:5–7.

———. "The Roosevelt Elk." *American Forests*, April 1936, 42:163–164.

Nash, Roderic. "American Environmental History: A New Teaching Frontier." *Pacific Historical Review*, August 1972, 41:362.

"A National Forest Policy." *American Forestry*, December 1919, pp. 1544–1546.

"National Park Improvement." *The Nation*, February 1, 1919, 108:157.

"National Park Legislation." Editorial, *American Forestry*, April 1917, p. 242.

"A National Park Service." Editorial, *The Independent*, May 29, 1916, 86:321.

"A National Park Service." *The Outlook*, February 3, 1912, 100:246.

"National Park Service Organized." *American Forestry*, June 1917, p. 437.

"National Park Standards — As Required by the Campfire Club of America." *American Forests*, August 1929, 35:476.

"The National Parks: A Conference." *The Outlook*, September 30, 1911, 99:255.

"National Parks and National Forests." Editorial, *American Forests*, August 1929, 35:499.

"National Parks versus National Forests." *American Forestry*, January 1917, 23:48–49.

"National Recreation Enthusiastically Planned." *National Parks Bulletin*, June 10, 1924.

Nelson, E. W. (Chief Bureau of Biological Survey). "Conservation of Game in National Forests and National Parks." *American Forests*, March 1917, 23:139–145.

Neuberger, Richard L. "How Much Conservation?" *Saturday Evening Post*, June 15, 1940, 212:12–13.

———. "The Olympics — Cockpit of Controversy." *American Forests*, December 1947, 53:537.

"New National Parks and Their Administration." Editorial, *American Forestry*, June 1916, 22:366–367.

"The New Olympic National Park." *Colliers*, April 10, 1909, 43:12.

Norcross, Charles P. "Weyerhaeuser — Richer than John D. Rockefeller." *Cosmopolitan*, 42:252–259 (1906–07)

Olmstead, Frederic Law. "The Yosemite Valley and the Mariposa Big Trees, A Preliminary Report, 1865." *Landscape Architecture,* October, 1952, 43(1): 12–25.

"Olympic Forest Reserve." *Scientific American Supplement No. 1365,* March 1, 1902, 53:21882–21883.

"The Olympic Issue." Editorial, *American Forests,* December 1947, 53:535.

"Olympic Park Boundaries Criticized by Washington's Governor." Editorial, *American Forests,* May 1938, 44:220.

"Olympic Park Pot Boils." *The Lumberman,* October 1953, p. 57.

"The Olympic Primitive Area." Editorial, *Pacific Pulp and Paper Industry,* September 1936, 10:16–17.

Osborn, Henry Fairfield. "Preservation of the Wild Animals of North America." *Forest and Stream,* April 16, 1904, 62:312–313.

"Our National Parks and the New Congress." *National Parks Bulletin,* December 1, 1923.

"An Outpost of the Wilderness." *Nature,* July 1935, 25–26:34–37.

Pack, Arthur N. "Let's Get Together." *Nature,* January 1936, 27–28:46–47.

Pack, Arthur Newton. "We are Taken to Task." *Nature,* March 1936, 27:177.

Park, Charles F., Jr. "The Spilite and Manganese Problems of the Olympic Peninsula, Washington." *American Journal of Science,* May 1946, 244:305–323.

Peters, William Harrison. "In the Forests of the Olympics." *American Forests,* April 1936, 42:170–176.

Peyton, J. S. "Progress in National Forestry." *Forestry and Irrigation,* April 1903, 9:194.

Pinchot, Gifford. "How the National Forests Were Won." *American Forests and Forest Life,* October 1930, 36:615–619.

———. "The Forester and the Lumberman." *Forestry and Irrigation,* April 1903, 9:176–178.

———. "A Plan to Save the Forests." *Century,* February 1895, 49:630.

"The Predatory View," *Nature,* April 1955, 48:201.

"Proceedings Meetings of the Ecological Society of America." *Ecology,* April 1922, 3:166–171.

"Proposed Mount Olympus National Park." *Planning and Civic Comment,* January–March 1937, pp. 7–11.

Rakestraw, Lawrence. "Conservation Historiography: An Assessment." *Pacific Historical Review,* August 1972, 41:271.

———. "Sheep Grazing in the Cascade Range: John Minto vs. John Muir." *Pacific Historical Review,* 1958, 27(4): 371–382.

Reed, Franklin. "The Proposed Mount Olympus National Park." *Journal of Forestry,* June 1936, 34:626–628.

Reedy, William Marion. "Our Bureaucratic National Park." *Reedy's Mirror,* St. Louis, March 4, 1920.

Richardson, Elmo R. "Olympic National Park—20 years of Controversy." *Forest History,* April 1968, 12:6–15.

Roloff, Clifford Edwin. "The Mount Olympus National Monument." *Washington Historical Quarterly,* July 1934, 25:214–228.

Roosevelt, Theodore. "The Importance of Practical Forestry." *Forestry and Irrigation,* April 1903, 9:169–172.

———. "A Plan to Save the Forests." *Century,* February 1895, 49:629–630.

"Saving the Yosemite Park." *The Outlook,* January 30, 1909, 91:234–236.

Schmeckebier, Laurence F. "The National Parks from the Scientific and Educational Side." *Popular Science Monthly,* June 1912, 80:530–547.

Schmitz, Henry. "Our Chips Are on the Table." Editorial, *Journal of Forestry,* October 1940, 38:751.

Schulz, William G. "Olympic Wonderland." *Christian Science Monitor Weekly Magazine Section,* December 22, 1937, pp. 8–9.

Schwartz, John E. and Glen E. Michell. "The Roosevelt Elk on the Olympic Peninsula, Washington." *The Journal of Wildlife Management,* October 1945, 9:(4).

"Scientific Notes and News." *Science,* June 25, 1909, 29:995–996.

"Secretary Noble's Monument." Editorial, *Field and Stream,* March 9, 1893.

"Secretary Work Defines National Park Policy." *National Parks Bulletin,* January 21, 1924.

"Shall the National Forests Be Made Self Supporting." Editorial, *American Forestry,* May 1917, 23:305–306.

"Shall We Cheapen Our National Parks." *American Forestry,* February 1917, 23:112–113.

Sherman, A. E. "The Department of Agriculture Replies." *The New Republic,* February 7, 1923, p. 288.

Silcox, F. A. "Forestry—A Public and Private Responsibility." *American Forests,* April 1935, 41:160.

Skow, John. "In Washington: Lighthawk Counts the Clearcuts." *Time,* August 29, 1988.

Smith, George Otis. "The Nation's Playgrounds." *American Review of Reviews,* July 1909, 40:44–48.

Sparhawk, W. N. "The History of Forestry in America." *Trees: The Yearbook of Agriculture 1949,* pp. 702–714.

Sprunt, Alexander, Jr. "What Price—Fish?" *Nature,* October 1935, 25–26:235–236.

Story, Isabelle F. "The New Director." *American Forests,* August 1929, 35:486.

"Strangely Interesting Mountains." *The Northwest Magazine,* February 1899, p. 39.

Stuart, R. Y. "The National Forests Today." *American Forests and Forest Life,* July 1930, 36:405–407.

Swain, Donald C. "Harold Ickes, Horace Albright and the Hundred Days: A Study in Conservation Administration." *Pacific Historical Review,* November 1965, 34:455.

———. "The National Park Service and the New Deal." *Pacific Historical Review,* August 1972, 41:312.

Taylor, Robert Lewis. "Oh Hawk of Mercy!" *New Yorker,* April 17, 1948.

Tomlinson, O. A. "Park Roads that Lead to Scenic Spots." *Washington Motorist,* October 1927, p. 8.

Twight, Ben W. and Fremont J. Lydon. "Multiple Use vs. Organizational Commitment." *Forest Science,* June 1988, vol. 34, no. 2.

Van Name, Willard G. "Danger to the Crater Lake National Park." *Science,* July 23, 1926, p. 91.

———. "A Grab for Half a National Park." *The New Republic,* February 7, 1923, p. 286.

———. "A Menace to the National Parks." *Science,* December 22, 1922, 56:705–707.

———. "The Barbour Roosevelt Sequoia Park Bill." *The New Republic,* February 14, 1923, p. 322.

———. "Letters." *Science,* August 17, 1928, 68:157.

"Wanted a National Park Service." *The Outlook,* March 1, 1916, 112:491.

"Wanted a National Primeval Park Policy." Editorial, *National Parks Bulletin,* December 1937, p. 13.

Ward, Henry Baldwin. "Origin and Objectives of the National Parks Association." *National Parks Bulletin,* July 1940, pp. 5–6.

———. "Maintaining the Standards and Scientific Usefulness of the National Parks." *Science,* January 4, 1929, 69:14–15.

Waver, Roland H. and William R. Supernough. "Wildlife Management in the National Parks—An Historical Perspective." *National Parks Bulletin,* July–August 1983, pp. 12–13.

Waugh, Frank H. "A National Park Policy." *Scientific Monthly,* April 1918, 6:305–318.

———. "Technical Problems in National Park Development." *The Scientific Monthly,* June 1918, 6:560–567.

Wharton, William P. "Preservation Requires Classification." Editorial, *National Parks Bulletin,* July 1940, pp. 3–4.

_____. "Why National Primeval Parks." *National Parks Bulletin,* December 1938, pp. 3–7.

"Where Experts Disagree." *The Outlook,* March 23, 1923, p. 567.

Wickersham, James. "A National Park in the Olympics . . . 1890." *The Living Wilderness,* Summer–Fall 1961.

Wilbur, Ray Lyman. "National Parks — An American Institution." *American Forests,* August 1929, 35:451.

Wilkinson, Charles F., and H. Michael Anderson. "Land and Resource Planning in the National Forests." *Oregon Law Review,* vol. 64, 1985.

Willis, Bailey. "The Mount Rainier National Park." *The Forester,* May 1899, 5:97–103.

Wood, Robert L. "Keep This Wilderness." *National Parks Magazine,* April–June 1949, 23:26–27.

Yard, Robert Sterling. "The National Parks Peril." *The Nation,* August 21, 1920, 3:208.

"The Yellowstone Grab." *The Outlook,* December 29, 1926.

Yeon, John B. "The Issue of the Olympics." *American Forests,* June 1936, 42:255–257.

Zalesky, Philip. "Mountaineer Conservation: Contribution to Destiny." *The Mountaineer,* 1966, pp. 53–93.

MANUSCRIPTS

Beezley, B. F. *Report of Investigation to Determine Eligibility of Dosewallips — East Fork Route and North Fork — Elwha for Classification as Forest Highway.* Olympic National Forest, September 1926, Bureau of Public Roads.

Beyers, William B. *An Economic Impact Study of Mt. Rainier and Olympic National Parks.* Department of Geography, University of Washington, February 1970.

Brant, Irving. *Adventures in Conservation.* Autobiographical account of the conservation activities of Brant's career. This manuscript, edited and shortened, has been published under the title *Adventures in Conservation with Franklin D. Roosevelt.* Flagstaff: Northland Publishing, 1988.

A Brief Asking the Federal Forest Service for the Allocation of Timber in the Olympic National Forest. March 1, 1929, Chambers of Commerce of Grays Harbor County.

Cox, John H. *Organization of the Lumber Industry in the Pacific Northwest,* Ph.D. dissertation, University of California, 1937.

Edge, Rosalie. *An Implacable Widow.* Autobiographical account of Edge's conservation activities.

Fringer, Guy. *Olympic National Park Administrative History.* National Park Service, 1986.

Gilligan, James. *Wilderness Policy Development in the United States.* Ph.D. dissertation, University of Michigan, 1954.

Graves, Henry S. *Need for Practice of Forestry on Private Lands.* Unpublished manuscript in H. L. Plumb papers.

Horning, W. H. *The Proposed Mount Olympus National Park and Its Probable Effect upon the Olympic National Forest and the Economic Interests of the Olympic Peninsula.* National Park Service, July 1936.

Hrubes, Robert John. *The USDA Forest Service in the Environmental Era: Institutional and Pragmatic Change.* Ph.D. dissertation, University of California, Berkeley, 1981.

Ingham, Meredith B., Jr. *Olympic National Park — A Study of Conservation Objectives Relating to Its Establishment and Boundary Adjustments.* National Park Service, 1956.

McCormick, Jack, and Associates. *Cultural Resource Overview of the Olympic National Forest, Washington,* 1978.

Mumaw, W. C. *The Possibilities of a Pulp Development on Grays Harbor.* Aberdeen, 1943. In H. L. Plumb papers.

Munger, Thornton T. "Recollections of My Thirty-eight Years in the Forest Service, 1908–1946." *Timber Lines,* Portland: Region Six Forest Service Thirty-year Club, 1962. Supplement to Volume XVI, December 1962.

O'Leary, Joseph Thomas. *Community Conflict and Adaption: An Examination of Community Response to Change in Natural Resource Management and Policy Strategies.* Ph.D. dissertation, University of Washington, 1974.

Overly, Fred J. *Sitka Spruce in Olympic National Park.* National Park Service, April 25, 1941.

Overly, Fred, and Jack Dodd. *Sitka Spruce in the Olympic Acquisition Area.* National Park Service, February 14, 1941.

_____. *Review of the Economic Availability of Timber in Olympic National Park 1947.* National Park Service, April 1947.

Plumb, H. L. *Memorandum Regarding the Creation of Olympic National Park.* 1953. In H. L. Plum papers.

Rakestraw, Lawrence. *A History of Forest Conservation in the Northwest 1891–1913.* Ph.D. dissertation, University of Washington, 1955.

Renton, Donald A. *Preference Representation and Conflict in the U.S. Forest Service.* Ph.D. dissertation, Colorado State University, 1975.

Sample, Tex S. *Paradigm on Consensus and Conflict Strategies: A Polar Typology.* A thirteen-page manuscript otherwise unidentified.

Sarlin, Reino R. *The Availability of Vital Woods which Can Be Contributed to War Needs by the National Park Service Within the Olympic Peninsula.* National Park Service, November 1942.

_____. *Preliminary Report on the Availability of Sitka Spruce and Douglas Fir in the Queets Corridor Section of the Olympic Public Works Project for National Defense Requirements.* National Park Service, July 1942.

_____. *Spruce Aircraft Lumber Recovery, Based on the Berfield Method of Log Riving.* National Park Service, January 1944.

Schwartz, John E. *Range Conditions and Management of the Roosevelt Elk on the Olympic Peninsula.* U.S. Forest Service, undated, early 1940's.

Sheltmire, Jack C. *The Contributions of Gifford Pinchot to the Development of the Contemporary Philosophy of Outdoor Recreation on Public Lands.* Ph.D. dissertation, State University of New York, 1981.

Skinner, Milton P. *Report on Roosevelt Elk, Olympic Peninsula, Washington.* Prepared for the Committee on the Olympic Peninsula of the Boone and Crockett Club, New York, 1934.

Sommarstrom, Alan Ralph. *The Impact of Human Use on Recreational Quality: The Example of the Olympic National Park Backcountry User.* M.A. thesis, University of Washington, 1966.

Twight, Ben Whitfield. *The Tenacity of Value Commitment: The Forest Service and the Olympic National Park.* Ph.D. dissertation, University of Washington, 1971.

Van Name, Willard G. *Report on Forests and Wildlife Protection in the Olympic Peninsula, Washington.* Submitted to Olympic Peninsula Committee of the Boone and Crockett Club, New York, 1932.

PAMPHLETS

The Administration of the National Parks. The Mountaineers, 1922, WLJ.

Brant, Irving, *Compromised Conservation—Can the Audubon Society Explain?* ECC October 1930, 2nd ed., September, 1931, CL.

_____. *The Olympic Forests for a National Park.* ECC pub. #68, January 1938, CL.

_____. *Protect the Roosevelt Elk.* ECC, March, 1938 (eight-page abstract from *The Olympic Forests for a National Park*), CL.

_____. *Shotgun Conservation.* ECC, October 1931, CL.

_____. *Unsportsmanlike Sportsmen.* ECC, February, 1931, CL.

Clark, Irving. *Our Olympic Heritage and its Defense.* Reprint from June 1947 issue of *The Living Wilderness,* Wilderness Society.

_____. *Will the Olympic National Park Get the Ax?* The Committee to Save Olympic National Park, 1947, CL.

Edge, Rosalie. *The Audubon Steel Trapping Sanctuary.* ECC, September, 1934, CL.

———. *Conservation—Come and Get It.* ECC Report for 1938, March 1939, CL.

———. *Conservation for Victory.* ECC Report for 1942, April, 1943, CL.

———. *Double Crossing Mount Olympus National Park.* ECC, March 1937, CL.

———. *Our Nation's Forests.* ECC pub. #73, September 1938, CL.

———. *The Raid of the Nation's Olympic Forests.* ECC, 1947, CL.

———. *Roads and More Roads in the National Parks and National Forests.* ECC, March, 1936, CL.

———. *The Slaughter of the Yellowstone Park Pelicans,* ECC, March, 1936, CL.

———. *Steel Trapping by the Audubon Association.* ECC, September, 1932, CL.

———. *Twelve Immediately Important Problems of the National parks and Wildlife Conservation.* ECC, June, 1935, CL.

Investigate Please. Joint publication of Grays Harbor Industries and Port Angeles Chamber of Commerce, 1948, CL. (No identification of source on this timber-industry pamphlet.)

An Olympic Peninsula Answer to the Wallgren Bill HR 7086. Olympic Peninsula Conservation Committee of Clallam, Grays Harbor, Jefferson and Mason Counties, 1936, CL. (The only known reference to this committee is on this timber-industry pamphlet.)

The Olympic National Park: Is it Too Large? No Says Newton B. Drury. Distributor unknown (reprint from University of Washington Forest Club Quarterly, vol. 21, no. 3, 1947–48).

"A Park for Mt. Olympus." ECC editorial reprint from *New York Herald Tribune,* March 22, 1936.

Thompson, Margaret. *A Real or a Sham Park in the Olympic Peninsula.* Bulletin of the Northwest Conservation League, January 1937.

Trouble on Olympus: A Defense of Olympic National Park. Sierra Club, 1947, CL.

Van Name, Willard G. *A Crisis in Conservation.* ECC, June, 1929, CL. (Also signed by W. DeWitt Miller and David Quinn.)

Van Name, Willard G. *Doomed Yosemite Forests,* ECC, December, 1931, Anonymous, CL.

———. *Hands Off the National Parks.* Privately published, February, 1926, HW.

———. *It's Alive! Kill It! The Present Policy Towards Native Birds and Animals of North America.* ECC, April, 1932, 2nd printing, May 1932, Anonymous, CL.

———. *Logging Operations in the Yosemite National Park.* Privately published, June, 1926, HW.

———. *A New Raid on the Yosemite National Park.* Privately published, November, 1927, HW.

———. *The Proposed Olympic National Park.* ECC, April, 1934, Anonymous, CL.

———. *Raid on Yellowstone National Park.* Privately published, February, 1929, HW.

———. *The Redwood Mountain Sequoia Grove.* Privately published, February, 1927, HW.

———. *Save the Yosemite Sugar Pines.* ECC, October, 1932, Anonymous, CL.

———. *The Sequoia National Park.* Privately published, February, 1927, HW.

———. *The United States Biological Survey: Destruction, Not Scientific Investigation and Conservation, Now its Chief Activity.* ECC, May, 1930, Anonymous, CL.

———. *The United States Bureau of Destruction and Extermination—The Misnamed and Perverted "Biological Survey."* ECC, September, 1934, Anonymous, CL.

GOVERNMENT DOCUMENTS

Dodwell, Arthur, and Theodore Rixon. *The Olympic Forest Reserve, Washington.* Washington, D.C.: Government Printing Office, 1900.

U.S. Congress. House. *Annual Report of the Commissioner of the General Land Office for 1901.* 57th Cong., 1st sess., H. Doc. 5, Serial 4289.

Dodwell, Arthur, and Theodore Rixon. *Forest Conditions in the Olympic Forest Reserve, Washington.* Washington, D.C.: Government Printing Office, 1902.

U.S. Congress. House. *Annual Report of the Commissioner of the General Land Office for 1902.* 57th Cong., 2nd sess., H. Doc. 5, Serial 4457.

426 *Bibliography*

U.S. Congress. Senate. *Investigations of the Department of Interior and the Bureau of Forestry, January–April, 1910.* 61st Cong., 3rd sess., S. Doc. 719.

Proceedings of the National Park Conference held at the Yellowstone National Park, September 11 and 12, 1911. Washington, D.C.: Government Printing Office, 1912.

U.S. Congress. Senate. *Hearings Before the Committee on the Public Lands on S. 3463, a Bill to Establish a Bureau of National Parks, April 17, 1912.* 62nd Cong., 2nd sess., Washington, D.C.: Government Printing Office, 1912.

Proceedings of the National Parks Conference Held at Yosemite National Park, October 14, 15 and 16, 1912. Washington, D.C.: Government Printing Office, 1913.

U.S. Congress. House. *Hetch Hetchy Dam Site Hearing on HR 6281 Before the Committee on the Public Lands, June 25, 1913.* 63rd Cong., 1st sess., Washington, D.C.: Government Printing Office, 1913.

U.S. Congress. House. *Hearing Before the Committee on the Public Lands on HR 104, a Bill to Establish a National Park Service, April 29, 1914.* 63rd Cong., 2nd sess., Washington, D.C.: Government Printing Office, 1914.

Proceedings of the National Park Conference held at Berkeley, California, March 11, 12 and 13, 1915. Washington, D.C.: Government Printing Office, 1915.

Mather, Stephen T. *Progress in the Development of the National Parks.* Washington, D.C.: Government Printing Office, 1916.

U.S. Congress. House. *Hearing Before the Committee on the Public Lands on HR 434 and HR 8668, Bills to Establish a National Park Service, April 5 and 6, 1916.* 64th Cong., 1st sess., Washington, D.C.: Government Printing Office, 1916.

Proceedings of the National Parks Conference Held in the Auditorium of the New National Museum, January 2–6, 1917. Washington, D.C.: Government Printing Office, 1917.

U.S. Congress. Senate. *Proceedings of the National Conference on Outdoor Recreation, 1924.* 68th Cong., 1st sess., S. Doc 151. Washington, D.C.: Government Printing Office, 1924.

Proceedings of the Meeting of the Advisory Council of the National Conference on Outdoor Recreation Held in the Assembly Hall of the American Red Cross Building, Washington, D.C., December 11 and 12, 1924. 68th Cong., 2nd sess., 1925, S. Doc. 229. Washington, D.C.: Government Printing Office, 1925.

Report of the Joint Committee on Recreational Survey of Federal Lands of the American Forestry Association and the National Parks Association to the National Conference on Outdoor Recreation. Washington, D.C.: National Conference on Outdoor Recreation, 1928.

U.S. Congress. Senate. *Deforested America: Statement of the Present Forest Service Situation in the United States. Report prepared by George P. Ahern.* 70th Cong., 2nd sess., 1929, S. Doc. 216. Washington, D.C.: Government Printing Office, 1929.

————. *A National Plan for Forestry: The Report of the Forest Service of the Agriculture Department on the Forest Problems of the United States.* 73rd Cong., 1st sess., 1933, S. Doc. 12. Washington, D.C.: Government Printing Office, 1933.

Wright, George M., and Ben H. Thompson. *Wildlife Management in the National Parks.* Washington, D.C.: Government Printing Office, 1935.

The Proposed Mount Olympus National Park: A Land Use Study of Public Lands on the Olympic Peninsula. Olympia: Washington State Planning Council, 1936.

U.S. Congress. House. *Mount Olympus National Park Hearing Before the Committee on the Public Lands on HR 7086, April 23–May 5, 1936.* 74th Cong., 2nd sess., Washington, D.C.: Government Printing Office, 1936.

Brant, Irving. *Report on the Enlargement of Olympic National Park.* Library of Congress, 1938.

U.S. Congress. House. *Hearings Before the Committee on the Public Lands on HR 10024 to Establish the Olympic National Park in the State of Washington, April 19, 1938.* 75th Cong., 3rd sess. Washington, D.C.: Government Printing Office, 1938.

U.S. Congress. Senate. *Forest Lands of the United States: Report of the Joint Committee on Forestry.* 77th Cong., 1st sess., S. Doc. 32. Washington, D.C.: Government Printing Office, 1941.

U.S. Congress. House. *Hearings Before the Committee on Public Lands Pursuant to HR 93, September 16 and 17, 1947.* Lake Crescent, Washington. 80th Cong., 2nd sess., Washington, D.C.: Government Printing Office, 1948.

Rogers, Edmund B. (compiler). *History of Legislation Relating to the National Park System Through the 82nd Congress.* National Park Service, 1958.

Compilation of the Administrative Policies for the National Parks and National Monuments of Scientific Significance. Washington, D.C.: Government Printing Office, 1968.

MANUSCRIPT AND OTHER COLLECTIONS

I would like to thank the many staff members from the libraries and archives below for the generous and courteous assistance that was always available to me. Special thanks has to go to Karyl Winn and her staff in the Manuscript Division of the University of Washington library, which was the major depository for the data in this study. Without their supportive assistance this book could not have been written.

Thomas T. Aldwell papers, Manuscript Division, Library, University of Washington, Seattle, Washington.

American Museum of Natural History, Mammal Department files, New York.

Board of Geographic Names files, Reston, Virginia.

Irving Brant papers, Manuscript Division, Library of Congress and selected parts on microfilm, Manuscript Division, Library, University of Washington, Seattle, Washington.

Richard Brooks, Olympic papers in possession of the author.

Irving Clark papers, Manuscript Division, Library, University of Washington, Seattle, Washington.

College of Forest Resources, University Archives, University of Washington, Seattle, Washington.

Asahel Curtis papers, Manuscript Division, Library, University of Washington, Seattle, Washington.

Emergency Conservation Committee files, New York, now in the possession of the Western History Department of the Denver Public Library.

Brock Evans papers, Manuscript Division, Library, University of Washington, Seattle, Washington.

Forest Service, Washington, D.C.

Forest Service, Regional files, Seattle, Washington.

Rudo L. Fromme papers, Manuscript Division, Library, University of Washington, Seattle, Washington.

Glenn Gallison papers, in possession of Gallison, Port Angeles, Washington.

Emily Haig, Olympic papers in possession of the author.

Henry M. Jackson papers, Manuscript Division, Library, University of Washington, Seattle, Washington.

Wesley L. Jones papers, Manuscript Division, Library, University of Washington, Seattle, Washington.

Carsten Lien papers, in possession of the author, Seattle, Washington.

Preston P. Macy papers, Manuscript Division, Library, University of Washington, Seattle, Washington.

Warren G. Magnuson papers, Manuscript Division, Library, University of Washington, Seattle, Washington.

Gordon Marckworth papers, University Archives, University of Washington, Seattle, Washington.

Elliot Marks Olympic papers, relevant copies in possession of author.

Edmond S. Meany papers, University Archives, University of Washington, Seattle, Washington.

Hugh B. Mitchell papers, Manuscript Division, Library, University of Washington, Seattle, Washington.

National Archives, Washington, D.C., and Seattle, Washington.

National Park Service, National Archives, Washington, D.C.

National Park Service, Regional files, National Archives, Seattle, Washington.

Olympic National Forest, Region Six, National Archives, Seattle, Washington.

Olympic National Park, Port Angeles, Washington.

John Osseward papers, Manuscript Division, Library, University of Washington, Seattle, Washington.

Fred Overly papers, Manuscript Division, Library, University of Washington, Seattle, Washington.

Pacific Northwest Loggers Association, Manuscript Division, Library, University of Washington, Seattle, Washington.

Gifford Pinchot papers, Library of Congress, Washington, D.C.

Herbert L. Plumb papers, Manuscript Division, Library, University of Washington, Seattle, Washington.

Paul Shepard Olympic papers, in possession of author.

Sierra Club papers, Manuscript Division, Library, University of Washington, Seattle, Washington.

Owen A. Tomlinson papers, in possession of author.

Ben Twight papers, Manuscript Division, Library, University of Washington, Seattle, Washington.

United States Forest Service, National Archives, Washington, D.C.

Washington State Archives, Olympia, Washington.

Washington State Historical Society, Tacoma, Washington.

Hugo Winkenwerder papers, University Archives, University of Washington, Seattle, Washington.

Philip H. Zalesky papers, Manuscript Division, Library, University of Washington, Seattle, Washington.

EMERGENCY CONSERVATION COMMITTEE PUBLICATIONS

An analysis of the archives and the publications of the ECC suggests it was involved in seven distinct conservation thrusts. For ease of reference, the publications of the ECC have been categorized into these same seven categories plus two additional categories: one to contain the annual reports which themselves were issued as conservation documents and a list of Willard Van Name's printed published pamphlets. Authorship was often omitted from the ECC's pamphlets, especially from those authored by Willard Van Name, so authorship as indicated here is sometimes from sources other than the pamphlets themselves. A complete set of the ECC pamphlets is available in the Special Collections Division of the University of Washington library, a gift of Peter Edge.

REFORMING THE NATIONAL AUDUBON SOCIETY

Baldwin, Roger, Irving Brant, and Rosalie Edge. *To the Members of the National Association of Audubon Societies.* August, 1932.

Baldwin, Roger, Irving Brant, and Davis Quinn (Van Name). *To the Members of the National Association of Audubon Societies.* September, 1932.

Baldwin, Roger, Irving Brant, Rosalie Edge, and Davis Quinn (Van Name). *To the Members of the National Association of Audubon Societies.* September, 1932.

Brant, Irving, *Compromised Conservation: Can the Audubon Society Explain?* Pub #6, October, 1930; Second Edition, Pub #14, September, 1931.

Breck, Mrs. Edward. *Blood Money for the Audubon Association.* Pub #33, reprinted by the ECC from *Anti Steel Trap News,* December, 1932, Journal of the Anti Steel Trap League, Washington, D.C.

Edge, Rosalie. *The Audubon Steel-Trapping Sanctuary.* Pub #38, September, 1934.

_____. *The Ducks and the Democracy.* Pub #87, 1942 (also listed under Saving the Waterfowl).

_____. *Live and Let Live.* Newsletter No. 1, Pub #39, August 1934 (also listed under Changing Public Policy — multi-topic).

_____. *To the Members of the National Association of Audubon Societies.* October, 1933.

_____. *Steel Trapping by the Audubon Association.* Pub #26, November, 1933.

Van Name, Willard G. *A Crisis in Conservation.* Pub #1, June 1928. Also signed by DeWitt Miller and Davis Quinn but authorship was Van Name's. A second edition, same date, was issued for the New Jersey Audubon Society. A fourth edition, Pub #13, September, 1931, was targeted for Audubon Society members.

SAVING THE WATERFOWL AND MIGRATORY BIRDS

Brant, Irving. *The Collapse of Waterfowl Protection: Danger of Immediate Extinction of Various Species.* Pub #50, June, 1935.

_____. *The Drought-Stricken Waterfowl: An Open Letter.* Pub #57 July, 1936, (broadside).

_____. *The Future of Waterfowl Protection.* January, 1936. A paper read by Brant at the Wilson Ornithological Club, December 30, 1935.

_____. *The Last Plea for Waterfowl.* Pub #28, January, 1934.

_____. *Shotgun Conservation.* Pub #12, October, 1931.

_____. *"Sportsmen's" Heaven is Hell for Ducks.* Pub #71, June, 1938.

_____. *To the Rescue of the Waterfowl.* Pub #91, January, 1945.

_____. *Unsportsmanlike Sportsmen.* Pub #8, February, 1931.

_____. *Waterfowl and Common Sense.* Pub #64, April, 1937.

Edge, Mrs. C.N. *Baiting and Live Decoys.* Pub #10, June, 1931.

Edge, Rosalie. *The Ducks and the Democracy.* Pub #87, 1942 (also listed under Reforming the National Audubon Society).

_____. *For Your Information.* September, 1931 (broadside).

Edge, Mrs. C.N. *Gambling with the Ducks.* Pub #82, February, 1941.

Edge, Rosalie. *Good News on Wildfowl.* October, 1933 (broadside).

_____. *Montana's Sanctuary for Duck Killers.* Pub #33, April, 1934.

_____. *Souvenir of the American Wildlife Conference.* April, 1942.

Edge, Mrs. C.N. *To Save the Trumpeter Swan.* Pub #83, February, 1941.

_____. *Waterfowl Crisis.* Broadside opposing S.3611 to permit baiting (no date).

Edge, Rosalie, *The Waterfowl Are Yours.* Pub #52, January, 1936.

_____. *The Wildfowl Get a Raw Deal.* Pub #40, April, 1934.

Hornaday, Dr. William T. *Is It "Good-bye" to America's Waterfowl?* Pub #45, March, 1935.

Lumley, Ellsworth D. *The Shortage of Waterfowl.* Unit 1 of Teaching Units 1940 (also listed under Teaching Conservation).

Talbot, L. Raymond. *Where Do You Stand on the Matter of Shooting?* Pub #44, reprinted from the Brookline Bird Club Bulletin (no date).

SAVING TREES AND MAKING PARKS

Brant, Irving. *The Olympic Forests for a National Park.* Pub #68, January, 1938. Second printing, Pub #68A, February 1938.

_____. *The Proposed John Muir--Kings Canyon National Park.* Pub #74, January, 1939.

_____. *Protect the Roosevelt Elk.* Pub #69, March, 1938. An extract from *The Olympic Forests . . .* (also listed under Saving Mammals). Special separate editions were made for the New York Zoological Society, The American Wildlife Institute, The American Bison Society and Jay N. Darling.

_____. *Protect the South Calaveras Sequoia Grove.* Pub #86, June, 1942.

Edge, Mrs. C.N. *Double Crossing Mount Olympus National Park.* Pub #63, March, 1937.

Edge, Rosalie. *The Impending Ruin of Kings Canyon.* Pub #77, June, 1939.

_____. *Latest Information on the Olympic Park Bills.* Pub #69A, March, 1938 (broadside).

_____. *Our Nation's Forests.* Pub #73, September, 1938 Teaching Unit 6 (also listed under Teaching Conservation).

_____. *The Raid on the Nation's Olympic Forests.* Pub #93, 1947.

Edge, Mrs. C.N. *Save Kings Canyon From Power Dams.* Pub #76, April, 1939 (broadside).

_____. *The Wallgren Mount Olympus National Park Bill HR 7086.* Pub #49, June, 1935.

McAtee, W.L. *The Grandeur of the Mighty Tree.* Pub #62, February, 1937.

Van Name, Willard G. *Doomed Yosemite Forests.* Pub #15, December, 1931.

_____. *The Proposed Olympic National Park.* Pub #35, April, 1934. Second edition, Pub #35A, June, 1934.

_____. *Save the Yosemite Sugar Pines.* Pub #21, October, 1932.

Unknown author. *A Hemlock National Park.* Editorial reprint from *New York Herald Tribune,* March 17, 1938.

_____. *A Park for Mt. Olympus.* Editorial reprint from *New York Herald Tribune,* Pub #55, March 22, 1936.

SAVING BIRDS OF PREY, FISH EATERS AND SCAVENGERS

Broun, Maurice. *The First Hawk Sanctuary.* Reprint from January, 1935, issue of the Bulletin of the Massachusetts Audubon Society, December, 1934.

_____. *Three Seasons at Hawk Mountain Sanctuary.* Pub #61, a paper read by Broun at the Wilson Ornithological Club, Chicago, November 17, 1936.

Edge, Mrs. C.N. *Blacker Thou the Crow.* Pub #23, February, 1933.

Edge, Rosalie. *The Duck Hawk and the Falconers.* Pub #90, April, 1944.

Edge, Mrs. C.N. *The Slaughter of the Yellowstone Park Pelicans.* Pub #20, September, 1932.

Edge, Rosalie. *The White Pelicans of Great Salt Lake.* Pub #47, May, 1935.

Edge, Rosalie, and Ellsworth D. Lumley. *Common Hawks of North America.* Pub #81, September, 1940.

Edge, Mrs. C.N., and Ellsworth D. Lumley. *Man's Friend: The Crow.* Pub #65, September, 1937.

Lumley, Ellsworth D. *Eagles.* Unit 3 of Teaching Units, February, 1935 (also listed under Teaching Conservation).

_____. *Fish Eating Birds.* Unit 4 of Teaching Units, May, 1935 (also listed under Teaching Conservation).

_____. *Hawks.* Unit 2 of Teaching Units, March, 1934 (also listed under Teaching Conservation).

_____. *Owls.* Unit 5 of Teaching Units, September, 1937 (also listed under Teaching Conservation).

_____. *Save Our Hawks: We Need Them.* (undated).

_____. *The Two Eagles of North America.* Unit 3 of Teaching Units. Revision of earlier *Eagles,* 1939 (also listed under Teaching Conservation).

McAtee, W.L. *Preface to Fish Eating Birds.* Pub #51, May, 1935.

Reed, Charles A., and Michael Kelly. *The Hawk* by Reed and *The Caged Falcon* by Kelly, a pamphlet in memory of Ellsworth D. Lumley on the occasion of his death, 1950.

Roosevelt, Franklin D. Broadside reproduction of a letter to Irving Brant praising Conservation Teaching Unit 3, *Eagles.*

Van Name, Willard G. *The Bald Eagle, Our National Emblem.* Pub #4, April, 1930.

_____. *Framing the Birds of Prey.* Pub #3, December, 1929, signed by Davis Quinn fronting for Van Name but was authored solely by Van Name. Revised in a fourth edition April, 1932, Pub #15 and as Pub #55 in a fifth edition, April 1936, also signed by Davis Quinn.

_____. *The Last of the White Pelican.* Pub #111, June, 1931.

_____. *Save the Bald Eagle! Shall We Allow Our National Emblem to Become Extinct?* Pub #41, January, 1935.

Unknown author. *Enter Hawk—Exit Mouse.* No file copy available.

_____. *Peace at Hawk Mountain Sanctuary.* No file copy available.

SAVING MAMMALS

Brant, Irving. *Protect the Roosevelt Elk.* Pub #69, March, 1938, an extract from *The Olympic Forests for a National Park,* March, 1938 (also listed under Saving Trees and Making Parks).

Edge, Rosalie. *Finishing the Mammals.* Pub #59, October, 1936.

Edge, Rosalie, and Dick Randall. *The Tragic Truth About Elk.* Pub #32, April, 1934.

Hall, E. Raymond. *The Coyote and His Control.* Reprint from April, 1934, issue of *Outdoor Life.*

McGuire, Harry. *Goodbye, Old Grizzly.* Reprint of an editorial in October, 1933 issue of *Outdoor Life.*

_____. *Sham Protection for the Alaskan Brown Bear.* Reprint from the February and March issues of *Outdoor Life* (undated).

Van Name, Willard G. *The Antelope's SOS.* Pub #7, October, 1930, signed by Davis Quinn, fronting for Van Name.

_____. *Disaster to the Yellowstone Park Elk Herds.* December, 1933.

CHANGING PUBLIC POLICY

Brant, Irving. *Your Land and Mine: An Open Letter to Governor Dewey.* Reprint from the *New York Star,* July 28, 1948.

Edge, Rosalie. *Defiance of State and Federal Governments by the Pickering Lumber Company,* April, 1915 (broadside).

_____. *Important Bills Pending in the New York State Legislature.* March, 1950 (broadside).

_____. *Live and Let Live.* Newsletter no. 1, August 13, 1934 (also listed under Reforming the National Audobon Society—multitopic).

_____. *The Migratory Bird Treaty with Mexico,* Pub #56, May, 1936.

_____. *Preserve the Lake Region between Minnesota and Ontario.* June, 1933 (broadside).

_____. *Roads and More Roads in the National Parks and National Forests.* Pub #54, March, 1936.

Edge, Mrs. C.N. *Twelve Immediately Important Problems of the National Parks and Wildlife Conservation.* Pub #48, May, 1935.

_____. *The Wily and Wasteful Proposal for the Echo Park Dam.* Pub #94, March, 1955.

Edge, Rosalie. *Yellowstone Park Is in Danger.* May 12, 1938 (broadside).

McAtee, W.L. *Conservation of Game or of Wildlife—Which?* Reprint from *The Scientific Monthly* (no date).

_____. *A Little Lesson on Vermin.* Pub #17, reprint from *Bird Lore* (undated—early 1930's).

_____. *Sanctuary—Do We Mean It,* Pub #37, September, 1934.

McGuire, Harry. *Behold—The Innocent Blatter!* Reprint from February, 1934 issue of *Outdoor Life,* opposes sheep in the National Forests.

_____. *Who Is Right About Poisoning?* Reprint from December 1932 issue of *Outdoor Life.*

Oberholtzer, Ernest C. *The Challenge of the Border Lakes.* Reprint from April–May 1933 issue of *Outdoor America.* Mailed with Edge broadside *Preserve the Lake Region* . . .

Van Name, Willard G. *Hands Off Yellowstone Lake.* Pub #25, February, 1933.

_____. *It's Alive!—Kill It! The Present Policy Toward Native Birds and Animals of North America.* Pub #19, April, 1932. Second edition, May, 1932.

_____. *Poison for Our Wildlife: An Answer to the Biological Survey.* Pub #9, May, 1931.

_____. *The United States Biological Survey: Destruction, Not Scientific Investigation and Conservation, Now Its Chief Activity.* Pub #5, May, 1930.

_____. *The United States Bureau of Destruction and Extermination: The Misnamed and Perverted "Biological Survey."* Pub #36, September, 1934.

Unknown author. *Grasshoppers.* Editorial reprint from *St. Louis Star* of August 5, 1931, regarding Biological Survey use of poison (author probably Irving Brant).

_____. *The Poisoner Again.* Reprint from *Outdoor Life,* no file copy available.

_____. *Report of the Special Committee on Predatory Mammal Control.* No file copy available.

TEACHING CONSERVATION

Lumley, Ellsworth D. *The Shortage of Waterfowl.* Unit 1, Pub #30, March, 1934. Revised as Pub #58, September, 1936 and as Pub #79 in 1940.

_____. *Hawks.* Unit 2, Pub #31, March, 1934. Second edition Pub #66, September, 1937.

_____. *Eagles.* Unit 3, Pub #43, February, 1935. Revised as *The Two Eagles of North America,* Pub #78, 1939.

_____. *The Fish Eating Birds.* Unit 4, Pub #46, May, 1935. Revised as Pub #72 (no date).

_____. *Owls.* Unit 5, Pub #67, September, 1937.

Edge, Rosalie. *Our Nation's Forests.* Unit 6, September, 1938.

Tippett, James S. *Research Is Needed to Determine Educational Procedure in Conservation.* Broadside (no date).

ECC ANNUAL REPORTS

Edge, Rosalie. *Conservation Today.* Pub #24, Report for 1932.

_____. *Emergency Conservation Committee Report for 1933.* Pub #24, February, 1934.

_____. *Fighting the Good Fight.* Pub #42, Report for 1934, February, 1935.

_____. *Forward into Battle.* Pub #53, Report for 1935, January, 1936.

_____. *Facing Conservation Facts.* Pub #60, Report for 1936, January, 1937.

_____. *The Advance of Conservation.* Pub #70, Report for 1937, March, 1938.

_____. *Conservation—Come and Get It.* Pub #75, Report for 1938, March, 1939.

_____. *Conservation—How It Works.* Pub #80, Report for 1939, March, 1940.

_____. *Conservation and Defense.* Pub #84, Report for 1940, April, 1941.

_____. *Conservation by the People.* Pub #85, Report for 1941, February, 1942.

_____. *Conservation for Victory.* Pub #88, Report for 1942, April, 1943.

_____. *Conservation in Action.* Pub #89, Report for 1943, April, 1944.

_____. *Conservation—Up and Doing.* Pub #92, Report for 1944, April, 1945.

Unable to categorize and unknown authorship:
An International Appeal, no file copy available.
Is Nature Wasting Safe? no file copy available.

WILLARD VAN NAME'S PRE-ECC PAMPHLETS

The Emergency Conservation Committee was created originally to enable Willard Van Name to continue his pamphleteering by providing the cover he needed to retain his position at the American Museum of Natural History. Because Van Name's pamphlets provided the ECC with its pamphleteering model when it started in 1930, his pamphlets are listed here in the order they appeared. All of them were published and distributed by Van Name with his own money.

February 1926, *Hands Off the National Parks*
June 1926, *Logging Operations in the Yosemite National Park*
February 1927, *The Redwood Mountain Sequoia Grove*
February 1927, *The Sequoia National Park*
November 1927, *A New Raid on the Yosemite National Park*
June 1928, *A Crisis in Conservation* (later reissued by the ECC)
February 1929, *Raid on Yellowstone National Park*
1929, *Vanishing Forest Reserves: Problems of the National Forests and National Parks.* Although published as a book, *Vanishing Forest Reserves* was actually a long pamphlet in the same style as the others. It was his last pre-ECC effort.

INTERVIEWS

All interviews were conducted in 1986 in the locations indicated. The interviews provided important linkages and other information and by so doing enriched the content of this work. The generous time the following gave is appreciated and gratefully acknowledged.

Richard Brooks, Citizen Activist, Seattle, Washington.
Floyd L. Dickinson, Former Olympic National Park Forester, Port Angeles, Washington.
Polly Dyer, Citizen Activist, Seattle, Washington.
Rosalie Edge, Emergency Conservation Committee Chairman, New York, July, 1959.
Gunnar Fagerlund, Former Olympic National Park Chief Naturalist, Sequim, Washington.
Frances Fagerlund, Wife and Associate, Sequim, Washington.
Glenn Gallison, Former Olympic National Park Chief Naturalist and Former National
    Park Service Associate Regional Director, Port Angeles, Washington.
Patrick D. Goldsworthy, Citizen Activist, Seattle, Washington.
Robin Lodewick, Daughter of Irving Brant, Eugene, Oregon.
Sid Malbon, Olympic National Park and Bureau of Outdoor Recreation Associate of Fred
    Overly, Seattle, Washington.
Harvey Manning, Citizen Activist, Bellevue, Washington.
Elliot Marks, Governor Daniel Evans' Assistant, Seattle, Washington.
Jack Nattinger, Former Olympic National Park Forester, Port Angeles, Washington.
Fred Packard, National Parks Association, Port Angeles, Washington, October, 1956.
Grant Sharpe, Former Olympic National Park Seasonal Naturalist and Professor of Forestry, Seattle, Washington.
Philip Zalesky, Citizen Activist, Everett, Washington.

INDEX

Founded in 1906, The Mountaineers is a Seattle-based non-profit outdoor activity and conservation club with 15,000 members, whose mission is "to explore, study, preserve, and enjoy the natural beauty of the outdoors . . . ." The club sponsors many classes and year-round outdoor activities in the Pacific Northwest and supports environmental causes by sponsoring legislation and presenting educational programs. The Mountaineers Books supports the club's mission by publishing travel and natural history guides, instructional texts, and works on conservation and history. For information, call or write The Mountaineers, Club Headquarters, 300 Third Avenue West, Seattle, Washington, 98119; (206) 284-6310.

Other titles you may enjoy from The Mountaineers Books:

100 HIKES IN™ SERIES: Best-selling guidebooks with detailed information on every trail including access, mileage, elevation, hiking time, and the best season to go.

- **50 HIKES IN™ MOUNT RAINIER NATIONAL PARK, 4th Edition,** *Ira Spring & Harvey Manning*
- **100 HIKES IN™ WASHINGTON'S NORTH CASCADES NATIONAL PARK REGION, 3rd Edition,** *Ira Spring & Harvey Manning*
- **100 HIKES IN™ WASHINGTON'S ALPINE LAKES, 3rd Edition,** *Vicky Spring, Ira Spring & Harvey Manning*
- **100 HIKES IN™ WASHINGTON'S SOUTH CASCADES & OLYMPICS, 3rd Edition,** *Ira Spring & Harvey Manning*

100 CLASSIC HIKES IN™ WASHINGTON, *Ira Spring & Harvey Manning*
A full-color guide to the state's finest trails by the respected authors of more than thirty Washington guides, written with a conservation ethic and a sense of humor.

SACRED BALANCE: Rediscovering Our Place in Nature,
David Suzuki with Amanda McConnell
This powerful, deeply felt narrative gives concrete suggestions for how we can meet our basic needs and create a way of life that is ecologically sustainable, fulfilling, and in balance with nature and our surroundings.

OLYMPIC MOUNTAINS TRAIL GUIDE: National Park and National Forest, 3rd Edition, *Robert L. Wood*
This thorough guide covers each trail of all skill levels in Washington's magnificent Olympic Mountains. Features include information blocks for each hike, numbered hikes for quick reference, and weather information for each section of the Olympics.

TREE HUGGERS: Victory, Defeat & Renewal in the Northwest Ancient Forest Campaign, *Kathie Durbin*
Presents the history of logging on public lands, traces scientists' efforts to understand old-growth ecology, and introduces forest activists and the politicians who tried to thwart their efforts. Valuable reading for anyone concerned about the fate of our forests and the future of public land management.

HIKING WASHINGTON'S GEOLOGY, *Scott Babcock & Bob Carson*
Explores the geologic history of Washington's dramatic landscape. Four to thirteen hikes are listed for each of eight different regions exemplifying the major events that have shaped the area.